PASSAGE
OF CHANGE

PASSAGE OF CHANGE

LAW, SOCIETY AND GOVERNANCE
IN THE PACIFIC

edited by
Anita Jowitt and Dr Tess Newton Cain

ANU
THE AUSTRALIAN NATIONAL UNIVERSITY

E PRESS

ANU
E PRESS

Published by ANU E Press
The Australian National University
Canberra ACT 0200, Australia
Email: anuepress@anu.edu.au

This title is also available online at: http://epress.anu.edu.au/passage_change _citation.html

National Library of Australia Cataloguing-in-Publication Entry
    Title: Passage of change : law, society and governance in the Pacific / edited by Anita Jowitt and Tess Newton Cain.
    ISBN: 9781921666889 (pbk.) 9781921666896 (eBook)
    Notes: Includes bibliographical references.
    Subjects: Jurisprudence--Pacific Area.
            Customary law--Pacific Area.
            Pacific Area--Politics and government.
            Pacific Area--Social conditions.
    Other Authors/Contributors:
            Jowitt, Anita.
            Cain, Tess Newton.
    Dewey Number: 340.5295

Cover design by Emily Brissenden
Printed by Griffin Press

CONTENTS

ACKNOWLEDGEMENTS

The editors wish to thank all of the authors who have contributed to this collection for their ongoing commitment, patience and cheerful acceptance of editorial suggestions.

Thanks also go to Ian Templeman, Emily Brissenden and the staff at Pandanus Books who embraced the project with warmth and enthusiasm.

Tess would like to thank Anita for having the idea in the first place and Anita would like to thank Tess for her invaluable input on the sbject of capital letters!

The enduring accommodation and understanding of Grant and Bernie are duly acknowledged.

TABLE OF ABBREVIATIONS

AusAID: Australian Agency for International Development
BCA: Bougainville Constituent Assembly
BLV: Bose Levu Vakavanua (Fiji)
BRG: Bougainville Reconciliation Government
CARMA: Community Area Resource Management Approach (Vanuatu)
CCAMLR: Convention on the Conservation of Antarctic Marine Living Resources
CDC: Constitutional Development Commission (PNG)
CEDAW: Convention on the Elimination of all forms of Discrimination Against Women
CLS: Critical Legal Studies
CPC: Constitutional Planning Committee (PNG)
CPC: Criminal Procedure Code (Vanuatu)
CPLCC: Central Polynesian Land and Commercial Company
CRC: United Nations Convention on the Rights of the Child
CRP: Comprehensive Reform Programme (Vanuatu)
CRT: Critical Race Theory
CS: Correctional Service (PNG)
DAP: Democratic Alliance Party (Cook Islands)
DWFN: Distant Water Fishing Nation
ECHR: European Convention on Human Rights
EEZ: Exclusive Economic Zone
EIA: Environmental Impact Assessment
FFA: Forum Fisheries Agency
FFC: Forum Fishery Committee
FSM: Federated States of Micronesia
IATTC: Inter American Tropical Tuna Commission
IFF: Isantabu Freedom Fighters (Solomon Islands)
INA: Institute for National Affairs (PNG)
IUCN: International Union for the Conservation of Nature
LMS: London Missionary Society
LRC: Law Reform Commission (PNG)
LUPO: Land Use Planning Office (Vanuatu)
MHLC: Multilateral High Level Conference
MIRAB: Migration, Remittances Aid and Bureaucracy

MP: Member of Parliament
MTCs: Minimum Terms and Conditions
MSY: Maximum Sustainable Yield
NAP: National Alliance Party (Cook Islands)
NEC: National Executive Council (Papua New Guinea)
NGDP: National Goals and Directive Principles (Papua New Guinea)
NGOs: Non-Governmental Organisations
NLTB: Native Land Trust Board (Fiji)
NM: Nautical Miles
PIC: Pacific Island Country
PILOM: Pacific Islands Law Officers' Meeting
PNA: Peoples' National Alliance (PNG)
PNG: Papua New Guinea
SI: Solomon Islands
SPC: Secretariat of the Pacific Community (Formerly the South Pacific
            Commission)
SPREP: South Pacific Regional Environment Programme
SVT: Soqosoqo ni Vakavulewa ni Taukei (Fiji)
TAC: Total Allowable Catch
UDT: Underdevelopment Theories
UN: United Nations
UNCED: United Nations Conference on Environment and Development
UNCHR: United Nations Centre for Human Rights
UNCLOS: United Nations Convention on the Law of the Sea
UNDP: United Nations Development Programme
UK: United Kingdom
US(A):   United States (of America)
USP: University of the South Pacific
VANRIS: Vanuatu Resources Information System
VMS: Vessel Monitoring System
VNPF: Vanuatu National Provident Fund
WCPO: Western and Central Pacific Ocean

TABLE OF CASES

TABLE OF
INTERNATIONAL
CONVENTIONS,
DECLARATIONS AND
TREATIES

TABLE OF
LEGISLATION

NOTES ON CONTRIBUTORS

BOTHMANN S. Susan Bothmann was born in Denmark and grew up in Australia. She spent 17 years practising law in Vanuatu. She now works in the Aboriginal Legal Service in rural New South Wales. She obtained her Law degree from Melbourne University in 1973 and has recently completed her Master of Laws at QUT. Appointed a Commissioner on the first Legal Aid Commission in Victoria in 1979 she also served on the Law Council of Vanuatu in 1996. She was elected President of the Vanuatu Law Society in 1998. She has lectured at USP in the undergraduate law programme and written extensively on issues concerning indigenous peoples and the law.

CORDONNERY, L. Dr Laurence Cordonnery has been lecturing in Public International Law and Environmental Law at the University of the South Pacific since 1998. She has a wide ranging interest in environmental law issues using a multidisciplinary approach and particularly information technology to address issues such as environmental protection and protected area management in Antarctica, the subject of her PhD, patagonian toothfish illegal fishing and incidental mortality of seabirds in the Southern Ocean. Since 1998 her academic research interests have focussed on achieving sustainability in natural resources management through community-based participation and institutional strengthening, good governance and increased regional cooperation amongst Pacific Island Countries.

DINNEN, S. Dr Sinclair Dinnen is a Fellow on the State Society and Governance in Melanesia Project in the Research School of Pacific and Asian Studies at The Australian National University. He received his PhD in law from the same university. His current research focuses on conflict and conflict management in the Melanesian countries of the South West Pacific. He has previously taught at the Law Faculty of the University of Papua New Guinea and was head of the Crime Studies Division at the National Research Institute in Port Moresby between 1992–1994. Between August and December 1999 he worked in the PNG Department of National Planning and Monitoring as a Law and Justice adviser to the government of Papua New Guinea. He is co-editor (with Allison Ley) of the recently published *Reflections on Violence in Melanesia* (Hawkins Press and Asia Pacific Press) and is author of *Law and Order in a Weak State — Crime and Politics in Papua New Guinea* published by University of Hawai'i Press.

FRASER, I. Ian Fraser began teaching law in Canada, his home country, and came to the School of Law at the University of the South Pacific in 1999 after five years at the University of Papua New Guinea. He teaches Torts and Jurisprudence. His interests include legal theory and the roles of law in Melanesia.

HASSALL, G. Dr Graham Hassall is Associate Dean, Undergraduate Studies, Landegg Academy, Switzerland. From 1990–2000 he was Research Fellow and Director of the Asia-Pacific program in the Centre for Comparative Constitutional Studies at the University of Melbourne Law School. He has a particular interest in electoral systems, conflict resolution, and methods of constitutional dialogue and change. In recent years he has been an official observer at general elections in Cambodia (1998) and Indonesia (1999), and in 1999 undertook research in Papua New Guinea, Philippines, and Japan.

HILL, E. Edward Hill is the Law Clinic Supervisor at the University of the South Pacific School of Law. He has also practised law in Canada, been a lecturer at the University of Papua New Guinea and served as a fellow of the Institute of Justice and Applied Legal Studies in Suva. He has acted as a consultant for a number of institutions in the South Pacific region, including the Ombudsman of Vanuatu.

HUGHES, R. Professor Robert Hughes became the Head of the USP School and Department of Law at the beginning of 1997. Before that he was the Director of the School of Law at the University of New England, Armidale, Australia. He was admitted as a solicitor of the Supreme Court of New South Wales in 1973. His books include *The Law of Public Unit Trusts, Identity, Law and Politics, Introduction to Trusts, Australian Legal Institutions, Law of Succession in the South Pacific, Trust Law in the South Pacific* and the 'Plant Industries' section for *Halsbury's Laws of Australia*.

JESSEP, O. Owen Jessep is an Associate Professor at the Faculty of Law of the University of New South Wales. His research interests include family law, children and the law, Pacific legal systems and customary law. He has published several books on family law in Papua New Guinea and is a co-editor, along with Anthony Regan and Eric Kwa, of the recently published *Twenty Years of the Papua New Guinea Constitution.*

JOWITT, A. Anita Jowitt joined the University of the South Pacific in 1997 and is a Lecturer in Law. She is undertaking her PhD through USP on the regulation of employment contracts in Vanuatu, Samoa and Fiji. Her other research interests include HIV/AIDS and the law.

NAIDU, V. Dr Vijay Naidu is Professor and Director of the Centre of Development Studies in the School of Social and Economic Development at USP. He obtained his BA and MA (with distinction) degrees from USP and his D.Phil from the University of Sussex in England. He has taught social science subjects, politics and sociology at pre-degree, undergraduate and graduate levels for more than 25 years. He has published widely on Fiji and the region. He has acted as a consultant to government, non-government, regional and international organisations in the areas of his specialist interests. These include social development, poverty and poverty alleviation, population mobility, ethnicity and conflict resolution, youth development and state policies. He is actively involved in civil society organisations as chair of the Citizens' Constitutional Forum and through his association with the Fiji Council of Social Services, the Fiji Women's Crisis Centre and the NGO Coalition on Human Rights. He is a member of Fiji's Legal Aid Commission.

REGAN, A. Anthony Regan has been a Fellow in the State Society and Governance in Melanesia Project in the Research School of Pacific and Asian Studies at The Australian National University since 1997. Between 1981 to 1997 he worked as a government lawyer, researcher and law teacher in Papua New Guinea for 14 years, and as a constitutional adviser in Uganda for 3 years. From 1998 to 2001 he was a constitutional adviser to the Bougainville parties in the Bougainville peace process. He has had involvement in the Solomon Islands peace process and in the constitution-making process for an independent East Timor. His research and writing concerns autonomy arrangements in 'developing' countries, the relationships of constitutions and political, economic and cultural forces and the Bougainville conflict and peace process.

NEWTON CAIN, T. Dr Tess Newton Cain graduated in Law from the University of Wales in 1993 and was awarded a PhD in Criminology by the University of Wales in 2000. From January 1997 to August 2001 she was a Lecturer in Law at the University of the South Pacific. She is a co-author of *Introduction to South Pacific Law* and a co-convenor of the 'Legal Developments in the Pacific Island Region' conference series. She has written extensively on law and legal issues pertaining to the South Pacific Region. She is currently based in Vanuatu as a private consultant.

ZORN, J. Jean G. Zorn is a Professor of Law and Director of the Legal Skills and Values Program at Florida International University College of Law. Prior to that she was a member of the Law Faculty of the University of Papua New Guinea, where she developed and taught courses in customary law and in law and development, and was a principal legal officer of Papua New Guinea's Law Reform Commission. She developed and for several years taught the extension course in Custom and Customary Law for the University of the South Pacific's Pacific Law Unit and has also taught (too briefly, she says) at the Law School of the University of the South Pacific in Vanuatu. She has written extensively on the customary laws of the Pacific Islands region and on the integration of custom into the state legal system.

INTRODUCTION

This book aims to introduce readers to some significant areas of 'modernisation inspired' legal changes or challenges that are currently being faced by Pacific island countries. These challenges are largely arising because of tensions between the legal, political and social systems introduced by various colonial powers and the legal, political and social systems of indigenous cultures. It may seem that indigenous cultures are becoming obsolete, a piece of tradition that, increasingly, belongs in the past. From such a viewpoint introduced systems must ultimately prevail in order that Pacific island nations are able to 'progress' and to participate in the global economy. Such a picture, though, rests on a static concept of culture which fails to realise that cultures adapt to change and that the meeting of different cultures is a catalyst for change in all of them. Throughout the Pacific these different systems are currently struggling to find ways to co-exist, to adjust to and accommodate each other. The aim of this struggle is to realise systems that are both reflective of culture and allow for participation in the modern global environment.

Law, as the multifaceted institution that 'sets the rules' for society, must be examined if a resolution to this struggle is to be achieved. This is no easy task. There are numerous 'big questions' to be answered. What is the role of law in Pacific societies, and what should it be? What needs to be done in order to make people within the Pacific respect the law? How can we make law become more relevant to people in Pacific societies? What do we mean by 'law' in a Pacific context? It is questions such as these that need to be addressed in order to develop a Pacific jurisprudence or philosophy of law.

There are also problems to be solved. Policy makers and legislatures are being called upon to address a number of significant issues in a wide range of areas of substantive (or practical) law. How can we manage our natural resources in a sustainable manner? How can we cease the seemingly endemic corruption amongst politicians? How can we translate human rights obligations into domestic law? The number of practical areas in which the law (either in its content or in its administration) may be deficient are simply too numerous to begin to list in any comprehensive manner.

Whilst the development of a body of Pacific jurisprudence or theory about law is undoubtedly helpful for solving practical law problems, practical law reform exercises also contribute to the development of theory. Whilst there may be methodological debate about whether it is preferable to work from concrete problems 'upwards' to create a generalisation or theory, or to work from theory 'downwards' to create solutions to particular problems, such a debate is not very helpful in practice. The reality of contemporary Pacific societies is that a number of very difficult practical legal problems are being faced, and that these problems do, often, require one to question the very nature and role of law. Given the large number of issues of all kinds that are being faced within the contemporary Pacific and the urgency with which some of these issues must be addressed approaching them from a number of perspectives is to be encouraged.

With these things in mind this book aims to provide readers with both theoretical and practical discussion of some of the issues facing Pacific societies and legal systems. There are, as already indicated, a huge number of issues that could be included in a book that has the aim of discussing current legal issues in the Pacific islands. We have tried to focus the content of the book on some specific themes or areas of current legal controversy that allow for the writers to both discuss theoretical issues and to discuss practical problems within that theme. In the end we also had to be guided by the areas in which our contributors wished to write. This book covers issues of governance and corruption, human rights and customary law, resource issues and the (re)building of social order in Pacific societies. These are, perhaps, some of the most controverisal issues currently being faced within the Pacific, although we freely acknowlege that there are many other issues that we are not including in this volume.

The first section discusses the notion of modernisation and some of the ways that we can see modernisation affecting Pacific societies. It provides readers with a broad context in which to consider specific legal issues arising in the contemporary Pacific.

The second section examines corruption. Chapters consider what corruption is, whether it is necessarily a bad thing and why it is that corruption is seemingly endemic within the Pacific. It also considers a specific practical measure to combat corruption – an ombudsman

The third section of this volume focuses specifically on some issues surrounding the place of custom and customary law in the legal systems of the South Pacific region. That is not to say that issues of custom are not relevant to the discussions elsewhere. Indeed, many of the chapters in other parts of the book will touch on issues related to those raised here. The content in this section serves to illustrate the complexities that are rife in any meaningful discussion of the relationship between custom and law. The authors do not necessarily seek to provide definitive answers. Rather, they assist the reader in forming appropriate and incisive questions.

The content of the fourth section, discussing human rights, is, in many ways, a continuation of the discussions that commenced in section 3. The apparent incompatibility between human rights and custom is perhaps the most visible clash between the different values found in the introduced and indigenous legal systems. This section highlights the numerous complexities and subtleties that underpin that basic question of 'what is the place of human rights in the South Pacific'?

The fifth section considers natural resource issues. Whilst Pacific land tenure has long been widely recognised as an area of considerable general interest for Pacific legal scholars, particularly because of the predominant role of customary law in this area, the management of other natural resources has been seen more of a specialist area. However, given the number of threats that the natural resources of the Pacific are facing and the centrality of these resources to Pacific lifestyles and economies natural resources issues are becoming of increasing interest and importance.

The sixth and final section of this book examines issues of disorder. Coups in Fiji Islands and Solomon Islands and high levels of criminal behaviour in Papua New Guinea are extreme expressions of the lack of respect for the rule of law that is to be found throughout the Pacific. Issues of disorder are, perhaps, the manifestation of tensions discussed elsewhere in this book. Issues of disorder are also, possibly, the greatest threat to the development of Pacific states. Reasons for the apparent lack of legitimacy of the state and possibilities for a new conception of statehood suggest ways for Pacific countries to respond to this threat and find a new way forward.

Whilst there are, of course, overlaps between the content of each theme, the book has been arranged into thematic sections in order to assist readers to appreciate the multiple approaches to a particular issue that can be taken. We have also provided introductions to each thematic section. This allows us to make some commentary on the theme and to highlight some of the important ideas within the chapters and links between them.

It is hoped that students of law, sociology and development studies will find this book helpful in introducing them to some of the current legal issues facing Pacific island countries. To assist students each chapter begins with a box defining some key terms that readers will meet in the chapter. This is done both to assist in ensuring that key terms are understood and to assist students in focusing upon the key issues contained within each chapter. Each section concludes with a series of thought provoking questions and some additional readings that would provide a good place to begin further investigation into the particular topic.

It is also hoped that this book will find a much wider readership than students. The authors contributing to this book all have strong academic backgrounds, and present their material in such a way that should be of interest to policy makers, aid donors and any others who have an interest in contemporary issues facing Pacific island legal systems and societies. The book also has relevance to readers who have more general interests in the nature of law and the state. Within the Pacific, because of the clash of introduced and traditional cultures, issues surrounding the relationship between law and the state are, maybe, more apparent than in other countries, as they manifest themselves as practical problems of disorder. Our experiences within the Pacific can make a valuable contribution to general political theory and philosophy by contributing fresh examples and perspectives to the global debate on the nature of law and the state. As such this book is not only limited to an audience with a specific interest in the Pacific region.

In a region and subject area in which there are so many interesting changes taking place it is inevitable that we can only touch briefly upon a few issues. Hopefully in the near future futher Pacific island focused publications of a socio-legal nature will fill some of the many gaps that this volume has to leave.

ANITA JOWITT
DR TESS NEWTON CAIN

Editors

SECTION 1
THE CONTEXT OF CHANGE

1. MODERNISATION AND DEVELOPMENT
IN THE SOUTH PACIFIC
Vijay Naidu

The changes that Pacific island countries are currently experiencing can largely be attributed to the impacts of modernisation. Whether modernisation is conceptualised as a process of development and progress or as a more chaotic situation during which traditional and introduced systems meet or are forced together with the result that both systems have to adjust, modernisation connotes change. These changes are far reaching. It is not only legal systems that are put into a state of flux because of modernisation, but all social systems, including political systems, family systems, education systems and religious systems.

The chapter by Professor Naidu aims to provide readers with some appreciation of the broad nature of changes that are currently taking place throughout the Pacific region. Such an appreciation is necessary in order to put legal change into its wider context. There are, of course, many potential interpretations of the changes and many variations in the experiences of different countries. This chapter does not pretend to be exhaustive in its exploration of the topic.

Complementing this discussion of change in the Pacific is a discussion of various theoretical approaches or perspectives on the nature and process of modernisation and change. The multifaceted nature both of change in the Pacific and of theoretical perspectives for conceptualising this change is thereby highlighted.

1. MODERNISATION AND DEVELOPMENT IN THE SOUTH PACIFIC

By: Professor Vijay Naidu

KEY TERMS AND PHRASES

Modernisation

Modernisation is popularly used to describe a process of societal change from 'primitive' to 'developed'. 'Developed' is usually equated with 'westernised'. As such the popular concept of the process of modernisation is not neutral, but is loaded with assumptions about what a modern society should look like and the desirability of attaining this modern model of society. A number of specific academic theories have arisen around the concept of modernisation. These theories may use the term in different or more precise ways than the popular definition of modernisation.

Indigenisation

Indigenisation can be used to describe a process whereby the values of an indigenous culture change another (introduced) culture to reflect or incorporate the values of the indigenous group. It is often used in the context of discussing how indigenous cultures affect the model of western culture as reflected in modernisation processes.

Dichotomy

A dichotomy is a division into two seemingly mutually exclusive or contradictory groups. Tradition and modernisation are often viewed as dichotomous concepts.

INTRODUCTION

Over the past century and a half Pacific island societies have undergone very significant changes. These changes are institutional, and have affected values, beliefs and attitudes and individual and group behaviour. They have transformed the political, economic and social dimensions of these societies. The extent and scope of societal change has varied from society to society but everywhere, from the remotest of villages to the not so sleepy towns, social change and its consequences are present. At the same time, however, in all Pacific island societies earlier and apparently more traditional structures, norms and values persist. The resilience of traditional institutions and their adaptations to the forces of change is remarkable. In the current era of globalisation which is driven by strong states, powerful corporate forces and the communication revolution, Pacific island countries are faced with numerous challenges as their governments seek to secure higher standards of living for island peoples. Islanders themselves have also established a transnational network of family and kin with flows of people, money and goods in an extension of socio-cultural values and institutions that is centred in the homeland and yet globalising.

Numerous contradictions and conflicts abound between established norms and new ways of doing things. Individualism exists in tension with more collective obligations; communal customary forms of land and the ownership of other natural resources co-exist with private ownership and individual accumulation of capital; market forces collide with the regulatory powers of the state; the nominal equality of citizenship underwritten by modern day constitutions conflicts with traditional and contemporary status inequality based on ethnicity, gender, status by birth and region of origin; traditional forms of authority sit uncomfortably with electoral systems and other paraphernalia of democracy; introduced systems of meritocracy conflict with traditionally ascribed statuses; inter-generational conflicts both latent and overt are ubiquitous; and disparities between urban and rural places, between regions of a country and between groups of people underlie the tensions and conflicts in the not so pacific Pacific.

The first part of this chapter briefly considers the concepts of evolution, modernisation and development and their relevance to the changes wrought in Pacific societies. The second part of this chapter provides an account of these changes and their significance for Pacific communities. In attempting to provide an overview it is likely that the unique and special experiences of some island societies may be omitted. However, it is hoped that the broad patterns of change that are identified provide insights into both change and continuity in Pacific societies.

EVOLUTION, MODERNISATION AND DEVELOPMENT

The changes that have overtaken island societies with increasing intensity over the last two centuries have their origins in Europe. Feudalism as a mode of production based on agriculture and the manor with the labour of serfs was displaced by urban-based manufacture of finished products for private profit. Rural agrarian production largely for consumption was superceded by industrial production for exchange. Agricultural labour coerced by the feudal lord was replaced by town and city based wage labour. In a short span of time the English landscape was changed by the massive shift of the mass of rural people to the emergent industrial towns and cities. This "great transformation" in which the "satanic mill" became central to peoples' livelihood caused widespread social dislocation, misery and hardship.[1] European societies underwent radical changes in their social structures and class character. A reading of the novels by Charles Dickens and accounts of poverty at the turn of the twentieth century[2] provide vivid images of the enormity of societal changes and the impact that these changes had on the lives of people. Agricultural revolution was followed by the industrial revolution, which was accompanied by political revolution. Scholars in Europe became preoccupied by the social, economic and political changes and events taking place all around them. To paraphrase McKee, scholars could not avoid being involved in the events of their time and this involvement always left its indelible marks on their disciplines.[3]

Scholarly interest in social change has led to the development of a number of theories about the nature of social change. The initial theoretical trend was to use evolutionary models to explain change. The evolutionary models were later complemented by (then superceded by) modernisation theories. Recently these models have been rejected as being too biased towards western lifestyles and a range of underdevelopment and other theories have arisen.

Evolutionary Theories

By the mid-nineteenth century European scholars were also aware of peoples elsewhere. The latter lived in a variety of societies that exhibited different levels of technology and political organisation — from small scale preliterate hunter-gatherer bands to tribes practising various forms of agriculture ruled by chiefs or elders to relatively large civilisations in Egypt, China and India. European social and political philosophers sought to explain societal change in terms of stages of human progress from the relatively simple, small and primitive conditions of paleolithic hunters and gatherers to the complex, large and industrialising societies of their time. Adam Smith (1723–1790), Herbert Spencer (1820–1903), Ferdinand Tonnies (1835–1936), Emile Durkheim (1858–1917), Karl Marx (1818–1883) and Max Weber (1864–1920), amongst others, contributed to explanations about how human societies had changed.

Many of them used evolutionary precepts in their explanations. Sahlins and Service[4] provide a comprehensive account of evolutionary theories. At the core of these explanations was the idea that human societies change from small and simple to become large and complex and from having the one institution of kinship playing multiple functions — including economic, social, political, legal and religious functions — to specialist institutions carrying out each of these functions. Mechanisms of change varied: population increase and competition over resources, environmental adaptation, warfare, new technology, literacy, political centralisation, class struggle and religion were some of the various mechanisms, instruments or catalysts for change identified by different theorists. For the evolutionists all human societies could be put at different stages of evolution, with contemporary European society being the most advanced. The adaptability of European societies together with their technology and social organisation made it possible for Europe to subordinate the rest of the world. In its extreme form evolution took the garb of Social Darwinism which not only perceived the manifest destiny of the white man to dominate the world but also rationalised the demise of indigenous peoples as losers in the competition for the survival of the fittest. In short, evolutionists chalked out the stages and mechanisms of change in human societies from 'primitive savagery' to post-enlightenment European 'civilisation'.

An evolutionary conceptualisation of human development was applied to Pacific island peoples by different categories of Europeans who arrived in the Pacific during the late eighteenth and nineteenth centuries. While there was a tendency to regard island societies as being at a more 'primitive' stage, early explorers commented positively on the relative health, tranquility and openness of islanders. Rousseau's conceptualisation of the noble savage living in harmony with nature was commonly used. Missionaries discerned the difference between the centralised chiefdoms of Polynesia from the relatively egalitarian Melanesia. Many early clergymen assumed the lighter skinned Polynesians with their aristocratic classes were closer to their own feudal origins. They sought to save the souls of island people by converting them to Christianity, an obviously superior religion from the heathen paganism that prevailed. Early Victorians believed that islanders had been lost to Christendom because of the influence of the devil and that it was incumbent on the missionaries to save them.

Islanders also had to be protected from evil Europeans who sought to exploit them and who brought wicked and corrupting influences. In this regard island peoples were seen as children who could be led into harm by unscrupulous adults. Missionaries campaigned against the sale of alcohol, arms and ammunition to islanders. They also firmly opposed immoral behaviour such as prostitution.

Settlers who came in the late nineteenth century saw island people as occupants of land that could be better utilised commercially and as potential plantation labour. They tended to regard islanders as an inferior race impeding progress. Openly racist organisations such as the British Settlers' Mutual Protection Society and the Ku Klux Klan were formed in Fiji.[5]

Modernisation

During the 1950s and 60s American and European social scientists sought to use Weber's ideas to explain the disparities between western and non-western societies and to chalk out road maps for modernising or developing the latter.[6] Their approach was a model of development that perceived change as the transformation of traditional social order through a process of modernisation. This meant the changing of values and attitudes, institutions and societal orientation to those prevailing in the industrialised liberal democracies of the West. Modernisation essentially meant

Westernisation. The theoretical perspectives included Parsons's pattern variables, various elite theories, modernising institutions, Easton's input-output model and empirical development indicators.

In general modernisation theories from the different social sciences stressed the significance of changes in values, norms and beliefs and individual motivations. These changes had fostered industrialisation and development of mass consumption societies in Europe and North America.[7] With suitable changes in values, institutions, leadership, technology and rates of savings, post-colonial societies could follow. These changes could be made possible through the diffusion or transplanting of ideas, institutions, values, capital and technology to the less developed world. Modernisation through diffusion had already began to take place with education, urbanisation, nuclear households, increased awareness through mass media, heightened political awareness and participation in democratic systems, replacement of traditional authorities with national system of laws coupled with representative government and the increase in earnings and savings for investment.

Most writings on change in the Pacific between the 1950s and 1980s can be placed in the modernisation paradigm. Teo Fairbairn, the prominent Samoan economist, epitomises this approach:

> ...the individual communities in the region have much in common. The force of tradition has tended to remain strong despite increasing exposure to the outside world; economic patterns are dominated by agriculture with subsistence production playing a major role though an ever-increasing demand for the goods and services of the cash economy is evident... Throughout the region the dominant physical disadvantages are isolation from large metropolitan centres, the highly dispersed nature of many individual groups, smallness of population and with a few notable exceptions, lack of basic mineral and industrial raw materials. On the economic side one is confronted with generally low levels of income and rates of savings, indigenous populations lacking in all but the most rudimentary managerial and technical skills, and methods of land tenure and social organizations that have their roots in traditional systems. In addition, heavy dependence on one or two agricultural export products renders them vulnerable to fluctuations in world markets for primary commodities as well as to the hazards of adverse weather. The combination of rapidly growing populations and rising expectations for the goods and services of the modern monetary economy, poses further challenges.[8]

More recently he has remarked that:

> In general, the severe shortage of skills experienced by most of the island countries weakens their capacity to absorb and apply modern technology and undermines the growth potential of all sectors, particularly the private sector which is potentially the most dynamic in promoting growth. In addition, cultural traditions are still a powerful force and tend to weaken the modernisation process and slow the development effort. The constraining influence of customary land

tenure systems on agricultural development is a notable example, while traditional beliefs often dominate attitudes towards savings, business endeavours and population control.[9]

Underdevelopment Theories

The modernisation perspective of blaming tradition within a country was turned over its head by underdevelopment theorists who blamed external forces for constraining and impeding development in the Third World.

'Dependency' and Underdevelopment Theories (UDT), which emerged in the late 1960s, maintained that metropolitan Europe's progress relied heavily on the exploitative chain-like relations with post-colonial satellite states. In its extreme form UDT maintained that the development of Europe led to the underdevelopment of the Third World. The notion of an expanding metropolis (core) and exploited post-colonial countries (periphery) was incorporated in Immanuel Wallerstein's World System's Theory. Wallerstein maintained that a world system emerged with the expansion of European capitalism. Former mini-systems (tribal societies) and empires (for example, China) were penetrated by and integrated into the capitalist world system. The world system itself comprises core countries that are industrialised and powerful, semi peripheral states which are partially industrialised but still dependent on agriculture and forms of non-wage labour and peripheral countries which are entirely dependent on agriculture and raw material production based largely on 'unfree' labour. The world system was managed by powerful states for their own benefit.

Several scholars of Pacific island societies have used UDT in explaining change. Amarshi, Good and Mortimer[10] have pointed to how Papua New Guinea's natural and human resources have become increasingly harnessed to the exploitative interests of transnational, often Australian capital. In his analysis of law and the state in Papua New Guinea, Fitzpatrick has noted that the pre-capitalist modes of production subsidised emerging capitalist enterprises in the country.[11] Rokotuivuna,[12] Utrecht[13], Narsey,[14] Narayan,[15] Durutalo[16] and Sutherland[17] have pointed to the extraction of monopoly profits from Fiji, the emergence of a class of collaborator capitalists or compradors and the emergence of the country as an Australian economic colony. Shankman[18] concluded from his study of Samoan emigration that (Western) Samoa was being underdeveloped by the loss of its skilled and professional human capital to metropolitan countries. The Cook Islands was examined by Bellam[19] using a similar perspective and he reached a somewhat similar conclusion that this country's interests had been subordinated to the interests of New Zealand capital. For all the smaller international migration and remittance dependant economies, referred to as MIRAB countries, the UDT approach can be applied. On a region wide basis, Howard et al[20] have used this paradigm as well as the perspective of world system theory and the articulation of modes of production. Naidu has used a similar approach in his analysis of Samoan and Fijian political economy.[21] On an individual country and region-wide basis the story told is similar, there has been a subordination of island economies and societies to transnational capital and interests.

Alternative Development Perspective

Most recently post modernist writers have attacked attempts at meta or grand theorising and have instead advocated for accounts that capture the diverse and complex character of human experiences. Alternative development perspectives vary in their emphasis on particular aspects of development and in their orientation. Writers such as Amartya Sen, Dudley Seers, Paul Streeten and Mahbubul Huq have sought to emphasise poverty eradication, employment generation, social justice, equality and human development aspects over preoccupation with economic growth. Still others have seen an attempt by the West to impose its values and norms upon non-western societies in the push for development. Schumacher's 'Small is Beautiful' type of approaches in turn have emphasised the role of small communities based on small scale agriculture and appropriate technology providing a more nurturing environment for all creatures. Eco-development and sustainable development advocates have pointed to the need for sound environmental management and social integration for long-term survival. They publicise the potential dangers posed by unsustainable capitalist industrial development. Intergenerational and international equity issues have been raised by them. Feminist writers have identified gender inequalities in policy and decision making, property rights, legal systems, access to opportunities, division of labour and the double burden of paid employment and unpaid domestic labour.

A number of Pacific writers have been most critical of the changes brought in the wake of capitalist development in the South Pacific. A number of them do not see any material gain in the transition of island people from small holder farmers or peasants to wage workers.[22] Others have pointed to the dangers of moving away from biodiverse and environmentally friendly horticulture to mono-cropping.[23] Sectoral development in tourism, mining, forestry, fisheries and physical infrastructure has come under critical scrutiny. Regional organisations such as the South Pacific Regional Environmental Programme (SPREP), the Forum Fisheries Agency (FFA) and the Secretariat of the Pacific Community (SPC) have been pushing for sustainable development of natural resources as well as for community development. Scholars who use these approaches tend to be very critical of elements of capitalist development but do not provide systematic and viable alternatives.

Evolutionary, modernisation and other development theories have sought to explain societal change. Their wide diversity is indicative of the complex and multifaceted nature of change. It is also indicative of the lack of theoretical unity or of a dominant theoretical perspective in the area of development studies.

SOCIAL CHANGE AND DEVELOPMENT IN PACIFIC ISLAND COUNTRIES

No society is static. However, social change was gradual until the advent of European incursion from the seventeenth century onwards, and has been especially apparent since the early nineteenth century. By this stage some Pacific societies, such as those in Polynesia, had evolved into centralised chiefdoms and proto-states. In Tonga and Hawaii certain chiefly lineages were deified while others were bestowed with rights to secular rule. Specialist craftsmen, canoe makers, warriors, priests and rulers emerged. The ranks of nobles, priests, subjects and slaves existed.[24] Polities in the Pacific ranged from those with a few dozen people in hunter and gatherer bands, to a few hundred in smaller chiefdoms to as many as several thousands in the centralised proto-states of Polynesia.

It is evident that in the post-contact period societal changes intensified over time. These changes can be divided and periodised into pre-colonial, colonial, post-colonial and contemporary changes. Changes during the pre-colonial period varied but generally did not cause significant transformation of Pacific island societies, with the possible exception of communities that were involved in the so-called labour trade.[25] In contrast, most significant structural changes were brought about in island societies during the decades of direct colonialism by metropolitan powers. The post-colonial period saw a resurgence of supposedly indigenous values but underlying structural changes persisted. In the contemporary era, economic and technological forces have engendered greater integration in the global market and significant social changes are causing political instability.

In this part of the paper, changes during the pre-colonial, colonial, post-colonial and contemporary periods will be outlined sequentially. Obviously, structural changes in one period will overlap into other periods. This division into periods is to help in the understanding of the nature and extent of change.

PRE-COLONIAL CHANGES

Pacific historians point to the fur hunters, whalers, sealers, ship wrecked sailors, castaways, escaped convicts, beachcombers, traders, missionaries and settlers arriving in the island in the 1800s as being the first outside agents of change. Up to the mid-1850s their impact on island societies was minimal in the sense that these societies remained intact. Indeed trading activities tended to reinforce existing social structures. Even the large scale collection and processing of sea slug or *beche-de-mer* did not alter island communities. However, many island societies were seriously threatened by the large increases in mortality rates and the population depletion that occurred as they had no immunity to diseases of European and Asian origins.[26] Alcohol and warfare also contributed to their demise. Iron and steel tools, knives and axes, rifles and double barreled guns, ammunition, and other manufactured commodities including clothes, drapery and items of adornment were in great demand in the islands. The ubiquity of these goods led Thurston, a settler and future

Governor of Fiji to declare that "the bow and arrow and stone age [was] disappearing at an astonishing rate."[27] Beachcombers and missionaries contributed to a change in local balance of power between chiefdoms, coastal and rural people. The sites for new exploitation of natural resources such as sandalwood and *beche-de-mer* made local rulers and their allies more powerful. Thus Bau and Bua in Fiji emerged as powerful chiefdoms by the 1830s. Missionaries backed the more powerful chiefs to extend their authority over neighboring polities. During this period several theocratic kingdoms backed by Wesleyan, London Missionary Society (LMS) and Catholic missionaries sprang up. The growing numbers of Europeans and their often disruptive activities drew the attention of their respective countries. These imperialist countries soon became embroiled in a scramble for colonies, which led to the carving of Oceania amongst them.

COLONIAL PERIOD

Colonies have been divided in terms of colonies of settlement, colonies of partial settlement and colonies of exploitation. All three forms of colonies were to be found in the Pacific. Australia, New Zealand and Hawaii became colonies of settlement with the almost complete displacement of indigenous peoples. Fiji, New Caledonia, Samoa and Tahiti were only partially occupied. Colonies of exploitation included Nauru and Ocean Islands, which were stripped of their topsoils, and Solomon Islands, which was depleted of its labour resources.

Many of the seeds of future changes were planted in the previous period of contact with European missionaries and traders. Missionary enterprise aimed at inculcating islanders with work ethics consistent with commerce. Coconut oil, copra, bananas, cocoa, coffee, pumpkin and other vegetables were cultivated and poultry, pigs and cattle raised for sale so that congregations could shave regularly and meet missionary dress codes, purchase the Bible and give generously to the mission. It became a matter of course for the colonial state to introduce a head tax, poll tax or hut tax to ensure that the islanders extended their revenue generation activities for government coffers as well. Islanders also engaged in commercial production of copra and coconut oil, bananas and other produce to meet their own needs of items of clothing, iron and steel tools, pots and pans, cutlery, matches, *et cetera*. Money in the form of colonial currency became increasingly the medium of exchange. In this manner islanders become peasant producers subjected to market and state pressures.

Economic and Social Changes during the Colonial period

With the establishment of colonial rule, government officials did not regard either native or small European settler productive activities as sufficient to meet the needs of the state for revenue. Merchant houses such as Godeffroy and Sons, Burns Philip and the Colonial Sugar Refining Company of Australia were drawn into setting up plantations and agricultural processing operations in the islands. In New Caledonia, settler plantations were overshadowed by the mining of nickel. Plantations required five ingredients to be successful — a plentiful supply of arable land, a plentiful supply of cheap labour, efficient management and capital, a secure market for products and necessary infrastructure. Plantation agriculture, and to a lesser extent mining, changed the face of some island colonies. Other island colonies were changed as they formed a vast pool of labour for these plantations and mines.

Land in the colonial and contemporary eras

Land ownership as in freehold private property for the exclusive use of the individual property rights holder in perpetuity was an alien concept amongst island people. It was first introduced by Christian missionaries who sought to maintain the exclusivity of their land acquisition by fencing it. Some small scale land alienation had taken place before the 1860s but trading in land together with disputes and outright conflicts over land escalated during the 1860s and 1870s. The American Civil War was accompanied by the blockade against cotton producers in the South. European textile mills starved of cotton sought it elsewhere in the world with high prices. Settlers arrived in Fiji and Samoa in their thousands to make a fortune in cotton. The South Seas Island variety of cotton proved initially to be a favourite. Acquisition of land was made possible by the rivalry amongst ambitious chiefs who sought to subordinate their opponents. They willingly parted with some of the best arable lands of their subjects as well as their opponents.[28] In return they received European goods, guns and ammunition and boats as well as assistance in warfare. Ironically, as the Civil War ended in America, arms and ammunition were collected by the Central Polynesian Land and Commercial Company (CPLCC) from the battle fields for sale to island chiefs.

One of the first acts of colonial governments in the island colonies was to regularise land deals as these were causing disputes and outright conflicts. In Samoa, where the total land area amounted to 950,000 acres, settlers claimed 1,691,893 acres.[29] Land Commissions were established to investigate land claims being made. The authenticity of property sales and legal documents were investigated and finalised. The flexible and fluid nature of customary ownership of land, which reflected demographic changes amongst lineages in a locality and their respective strengths, was lost with the documentation of ownership. This loss of flexibility together with the alienation and commercial leasing of some of the best lands contributed to land shortages among islanders. Land remained a major source of disputes during the colonial period.

Labour

The second significant act of some colonial governments was to regularise the recruitment, engagement, terms and conditions and repatriation of migrant labour. As the colonial enterprise in plantations and mines took root in the islands much of the western and central Pacific was converted into a large labour reserve. Blackbirding and labour trading took thousands of labourers from Melanesia and Micronesia to Queensland and New South Wales in Australia, Hawaii, New Caledonia, Samoa, Fiji and to central and south America. By the 1870s it was realized that island labour was inadequate for further plantation growth. The colonial governments of Fiji, Samoa and Tahiti readily engaged in recruiting labour from Asian sources. In Hawaii the plantocracy also opted for labour from neighbouring Asia. Thus immigrant labour for producing cotton, sugar, coffee, bananas, pineapples, nickel and gold contributed to the further growth in multi-ethnic societies in the islands. Melanesian labourers were followed by and worked together with Chinese labourers in Samoa and Indian labourers in Fiji. Chinese, Japanese, Filipino and Portuguese labourers were imported to work in Hawaii's plantations. Chinese were imported into Tahiti. Arabs, Indians, Chinese, Indo-Chinese, Ni-Vanuatu and Wallis and Futuna people were drawn to the mines and plantations of New Caledonia.

Urbanisation

Port towns began as trading outposts grew in number and size throughout the island world from the 1800s. Some of the 'hell holes' of yesteryear, such as Apia and Levuka, settled down to being modest centres of government, trade and commerce, education and other services. Besides government officials and merchants a professional class of surveyors, lawyers, doctors and teachers emerged in these urban centres as did a category of waged workers, domestic servants and garden boys.

New Social Categories and Classes

Wage labour and urbanisation had a considerable impact on social organisation. During the colonial period new categories of people emerged in the islands. Apart from colonial officials, planters, a smattering of merchants and professional people who were whites occupying the apex of society, there appeared in these societies new groups of island people. Catechists, pastors and missionaries trained by the various Christian denominations increased amongst islanders. Employment as interpreters, court clerks, policemen, low ranking civil servants, stevedores, public works departments labourers and in merchant houses produced islanders with different work habits, life styles and orientations to their rural cousins. To these were added, particularly in the post World War II era, teachers, nurses, medical officers (then doctors), higher level civil servants, businessmen (usually mixed race, European or Asian) and just before the end of colonialism, politicians. Professional bodies, trade unions and social clubs were formed to enhance these new categories of islander interests and aspirations.

Infrastructure

Plantation and mining enclaves also impacted on island economies by their demand for infrastructure. Wharves, jetties, lighthouses, beacons, roads, railway lines and bridges had to be built and maintained. In order to fund the building and maintenance of infrastructure and to sustain the nascent government institutions — the civil service, police force, magistrates and other law enforcement officers, prisons and the governing executive — revenue had to be collected. Direct and indirect taxes, excise duties and import-export taxes were imposed. The colonial state also became the sole determinant of colonial currency and its value.

Political Changes during the Colonial period

The Pacific has been called a European artifact in so far as its exploration, extent and identification have been a recent European endeavour.[30] In another and even more direct sense it is a European creation as the countries of Pacific have largely gained their territorial integrity and their names through direct colonialism. The partition of the Pacific took place in tandem with the carving up of Africa. Indeed at the Berlin Conference (1889) Britain and Germany exchanged parts of their Pacific and Africa possessions! The territorial boundaries of most Pacific island countries reflect the maps drawn by their colonisers. All Melanesian countries were fragmented into much smaller tribal polities until direct colonialism. The division of the island of Papua New Guinea between the Dutch and the British/Australians remains to this day as Indonesian occupied West Papua and the independent state of Papua New Guinea. Bougainville, which is culturally related more closely to Solomon Islands, was ceded by the British to the Germans. Fiji had forty more or less powerful chiefdoms and polities at the time of European contact. It took the British a war of pacification to subdue the fiercely independent interior people of Viti Levu. Samoa was divided between Germany and the United States and remains split between American Samoa and the independent state of Samoa. Tonga's expansionism and incorporation of parts of the Fiji group was stalled by the British. Colonial rule ended the internecine warfare that erupted throughout the Pacific during early contact.

The Colonial State

With the possible rare exception most Pacific island states' political boundaries are no more than a hundred years old and established by the colonial power. In virtually all cases there has been an expansion in the size of the polity from pre-colonial times. Local and island-based autonomy gave away to centralised systems of political control. The declaration of crown colony, protectorate or trusteeship by colonial powers as well as treaty agreements not only defined the territorial limits of the colonial possession but also established the new politico-administrative and legal order. Colonial rule was about law and order as perceived by the representative of the imperialist state, the colonial governor. The colonial state imposed an administrative order and a legal framework, including a system of courts and police. Autocratic and authoritarian rule prevailed until almost a decade before independence. Politics was discouraged. However, the exigencies of ruling remote colonies and the balance of forces in the colonised territories required in most cases the co-optation of indigenous chiefs and aristocracy.

Although chiefs had some advisory function and influence in the executive of colonial Government, political representation and participation by the majority of islanders came fairly late in the period of colonialism. It was not until the 1962 independence constitution that voting for the Fono of Faipule was introduced in Samoa, but even then only on the basis of exclusive matai suffrage. Adult ethnic Fijians voted for the first time in 1965. By this stage Westminster-type institutions were transplanted to island countries that were ruled by the British, Australians and New Zealanders.

Similar transfer of political institutions occurred in American and French territories. Executive, legislative and judicial branches of the state were more clearly identified and separated and a civil service established.

Indirect Rule

In Fiji and Samoa, councils of chiefs were established at the colony-wide level. Local chiefs were used to provide a relatively inexpensive but effective administration through systems of indirect rule. The incorporation of the chiefly order within the colonial state meant that although the chiefly structure remained ideologically traditional, in reality it was being transformed into a foreign-controlled instrument of domination over 'commoners'. But this point should not be taken too far as earlier governors remained sensitive to chiefly interests. Thus Fiji's Governor Des Voeux (1880–1885) maintained that, "...the chiefs represent the army and navy, and practically the police of the country. The maintenance of their interest is therefore necessary even on these somewhat selfish grounds alone."[31] Pre-existing political entities such as hamlets, villages, districts and confederacies were modified and consolidated through the system of indirect rule. Likewise, while labour services, tributes and other presentations to elders and chiefs were either prohibited or modified to suit the colonial authorities (for example the taxation in kind imposed by Governor Sir Arthur Gordon in Fiji), 'customs of respect' to those in authority were reinforced.

Anti-Colonial Struggles

The centralised colonial order was also a racist one. A system of racial hierarchy was established based on differential incorporation, economic stratification and racial segregation. A racial division of colour situated managers of merchant houses, traders, plantation owners, senior public servants and other owners of capital who were generally white at the highest rank. In the middle were Asians, chiefs and mixed race business people and at the bottom of the pile were immigrant workers and indigenous peasants whose involvement in the mainstream economy was subject to strict controls. Taxation and restrictive controls over day-to-day life proved to be irksome to many. Anti-colonial struggles took many forms: restorative rebellious of an atavistic kind attempting to reassert past social order; religious movements that syncretised Christian teaching with indigenous beliefs and rituals predicting the arrival of a redeeming (liberating) leader; economic and industrial protests by urban workers, small holder farmers, plantation workers and peasant producers over what they earned from their labour or produce; and political struggles (which combined elements of the other types of struggles) calling for an end to colonial rule.

POST-COLONIAL AND CONTEMPORARY PERIODS

These economic and political changes, which had their roots in colonial rule, have continued to affect contemporary Pacific island societies in a number of ways, as discussed below.

Social and Economic Change

Multiethnic Societies

During the colonial era, changes had taken place in the population composition, residential and work patterns, marriage and family structure, social mobility and gender relations in the islands. To begin with, over the last century demography patterns have been transformed. Fiji, Hawaii, New Caledonia, Samoa and Tahiti became more complexly multi-ethnic with the settlement of peoples of Asian and European origins. Categories of mixed race people have now emerged in virtually all the islands. Most PICs have become multicultural.

Land

In the contemporary era changes in land tenure rooted in colonial history have led to outright conflicts. Relatively small parcels of alienated free hold and state owned land (in many islands, the British concept of state ownership dubiously exists and extends to the tidal water mark) sit amidst customary owned land. Where land boundaries among indigenous landowners have not been surveyed and documented there are many disagreements over where one group's land rights end and another group's begin. Such disputes often become violent. Land tribunals and courts have been established to handle such problems in most Pacific Island countries (PICs). In Fiji Islands the Native Land Trust Board (NLTB) was formed in 1940 to oversee the usage of customary owned land and its leasing to agricultural and other commercial interests. However, group ownership of such land has led to difficulties over decision making and the sharing of rent monies. Where customary title holders or chiefs are the primary recipients of land rents the succession to chiefly title has increasingly become contentious. These disputes continue to be dealt with by land and titles tribunals established by the colonial state. Communal or collective ownership has also made it almost impossible to obtain credit from commercial banks because customary owned land has little value as collateral. Disagreements also occur over the amount of rent that ought to be charged. Some members of the land-owning group have taken it upon themselves to seek additional payments in cash and in kind from leaseholders. In some instances, as in Guadalcanal in the Solomon Islands, individuals have legally sold customary land to Malaitans. This has put the buyer in considerable hardship as the group itself has refused to accept the legality of the transaction. With the recent violent political conflict, many migrant islanders have found their property rights seriously jeopardised.

In many Pacific countries there is potential for serious tensions and conflicts between resident land owners in urban and peri-urban areas and localities of enclave development and migrant islanders. Informal traditional or customary arrangements between owners and migrants place the latter into a category of tenants at will. With a growing number of migrants there has been pressure on resident groups. The competition over land for housing and gardening and over neighbouring marine resources is likely to spill over into open conflicts.

Urbanisation

Residential patterns have changed. Over the last forty years and especially in the last two decades there has been an intensification of population mobility. Islanders have moved from outlying islands and inland areas to coastal regions and urban places. Several PICs are predominantly urban. Much of Polynesia and Micronesia has experienced an urban shift and the rate of urbanisation throughout more rural parts of Micronesia and Melanesia is double the rate of population growth. Ward points to how urbanism — town and city life — has become integral to the lives of islanders.[32] This has involved shifts away from agrarian livelihoods to employment in government, business, manufacture, transportation and tourism. Being well connected to metropolitan centres, urban centres are places for new ideas, life styles and fashions. Segregated residence has been replaced by socio-economic division as the major determinant of residential patterns.

The attraction of opportunities in towns and cities has led to rapid urbanisation and associated problems. Inadequate housing has resulted in the growth of squatter settlements and informal housing. Public water supply and the disposal of garbage and sewerage in towns and cities have become critical environmental and community health matters. Other infrastructural bottlenecks include roads, electricity supply, transport connections between islands and to remote localities in larger islands as well as educational and health services.

As indicated earlier, the pressure on urban land is causing tensions between landowners and immigrant groups. Most Pacific states do not appear to have the capacity to address this very serious problem.

A consideration of urbanisation and urbanism will be inadequate without reference to international migration of islanders. Auckland has become the largest Polynesian city and Vancouver has more Indo-Fijians than the second largest city of Lautoka in Fiji. Emigration and remittances have become critical in the lives of Micronesians and Polynesians. Bertram and Watters[33] have coined the acronym MIRAB to describe societies dependent on migration, remittances, aid and relatively large bureaucracies. Micronesians have been migrating to Guam, Hawaii and the west coast of mainland USA. Cook Islanders, Niueans, Samoans, Tokelauans and Tongans have sought opportunities in New Zealand and Australia. Samoans and Tongans have also settled in the United States. International kinship networks have emerged with flows of people, goods and services as well as money. Going abroad and making a living as well as supporting families back home in the islands has become a pivotal strategy for many island people. In this regard island people not only avail themselves of the opportunities in metropolitan rim countries for education and training, employment and improved material standards of living, they are also exposed to stresses of urban life styles and to the problems of substance abuse, urban gangs, gambling and inter-generational conflicts. Most islanders find themselves in an underclass of semi skilled and unskilled workers in Auckland, Sydney, Los Angeles and other cities.[34]

Classes

The dominant classes that inherited state power on the eve of independence comprised educated chiefs, a coterie of professionals (teachers, lawyers, ministers of religion and former civil servants) and businessmen politicians. These elements continue to control the contemporary state. During the first decade of political independence there was much euphoria and rhetoric about following a unique Pacific style of development. Leaders and writers spoke about the "Pacific Way" and "Melanesian socialism". However, after the initial expansion in the economies of island countries and their labour markets the limitations of being small, isolated, vulnerable and poorly governed micro-states have thwarted development prospects.

In most PICs' constitutions the position of traditional chiefs is entrenched. This is another reason why in several instances there has been intense rivalry for prominent chiefly positions. In Fiji the *Bose Levu Vakavanua* (BLV) or Great Council of Chiefs has played a retrograde role in holding back political development. The chiefs with their allies in the state and in the private sector have supported three military coups that have toppled left of centre governments or coalitions. On each occasion the justification for the extra-legal military intervention has been ethnicity when in fact the real reason was to maintain and even extend the privileged position of chiefs, senior civil servants and certain business interests. Rampant racism has been the cover for maintaining class privileges. In virtually all PICs political power has led to and is perceived as the most potent avenue for acquiring economic wealth. In the short term it has allowed state power holders to enjoy lifestyles well beyond the imagination of their fellow country people. In many instances, those who are politically powerful sit as members of corporate boards of large local and international companies. Private companies in Fiji Islands have tended to employ persons of chiefly status as personnel and public relations managers because of their standing and influence.

During the post-colonial and contemporary periods there has been a tendency on the part of first generation state power holders to extend their privileges to their children. The latter have been sent to local elite schools and to secondary and post-secondary institutions abroad. The children of other sections of the middle class have also been educated. Prominent among the socially mobile are children of church ministers. The competition for employment in the public service is relieved by international migration but nepotism affects selection based on merit. There is some indication of 'elite closure' in this regard as those in privileged positions seek to reserve similar privileges for their offspring.

The class of wage earners has increased only slowly in the post-colonial period because of limited expansion in the labour markets of island countries. This has been due to depressed economic conditions in virtually all the island states for the last thirty odd years. Small local markets and limited resources have stifled growth in the smaller countries. Environmental degradation and conflict arising over the sharing of proceeds from resource exploitation has damaged prospects in the larger PICs. However, in many island countries the workers have organised themselves in trade unions which have sought to better their wages and terms of employment in spite of the adverse economic situation.

Slow growth or no-growth has meant that many young people have to turn to agriculture and other informal sector activities to make their livelihoods. Semi-subsistence small holder farming has continued to absorb and support growing populations. In one sense there is a large army of reserve labour in the islands. Other informal sector activities include roadside vendoring, domestic work, shoe shining, the selling of garlands (leis), backyard garages, commercial sex and retailing of drugs.

Status changes

New livelihoods, the acquisition of new knowledge and skills, alternative life styles, the changing status of women and socially (and physically) mobile young people have somewhat modified the pre-existing forms of power, prestige and wealth.

Decision-making is no longer the exclusive preserve of male elders, chiefs and aristocrats. It is more diffused with educated common people and women having a role in positions of power and influence. Employment outside villages and agriculture has given a whole lot of people incomes and purchasing power beyond that of village headmen and district chiefs. Remittances have reinforced this trend. In some cases those of chiefly origins have acquired education and are in very powerful positions but in many instances tradition bound chiefs have had limited education and their influence limited to the local level. Urbanisation has also changed values and norms of people. A degree of anonymity and impersonal relations have led to changes in attire, as well as behaviour patterns not envisaged in village surroundings. Young people especially value the freedom of towns and cities.

Education

The introduction of formal education, beginning with largely mission and community run primary schools, then a few secondary schools, followed by teachers' colleges, nursing schools and other post-secondary institutions had a profound effect on island peoples' levels of knowledge and skills, perceptions, aspirations and orientation. One's future was no longer entirely dependent on one's kinship group and that group's access to land. Education opened up a new world of opportunities, initially in the public service but later on in the professions, in business and overseas. Whilst most islanders spent only a few years in schools, enough to read the vernacular Bible and return to their family plots, others in ever growing numbers sought the highest levels of education available. A fortunate few went abroad for further education. Regional tertiary institutions such as the Fiji School of Medicine, Universities of Papua New Guinea and the South Pacific, the Pacific Regional Seminary and the Pacific Theological College have contributed to regional awareness. In the islands of Polynesia, education was especially valued and literacy rates are generally above 80 percent. Melanesian countries have much lower literacy rates because of the later introduction of formal education and the shortage of facilities in the context of larger fragmented populations.

In Polynesia and much of Micronesia education is very highly valued. There is a good spread of primary schools and a few secondary schools. Elite mission and public schools draw the top students from primary schools. These tend to be the children of upper and middle class families. Upon finishing high school a large number of them are sent abroad for tertiary education. Most of them do not go to tertiary institutions and universities in the region, preferring metropolitan country institutions. Many of them do not return to their island countries. Indeed, with public sector reforms and the huge cuts made in the number of positions, overseas education is seen as a passport to life abroad.

In Fiji Islands a large proportion of non-ethnic Fijian students attending the University of the South Pacific as well as those going abroad for further post secondary studies do so to obtain qualifications that will get them abroad. The reason for this state of affairs is that the Fijian state practises institutionalised racism. There is systematic discrimination in the allocation of scholarships, in employment in the public sector and in the prospects for promotion. The periodic and what appears to be regular extra-legal interference of the Fijian military in national politics, reinforces uncertainty and the inclination to emigrate.

Unlike the grave shortage of teachers in schools in Fiji Islands because of emigration, the shortage of teachers in Melanesian countries is a consequence of a poorly developed educational system. There has been a lack of trained teachers at all levels because not many people have gone beyond primary school. Indeed, as indicated above until recently more than 50 percent of school age children did not attend school. With the relatively high population growth rates and the demand for education, there is a severe shortage of both schools and teachers in Melanesia. The prospect for girls being educated in larger numbers continues to be limited in the Melanesian countries.

Family and Marriage

Education and the new modes of social and physical mobility have changed the life styles of educated islanders. Clubs, dance halls, nightclubs, cinemas and pubs have become centres for socialising. Whilst wider kinship ties remain significant, over the last 30 years nuclear families have gained distinct identity and importance in urban and peri-urban localities. In Fiji Islands more than half the total households are comprised of nuclear families. In the context of the financial demands of urban living, larger families and wider kinship network obligations are perceived as burdensome. Arranged marriages have been increasingly displaced by love marriages. Marriage partners in urban areas can be from distant regions and different linguistic and ethnic groups. The status of women has also undergone change. With proselytisation to Christianity, polygamy was proscribed and eventually prohibited by law. Monogamous families were encouraged, although not entirely successfully. Women who had earlier had been major producers of food and artifacts as well as 'beasts of burden' (in Melanesia) were pressured towards behaving like Victorian housewives. They were required to learn how to cook, sew, clean their homes and raise children along European patterns. This was in contrast to the considerable amount of female out-door livelihood activities in indigenous lifestyles. Previously with the men being responsible for cooking the day's large single meal in the earth oven the kitchen was not women's responsibility. Employment, albeit in particular professions relegated to women such as nursing, teaching and secretarial work, liberated women and also gave them higher status. A new generation of women professionals, senior civil servants, businesswomen, women in civil society organisations and women activists have been active in breaking gender barriers. Contraceptives and growing awareness of reproductive health have also helped in the liberation of women.

Cultural Change

The term culture is usually defined as the way of life of a people comprising material and non-material aspects. Material culture denotes technology, buildings, canoes and other artifacts, including personal possessions. Non-material culture denotes the symbolic, value, belief and institutional dimensions of the way of life. Whilst one may think that the changes discussed above would have negatively impacted on Pacific culture, this does not seem to be the case. Instead, as discussed below, Pacific cultures have continued to adapt and Pacific societies have retained cultures that, whilst not purely 'traditional' are still uniquely 'Pacific'.

Resilience of Tradition

Recently Anthony Hooper observed that "culture plays a much more significant role in national economies and national life of Pacific countries than it does in most other regions of the world."[35] This is because in most Pacific countries, "around 80 to 90 percent of land resources are under customary tenure, and the traditional sector accounts for around 50 percent of national GDP."[36] The entrenchment of customary land tenure and traditional social structures in national constitutions ensure their perpetuation and insulation from both market forces and state coercion. With customary control over most economic resources essential for development it is not "simply a matter of engineering a transition from substance to dynamic monetary economies."[37] In any case Hooper has argued that it is erroneous to characterise the traditional sector as subsistence because production is geared to fulfilling a diverse range of reciprocal and redistributive exchanges in networks of mutual obligations that integrate island people. Economies in the traditional sector for Hooper are "embedded in the society", with a large moral and ideological content.[38]

A second reason for the significance of culture in the island countries of the Pacific is because of its role in national politics. Hooper has pointed to the fact that politicians have to win the support of electors reliant on livelihoods in the traditional sector where "matters of custom and tradition carry considerable political clout."[39] National constitutions in Hooper's view assert legitimacy in terms of "distinctive culture and traditions" as much as they attend to "notions of democracy and individual rights". "In these ways", Hooper claims, "culture in one form or another is right at the heart of national and political life."[40]

Indigenisation of Modernity

Marshall Sahlins, in his chapter in the same book, has also argued that indigenous cultures have been resilient to change and that there has been an indigenisation of modernity. These cultures have not simply been transformed to being a mere reflection of the West but have adopted new technologies, money and goods in diverse ways to invigorate traditional values and norms, customary ceremonies and exchange relations. Far from being passive victims of colonialism and modernisation, indigenous people have responded positively "to harness the good things of Europeans to the development of their own existence."[41] Rural-urban, and even international migration streams are perceived as circulatory in nature. While the physical geography of the indigenous village is limited, there are no limits to the social geography of the village. In this regard even globalisation is seen as making possible the enlargement of the complex social network of kinship reinforced by flows of goods, people and cash. Purely rational economic decisions related to the maximisation of the return to labour are geared to the fulfillment of traditional obligations to family and kinsfolk in accord with cultural values.

Sahlins[42] maintains that the dichotomy between modernity and tradition is undermined by the fact that non-western peoples have sought to create their own cultural versions of modernity. In any case what is regarded as traditional has usually been neo-tradition, already a hybrid of the old and the new. Cultures have ways of adapting, changing, disappearing and reappearing in unimagined ways — culture is not simply a heritage, it is a project and a philosophy of life. As a philosophy of life, culture "is an exhaustible reservoir of responses to the world's challenges" in contrast to development which denotes "a scale of values, norms of conduct or models of behaviour transmissible from one society to another!"[43]

Language

While the dichotomy of tradition and modernity is false and simplistic (English common law is 'traditional') and indigenous socio-cultural systems incorporate and adapt to modernisation, there nevertheless have been considerable changes in Pacific societies. Besides indigenous islanders who in the Melanesian countries have considerable linguistic diversity, there are people of Asian and European origins. Pidgin and Bislama or a dominant dialect, as in Bauan Fijian, have become the lingua franca among them. The languages of former colonial rulers, English and French, have become official languages in post colonial Pacific states. English has become the medium of communication of the regional elite. It is the language of social mobility.[44]

Religion

With rare exceptions, islanders converted to Christianity. Catholic and various Protestant denominations predominate. Just about every village and settlement boasts a church. Sabbath is closely adhered to amongst islanders, particularly in rural areas. Prayer sessions, church choirs, grace before meals and other outward manifestations of religion are widespread. Pastors and priests are highly respected and, in most instances, very well rewarded. However, there continues to exist, in most Pacific communities, beliefs and rituals that predate proselytisation. Such beliefs range from a regard for ancestral spirits, sacredness of sites and objects, trees, totems, sorcery and witchcraft, spiritual powers of certain lineages and of chiefs as well as individuals continue to act as mechanisms for social control. Kava remains a sacred drink in Fiji Islands and Samoa at ceremonies and ritual functions. The incorporation of Christianity into the social structures and everyday lives of islanders has led to the view that there has been an indigenisation of this religion in this view. The Christian belief system, its moral codes and rituals have a distinct Pacific favour.

In multicultural Fiji Islands, 90 percent of the Indo-Fijian population are Hindus or Muslims. There has been a syncretisation of these religions with both Christianity and indigenous religious beliefs and rituals. In recent years there has been an Arabisation of Islam in Fiji and this is most evident in the attire of Muslim men and women.

Changes in Material Culture

At the level of material culture changes are obvious and marked. In much of Micronesia and Polynesia buildings, including family homes, have been constructed with concrete and/or wood in the western style. Corrugated iron has largely replaced thatch. Pacific style architecture such as the neo-traditional fale and the bure has been retained. In Samoa family homes, meeting places and public buildings display this architecture. Parliament buildings in Fiji Islands and Papua New Guinea have a distinct island character.

Modes of communication and transportation have changed. Traditional drums (such as the Lali and tamtam) and conch shells continue to be used symbolically and in ceremonies but telephones (including mobile phones), radio and to an extent electronic forms of communication have become more widely used. Pacific issues are discussed on line internationally. Tonga has claimed its share of satellite space and remote Tuvalu had the foresight to lay claim to its lucrative dot.com name. Land, sea and air transportation has been revolutionised in most islands. Motor cars, trucks, buses and vans crowd island roads and highways. Regular aircraft flights exist between most Pacific capitals to international destinations. In-country airline companies also operate to service inland and outlying locations. Helicopters are available in some of the bigger countries. Shipping services are provided by inter-island ferries as well as fibre-glass outboard powered boats. However, there are still island countries such as Tokelau and Niue as well as many outer islands of the larger archipelagoes where transportation continues to be irregular.

Modern communication and transport systems have facilitated cross boundary flows of people, ideas, capital, goods and services within and between countries. There is a demand on political leaders to provide higher materially comparable living standards found in metropolitan countries. The print media which exists in most countries of the Pacific, transistor radio, cinema and television together with inter-personal communication have made most islanders, particularly young people conscious of life styles and fashions in metropolitan centres. In Pacific towns and cities hair styles, attire, personal possessions and even the language used reflect fads and fashions elsewhere. In Fiji Islands both Hollywood and Bollywood have considerable influence in these matters. The music and songs in island popular cultures also reflect external influences but local compositions and styles do impact on the island and diaspora scenes. Island cuisines have been enriched by European and Asian dishes so that roasts, barbeques, chopsuey, chowmein, and curries complement *lovo* food at most feasts.

CONCLUSION

It is obvious that socio-economic, cultural and political changes have transformed Pacific island societies. Individualism, preoccupation with oneself and one's immediate family rather than the wider kinship network together with individual acquisitiveness has increased. It is also apparent that this transformation is not entirely in the likeness of the West, as propounded by evolutionary theorists and predicted by the diffusionist modernisation school. Development has improved standards of living (nutrition, health, life expectancy, housing, education) but has occurred in tandem with increased inequality amongst islanders. The co-existence and hybridisation of traditional and neo-traditional structures with modern institutions of the state and market have led to many contradictions, tensions and conflicts. As we look to the future these conflicts and tensions must be addressed so as to ensure the harmonious continuation of Pacific island states. However, it should be noted that addressing tensions is not the same as removing tensions through the homogenisation of cultures. The dualism and admixture that exists in Pacific societies has provided safety nets, security and equality, as well as new opportunities. There is a place in the Pacific both for countries and people both to be like Kavaliku's lokua, "small fish living in reef ponds cut off from the sea at tidal lows, but periodically replenished by ocean waters" and to explore oceans and their surrounding shores for new opportunities to sustain their homelands.[45]

ENDNOTES

1   Polanyi, K. 1957. *The Great Transformation*. Boston, MA: Beacon Press at p 31.

2   See Booth, C. *Life and Labour of the People of London* cited in McKee, J.B. 1969. *Introduction to Sociology*. New York: Holt, Rinehart and Winston Inc.

3   McKee, J.B. 1969. Above, n 2 at p 20.

4   Sahlins, M. and Service, E.R. 1960. *Evolution*. Ann Arbor Michigan: University of Michigan Press.

5   Scarr, D. 1973. *The Majesty of Colour: A life of John Bates Thurston, vol. 1, I, the very bayonet*. Canberra: Australian National University.

6   Max Weber's account of the transformation in Europe was based on a close examination of European social structure, culture and history. He maintained that the protestant ethic unique to Europe gave rise to capitalism. Calvinist anxiety over salvation led to abstinence from indulgence of any kind, an increase in savings and enterprise. Society became rationalised and bureaucratised with no place for superstition, magic and the satisfaction of baser needs. Society followed routines based on law and order, procedures, plans and predictability. Calculating in a rational way the outcomes of businesses and other activities became integral to the process of rationality.

7   Sahlins makes the sardonic observation that "Rostow must have been among the first to perceive that the culmination of human social evolution was shopping." See Sahlins, M. 2000. On the anthropology of modernity, or, some triumphs of culture over despondency theory. In Hooper, A. (ed), *Culture and Development in the Pacific*. Canberra: Asia Pacific Press, at p 46.

8   Fairbairn, T.I.J. 1971. Pacific Island Economies. *Journal of Polynesian Society* Vol. 80, No.1: 74–118 at pp 74–75.
    See also Nayacakalou, R. 1975. *Leadership in Fiji*. Melbourne: Oxford University Press; Belshaw, C.S. 1964. *Under the Ivi Tree*. Berkeley & Los Angeles: University of California Press; Watters, R.F. 1969. *Koro*. London: Clarendon Press.

9   Fairbairn, T.I.J. 1994. Pacific Island Economies. In Douglas, N and N. (eds) *Pacific Islands Yearbook, 17th Edition*. Suva: Fiji Times Ltd at pp 14–15.

10 Amarshi, A., Good, K. and Mortimer, R. 1979. *Development and Dependency: The Political Economy of Papua New Guinea*. Melbourne: Oxford University Press.

11 Fitzpatrick, P. 1980. *Law and State in Papua New Guinea*. London: Academic Press.

12 Rokotuivuna, A. 1973. *Fiji A Developing Australian Colony*. Victoria: IDA.

13 Utrecht, E. (ed) 1984. *Fiji: Client State of Australia?* Sydney: University of Sydney..

14 Narsey, W. 1979. Monopoly Capital, White Racism and Superprofits in Fiji: A case study of CSR. *The Journal of Pacific Studies* 5: 66–146.

15 Narayan, J. 1984. *The Political Economy of Fiji*. Suva: South Pacific Review Press.

16 Durutalo, S. 1985. Internal Colonialism and Unequal Regional Development: The case of Western Viti Levu, Fiji. Unpublished MA Thesis, Sociology Department, School of Social and Economic Development, University of the South Pacific, Suva.

17 Sutherland, W. 1992. *Beyond the Politics of Race*. Canberra: Research School of Pacific Studies, Australian National University.

18 Shankman, P. 1976. *Migration and Underdevelopment: The case of Western Samoa*. Boulder, Colorado: Westview Press.

19 Bellam, M. 1981. *The Citrus Colony*. Wellington: New Zealand Coalition for Trade and Development.

20 Howard, M. et al. 1983. The Political Economy of the South Pacific. *South East Asian Monograph Series. No. 13*. Townsville: James Cook University .

21 Naidu, V. 1988. State, Class and Politics in the South Pacific. Unpublished D.Phil Thesis, University of Sussex, Falmer.

22 See, i.e., Crocombe, R.G. 1971. *Land Tenure in the Pacific*. Melbourne: Oxford University Press.

23 Thaman, R. 1990. Challenges and constraints to sustainable development in the Pacific Islands. Presented to the UNDP Regional Workshop on Environmental Management and Sustainable Development in the South Pacific, Suva (17–21 April).

24 Vayda, A.P. (ed) 1968. *Peoples and Cultures of the Pacific*. New York: The Natural History Press.

25 Graves, A. 1984. The Nature and Origins of Pacific Islands Labour Migration to Queensland, 1863–1906. In Mark, S. and Richardson, B. (eds) *International Labour Migration*. Oxford: Oxford University Press.

26 Moorehead, A. 1966. *The Fatal Impact*. New York: Harper and Row.

27 Morrell, W.P. 1960. *Britain in the Pacific Islands*. Oxford: Clarendon Press.

28 France, P. 1969. *The Charter of the Land*. Melbourne: Oxford University Press.

29 Gilson, R.D. 1970. *Samoa 1830–1900, the politics of a multicultural community*. Melbourne: Oxford University Press.

30 Spate, O.H.K. 1978. The Pacific as an artefact. In Gunson, N. (ed). *The Changing Pacific. Essays in Honour of H.E.Maude*. Oxford: Oxford University Press, at p 32.

31 Fiji Royal Gazette 1884. Vol. 10.

32 Ward, R.G. 1997. Pacific Islands Urbanisation: Trends, Issues and Questions. Paper presented at the Conference on Management of Social Transformation in the South Pacific, UNESCO/MOST, USP, Suva, October 1997.

33 Bertram, I.G. & Watters, R.F. 1985. The Mirab economy in the South Pacific micro-states. *Pacific Viewpoint* 26(3):497–519.

34 McCall, G. and Connell, J. 1994. Pacific Islands Migration. In Douglas, N. and N. (eds),1994 Above n 9.

35 Hooper, A. 2000. Above, n 7 at p 2.

36 Hooper, A. 2000. Above, n 7 at p 2.

37 Hooper, A. 2000. Above, n 7 at p 2.

38 Hooper, A. 2000. Above, n 7 at p 3.

39 Hooper, A. 2000. Above, n 7 at p 3.

40 Hooper, A. 2000. Above, n 7 at p 3.

41 Hooper, A. 2000. Above, n 7 at p 3.

42 Sahlins, M. 2000. Above, n 7 at p 48.

43 Tour'e, cited in Sahlins, M. 2000. Above, n 7 at p 58.

44 Waddell, E., Naidu, V. and Hau'ofa, E. 1993. *A New Oceania*. Suva: School of Social and Economic Development and the University of the South Pacific in association with Beake House.

45 Hooper, A. 2000. Above, n 7 at p 12.

Review questions

1. Identify and evaluate the impact of the most important agents of societal change during the colonial era in a Pacific island society. (Examples of agents of change are religious missions, commercial interests, the colonial state, anti-colonial movements and trade unions.)

2. To what extent do you think it is valid to say that the personal relations found in small scale pre-European societies have given way to impersonal contractual relations in PICS? How do you think this change affects the maintenance of order in PICs?

3. "Social change is more likely to emerge from factories and towns than from farms and rural settlements." Discuss this assertion with respect to urbanisation and urbanism in a Pacific island society.

4. How would you explain or characterise the maintenance of law in order in pre colonial Pacific societies, colonial Pacific societies and post-colonial, contemporary Pacific societies?

Further readings

Crocombe, R.G. Neemia, U. Ravuvu, A. & Vom Busch, W. (eds) 1992. *Culture and Democracy in the South Pacific*. Suva: Institue of Pacific Studies, University of the South Pacific.

Hooper, A. (ed) 2000. *Culture and Sustainable Development in the South Pacific*. Suva: Institute of Pacific Studies, University of the South Pacific.

Martinussen, J. 1997. *Society, State and Market*. London: Zed Books.

Naidu, V. 1991. *Development, State and Class Theories: An Introductory Survey*. Suva: Fiji Institue of Applied Studies.

Waddell, E. Naidu, V. & Hau'ofa, E. (eds) 1993. *A New Oceania: Rediscovering Our Sea of Islands*. Suva: SSED, University of the South Pacific in association with Beake Press.

SECTION 2
CORRUPTION

Corruption is frequently blamed for the failure of countries in the Pacific and elsewhere to achieve their development goals. The presence of corruption in government and the public service is thought to indicate a number of problems, including lack of accountability, lack of transparency and a general failure to 'play by the rules' or follow the law. It is this last factor which is, perhaps, at the heart of concerns about corruption. If the authorities that are supposed to make and enforce the rules cannot follow them, how can the citizens and investors into that country hope to live in a stable and predictable environment in which they can be sure of having their rights upheld and protected?

Combatting corruption has been one of the central concerns of the donor community in recent years, and is at the heart of the good governance agenda that is currently driving development programmes. Legal and institutional reforms aimed at increasing accountability and exposing corruption, including leadership codes, ombusman's offices and financial accountability legislation have been proliferating in the Pacific island region. This section discusses the nature and causes of corruption, and examines the operation of some of the measures that have been taken to expose and thereby, hopefully, reduce corruption.

The first chapter, by Professor Hughes, provides us with a meaning for the term corruption. It also raises the question of whether corruption is necessarily a bad thing, or whether corruption can actually have beneficial results in some situations.

Hassall's chapter elaborates further on the point made by Hughes that whilst institutions of government are perceived to be largely irrelevant there is not going to be a commitment to uphold these insitutions or to follow their rules. His argument is that a lack of constitutional legitimacy caused by constitutions failing to be grounded in the will of the people has resulted in corruption and instability within the Pacific Island region. After discussing some notable expressions of this lack of legitimacy, he turns to consider what is necessary in order to regenerate a sense of legitimacy in the consitutional orders within the region.

Hill's chapter concludes this section by providing a study of the role and performance of the Ombudsman's Office in Vanuatu. This chapter complements the more theoretical chapters preceeding it by providing a discussion of what corruption means in practice in Vanuatu and the role that the Ombudsman's Office plays in such an environment.

2. CORRUPTION

By: Professor Robert Hughes

KEY TERMS AND PHRASES

Corruption

This term has no precise meaning, but is popularly associated with the abuse of power for personal gain. Within the popular conception of corruption, not only legal wrongdoing but behaviours that are seen as immoral can be considered to be corrupt.

Fiduciary

A fiduciary is a person who is subjected to special legal duties to act always in the interests on whose behalf he or she acts. Fiduciaries are also denied the possibility of making personal profits or gains from the carrying out of their functions. There are many types of fiduciary with different standards of responsibility. A trustee is the traditional kind of fiduciary and subjected to the highest duties.

Political legitimacy

Political legitimacy is concerned with the justification of a government or a system of government to operate within any particular society. The word 'legitimacy' has connections with legality, although now it is used in a broader sense as meaning something like the basis of political authority.

INTRODUCTION

Corruption in political systems is a pervasive international issue. The political systems of the South Pacific region are certainly not immune to corruption. It is not a phenomenon which only attends larger developed political systems. Certainly neither the smallness nor the communal atmosphere of the Pacific island states have prevented the occurrence of corruption on a relatively wide scale.[1] The phenomenon produces some basic themes which are seemingly incontrovertible. Corruption is one of the most significant threats to democracy world-wide. It produces instability and thrives on the social inequality to which it is a substantial contributor. It undermines the confidence of peoples in the legitimate institutions of government. It is a major contributor to social, cultural and economic decline of nation states. It is evanescent, perverse and consequentially difficult both to detect and eliminate.

To begin it is appropriate to seek some understanding of the concept of (political) corruption. As with many of our concepts in general use 'corruption' is a rather amorphous notion. It is not quite a term of legal art in the sense that it does not lend itself easily to a precise definition. It might sometimes be used to denote 'non-legal' corruption in the sense that it refers to acts which constitute abuses of power or the appropriation of advantage which, though not precisely illegal or criminal in nature, are nonetheless open to condemnation. Some have in mind the contemptible actions of public officials only whilst others would include corruption in the private sphere as a significant component of corrupt activity. From a legal point of view the focus has perhaps been on a special category of crime; namely that type of crime which is committed by public officers or which is, in some way, connected with the performance of public duties and functions.

What is corruption in some places might not be considered so in others. In a world where cultural relativism pretends considerable explanatory power one is often confronted with the possibility of misinterpretation of the acts of others. A condemnation of something as obviously corrupt, particularly by cultural outsiders, will often be met with a standard response; namely, that the perspective of the observer does not take account the cultural norms and values. In particular, it fails to take into account the system of privileges and favours which specific actors, especially the traditionally powerful, are entitled to within the culture concerned. Hence what might be treated as clearly a case of corruption in Australia or the United Kingdom might not readily be perceived as such in, say, Pacific cultures.

It is an unfortunate fact that thinkers from a Western tradition are not always attuned to these factors. Given a Western tradition of philosophical and political thought which pretends, be it cultural imperialism or not, the seeking out of universal patterns of thought and understanding, the cause of the error is obvious enough. No doubt, if the pretence of a universal moral order were still a realisable objective we would be on clearer ground. Some simple and universal understanding of corruption might exist which could direct our thinking on this issue and encourage our forthright condemnation of unacceptable behaviour. But corruption is not reducible to such a simple formula. That aside, most people carry with them certain clear assumptions about what corruption involves but then find it difficult to provide a reasonable definition of it or, at least, one which applies to all potential cases of corruption. In fact, there is no single definition which encompasses everything that people would want to take as corruption.

The regulation of corruption is rendered problematic by the fact that the understanding of corruption tends to vary from place to place and from jurisdiction to jurisdiction. Certainly cultural factors play a part in this. However, there are many interesting issues that arise in the context of corruption that are not confined to problems of definition. Does corruption involve only some positive action on the part of a particular person or can a failure to act also involve corruption? Are all forms of corruption intrinsically bad or can corrupt conduct be justified under some circumstances — for instance where it does no immediate harm or where it actively promotes some good, or perhaps more good than bad? Let us consider firstly some definitions of corruption and before turning to some of these questions.

THE MEANING OF CORRUPTION

As indicated above, the legal sense of corruption is somewhat unsettled.[2] Certainly the term has appeared in statutes and in cases from time to time. This has become more frequent over the last 30 years or so with the rise of efforts to combat corrupt behaviour of various sorts — usually as some aspect of maladministration. It can mean anything from the exercise of undue influence to the making of false declarations (e.g. for electoral purposes). Undue influence, or perhaps breach of fiduciary duties on the part of trustees or other fiduciaries, seems in fact the closest that private law comes to dealing with corruption. These breaches involve essentially a failure on the part of a person who is in a position of power to comply with the duties and obligations of office. Thus they involve a form of equitable fraud that very often leads to the imposition of a constructive trust. Whilst corruption is often seen as a public law issue there is some degree of similarity with principles of equity. I will return to this issue later on.

The term 'corruption' in everyday usage is likewise very broad in its meaning. It has many synonyms including decomposition, neology, foulness, disease, deterioration, imperfection, perversity, degeneration, improbity, fraud, deceit and vice. But whatever dictionary meaning the term has, it is now predominantly associated with a failure in the performance or observance of a public duty by someone who is considered to be am actor in the public sphere. A Commonwealth paper on corruption offers this working definition:

> Corruption... [is] the wrongful exercise of public duty for direct or consequential personal gain ... Quite apart from the harmful effects which corruption may have on the actual processes of democracy, government, the law and the judiciary, the corrupt act is inherently undemocratic.[3]

A document issued by the Independent Commission Against Corruption of New South Wales, Australia states:

> What is corruption? Corruption commonly involves the dishonest or preferential use of power or position which has the result of one person or organisation being advantaged over another. It includes the conduct of non public officials who cause public officials to misuse their power or position. The community expects public officials to perform their duties with honesty and in the best interests of the public. Corruption involves a breach of public trust and leads to inequality, wasted resources and wasted public money. A key notion when considering whether or not corrupt conduct has occurred is the misuse of public office in the public sector of New South Wales.[4]

There are some authorities which appear to suggest that the word 'corruptly' where it appears in legislation denotes merely action which is deliberate.[5] There are others that suggest that it imposes a requirement of purposefully doing the act that the legislation forbids.[6] These are authorities that are concerned with the offering of bribes to public officials which indicate that the innocent receipt of a bribe by the recipient does not constitute corruption.[7] The general tendency, however, is to say that the element of corruption does not require proof of any special element such as evil, immorality, dishonesty, wickedness, iniquity, improbity or deceit.[8] Something is corrupt simply if it "does something that the legislature forbids".[9]

The definition of corruption in section 8 of the *Independent Commission Against Corruption Act* 1988 (N.S.W.) in fact shows how broad the concept has become in terms of the types of conduct which can be considered corrupt. According to that section corruption includes: "official misconduct, bribery, blackmail, obtaining or offering secret commissions, fraud, theft, perverting the course of justice, embezzlement, election bribery, election funding offences, election fraud, treating (corruptly influencing a person's vote), tax evasion, revenue evasion, currency violations, illegal drug dealings, illegal gambling, obtaining financial benefit from vice engaged in by others, bankruptcy and company violations, harbouring criminals, forgery, treason or other offences against the Sovereign, homicide or violence and any conspiracy or attempt to conspire in relation to any of the above." Not all of these are in fact crimes. Where they are civil matters, however, the general tendency has been for the courts to require proof of corrupt activity according to the criminal standard of proof or something approximating it.[10] But it tends to be the fact that the relevant activity relates to a public official that brings out the association with corruption. It is this which also allegedly warrants special treatment of corruption within the legal system.

Corruption as a Legal Concept

There is no specifically designated crime of corruption in English law, although it might be an element in certain criminal conduct as we have seen — for example, something done with an intention to corrupt or done corruptly. In *Woolmington v the Director of Public Prosecutions*[11] the House of Lords gave recognition to a common law offence of corrupting public morals. The corrupting circumstance in that case was running a brothel, clearly an element of supposed immorality. This case is therefore sometimes displayed as an attempt to show that there often is a moral content to the law. This is a claim that stops short of the natural law claim that there is always a moral criterion that determines the validity of law. It also stops short of the contention that the legal condemnation of corruption is based essentially on moral grounds.

One of the primary legal senses of corruption has long been that of bribery. Put another way, bribery is perhaps the classical legal sense of corruption. Bribery conveys the basic idea of procuring or attempting to procure favourable actions on the part of a public official by the payment or offer of a reward. In English law the bribery of public officials was a common law misdemeanour. Bribery of and by agents was also recognised as a misdemeanour under the *Prevention of Corruption Acts* 1906 and 1916 (UK). There are now several statutes which deem corruption or bribery and corruption an offence — see in the UK for example, the *Public Bodies Corrupt Practices Act* 1889, the *Sale of Offices Acts* 1551 and 1809 and the *Representation of the People Act* 1949. There is now also legislation in some jurisdictions which prohibits the taking by public officers of secret commissions for the performance of their duties.[12]

There is no doubt that bribery has been regarded as a serious breach of public trust and, in criminal cases, has attracted the imposition of serious penalties. For example, in *R v Nath*[13] Perry J. said (at 119):

> A breach by persons holding public office of the duty to act honestly in the performance of their public duties is a most serious matter which should ordinarily attract a substantial penalty.

In *R v Challoner*,[14] a case involving fraud by a branch bank manager, Kirby P. said (at 375):

> There is no doubt that a long line of authority in this court lays down the principle that, in offences of this kind, by persons in a position of trust involving the manipulation of public monies, a custodial sentence is normally required.

The concept of corruption is now clearly much wider than mere bribery although, no doubt, this remains one of its primary senses. Although corruption is frequently linked with the activities of organised crime this is not necessarily the case. One thing that the link with organised crime does show us is that corruption need not involve something so simple as an isolated act undertaken by a public official done in return for the offer of a reward or payment. The techniques, and indeed the conduct, involved might be much more subtle than mere payment or offers of reward to procure particular outcomes.

It should be noted that now, particularly in those statutes constituting corruption investigation agencies, legal definitions appear which widen the concept of corruption considerably. Evidence of this has been provided above. The focus is now much more on maintaining the performance of duties and standards by public officials. This is not to say that it is only the acts of public officials that can be regarded as corrupt for the purposes of the law. The breach by a fiduciary (say a trustee or a corporate director) of his or her duty to act in the best interests of the entity which he or she controls is a significant form of corruption which the law, and more especially equity, has long sought to control. There are clearly parallels between the logic applied with respect to the corrupt activities of public actors and the principles of public law in the general area of equitable fraud, breach of fiduciary duty and so on.

In fact the two cases just mentioned (public and private corruption) are not so distinct as is sometimes thought. Fiduciaries are, by definition, persons who are obliged to act in the interests of others rather than in their own interest. They are obliged to avoid conflicts of duty and interest (including the payment of bribes). Public officials and politicians are really in the position of fiduciaries and, in some jurisdictions, they have been explicitly treated as such for some purposes. This has been taken as an implicit part of the conferral of political power for the purposes of administrative law. The power is conferred on trust. For example, in *Manunivavalagi Dalituicama Korovulasvula v Public Service Commission*[15] it was said

> The Common Law makes it clear that, generally speaking a statutory power conferred on any person or authority for public purposes is conferred as it were, upon trust and not absolutely. Accordingly the holder of such a power does not have an unfettered discretion in exercising the power.

Some of the bribery cases such as *R. v Nath* and *R. v Challoner* (both above) have treated the action in question as a breach of trust reposed in a public official. But that is not quite the same as enforcement as a fiduciary duty. Unfortunately, imposing a fiduciary duty on someone operates merely as an *ex post facto* attempt to rectify a breach of the duty on behalf of someone whose interest, usually a proprietary interest, has been affected. It has not been, and would not be, entirely effective in eliminating or perhaps lessening corruption. The anti-corruption measures, which we will examine in a moment, have a much broader purpose.

IS CORRUPTION ENDEMIC IN POLITICAL/LEGAL SYSTEMS?

There are divergent views on how far corruption is an inevitable part of all political systems. The ideologically conservative view is that corruption is part of human nature and therefore will be an aspect of all forms of human interrelationship. That is so whether the relationship be realised in national politics, Pacific as well as Western politics, commerce, village or local administration, corporations and clubs, families or other such forms of association. Yet such an answer is too simple, in my view. For one thing, corruption does not appear all the time, nor does it colour all forms of relationship at all times. The proposition that people are basically or primarily bad is, to anyone with any reasonable experience of human affairs, quite a naïve and untenable proposition. It would, of course, be just as naïve and untenable to claim that corruption and other forms of 'badness', do not exist at all. Corruption is, as has been conceded already, a prevalent aspect of contemporary life and, especially, public life.

However, corruption in the public sphere has sometimes been treated as if it were prevalent only in certain forms of society — for example in underdeveloped or third world societies. The impression has been, indeed that it was or is a characteristic of those societies; that is, corruption was or is institutionalised in them as an aspect of the stage of development. The causes are sometimes taken to be poor economic conditions, ineptitude of administration or the poor education of public officials. Sometimes it is the existence of the traditional structure of society that is inconsistent with the regime of public administration imposed by colonisers which is treated as the primary cause. According to this theory the assumption behind the neutral administrative role of a public service (bureaucracy) on the Western model does not work when it falls into the hands of those who have loyalties which lie elsewhere. Post-colonial societies such as India are often targeted for attention as examples.[16] Hargreaves, for example, once wrote of the Indian bureaucracy:

> One major element in the effective operation — and in the public image — of bureaucracy is corruption. Whilst most people continue to see government service as prestigious, their confidence in it is low. Public servants are described as ineffectual, self-seeking, and dishonest. In a survey of residents of Delhi State, almost 60 percent felt that at least half the government officials were corrupt. Corruption may be greatly exaggerated in India because economically frustrated individuals seek a scapegoat in official misbehaviour, but A.D. Gorwala argues that "the psychological atmosphere produced by the persistent and unfavourable comment is itself the cause of further moral deterioration, for people will begin to adapt their methods, even for securing a legitimate right, to what they believe to be the tendency of men in power and office". Moreover, the public may decry corruption, but traditional attitudes often condone it, and fatalism may lead many to accept it as inevitable. Nepotism is officially condemned, but in traditional terms it may be viewed as loyalty to one's family friends and community.[17]

On the other hand, the occurrence of corruption in Western societies is sometimes supposed to be rare or, at least, very occasional and nothing approximating its institutional occurrence in third world countries. It might still be the case that the occurrence of corruption in economically less developed countries is higher. But it is a significant factor in the developed countries as well. However, more recent experience has shown that corruption in Western societies has been much more regular and institutionalised than otherwise thought. Hence the pointing of the finger at underdeveloped or eastern countries alone was unfair. Confirming this, a recent report on OECD countries begins:

> OECD countries are concerned about declining confidence in government. This so-called "confidence deficit" has been fueled by well publicised "scandals", ranging from inappropriate actions on the part of public officials, to full-scale corruption. Few, if any, Member countries have escaped the taint, if not the reality of wrongdoing. As a result, ethics or standards in public life have become an important public and political issue.[18]

Some research has been published by the University of Goettingen and Transparency International on corruption in various countries throughout the world.[19] The report covers only 85 countries — less than half of the countries in the world. Unfortunately the South Pacific does not receive a mention at all. A score of 10 indicates the least level of perceived corruption. The lower the score the worse the perceived corruption level. The best rankings were: Denmark (10.0) Finland (9.6) Sweden (9.5) New Zealand (9.4) Iceland (9.3) Canada (9.2) Singapore (9.1) Netherlands (9. 0) Norway (9.0) Switzerland (8.9) Australia, Luxembourg, United Kingdom (8.7).The ten worst were : Vietnam (2.5) Russia (2.4) Ecuador (2.3) Venezuela (2.3) Colombia (2.2) Indonesia (2.0) Nigeria (1.9) Tanzania (1.9) Honduras (1.7) Paraguay (1.5) Cameroon (1.4).

This is an index compiled on the basis of perceptions of corruption held by members of the public, business and non-government organisations. It is not a survey of actual corruption which would, of course, be extremely difficult if not impossible to survey simply because much of it is undetected. It is a ranking only. Hence a score of 10 for Denmark does not indicate and absence of corruption in that country. It just means that it obtained the best score. Significantly, however, it appears that over fifty of the countries failed to attain a score of at least five which is a remarkably poor performance. One can merely conjecture how the South Pacific countries might have ranked given the many reported instances of corruption which have occurred in recent times. On recent indications they would certainly not rank very highly. If the exercise is one based on perception of corruption then one would expect the perception level of corruption throughout the Pacific to be high. For one thing these are small countries where often corruption is a matter of common knowledge. Additionally, that common knowledge or awareness simply does not seem to lead to an impetus to reform.

SHOULD WE ATTEMPT TO COMBAT CORRUPTION?

There was once a view that corruption, in certain sorts of environments, including bureaucratic environments, could be seen in positive terms. It achieved effective results where this was otherwise impossible or unlikely. One could argue, for example, that corruption in certain developing countries at least provided a means of getting the job done. Many large corporations have had the experience of dealing with bureaucracies in these countries in just this way. If bribery is necessary to get the corporate project under way then bribery as the means is justified by the end. To take another view of it, could one argue that if corruption benefits a majority of the community and harms no-one in particular and, as an aside, also gets things done, should it be condoned or at least tolerated?

Say, for example, that it is of importance that a particular bureaucratic action should be undertaken to ensure that a building project of major importance to the economic well-being of a section of the community in a small island state should be undertaken. Several jobs will result if the work goes ahead. It will produce considerable revenue for the people of the island state as a whole because it will dramatically increase the revenue of the country. The bureaucracy in the country is renowned for its inefficiency and incompetence. It has had the development application for over a year and nothing has happened. Wouldn't a small bribe by the developer to an official to get the job done be tolerable in the interests of the overall well being of the community concerned? What harm is there in producing effective bureaucratic action? Many would oppose such a view on the ground that corruption is *absolutely* wrong on moral grounds and ought to be opposed and condemned wherever it occurs on that basis. Corruption ought to be seen as a crime and it should be referred to criminal investigation divisions for investigation, detection and prosecution. In short, corruption must not be condoned. It must be rooted out and the corrupt brought to justice.

Corruption and ineffficiency

But whatever the moral issue involved, such a position of moral condemnation never seems to have worked very well. If anything it has been a realisation of the failure of the moral high ground position, just referred to, which seems to have produced somewhat more effective measures in combating corruption. The move in this direction came initially from large business organisations in the 1980s. There appears to have been an increasing awareness of the need to combat corruption. It was a recognition which went hand in hand with the so-called white collar crime phenomenon. White collar crime, or crime committed by officers and employees of corporations, had long been outlawed by corporations legislation and, for the most part, subjected to harsh criminal sanctions. But such crimes were notoriously difficult to prosecute successfully. Furthermore, they attracted unwanted attention to the corporation involved with the publicity potentially able to do damage to the public image of the company and, more especially, to the image of the corporation in financial or investment circles.

Hence an alternative strategy was thought appropriate in this area on the part of both corporations themselves and on the part of corporate legislators. Firstly, as noted already, the business corporations came to see corruption within a corporation as counter productive to the general nature of the enterprise. Corporations which had sound ethical business practices seemed to perform better on the stock exchange and to outperform those which didn't. In other words, big business started to adopt measures to combat corruption within organisations, not because it was perceived as morally wrong but because it was bad for business. In the business world moral issues rarely count. It is turnover and the competitive edge which matters most. Corruption was and is seen as counterproductive to business performance. This, of course, is not quite the same view opposing corruption that we might be used to.

On the other hand, corporate regulators, realising the ineffectiveness of hard-line criminal prosecutions in counteracting white collar crime, proceeded to create particular categories of quasi-criminal liability — what is in essence a form of civil liability. Certainly this measure facilitated proof against the delinquent officer but it also lessened the stigma attaching to the corrupt action against the corporation. The business management view of corruption — as something which was counterproductive to the enterprise and appropriate for alternative strategies of elimination — then seems to have filtered through to the public sector. One of the reasons for this was the adoption of the new approaches to public sector management which sought to adopt business strategies and private sector management techniques to improve the efficiency of the bureaucracy.

Corruption and Political Legitimacy

The prevention of corruption is not just a matter which goes to the achievement of efficiency in the operations of government. I think that this is of as little worth in explaining the phenomenon of corruption as cavalier condemnations of the immorality or evil of corruption. An important factor which is of greater signficance than either of these is that of maintenance of political legitimacy of the institutions within a given political and/or legal system. These are the institutions which are basic to the stability of the political system and the maintenance of some sense of order and regularity in it. The term 'institutions' here should be taken broadly enough to include not only the likes of parliament and the courts but the other institutions established by and as part of the operation of the law. Thus it would include such established principles as fundamental constitutional guarantees of human rights, due process and the like. Enshrined egalitarian principles are, indeed, the most immediately offended by corrupt activities because the latter provide access for some to advantages and benefits which are not capable of enjoyment by other citizens. It is clear enough that order and regularity within any politico-legal system are sometimes matters which are over-emphasised, most usually by conservatives, as factors necessary to human life. They have to be balanced against the need for innovation and change, but they are, nonetheless, important factors.

It is common enough to hear of crises of political legitimacy in the modern and post-modern worlds. The element of legitimacy means different things to different authors and indeed the causes of alleged crises in legitimacy is as debatable as the proposals for their rectification. But in one vital sense legitimacy does involve questions of the acceptance by the population at large of the place and the functions of established institutions. Corruption is clearly a major factor which has the potential to devalue the operation of these institutions and to characterise them in the public mind sometimes as worthless or unjust and sometimes as having fallen into disuse. To illustrate this, take the case of the judiciary. If the decisions of judges were the product of corruption on the part of occupants of judicial office, they would not be decisions according to law. They would not be impartial. They would be prejudiced. The consequence of this would clearly be that citizens, other than those initiating the corruption perhaps, would lose faith in the judicial system and most likely resort to extra legal means to resolve their disputes. That in turn would cause widespread instability in the political system itself.

It is not too difficult to draw out further examples of the destabilising effects of corruption relating to other primary institutions including those for the making and administration of law. Nor is it too difficult to see why corruption is perceived as a danger to the role of institutions of government whether we take them as strictly democratic in any complete sense or not. Just what constitutes a democracy is an arguable concept from the point of view of political theory. However if we assume, as many would do, that it has much to do with the effective role of a parliament, courts of law and a neutral executive, then the erosion of their legitimacy is also a challenge to democracy in that sense. There are other less acceptable alternatives and corruption clearly points us in the direction of some of the least desirable of these alternatives.

CORRUPTION, DEMOCRACY AND THE SOUTH PACIFIC COUNTRIES

We have seen how eliminating corruption is regarded by many as essential to maintaining democracy and the democratic process in various ways. It has significance for the legitimacy of political institutions. Its elimination encourages better business practice on the part of bureaucracies and governments. Corruption has the capacity to erode fundamental human rights to be enjoyed by people within the system and to undermine the rule of law and basic political institutions.

In this context it could be said that democracy assumes a predominantly liberal conception of a desirable system of government. On this view, government is seen as serving the interests of those individuals who are governed by it. In the so-called Western sphere it is premised on assumptions relating to the individual composition of society.

The democratic institutions of government, in this sense, were brought to the Pacific countries as part of the colonial inheritance. This is true enough, although it would be wrong to say that the original colonial institutions of government were themselves democratic. They were the agencies of colonial rule rather than agencies of popular government. Parliamentary democracy was slow to emerge in these countries and was only achieved through various stages leading towards independence. Many Pacific countries have subsequently adopted some anti-corruption measures and agencies along the lines of Western countries, although this has not been as extensive as elsewhere. There remains in fact a certain degree of both ambivalence and ignorance about these institutions, their basic functions and their objectives.

One reason for this is the lack of education and training of public officials (and the general public) in matters pertaining to codes of conduct, political responsibility, competence and ethics awareness. So far as politicians are concerned there have been few political systems which have required that political representatives have minimal educational qualifications to hold office. Yet the jobs they perform are often intellectually demanding, carrying high levels of financial responsibility and indeed often requiring considerable business acumen. It is not difficult to point to many instances where there have been Attorney Generals or their equivalents who hold no legal qualifications, Ministers of Finance who cannot understand a simple balance sheet and Ministers of Education who have no formal educational training at even the most basic level. There is an element of failure of any democratic system where those who are elected often do not have the simple competence to engage in informed and sensible debate concerning the future of a country and its people. No wonder that when they are forced into dealings which all manner of scheisters and articulate con-artists, they are often left short. This is a ready road to corruption. Apart from this there have been numerous areas in which persons who are elected to political office have no understanding of the responsibilities which attach to their office. Little wonder again that they perform in a manner which is wholly different from expectations. Unfortunately the same comments can often be extended to non-elected public officials who obtain office not on the basis of merit but through political patronage. Whilst these problems are not unique to South Pacific countries it is a considerable factor in the region, as with other so-called developing countries. Sometimes corruption on the part of public officials can be explained not by greed or criminal dispositions *per se*. It is often simply a matter of ignorance. People are elected from backgrounds which are steeped in customary obligations. They frequently have no idea what the nature of the office to which they are elected requires of them in terms of simple accountability and responsibility. Although this is not, of course, the only cause of corruption in South Pacific countries, it is a pervasive one.

A more fundamental reason for the ambivalence towards the existing political institutions is their perceived relevance. Why should one really set to work upholding institutions which appear rather remote from cultural experience in any event? It is a point which might well need addressing before effective moves to combat corruption can even begin. If we perceive corruption as simply something which is anti-democratic in the western liberal sense of that term then we will likely be drawn into numerous side issues about the relevance of democracy in that sense to these countries. Many Pacific societies are ordered according to traditional lines of authority which might be better called monarchic or oligarchic, but not democratic. If, for example, chiefly authority is a predominant factor in such societies, as it mostly is, the system cannot be understood as democratic in the liberal sense. If they are communally based societies as we are often told, then one couldn't say that the individual members of them are possessed of certain fundamental rights against those who rule. Their primary position is that they owe obligations to the community. It is on this basis that we often hear about concepts such as Asian style democracy or leader-democracy. The contention here is that developing or new countries, or those countries which are remarkably different from European countries in their social composition, cannot have the luxury of democracy on the Western model. If they are not to be called democratic on the Western liberal model does that mean that the elimination of corruption cannot be justified because it is democratic to do so?

To agree with the above statement is somewhat unpalatable if one accepts that corruption necessarily results in political instability. Rather, one might want to say that South Pacific countries are democratic but in a rather different sense from that understood elsewhere. Perhaps their makeup is more appropriate to a communitarian concept of democracy.[20] It is to be borne in mind, of course, that in most of the world it is better to be seen as democratic than not. The constitution of the former USSR proclaimed that it was a democratic constitution. So did that of Cuba. This may simply be because democracy is, as I have said, a 'good' word in international politics, just as perhaps communism is now a 'bad' word. However that might be, it is still arguable that democracy is just one form of government which does not necessarily require precise implementation of particular models draws from elsewhere. There can be just forms of government which might not conform closely to the liberal model of democracy. Would corruption still be condemned in such systems? I would think so on the basis of the destabilising effect of corruption on any such system. It is condemned because of its challenge to the legitimacy of basic political institutions whatever they might be.

In societies such as those of the South Pacific which are based to some considerable extent on custom one might think that there is some basic brake against corruption which is provided by the operation of the customary system which provides at least some restraint against interference with traditional values. But clearly custom is a fluid set of practices which can enhance the possibility of corruption in many ways. Clever leaders can, and often do, manipulate the appeal to customary practices and obligations to achieve purposes which are foreign to them.[21] In fact, the simple existence of introduced law alongside customary systems often creates what could best be termed a confusion of authority, which frequently lends itself to exploitative practices, distortion and misrepresentation by leaders and public officials who are determined to achieve particular ends of their own. It is not the mere existence of custom as such but the duality of the system in which it operates which creates this particular confusion.

As a final point we should perhaps acknowledge that the move to adopt anti-corruption measures of a particular type is not only a matter which is driven by national politics. Of course it could be questioned how high corruption would be on the agenda of South Pacific countries if the matter was simply left to these countries alone. There are, however, numerous external pressures for the adoption of reforms of a particular type. Much of the agenda of the small island states is written elsewhere. The pressures brought on a country can be direct or indirect. They might range from encouragement to diplomatic argument at various levels. Or countries might be encouraged by economic rewards — for example, tied grants of aid which are often made on the basis that a country will introduce systematic reforms including legal anti-corruption measures. The involvement of the European Union in bringing pressure through the sugar concession for human rights reform in Fiji is one pertinent example. The role of international development agencies such as the World Bank[22] and the Asian Development Bank as well as foreign government agencies in bringing about the Comprehensive Reform Programme in Vanuatu is another. True enough, many people see this as a form of interference in the local political makeup or political sovereignty of a country. But the fact is that the smaller players in international politics are often at the whim of the larger countries. This frequently leads to a situation where law reform is introduced which does not really reflect what we could call public opinion or the public mandate. And when it does occur in areas which are a challenge to established cultural values and practices then there is dissent about the need for reform in the first place. Put another way, there is apathy about what might otherwise be entirely justifiable commitment to reform.

Given the existing ambivalence towards political institutions that are perceived to be irrelevant impositions, it is hard to see how 'imposed' anti-corruption law reform agendas will achieve their desired effects throughout the Pacific. Instead it would seem that an approach that goes back to basics — first of all considering how political institutions can be structured to make them relevant for each Pacific island country, and then considering the meaning of corruption and the role of anti-corruption measures within these institutions — will be required to meaningfully address corruption within the Pacific.

ENDNOTES

1   See for example Larmour, P. 1997. Corruption and Governance in the South Pacific. *Discussion Paper No. 97/5 State Society and Governance in Melanesia Project.* Canberra: ANU at p. 1. The examples provided by Larmour can be supported by reference to many more recent instances in the South Pacific region. The content of various public reports of the Ombudsman of Vanuatu over the period from 1997–1999 give numerous accounts of corrupt practices by politicians. The National Bank scandal in 1997/1998 in Fiji provides another example, as do allegations of money laundering in Nauru in 1999/2000. It was allegedly allegations of corruption on the part of politicians in Samoa which was behind the assassination of a government Minister in 1999. In fact there are numerous other examples.

2   See Powles, G. 1998. Official Power and Corruption: The Abuse of Power and Accountability. Paper delivered at the Pacific Islands Legal Officers' Meeting. Canberra 20th October 1998.

3   Commonwealth Secretariat. 1998. Position paper on Corruption. Presented to the Pacific Island Legal Officers' Meeting. Canberra 20th October 1998. At p. 1.

4   From Independent Commission Against Corruption (N.S.W.).
Home Page http://www.icac.nsw.gov.au/frame.htm (Accessed March 1999)

5   See *Cooper v Slade* (1858) 6 H.L.C. 746 and *R. v Smith* (1960) 2 Q.B. 423.

6   See *R. v Wellburn, R v Nurdin, R v Randel* (1979) 69 Cr. App Rep. 69 at 73, 74.

7   See *R. v Carr* [1956] 2 All E.R. 979; *R v Mills* (1978) 68 Cr. App. Rep. 154 at 158.

8   See *Alisae v Salaka* [1985/86] SILR 31.

9   See *Alisae v Salaka*, above, n 8, at p 37.

10 See *Alisae v Salaka*, above n 8. This involved an allegation in an election petition of corrupt practices. The court held that the criminal standard was appropriate although this was essentially a civil action following *Menyamya v Open Parliamentary Election* [1977] PNGLR 302. The court distinguished *Tegatova v Bennett* [1983] SILR 34 and *In re*

Moresby Parliamentary Election No. 2 [1977] PNGLR 448 on the basis that these cases were concerned not with corrupt practices but with residential qualifications.

11 [1935] AC 462.

12 On the range of offences see *Halsbury's Laws of England*. 1990. London: Butterworths. Vol. 11, pp. 231ff. In the South Pacific see, for example, the various corruption offences specified in sections 106–108 *Penal Code* [Cap 17] (Fiji).

13 (1994) 74 A. Crim. R 115.

14 (1990) 49 A. Crim. R. 370.

15 Unreported, Fiji Islands Court of Appeal, Civil Appeal No 6/94.

16 See Hiro, D. 1976. *Inside India Today*. London: Routledge, Kegan and Paul, chapter 3. Hiro identifies modernisation and industrialisation of traditional society in India as the reasons the existence of wide scale corruption in that country after independence.

17 Hardgrave, R. 1980. *India: Government and Politics in a Developing Nation*. New York: Harcourt Brace Jovanovich pp. 75–76.

18 OECD 1999. *Ethics in the Public Service – Executive Summary*. Report at http://www.oecd.org/puma/gvrnance/ethics/pbs/eip96/execsum.htm. (Accessed March 1999)

19 The Corruption Perception Index is accessible at http://www.gwgd.de/uwvw/icr.html (Accessed March 1999)

20 This concept is relatively unexplored in the context of the Pacific.

21 See Field, M. 2000. Corruption Rife in the Pacific. *Fiji Times*. 2nd March 2000, p. 10.

22 On the World Bank's position in respect of corruption see its paper World Bank. 1997. *Helping Countries to Combat Corruption: The Role of the World Bank*. World Bank: Washington D.C.

3. GOVERNANCE, LEGITIMACY AND THE RULE OF LAW IN THE SOUTH PACIFIC

By: Graham Hassall

KEY TERMS AND PHRASES

Autocthonous

Something that is autocthonous is formed, or originates, in the place that it is found. In this context the term is used when discussing constitutions that have been home-grown rather than imposed by outsiders or borrowed from western constitutional models.

Governance

Governance comprises the traditions, institutions, mechanisms and processes that determine how power is exercised. The concept of governance extends beyond formal government institutions, and includes a consideration of the role of citizens and non-governmental organisations (often referred to as civil society) and the insitutitions and processes by which civil society participates in governance within a society.

Modern/modernity

Modernism is a complex term used by a number of disciplines, including art history, literature studies and political studies. Within politics it is often used to represent a particular order that is based on a number of concepts that are in themselves complex. These include the concepts of nationhood and the rule of law. Also characteristic of modernity is the use of rationality or reason and a belief in certainty. The concept of 'western' industrialised nations may be thought to be an expression of modernity.

Nationalism

Nationalism refers to a commitment to nationhood and represents a complex web of ideas about the nature of the state and membership of it. Nations are imagined to be geographical and political communities of limited boundaries that are in themselves sovereign. They are often imagined to be 'natural' phenomena, arising because of 'natural' ethnic unity.

The rule of law

There are a number of definitions of, or jurisprudential statements on, the rule of law, with the jurist Albert V. Dicey's conception of the rule of law being possibly the most familiar. Key elements of the concept are limits to the exercise of power, equality before the law, predictable and stable laws and procedures and the separation of powers between various state authorities.

INTRODUCTION

This chapter suggests that some of the difficulties now facing the states that came to independence in the South Pacific at different times in the second half of the twentieth century derive from the manner in which they were constituted. Although any state, at any time, may face political crises or economic setbacks, the seemingly endemic nature of corrupt practices by politicians and of societal unrest in such states as Papua New Guinea, Solomon Islands, Vanuatu and Fiji Islands suggests the presence of conflict at more fundamental levels. Concerns at the ability of new states to govern are not new. However, notions of quite recent origin that look at capacities for governance rather than just ideologies of political and legal legitimacy allow one to view the actual operation of constitutions in various Pacific island states in a new way. How well do the state systems that were established at independence provide governance to their citizens? If it is found that the institutions provided by the constitution create more disorder than order, deliver less justice than more, and result in deteriorating social and economic conditions rather than the reverse, then questions must be asked about regeneration of the constitutional foundations, as much as about their day-to-day operation.

In the South Pacific, where the essential aspects of the modern approach to law and constitution were adopted at independence, a survey of their subsequent operation suggests that capacities for governance remain limited, and that the legitimacy of introduced law remains contested. The multiple hindrances to the operation of introduced law include:

- how parliaments are functioning and how parliamentarians are acting (for instance legislative inaction, use of no confidence motions, use of electoral development funds, constituency representation);
- failures within electoral systems (for instance volatility of political parties, electoral violence);
- judicial scrutiny and activism (for instance controversy in the areas of finding the underlying law and protection of human rights, lack of judicial independence);
- the functioning of the executive, particularly cabinet ministers (for instance lack of accountability, difficulties in the provision of services such as health, education, transport and infrastructure);
- the functioning of a number of other executive agencies including the police and the defence forces; and
- the level of maturity of civil society.

How is it that new nations, defined so clearly in modern constitutions and laws, have not gained the moral authority promised at the moment of independence? This chapter suggests that one possible cause of so much contestation (and hence one crucial factor in establishing constitutional legitimacy) is the inadequate measures taken to 'ground' independence constitutions in the will of the people. Clearly, this is a question about values as much as about the efficacy of law. This chapter also proposes that the legitimacy of modern law and constitutions must be examined in the light of both normative considerations as well as more systemic approaches. Although modern states and law were introduced to the region from outside, with an expectation that the rule of law would be a sufficient support for development, modernisation, order and progress, insufficient attention was paid to the validity of the modern law system as a whole, or to the methods by which this system generated legitimacy in the eyes of those who are subject to it as citizens.

Constitutions and Governance

A constitutional system might be described as the sum of state and non-state actors that determine and affect the distribution and use of state power. The constitution channels the public power of the people. As described by Jan-Erik Lane, "...implicit in the concept of a constitution is the notion of restraints on State power".[1] Modern constitutions seek to be effective and to provide the legal framework for the activities of all citizens (and others) in the state. When I say effective, I mean that they intend to influence the behaviour of every member of society by making laws about what is permissible to do and what is 'illegal'. The extent of effectiveness of a constitution can, perhaps, be determined by examining governance in a particular country.

Governance refers to the exercise of economic, political and administrative authority to manage a country's affairs at all levels. It comprises the mechanisms, processes and institutions through which citizens and groups articulate their interests, exercise their legal rights, meet their obligations and mediate their differences.[2] The idea of governance is being promoted by states, intergovernmental agencies, and civil society.[3] It is also being explored in relation to Pacific island countries' constitutions, and the proper operation of government.[4] The concept of governance requires a state to find new ways of asserting its legitimacy and reinforcing its capacities to govern by consent. These new mechanisms include improving accountability, allowing for freedom of association and participation, providing free and fair legal frameworks in which individuals can act, allowing access to information, improving public sector efficiency, and boosting levels of cooperation between branches of government, the business sector and civil society.

Modernity and the Rule of Law

The constitutions that frame the exercise of state power in the new Pacific nations signify the legal norms of modernity. The term 'modern' has a particular meaning. It doesn't just mean contemporary, or in our times. Sociologist Anthony Giddens describes modernity as "...the institutions and modes of behaviour established first of all in post-feudal Europe, but which in the twentieth century increasingly have become world-historical in their impact".[5] For present purposes, modernity will be used to signify a complex network of social norms, economic models, and political ideals sometimes summarised as 'the rule of law'.[6]

The rule of law is a doctrine concerning the proper construction of law and application of law developed in the United Kingdom and exported to other legal jurisdictions by the forces of history.[7] Under the ideology of colonialism, the doctrine sought to impose reason on very different human societies. The ordering processes were known as pacification and development.[8] Modern conceptions of 'the constitution' and 'the law' have come to the Pacific as part of this world-historical process. They seek to establish a paradigm of relations between members of society, and between the individual, the community, and the state.

The doctrine states that all people must be treated equally before the law, even though they may be acting for the monarch. The doctrine states, furthermore, that power will only be exercised in accordance with law. In other words, power will not be used arbitrarily. Additionally, the doctrine presumes the presence and desirability of a number of fundamental rights of citizens, including rights to freedom of the person, of speech, of movement and association. To speak of the rule of law, in other words, is to conjure a matrix of legal rules, values, institutions, and procedures, the absence of any one of which will lead to calls for the restoration of/ adherence to/ upholding of the rule of law.

The term rule of law is often used when describing approval or disapproval of the action or inaction of a government or a court. The rule of law is also sometimes referred to as constitutionalism, which has as its principal motivation the "restraining of state power", and "protection of the relatively powerless (individuals and minorities) from oppression by the powerful."[9] The rule of law is thus a doctrine of legitimation for those who hold and exercise power in a constitutional state. Why is their tenure legitimate? Because they 'uphold the rule of law' (i.e., they restrain their use of power in accordance with the laws, which are made by them with the consent of 'the people').

THE LEGITIMACY OF MODERN LAW

The legitimacy of modern law derives from statements about the origin of law and about how the law is to be applied. The intention of modern law is to locate sovereignty in the people and treat every member of society equally before the law. The origin of the law, therefore, is said to be the will of the people, consenting to the law (through some sort of social contract) as it is a device to uphold their sovereignty and the rights that this entails. The second source of legitimacy, how the law is to be applied, is also a monitor of the legitimacy of the origins of the law, as law will only be effectively applied if it is popularly supported (in the absence of 'tyrannical' coercion).

In the initial decades following the attainment of independence by the small island groups in the South Pacific problems of colonial rule were supplanted by those of new nations. By the mid-1990s the stability of states was being challenged from within as much as from external factors. Ethnic conflict had destabilised Fiji, and separatist conflicts had greatly affected Papua New Guinea and Solomon Islands. Corrupt practices by politicians and public servants greatly occupied the media and state-agencies charged with upholding the law in these countries as well as such nearby states as Tonga, Vanuatu, Nauru, Cook Islands, French Polynesia and Samoa. The modern Pacific island state, like so many others beyond the Pacific region, gives the appearance of being populated by citizens who place more emphasis on self-interest than public service. Within this atmosphere of corruption and instability the law is patently ineffective. This ineffectiveness is not rooted purely in resource issues that hinder the timely application of the law. Rather, a more fundamental disrespect for the law and its origins is indicated.

The grounding of legitimacy in constitutional assent

Although modern law locates sovereignty in the people and seeks to treat every member of society equally before the law, the constitutions of Pacific island states were rarely founded on consent by the people. On the contrary, most states in the region can truly be regarded as post-colonial in that their constitutional values and practices were either copied from colonial authorities or established in reaction to them. Colonial authorities, believing that subject peoples had little understanding of the issues at hand (and seeking to economise on time and expenses), generally established expert commissions or at best constituent assemblies comprising people's representatives, to complete constitutional exercises on their behalf. On this point Ghai has written:

> In Papua New Guinea and Solomon Islands, vigorous attempts were made to consult with the people, through questionnaires and tours of the country by committees set up to recommend on the constitution for independence. However, the choices offered to the people, derived largely from the experience of the colonial powers, were complex, and their intricacies probably beyond the comprehension of most people. While this consultation lent an aura of legitimacy to the constitution, it did not significantly influence its contents.[10]

In the case of the British colonies, consultation within the colony was frequently limited to elite members of the various ethnic communities co-existing in the colony. The resulting constitutions were not the result of the free expression of the people but were rather the evidence of compromise between departing colonial masters and incoming national elites. In the cases of Solomon Islands, Gilbert Islands and Fiji, for instance, discussions on independence constitutions were held in London. Such constitutions, as a consequence, primarily allow access to the state by elites (usually recipients of western education or otherwise privileged under colonial rule), whether as representatives or as beneficiaries. The language of the law is not that of 'the people'.

There are other rationalisations than simple colonial paternalism for the lack of traditional concepts of governance being incorporated into Pacific island constitutions. By way of further rationalisation for such an approach Ghai has suggested:

> Despite consultation with the people and the active involvement of their leaders, the constitutions cannot be said to be rooted in indigenous concepts of power, authority, and decision making, for a number of reasons. These lie in the difficulty

of expanding these concepts, which are peculiar to an island or group, to the national scale; in the constitutional evolution over several decades of colonial rule along Western lines; in the emergence to eminence of an educated, Christianised and Westernised elite with a loyalty to and dependence on modern state institutions; and in the influence of successive bureaucrats and consultants. With them, notions of economic development and state management of resources had primacy, militating against experiments in participatory democracy.[11]

This modernist approach to nation-building through constitution-making had intended and unintended consequences. The resulting constitutions mirror those of the metropolitan powers, and almost all Pacific island states chose at independence a constitutional form familiar to them from the colonial era. Those associated with Britain, Australia and New Zealand operate parliamentary systems while those associated with France and the United States, presidential. They generally ignore the diversity of traditions within Pacific societies in their search for homogeneity and they are — consequently — elitist in nature, and valued more among the western educated than among the majority, whose constitutions (or systems of governance) continue to operate at village level. Perhaps most significantly, they don't fully come to terms with the orders of governance that pre-existed colonial rule and which continue to hold great significance (under the labels 'customary law' and 'traditional leaders') over the majority of the people.

At independence there was a vision of national parliaments replacing the foreign 'received' law with more relevant enactments and of national courts contributing law based more firmly on custom. Papua New Guinea's *Constitution*, for instance, expounds the doctrine of the 'underlying law', an indigenous common law that parliament and the judiciary were to create. This has not been the post-colonial experience, however, with programs of law reform faltering, and courts explaining that judgments based on custom were dependent on the quality of arguments placed before the courts that relied on such custom. John Gawi wrote in 1985 his view that the problem of Papua New Guinea's legal order was an institutional one. He suggested that the common law had become so entrenched in the country's legal system prior to independence, that it had become "an integral part of Papua New Guinean society":

> Because of the nebulous nature of our pre-existing institutions (traditional institutions), common law with its institutional structure was able to force the traditional institutions to conform to the framework of the common law. What, in effect, happened was that our traditional institutions had been subsumed into the institutional framework of common law. Therefore, before the Constitution came, the only way we were able to describe our traditional institutions was to describe them by labels imposed on them by common law…. Our only hope was the Constitution, but the Constitution has failed. In fact the forces of common law are such that the Constitution is now being forced to conform to the institutions of common law. Every constitutional provision purportedly

interpreted by the courts in Papua New Guinea is as good as a dead provision. As time goes by, and before we know it, the process of subsumption will be complete.[12]

Within the South Pacific region some progress has been made toward recovering an authentic constitution, or at least one which will not subjugate traditional orders of governance to western modes of order. When Solomon Islands conducted a constitutional review in the late 1980s, Prime Minister Alebua described the intention to his fellow parliamentarians:

> Mr Speaker sir... the Constitutional Review Committee was deliberately set up without any outside legal advisor. Because what we are trying to work towards is a constitution of and for the Solomon Islands. Once we start putting in foreign influences sir, certainly it won't be a Solomon Islands Constitution.[13]

Another interesting instance of a people attempting to re-establish an authentic constitutional order occurred recently in Vanuatu. In February 1997 custom chiefs from four villages on the island of Ambae produced their own constitution establishing the responsibility of chiefs of certain villages in the area to protect and safeguard the general welfare of their people, protect and promote traditional values, resolve disputes and disagreements and assist the police and other authorities, including churches, schools and other social welfare institutions. Vanuatu's *Constitution* recognises custom chiefs but does not define their role in decision-making about non-traditional matters.

Such attempts have not, however, resulted in any substantive or formal changes to Pacific island constitutions. As the modern constitutions remain divorced from traditional order so too does the origin of the law in the will of the people remain, in large part, a fiction. This issue is at the heart of the failure of legitimacy of the rule of law in Pacific island states.

Legitimacy, assent and nationalism

A further challenge to constitutional legitimacy comes from the often unacknowledged link between social and political philosophies and constitutional design and practice. While liberal approaches to constitutionalism express concern at the outcomes of socialist and communist constitutionalism, the impact of philosophies premised on nation, race and religion must also be considered. Nationalism, for instance, when translated into nation-building laws governing language, education and mobility has often sought to suppress or even eradicate the cultural diversity that constituted the pre-colonial states and societies. These philosophies complicate the notion of assent. Whilst at one level there may be assent to an ideal unity, on another level the relationship between this ideal and the reality of cultural diversity creates a tension, and possibly a negation of any assumed assent.

Legitimacy and performance

The second source of legitimacy, how the law is to be applied, also does not provide a basis for constitutional legitimacy. As already noted, success in establishing constitutional legitimacy has been hindered by problematic performance of constitutional duties in a number of South Pacific jurisdictions by various agencies.

Instability of political parties

Of particular note is the destabilising practice of strategic changes of political alliance by members of parliament (MPs). Democracies require (or imagine) communicative action, but through formalisation, legalisation and, increasingly, the constitutional recognition of party systems, democracies are increasingly beholden to strategic action. I say this because I see the following series of events being played out in a number of countries: peoples' representatives are elected to legislatures. Political parties (or interest groups) are established to marshal numbers in a bid to acquire more than 50% of the seats and therefore capture the executive (in some places, in a bid to capture the percentage of seats required to capture control over constitutional change). Loyalty to a party is premised on non-ideological factors and is increasingly liable to fluid movement of parliamentarians between parties. In an effort to promote executive stability, laws are being enacted to prevent party-hopping, or defection. Paradoxically, laws designed to promote political stability strike at the freedom of association that is at the heart of democratic societies. Paradoxically, too, the more that political practice is regulated by law, the more constrained the democratic process becomes.

The problem of stabilising political party systems is linked to two processes at the heart of constitutionalism: the performance of the legislative and executive branches of government. In a system in which the executive government is formed from within the legislature and in which political party affiliations are fluid, any executive government faces the challenge of maintaining the allegiance of its members. MPs may be enticed to cross the floor and, with the opposition groups, to form a new government with themselves in an improved situation. The necessity to form political party coalitions among parties — sometimes resulting in coalitions between a great number of parties — has significant impact on the capacity of parliaments and governments to carry out their duties.

An instance of the volatility of political parties occurred in Papua New Guinea in December 1999. A day after passage of the Budget for 2000, Prime Minister Morauta sacked the Deputy Prime Minister, John Pundari, and the Advance PNG Party, from the coalition government.[14] In response to the new political environment a number of existing parties announced the formation of a new political group, the Peoples' National Alliance (PNA).[15] There is other evidence in PNG that raises questions about the stability of the party system and its existence as anything more than a device that MPs use to marshal numbers within the Parliament. For more than two decades since Independence, for example, parties have not adhered to any system of legal registration other than as associations.[16]

Recent events in Cook Islands also demonstrate the problem. Although Cook Islands received assistance from several overseas agencies to improve electoral administration prior to general elections in July 1999, no amount of technical assistance could have prepared the country for the subsequent political turmoil. When incumbent Prime Minister, Sir Geoffrey Henry, appeared ready to form a coalition government with the leader of the New Alliance Party (NAP), Norman George, three members of Henry's Cook Islands Party defected after the ballot to help Joe Williams gain a majority in the 25-member Assembly. However, the Williams Government fell three and a half months later in a no-confidence vote that brought the Democratic Alliance Party (DAP) and the NAP coalition into government under Dr Terepai Moate.

In 1999 a three-member Commission of Political Review recommended a number of changes to Cook Islands political system to increase political stability and constitutional effectiveness.[17] The Commission's report also recommended fostering of public discussion of future options of Cook Islands system of government and recommended a "more comprehensive national political review to be undertaken" after the term of the next Parliament.

To an increasing extent, in part because of the instability of party politics, electoral contests and even votes within parliaments are being decided in the courts rather than through counting of the ballots. In Vanuatu, for instance, Parliament became dead-locked in November 1997 over a no-confidence motion against the government of Prime Minister Serge Vohor. President Jean Marie Leye ordered dissolution of the Parliament, and following the dismissal of a challenge to this dissolution by the Vanuatu Court of Appeal in January 1998, general elections were held on March 6 at which no single party won enough seats in the 52-member parliament to govern in its own right,[18] and following which numerous allegations concerning malpractices were made.[19]

There are several options for the regulation of political parties, but some create dilemmas in terms of democratic theory. The view is sometimes put that a smaller number of stable parties is preferable to a larger number of more fluid parties. But legislating to limit the number of parties is commonly regarded as being a restriction on democratic choice. Similarly, preventing the defection of MPs from one party to another by laws that require defecting members to resign their seats and recontest with their new party at the next election is similarly a restrictive measure. MPs are, firstly, representatives of the people rather than of political parties, and so there must be concerns about laws that place control over the legislature and the executive in the hands of the parties.

Constitutional reform in Papua New Guinea has sought to limit the impact of electoral contests by reducing the nomination period for candidates and reducing the formal campaign period.[20] After a long process the Parliament has also created an organic law concerning the integrity of political parties and candidates as required by sections 129 and 130 of the *Constitution*.[21] As a major cause of political instability since Independence has been the volatility of MP loyalty to political parties, the government is seeking to strengthen the party system and diminish the prevalence of 'party-hopping'. To achieve this, the *Organic Law* provides for the dismissal from Parliament of an MP who defects to a political party other than the one for which he or she was elected to Parliament.[22]

Political parties have expressed concern, however, that the draft provisions are too harsh and penalise MPs who seek to change parties with valid reasons. The Pangu Pati, one of the oldest political groups in Papua New Guinea, has suggested that the *Organic Law* should also restrict the formation of new political parties "on the floor of Parliament", and restrict the influence of independent MPs.[23] Melanesian Alliance leader, John Momis, who is one of the "Founding Fathers" of the Papua New Guinea *Constitution*, has also called for constitutional change, but has not defined the "radical measures" to the Westminster system he envisages.[24]

The functioning of the executive

The functioning of the executive is another area in which the inadequate performance of duties weakens the legitimacy of the constitution. In parliamentary systems executive power is exercised by or on advice from a cabinet, derived from the legislature. Since executive power is often regarded as the most powerful branch of government, it is often the most coveted by political interests. It is subject also to the most scrutiny by other public bodies, particularly the legislature, but also the courts, on application, and other offices such as that of the ombudsman and auditor-general.

In Pacific island states MPs tend to desire active roles in executive government. The traditional argument in favour of this involvement has been that MPs have been obliged to assist in the delivery of services in response to people's expectations of a 'big man'.[25] But it may be that the participation of MPs in the planning and delivery of services has unintended effects, such as drawing resources away from the line departments ordinarily responsible for such activities, or possibly leading to overlaps in the delivery of services. Furthermore, the involvement of MPs in service planning and delivery leaves them little time for other parliamentary duties, such as the development of legislation, committee service and scrutiny of government. A more sceptical view would be that MPs have simply sought to exercise control over budgets, specific programs and statutory bodies. In the long term, the role of the MP will require clarification, particularly as a more educated public begins to ask incisive questions concerning the ideal role of elected representatives.

In a number of Pacific island states there have been unprecedented incidents of public agitation against the corrupt and incompetent actions of executive governments. For instance, in Samoa in October 1998 five thousand people gathered to protest against the Alesana government. Principle concerns were the sacking of auditor-general Sua Rimoni Ah Chong in August, illegal sale of passports and the fact that the public accounts had not been audited for approximately eight years.[26]

INSTABILITY AND CONSTITUTIONAL LEGITIMACY

Civil violence is probably the most extreme expression of weaknesses in the constitution of countries and their law. Such violence is now becoming a familiar part of Pacific island politics, particularly in Melanesia, where expressions of violence have resulted in destabilised states. As the experience of Solomon Islands, Papua New Guinea and Fiji Islands indicate, instability is tied up with a lack of consistutional legitimacy.

Examining Solomon Islands first, this nation opted for a parliamentary democracy with the Queen as Head of State and her representative, the Governor General, elected by Parliament. There was to be a single chamber legislature and, recognising the hazards of party government in Solomon Islands, the Prime Minister was to be elected by and from the members of Parliament and could be removed only by a motion of no-confidence. But neither the Solomon Islands state, nor its constitution, nor the rule of law ideology has provided sufficient legal, administrative, or conceptual authority to prevent endemic corruption in public office or resurgent ethnic and political conflict.

Although long-standing separatist sentiments in Solomon Islands are well known, their eruption in the late 1990s has proven difficult to resolve. The escalation commenced with legal disputes between national and provincial politicians. In 1997 the High Court invalidated the *Provincial Government Act* 1996, which had sought to replace Provincial Premiers with elected provincial councils in an effort to decrease cost and improve the efficiency of government services. The Malaita and Guadalcanal Provincial Governments had threatened secession on passage of the Bill, and the successful challenge was made by the government of Guadalcanal. In 1999 the heads of the Solomon Islands' nine provinces recommended that the national *Constitution* and the *Provincial Government Act* 1996 be reviewed. Guadalcanal province commenced seeking compensation for the use of land, especially in and near Honiara, under use by the national government. Tensions on Guadalcanal between landowners and settlers from outer islands then became violent, and on June 16 1999 the government invoked a state of emergency.[27] Although Commonwealth special envoy to Solomon Islands, former Prime Minister of Fiji Sitiveni Rabuka, negotiated a peace accord, violence continued and the factors underlying the conflict remained unaddressed. On June 5 2000 members of the Malaita Eagle Force, along with a faction of police officers, the Seagulls, detained then Prime Minister Ulufa'alu and demanded his resignnation. On 13 June, Ulufa'alu submitted his resignation and on 30 June, Manasseh Sogavare was elected Prime Minister and a new government was formed. On 15 October 2000 the Townsville Peace Agreement was signed, the 7th peace agreement since June of 1999. Although this agreement has not restored stability it has created a cease-fire situation. Elections were held on 5 December 2001, and it is widely acknowledged that the first responsibility of the new government will be the rebuilding of order, or reconstitution of the state, in such a way as to ensure lasting peace.[28]

The myth of the modern constitution being written by the people is particularly prevalent in Papua New Guinea. However, almost thirty years after independence there is still uncertainty concerning the extent to which the nation of Papua New Guinea is governed by the rule of law. Here, as in Solomon Islands, corruption and ethnic conflict have weakened the basis of the state and called into question its capacity to govern and to apply the rule of law.

A crisis of legitimacy has been felt most severely in Bougainville. Since Independence conflict over the status of this province has been in part a conflict over the question of devolution of power. It is a question at the heart of the *Constitution* and its resolution can only be found through constitutional dialogue. The Bougainville Reconciliation Government (BRG), frustrated at the national Parliament's inability to put the Bougainville conflict above political in-fighting, convened a Constitutional Convention on 24 December 1998, at which a BRG Constitution was adopted by acclamation, to provide for the establishment of a Bougainville Constituent Assembly (BCA) as an advisory body ahead of the election of a BRG. The BCA met on 15–16 January 1999 and adopted the BRG Basic Agreement and the BRG Constitution. The National Executive Council (NEC) subsequently endorsed the BRG Basic Agreement but did not consider the BRG Constitution. In May 1999 the people of Bougainville elected 69 members to the Bougainville Reconciliation Government. Joseph Kabui was elected President. After a long process of peace talks, the Bougainville Peace Agreement, signed at Arawa on 30 August 2001 "provides for arrangements for an autonomous Bougainville Government operating under a home-grown Bougainville Consistution…"[29] This Bougainville-wide exercise, however, does not constitute a Papua New Guinea-wide constitutional reform exercise.[30]

Recent events in Fiji, where the *Constitution* has undergone the most significant processes of reform of any South Pacific state since independence, further illustrate the tenuous authority of the modern constitution and state. Negotiations with the British resulted in independence in 1970. Two military coups occurred in 1987, when Fijian interests perceived a threat to Fijian hegemony from Fiji–Indian interests.[31] Despite the promulgation of a new constitution in 1990 which met with the satisfaction of those who instigated the coups, a constitutionally mandated constitutional review undertaken by the Reeves Commission in 1997[32] failed to maintain this appeasement, and in 2000 the state was once again thrown into disarray when George Speight named the protection of Fijian interests as his paramount reason for storming the Parliament and attempting to overthrow the Mahendra Chaudhry government. Whilst the courts intervened in the situation and upheld the validity of the 1997 *Constitution* the ongoing disorder that was created by Speight's actions does little to create the impression of authoritative constitutional order in Fiji Islands.

THE REGENERATION OF LEGITIMACY

This instability is indicative of a need to reconsider the constitutions, and not just their day-to-day workings, in order to regenerate legitimacy and create lasting order. In a recent work, *Between Facts and Norms*, Habermas has sought the reasons for the large distance that sometimes appears between the ideal laws of a society and the actual practice of that society. He suggests, ultimately, that the 'most effective law' results from procedures that all who are affected by that law can participate in:

> From the standpoint of legal theory, the modern legal order can draw its legitimacy only from the idea of self-determination: citizens should always be able to understand themselves as authors of the law to which they are subject as addressees.[34]

Habermas and others have developed a theory of discourse ethics based on a distinction between strategic and communicative action. In strategic action:

> …actors are interested solely in the success, ie, the consequences of the outcomes of their actions, [and] they will try to reach their objectives by influencing their opponent's definition of the situation, and thus his decision or motives, through means by using weapons or goods, threats or enticements.[35]

Communicative action, on the other hand, is oriented toward reaching a common understanding rather than achieving personal success.[36] What is required is a paradigm shift, not simply a tinkering with the system. This involves new understandings of relations between law and power. When applied to the challenge of renewing the legitimacy of the constitutions in Pacific island jurisdictions, one major challenge will be to increase understanding of this distinction between communicative and strategic action. Some may conclude that communicative action remains an ideal and that all discourse, including constitutional discourse, is strategic in purpose. Yet the challenge remains of finding some form of discourse concerning the structure and operation of the constitution that keeps its interests beyond the party-political, beyond the interests of any particular group in that society.

It should be noted that there are difficulties in maintaining clear distinctions between communicative and strategic action. These difficulties can be observed in the recent history of Papua New Guinea's Constitutional Review Committee (later the Constitutional Development Commission (CDC)). MP Philemon Embel, having been appointed Chair of the Commission in May 1999, was recalled to Cabinet in July and replaced by MP Bernard Mollok. Charged with overseeing the drafting of an *Organic Law on the Integrity of Political Parties and Candidates* (as required by ss 129 and 130 of the *Constitution*), Mollok called on the government to undertake a total review of the PNG *Constitution*, rather than the "piecemeal approaches" which had occurred in recent years.[37] The Chairman identified existing electoral laws, and the behaviour that takes place during electoral periods, as indicative of the "foreign concepts" of governing that had created problems for the country.[38] However, when the Chairman began publicly to berate the government for giving the CDC inadequate resources and insufficient time to complete its work,[39] and eventually claimed that the government was not supporting the work of the CDC,[40] he was removed from the position.[41]

Mechanisms for amending constitutions

The most common ways in which a constitution can be amended are through a vote in parliament or through other means which allow 'the people' to have control over any changes such as referenda or constitutional conventions. Another mechanism, in which the role of public involvement can vary widely, is the expert commission, such as the Reeves Commission that reported on the Fijian *Constitution* in 1996.[42]

Constitutional conventions tend to be held when large-scale change to a constitution is envisaged, rather than change to specific provisions only. The idea is to allow for full consultation on the issues, or communicative action. Such conventions have been held in Pacific island nations such as the Federated States of Micronesia and the Marshall Islands. The Commonwealth of the Northern Mariana Islands, a nation that has chosen to be in free association with the United States, established a constitutional convention in 1974 following a vote by the people which gained 75% approval. A second constitutional convention held in 1984 proposed 44 constitutional amendments, all of which were approved by the people.

At Kiribati's first constitutional convention (March 2–6 1998) some 200 delegates consulted on a report prepared for the convention by a Parliamentary Select Committee. The convention's proposals and recommendations included increasing the members of the Council of State from three to either four or five, although different views were put as to who the additional members should be. The proposed amendments will be put to public comment before debate in Parliament, where they require a two-thirds majority to pass.

A constitutional convention may sound expensive to hold, but where they succeed in bringing together the people's representatives to discuss the foundations of the state system, they help to establish the legitimacy of the constitution. By ensuring that the constitution truly expresses the wishes of the people as they evolve over time, such a form of structured public dialogue as a constitutional convention consolidates legitimacy through communicative action, and in doing so, contributes to the attainment of such other goals as democracy, justice and prosperity. States that do not respond effectively to the need to consolidate legitimacy risk serious internal conflicts and social instability.

Legitimacy and related goals

The first goal of any exercise aiming to regenerate constitutional order is to establish legitimacy. As already indicated legitimacy refers to the acceptance of the foundational principles of a state and to the constitution of a state. A people who see its state and government as having legitimacy have a sense of constitutional unity. Without this sense of unity, a state is in danger of serious conflict, and even collapse. A government can establish this sense of legitimacy over time by meeting the needs of the people, and by building a sense of purpose and unity amongst them. The ability to build legitimacy depends partly on the quality of dialogue between the people and the state. The making of a constitution, and later reforming it, is part of this exercise of consolidating the legitimacy of a state. The legitimacy of a state provides the foundation for the operation of democracy.

Democracy is an ancient concept that continues to evolve over time. In a broad sense it refers to the election of leaders by the people. People who elect their own leaders are said to be 'free', although this 'freedom' refers to their agreement to act as they wish within the bounds of the rights and responsibilities that are determined by the society's legal system and public culture. The idea of democracy is not to achieve 'total freedom' — for such a thing is impossible — but to provide a social and political society in which individuals are able to pursue goals of their own choosing, to fully develop their personalities, abilities and talents, and to contribute the fruits of their efforts back to their society. There is not one approach to democratic structure and procedure, but many. The majority of contemporary democratic states opt for forms of 'representative' democracy, in preference to 'direct' democracy. In political terms, much of this 'representation' occurs through party systems. But in the process of constitution-making we must remain aware that the current approach to so-called 'democratic institutions' is but one among many. It could be argued that the more party systems are developed, the less represented the people become, as it is the parties, rather than the people, who come to determine policy. Such reservations maybe raise the need for a reconsideration of the form of democratic system selected. However, democracy offers both legitimacy and accountability, since the people have control over their leaders and over the laws that bind them. Where these conditions are met a government acquires authority, and, possessing authority, becomes effective in governing with a sense of justice.

The quest for legitimacy and democracy is, then, linked to the quest for justice. People have an innate sense of injustice, in the sense that they know when they have been wronged, or harmed. The ability to govern justly, however, is not innate in the same way, but only comes with experience, wide knowledge of current conditions and past circumstances, a sense of compassion and an ability to remain impartial. In many systems of governance the 'justice system' refers to the court system alone, but so-called 'access to justice' is a matter that extends beyond the courts. The laws of a country must be just, the administration of government must be just and disputes must be solved in a just manner. A just society exercises both reward and punishment and a just society ensures the fair distribution of both welfare and wealth.

A final challenge of contemporary governance is the generation of social and economic prosperity. This challenge requires more than 'economic development', more than industrialisation and increased consumption and more than the spread of material benefits. It refers to the attainment of the well-being of the people, through their acquisition of material development in accordance with their own plans, activities and priorities. It refers, that is, to the development of the people's personalities in accordance with their own volition and choice. Questions of prosperity become linked to issues like taxation and the provision of welfare services.

These four challenges, attaining legitimacy, democracy, justice and prosperity, confront all systems of government, no matter which hemisphere, and no matter which culture. They relate to the quest for human rights, transparency, accountability and non-discrimination. When they are lost sight of, the idea of governance is reduced to the struggle for so-called power and struggles over the acquisition and distribution of limited resources.

Meeting the challenges of contemporary governance requires an evaluation of the constitution which cannot be rushed, which must be impartial, which must involve wide participation of the people, and which must meet their needs in the context of an emerging regional and global order. Such an evaluation may well revisit and revitalise traditional values of consultation, reciprocity and social solidarity, and more critically examine introduced structures of governance which produce conflict rather than progress. This can be done, but not without imagination and universal participation.

ENDNOTES

1   Lane, J-E. 1996. *Constitutions and Political Theory.* Manchester & New York: Manchester University Press, p10.

2   Governance for Sustainable Human Development, a UNDP Policy Document.

3   Commission on Global Governance, 1995. *Issues in Global Governance*: papers written for the Commission on Global Governance: London & Boston: Kluwer Law International in association with the Commission on Global Governance. Agencies working at international level include ombudsmen, the Inter-Parliamentary Union, Electoral Authorities and Monitors, Transparency International, Human Rights Monitors, Media Monitors, International Institute for Democracy and Electoral Assistance, the United Nations and its many agencies.

4   Macdonald, B. 1996. *Governance and political process in Kiribati.* Canberra: National Centre for Development Studies; Paeniu, B. 1995. South Pacific: Traditional Governance and sustainable development in the Pacific. *Economic Division Working Papers (No. 6),* Canberra: ANU Research School of Pacific and Asian Studies; Taafaki, T. , & Oh, J. 1995. *Governance in the Pacific: Politics and Policy Success in Tuvalu.* Canberra: National Centre for Development Studies Australian National University.

5   Giddens, A. 1991. *Modernity and Self-Identity: Self and Society in the Late Modern Age.* Chicago: Stanford University Press, p14–15.

6   An example of the presuppositions of modernity in relation to electoral systems are articulated in Apter, D.E. 1961. Some Reflections on the Role of a Political Opposition in New Nations. *Comparative Studies in Society and History* 4: 154–168.

7   Dictionaries give the term "rule of law" a variety of meanings: "The Rule of Law, sometimes called "the supremacy of law", provides that decisions should be made by the application of known principles or laws without the intervention of discretion in their application" (*Black's Law Dictionary.* 1991, Minn: West Publishing);
"The principle that all citizens of this country are subject to the same laws, and that no one can be punished for something not expressed to be legal" (McFarlane, G. 1984. *The Layman's Dictionary of English Law.* Oxford: Pergaman Press. At p 252);

"The general condition of a state in which laws are accepted and observed." (Curzon, L.B. 1983. *A Dictionary of Law*. At p 211).

8   Yeatman has highlighted the position of anthropology in the front lines of colonial ordering, "situated as it is as the knowledge discipline which has informed and legitimised the modern western project of civilization/colonisation on a world-system scale." Yeatman, A. 1994. *Post-Modern Revisionings of the Political*. Routledge: New York & London, at p 32.

9   Regan, A. 1992. Constitutionalism, Legitimacy and the Judiciary. In James, R.W. & Fraser, I. (eds), *Legal Issues in a Developing Society*. Faculty of Law, University of Papua New Guinea, at p 15.

10 Ghai, Y. 1990. Constitutional Reviews in Papua New Guinea and Solomon Islands. *The Contemporary Pacific* 2:2, 313.

11 Ghai, Y. Above n 10 at p 315.

12 Gawi, J. The Status of the Common Law under the Constitution, 13–14.

13 Solomon Islands Parliament. *Hansard*. 3rd Session, 19th Meeting, 21 March–12 April 1988, p305.

14 Five other parties remained in the coalition: the National Alliance, the Peoples' Progress Party, the Peoples' Action Party, the Melanesian Alliance and the Pangu Pati.

15 The parties involved are the Melanesian Alliance (MA), the National Alliance (NA), the Peoples' Action Party (PAP), the Movement for Greater Autonomy (MGA) and a number of Independents.

16 "No Party Registered", *Post Courier* (22 October 1999).

17 "Reforming the Political System of the Cook Islands". The report suggested reducing the term of Parliament from 5 years to 4; abolishing the Overseas Constituency, and reducing the number of Members of Parliament from 25 to 17. It also made recommendations concerning the qualifications of voters and candidates, switching to a preferential electoral system, reducing the campaign period and tightening the accountability of political party finances, including a system of recall, limiting the length of consecutive term of MPs to 16 years (including up to 12 years as a Minister and/or 8 years as Prime Minister), and introducing a leadership code.

18 The Vanua'aku Pati won 18, the Union of Moderate Parties 12, the National United Party 11, the Melanesian Progressive Party 6, the John Frum Movement 2, independent candidates 2, and the Vanuatu Republikan Pati 1 seat. A coalition government was formed by Donald Kalpokas (President of the Vanua'aku Pati), together with members of the Vanua'aku Pati (VP) and the National United Party (NUP).

19 The events of 2001 during which the Speaker of the Parliament, Paul Ren Tari, closed a session of Parliament in order to prevent debate on a a no-confidence motion against the then Prime Minister Barak Sope provide another example of the courts becoming involved in parliamentary business. The members of the oppostition filed a petition in the Supreme Court to require the Speaker to convene Parliament and allow the motion to be debated. The judgments relating to this issue can be found at http://www.vanuatu.usp.ac.fj/journal_splaw/Special_Interest/Vanuatu_2001/Main.html (Accessed 30/10/01).

20 Constitutional Amendments 18 (concerning the Commencement of Constitutional Amendments Nos. 16 and 17) and 19 reduced the period for nomination of candidates from 35 to 28 days, reduced the formal campaign period, created provision for postal votes by citizens resident abroad, and for the holding of direct elections for local-level government council presidents. The amendments replaced the *Organic Law on National Elections*, the *Organic Law on Elections (Amendment No 1)*, *Electoral Regulation* 1977, *Electoral (Amendment) Regulation* 1987 the *Local Government (Electoral Provisions) Regulation* and other related legislation.

21 *Organic Law on the Integrity of Political Parties and Candidates.* Parts I, II, II, IV & VIII came into effect on 22/2/01. The rest of the Act came into effect on 22/2/02.

22 Other sections of the law require a political party to have more than ten Members of Parliament in order to be registered and receive State funding; to deny registration to a party that is regionally rather than nationally based, which does not portray nationalism, or which "portrays sinister tactics designed to work against the National Constitution"; to require all registered political parties to have a registered office, a Constitution, a secretariat and a National policy; and require transparency of the sources of party funds "Defector MPs Face Instant Dismissal", Post Courier (20 October 1999).

23 "Pangu Offers New Ways", *Post Courier* (20 October 1999).

24 "Architect Urges Radical Change", *Post Courier* (20 October 1999).

25 Throughout the Pacific, but particularly in Melanesia, 'big man' is used to refer to an important public figure. Theconcept combines elements of contemporary politics with traditional notions of the obligations of people holding high status.

26 For further examples, Hill, T. The Vanuatu Ombudsman, in this volume, details instances of public agitation because of corruption within the executive within the Vanuatu context.

27 The military activities of the Isantabu Freedom Fighters (IFF) resulted in the departure of at least 10,000 Malaitans — although they also disrupted the economic and political stability of the entire country.

28 For more information on the background to the situation in Solomon Islands and current updates see ttp://rspas.anu.edu.au/melanesia/index.htm (Accessed 31/10/01); http://www.peoplefirst.net.sb/Default.htm (Accessed 31/10/01).

29 Clause 1.

30 For more information on the background to the situation in Bougainville and current updates see http://rspas.anu.edu.au/melanesia/bougainvillepeacedocs.htm (Accessed 31/10/01); http://www.unpo.org/member/bougain/bougain.html (Accessed 30/10/01).

31 Ghai, Y. A Coup by Another Name? The Politics of Legality. *The Contemporary Pacific* 2:1, 11–35.

32 The key issues dividing the major political parties were the "paramountcy" of Fijian chiefs, the electoral system (a communal system, which did not allow cross voting), the existence of and powers of the senate (many of whose number were appointed by the Great Council of Chiefs). The Constitutional Review Commission received more than 700 submissions

from the major political parties and the public at large. The submission of the ruling *Soqosoqo ni Vakavulewa ni Taukei (SVT)* stated emphatically that the 1990 constitution, which weights the allocation of political power in favour of ethnic Fijians, must continue to form the basis of Fiji's constitutional order. The submissions of the chief of Rotuma's Royal Malmahan Clan indicated that Rotumans did not want to be mentioned in the Constitution, and preferred some form of free association.

34 Habermas, J. (trans. Rehg, W.) 1995. *Between Facts and Norms.* MA: MIT Press. At p 449.

35 Habermas, J. 1995. Moral Consciousness and Communicative Action. In Lenhardt, T. and Weber Nicholsen, S. (trans) *Moral Consciousness and Communicative Action.* Cambridge MA: MIT Press. p 116.

36 Habermas, J. (trans. McCarthy, T.) 1981. *The Theory of Communicative Action* Boston: Beacon Press.

37 "Mollok Wants a Total Review", *Post Courier* (20 October 1999); "Political Change Vital (Mollok", *Post Courier* (22 October 1999).

38 "Western Ways 'Source of Strife'", *Post Courier* (22 October 1999).

39 Mr Mollok said the importance of the proposed Organic Law should not be rushed "The convention has revealed that the proposed law is being rushed and that it may end up being unworkable in many aspects as is the case with the Organic Law on Provincial and Local Level Governments." He said that "while there was wide support for the proposed law to be enacted, there were suggestions that the Government might not have a consolidated number on the matter. This was illustrated by the differing views expressed by leaders of the current coalition party. The CDC had been told to come up with this historic piece of legislation but it seemed the Government was not really showing its genuineness by rushing the Bill, instead of allowing for adequate public awareness and adequate funding for the commission to carry out this task": "CDC Chief Calls on Govt to Take Lead", *Post Courier* (22 October 1999). See also, "Law to Control Politicians a Must (CDC Chairman)", *Post Courier* (25 October 1999).

40 "Mollok Calls for More Time, Funds", *Post Courier* (25 October 1999).

41 "Sacked Chairman Cries Foul", *Post Courier* (16 November 1999).

42 Lal, B.V. 1998. *Another Way: the Politics of Constitutional Reform in Post-Coup Fiji.* Canberra: National Centre for Development Studies.

4. THE VANUATU OMBUDSMAN

By: Edward R. Hill

KEY TERMS AND PHRASES

Generic Model

A generic model is a general or standard model or structure that is applied in a number of situations. When talking about laws we sometimes find that 'generic models' of particular laws have been transplanted from other legal systems, and maybe modified to fit the particular situation of the jurisdiction adopting the generic model.

Ombudsman

According to the generic model of the ombudsman, an ombudsman is an independent person appointed by and responsible to either the Head of State or the parliament of a jurisdiction. The ombudsman acts on the complaints of members of the public and has powers of investigation. The focus of the ombudsman's jurisdiction is the fair and efficient administration of the laws.

INTRODUCTION

The 1980 Vanuatu *Constitution* provides a number of features that are common to many other constitutional democracies. These include entrenched individual rights and freedoms, an independent judiciary and a democratically elected government. The *Constitution* also includes provision for an ombudsman. In 1994, fourteen years after the *Constitution* came into effect, the first Ombudsman was appointed in Vanuatu. Since then, the Office of the Ombudsman has had a high profile in the country, exposing misconduct, corruption and mismanagement within the government and public sector and, in the process, creating widespread controversy. In this short time the Office of the Ombudsman has undergone a number of changes. In 1999, the first Ombudsman's term of appointment expired and a second Ombudsman succeeded her. There have also been two *Ombudsman Acts* since 1995 and a term of approximately a year during which the Ombudsman operated without any supporting legislation apart from the *Constitution*.[1] This chapter describes the mandate and the role of the Office of the Ombudsman in Vanuatu and the environment in which it has operated during its first 6 years of operation. It also examines some types of misconduct that it has revealed. Particular emphasis is placed on the relationship of the Ombudsman and the politicians and other leaders of Vanuatu.

What is an Ombudsman?

The International Bar Association defines 'ombudsman' as, "an office established by Constitution or statute, headed by an independent, high-level, public official, who is responsible to the Legislature or Parliament, who receives complaints from aggrieved persons against government agencies, officials and employers, or who acts on his own motion, and has the power to investigate and recommend corrective action and issue reports."[2] This definition describes what might be referred to as the generic model of the ombudsman's office. In this model an ombudsman provides a means for people to bring to the attention of an official who is independent of the government complaints about any unfair treatment by the government or any unfair ways in which laws have been applied to them. An ombudsman then provides assistance in the form of information, mediation or recommendations to the relevant authority. In most jurisdictions, the ombudsman also publishes reports exposing problems and recommending solutions. In most stable democracies the existence of an ombudsman's office is largely an uncontroversial feature of governance.

The offices of ombudsmen in numerous jurisdictions are based on this model. The scope of inquiry of an ombudsman operating in such a model is restricted in certain ways. For instance, the Head of State and the judiciary are usually beyond the jurisdiction of most ombudsmen.[3] An ombudsman typically has a mandate to make reports and recommendations arising from complaints but does not have the jurisdiction to enforce recommendations or engage in criminal prosecutions.[4] An ombudsman is either appointed or elected by the government or Head of State. To be effective, an ombudsman must be free of political pressures in the conduct of investigations and reporting. It is also important that an ombudsman be seen to be neutral, of high integrity and equipped with the expertise and courage to tackle issues which may not be politically popular. As we shall see, Vanuatu's Office of the Ombudsman has, under both Acts, been largely based on the generic model.

The first country to have an Office of the Ombudsman was Sweden. The Swedish Parliament elected the first Ombudsman in 1809. His role was to supervise the observance of laws and regulations by all officials and judges.[5] More than a century later, the appointment of a Danish Ombudsman spurred interest in other countries.[6] New Zealand appointed an Ombudsman in 1962. Canada and Australia established Offices of the Ombudsman in the 1960's and 1970's. Since that time ombudsman's offices have been established in over 80 countries.

The ombudsman model is no longer limited to a role of 'government watchdog' and has been applied in a wide range of contexts. For instance, there are ombudsmen whose mandate is restricted to housing, long term care, funerals, victim-offender disputes, hospitals, health care, insurance, investments, pensions and police. There are also private mediators who offer their services in particular areas. 'Ombudsman' as a keyword in any search of the World Wide Web produces an abundance of examples.

The Vanuatu context

Although Vanuatu has adopted the generic model of the ombudsman, its unique colonial history, development status, geography and cultural roots create a challenging environment for the Office of the Ombudsman to operate within. Vanuatu is a small South Pacific country comprising approximately 65 inhabited islands and more than 100 indigenous languages. It is one of the most culturally diverse nations in the world. The cultures of Vanuatu are deeply rooted in traditional beliefs and ways of living. A majority of the population lives in tribal, non-urban and largely subsistence communities. Kinship is an important factor in social relationships. The influence of the modern world, technology and the cash economy is centred in Port Vila, the capital of Vanuatu, together with several other smaller towns.

For 73 years, until independence in 1980, the British and the French ruled the islands jointly as a condominium, in one of the more unique arrangements in colonial history. Neither colonial power had exclusive sovereignty. The legacy of these two competing foreign powers is still strongly felt today with political parties and the education system divided along old colonial lines. In addition, language, culture and economic disparities continue to be divisive factors in Vanuatu society. As is the case with other Pacific island countries, foreign donors continue to play a significant role in the economy.[7]

The President is Head of State and there is a Parliament consisting of 52 elected representatives. Elections are held every 4 years. This model of government (and indeed the notion of a nation state itself) is foreign to the pre-existing social and political fabric of Vanuatu society. While the model of government incorporates the major features of the colonisers' own governments and most 'western' democracies, it was, and to a large extent continues to be foreign to a large proportion of ni-Vanuatu people. The process of social and political adjustment to the new order is a continuing one.

Since 1995 the Government of Vanuatu has been particularly unstable, with several cabinet shuffles, the formation of new political parties, the re-alignment of others, an election, no-confidence motions, frequent changes of government, changing alliances among political parties and the kidnapping of the President. There appears to be an increasing inability or unwillingness on the part of government to provide for the social needs of the population, which is resulting in unemployment, inequity and poverty.[8] There have been numerous instances of abuse of political power for personal or political reasons. It is in this environment that the Ombudsman of Vanuatu operates.

The Constitutional foundation of the Ombudsman

The *Constitution* of Vanuatu creates a generic model for the Ombudsman in Vanuatu. Article 65 provides for the independence of the Ombudsman and his or her freedom from supervision and control. The Ombudsman is appointed for a 5-year term by the President, on advice from the Prime Minister and leaders of other political parties.

Article 62 provides that an inquiry may be conducted by the Ombudsman into the conduct of any level of the government, public service or public authorities with the exception of the judiciary and the President. Inquiries may be commenced on the basis of a complaint by a member of the public, a member of parliament, the National Council of Chiefs, a local government or on the Ombudsman's own initiative.[9]

Article 63 of the *Constitution* provides that where the Ombudsman finds that conduct being investigated was defective a report of the findings shall be made to the Prime Minister and the person in charge of the relevant public service. A decision and reply is required of the Prime Minister or the person in charge.[10]

With two notable exceptions, the Office of the Ombudsman, as shaped by the *Constitution,* contains few provisions specific to the circumstances of Vanuatu. Article 64 imposes responsibility on the Ombudsman with respect to the three official languages of the country.[11] A person who is aggrieved in connection with the use of an official language may complain to the Ombudsman who is obliged to launch an investigation. The Ombudsman also reports to the Parliament on a yearly basis about the observance of multilingualism.[12] Article 62(1)(b) is also specific to the circumstances of Vanuatu in providing that an Ombudsman's inquiry may be launched at the instance of the National Council of Chiefs.

OMBUDSMAN ACT 1995

Vanuatu's first Ombudsman was appointed in 1994.[13] The first *Ombudsman Act* came into force on August 18, 1995, nearly a year after the first Ombudsman had been appointed. It both strengthened the independence of the Ombudsman and provided tools for the effective investigation of complaints.[14]

Independence

The Act enhanced the independence of the Ombudsman in three ways. Firstly, he or she could have no political affiliations or trade or profession during his or her term. Secondly, it provided protection against dismissal except on specific grounds such as bankruptcy, a criminal conviction or gross misconduct.[15] Independence was further enhanced with the provision that staff be appointed directly by the Ombudsman rather than through the Public Service Commission.[16]

Scope of inquiries

Section 14 of the 1995 *Ombudsman Act* articulated and expanded the method of inquiry provided by Article 62 of the *Constitution*. The Ombudsman could inquire into any government body or body supported mainly out of public moneys, or any employee of such a body. Such inquiry could be into any defects in any law or administrative practice or any alleged discriminatory practice or any suspected breach of the Leadership Code.[17]

Powers and procedures

The 1995 Act provided the power to compel testimony and the disclosure of documents in the course of an inquiry. It also created powers of search and seizure pursuant to a warrant.[18] Obstruction of the Ombudsman in the exercise of his or her duties was made an offence.[19]

Where an inquiry concluded that conduct was contrary to section 63(2) of the *Constitution*, was discriminatory or that a law or practice was defective, section 22 directed that the relevant authority be notified. It also required that reports be forwarded to the Prime Minister, the President and in some cases to the head of the department of the public service or to the Leader of the Opposition.

The 1995 Act ensured that inquiries and reports of the Ombudsman could not be ignored by the government. In response to a report the Prime Minister was required to provide not only a decision but also information about the steps that were proposed in relation to the Ombudsman's recommendations.[20] Where there was no response to the Ombudsman's recommendations, she or he was empowered by section 30 to apply to the Supreme Court for an order that the recommendations be implemented.[21] These provisions provide the Ombudsman with significant powers of enforcement that are beyond those found in the generic model described above.[22]

THE FIRST OMBUDSMAN – A NEW PRESENCE

The first Ombudsman, Marie-Noelle Ferrieux Patterson, is a naturalised citizen of Vanuatu, originally from France. She lost no time in commencing inquiries in response to complaints. The resulting public reports were unprecedented in the short history of Vanuatu. Never before had leaders been subjected to such scrutiny and, in some cases, to such unflinching and sustained criticism. The number of complaints that fell within the Ombudsman's jurisdiction dramatically increased from 59 in 1994/1995 to 542 in 1998/1999.[23]

At the time of her appointment, the first Ombudsman had no office, no staff and few resources.[24] This state of affairs continued during the first year of the first Ombudsman's appointment and created a challenge for her. This itself became a public issue. In describing the efforts to make suitable arrangements for the accommodation of herself and her office the Ombudsman lashed out at the government for its ineptitude and resulting waste of energy and time.[25] This set the tone for the ensuing relationship between much of the governing elite and the Ombudsman.

The lack of resources was, however, only temporary. It is worth noting by way of comparison that while the Ombudsman's staff quickly grew to more than 20 full time employees and occupied 2 floors of a downtown Port Vila office building, the Office of the Public Solicitor, which is constitutionally responsible for providing legal assistance to "needy persons",[26] has continued to work with less than 5 staff. Similarly, the Office of the Public Prosecutor, responsible for all criminal prosecutions within the country, has continued to work with a handful of staff. Much of the funding that has allowed the Office of the Ombudsman to grow so rapidly has come from the international donor community who obviously saw a significant need for such an institution.[27]

The Ombudsman as an outsider

This outside funding has, in part, contributed to a perception that the Office of the Ombudsman is an imposed institution, serving foreign interests. The first Ombudsman placed considerable importance upon the need to maintain an environment that will attract foreign assistance and investment:

> It is vital for the public to face the fact that it is foreign money which constitutes the only hope in Vanuatu's present financial crisis. Foreign aid from such countries as Australia and others makes up almost 50% of Vanuatu's entire budget (recurrent plus development). This aid is in danger of being drastically reduced as a result of the irresponsible antics of some leaders here. It is therefore vital for us citizens to be aware of who our best friends are, and who are actually our biggest enemies and drawbacks.[28]

The obvious interest by the first Ombudsman in attracting foreign investment and the favour of foreign donors may be justified. However it provided a potential for characterising her as an outsider with outsider's interests. This view has indeed been evident among members of the political elite. For example, one senior bureaucrat, Father Leymang, after an unsuccessful legal challenge to the right of the Ombudsman to compel disclosure of information pursuant to section 30 of the 1995 Act, wrote a letter that was published in the *Vanuatu Trading Post* on February 18, 1998. In it he called for the confiscation of the Ombudsman's passport and her deportation (notwithstanding that she is a ni-Vanuatu citizen). He stated further that:

> Mrs Marie Noelle Ferrieux Patterson stands there like a European-style teacher, stern and harsh, wielding a big stick fashioned by foreign powers to punish the young Melanesians (the politicians).[29]

The public acceptance of the Ombudsman's findings and recommendations have eroded in accordance with the degree that this view of her as an outsider, imposing outsiders' views and promoting their interests, is perceived to be correct. One of the justifications for the repeal of the first *Ombudsman Act* used this characterisation. The Prime Minister, interviewed on television in connection with the repeal of the Act stated that indigenous people should run their own country and not allow "former colonialists" to decide their future.[30] Again, this characterisation is not without its foundations.[31]

Being a woman undoubtedly also had an impact on how the first Ombudsman was perceived in a society where the preponderance of political power is wielded exclusively by men. This was evident in the Parliamentary debate during the repeal of the *Ombudsman Act* 1995. Mr Barak Sope, a Minister who had been subjected to intense scrutiny and criticism by the Ombudsman, defended his support of the Bill to repeal the first *Ombudsman Act* because, in his view, Melanesian culture does not allow women to criticise men.[32] It is questionable that this view of Melanesian culture is in fact correct in any event.[33]

The moral imperative

The reports of the first Ombudsman do more than dispassionately and objectively reveal wrongful conduct. The tone of the reports themselves is bombastic, combative and moralistic.[34] The reports contain mention of the personal revulsion of the Ombudsman and severe moralistic reprimands of those found to be corrupt or criminally responsible for their actions. Reports were routinely prefaced with biblical quotes.[35] The implication of the biblical quotes together with other editorialising, particularly in the preambles of the reports, is that the Ombudsman has the role of a moral judge supported in her opinions by biblical authority. The first Ombudsman has been criticised for taking on this role.[36] However, she made no secret of her moral approach to her duties. In her 1996 Annual Report, she had this to say at page 5:

> I expect to be attacked again for attempting to "lecture" the public, but I make no apology for sounding out these warnings in an attempt to secure the enlightenment and education of the public in these important matters. It is of course one of the specific duties of the Ombudsman to inform the public of what is done "officially" in their name. It is not a **political** revolution that is needed in my opinion, but a moral and ethical one.

The first Ombudsman's legal battles

The struggle between the first Ombudsman and the political elite was also played out in court. There have been several attempts by the Ombudsman to compel the disclosure of information pursuant to section 30 of the first *Ombudsman Act*.[37] There has also been an application by the Ombudsman to have her recommendation made enforceable by order of the court pursuant to section 30. This concerned an attempt to force the repayment of *ex gratia* payments to certain politicians.[38] In response, the Council of Ministers (which included many of those who were the subject of the section 30 application) attempted to dismiss the Ombudsman from office by resolution. This resolution was challenged in court by the Ombudsman and was eventually held to be "invalid in law and thus unlawful and of no legal or other effect."[39] This entire episode attracted media attention throughout the region.

THE REPLACEMENT OF THE OMBUDSMAN AND A NEW OMBUDSMAN ACT

The first Ombudsman's style was tenacious and in her reports, she provided no quarter to her *opponents* — those among the political elite of the country whose conduct formed the basis of her reports. In disclosing the existence of corruption and incompetence, she left little opportunity by which those involved could save face.[40] On June 26, 1998, after three years of operation, the exposure of widespread corruption and misuse of power, and vigorous opposition from the Council of Ministers, the *Ombudsman Act* of 1995 was repealed by Parliament. Given the opposition among the political elite to the Ombudsman personally and to her role this drastic action is not surprising. Notwithstanding this, the Ombudsman continued to operate, solely on the basis of the Constitutional provisions and her continuing appointment.

After a period without any specific legislation, a new Act came into force on January 11, 1999. Later that year, the first Ombudsman's 5 year term of office expired and, despite her application to have her position renewed, Mr Hannington Alatoa, an indigenous citizen, was appointed as Vanuatu's second Ombudsman. The appointment of the second Ombudsman created a division of opinion between supporters of the first Ombudsman's rigorously investigative approach and those who favoured a more conciliatory approach.

THE SECOND OMBUDSMAN ACT

In several respects, the new legislation lacks the force of the first Act and therefore represents less of a potential threat to those whose conduct is likely to be scrutinised.

No longer are appointments to the staff of the Ombudsman made directly by the Ombudsman and independently of the Public Service. Under the new Act, employees are appointed as part of the Public Service and subject to the same control as are other government employees who are appointed through the Public Service. This creates the potential for employees of the Ombudsman to be intimidated where their work is critical of or threatens someone who has control over the employment of public servants.[41]

The new Act restricts the use of inflammatory language and prohibits allegations of criminal wrongdoing without stating the alleged offence and providing evidence to support the allegation.[42] Interestingly the Act does not specify what form the evidence must take or what standard of proof must be satisfied in order to make an allegation of criminal wrongdoing. It is reasonable to conclude, however, that this provision found its way into the new Act in response to the many comments of the first

Ombudsman which could be construed as inflammatory and the many allegations of criminal wrongdoing made by her. Whilst reports published by the first Ombudsman prior to the second *Ombudsman Act* coming into force do not hesitate to draw unequivocal conclusions that leaders breached the Leadership Code, those published after the passing of the second Act qualify allegations with the phrase, "may have" to condition a conclusion that the Code was breached.[43]

Another significant change made by the second *Ombudsman Act* is the requirement that notice be given to the person in charge of the relevant government agency or the relevant leader before an inquiry is launched, except where the Ombudsman has reasonable grounds for believing that to do so would interfere with his or her inquiry.[44] Such notice could serve to give the agency or leader being investigated an opportunity to take steps to minimise the effectiveness or impact of an inquiry.

The 1995 Act provided that the Ombudsman could apply to the Supreme Court for an order giving effect to a recommendation of the Ombudsman where the Prime Minister (or other relevant person required to do so) did not respond to the Ombudsman's recommendations with a decision and an indication of what steps were to be taken to deal with the recommendations. This power is lacking in the new Act. This change (which represents a retreat to the generic model) alters what might be considered to be the balance of power between the Ombudsman and the government in favour of the government.

The Ombudsman's access to restricted or "prohibited information" is limited by section 27 of the new Act. This is defined in the Act to include "information that is prohibited or restricted under or by any recognised duty of professional confidentiality or privilege." This definition begs questions concerning the nature of "professional confidentiality or privilege" which have yet to be clarified by any judicial consideration.

Mediation

Another significant way in which the new *Ombudsman Act* 1998 differs from the 1995 Act is its inclusion of provisions enabling the use of mediation in the resolution of disputes arising from complaints to the Ombudsman. Although mediation has been informally used by other ombudsman offices, Vanuatu appears to be the first jurisdiction to formally include it within the scope of an ombudsman's powers and duties.[45]

The Ombudsman is required to mediate where requested to do so and where practicable.[46] If the Ombudsman believes that it would not be practicable to mediate, he or she must give reasons in writing to the person who requested mediation. The use of mediation has not yet become widespread in the work of the Ombudsman. However, it is expected to increase as a means of resolving complaints in appropriate cases.[47] In order to facilitate the use of mediation, the image of the Ombudsman as an adversarial presence, which was created in the first 5 years of the existence of the Ombudsman's office, will require moderation. The more like an accuser or adversary the Ombudsman is, the less effective he or she will be in the role of a neutral agent who is able to facilitate the resolution of disputes.

It has been suggested that mediation, as a means of conducting the work of the Ombudsman, is inappropriate.[48] The basis for this criticism is that an invitation to mediate early in an investigation would give the party to the mediation whose conduct is being investigated an opportunity to hide or destroy incriminating evidence. It has also been suggested that common sense favours the view that a conciliatory approach would not work in cases where there has been an apparent misuse of official power. While this may be so in some cases, mediation could provide a useful tool in cases where these factors are not present.

New image

The second Ombudsman has in fact begun to cultivate an image consistent with the use of mediation and at variance with that cultivated by the first Ombudsman. The use of biblical quotes in prefaces of public reports has been discontinued. Personal reactions of the Ombudsman, particularly expressions of outrage, are less apparent in the text of public reports than was previously the case. As indicated above, categorical judgements about the commission of offences by leaders and politicians are no longer included in the text of public reports. There is less evidence of moral indignation and a greater emphasis on co-operation and the implementation of mediation as a means of resolving appropriate disputes. Accompanying these changes is a discernable lessening of public attacks by politicians and others on the Office of the Ombudsman and the Ombudsman personally.

PATTERNS OF MISCONDUCT REVEALED

Before the end of 2000, the Ombudsman published more than 70 public reports arising from individual inquiries. Not all of the reports deal with deliberately improper conduct. Many reports reveal systemic weaknesses and deficiencies in administrative practice and procedure. Examples of these types of reports include inquiries into the condition of prisons and the use of disciplinary procedures in prisons.[49] Others include inquiries and reports concerning the incompetence of the Vanuatu Fire Service[50] discrimination inherent in the *Citizenship Act* [Cap 112],[51] the language of instruction at a particular school,[52] and discriminatory criteria applied by the National Exam Board for admission into grade 7.[53]

However, a large proportion of investigations and public reports do reveal improper conduct, particularly on the part of politicians and senior public servants. It is difficult to neatly categorise this conduct as the revelations of single reports often include a wide range of improper conduct. However, using several reports as examples, it is possible to identify some recurring themes. Some of the major ones are illustrated below.

The rule of law under attack

One aspect of improper conduct that is revealed by the public reports of the Ombudsman is the degree to which political leaders consider themselves to be free to make decisions and engage in conduct without regard to the bounds of their statutory powers. Ministers of the Government have, on numerous occasions, made decisions that purportedly bind the government (particularly involving the spending of public money) without a legal foundation for doing so. Proper procedures are often bypassed in order to achieve results. The Minister of Finance, in response to an investigation by the Ombudsman, puts a couple of revealing rhetorical questions in which he justifies his actions with an appeal to what he considers to be democratic principles:

> Why doesn't the Office of the Ombudsman ask here the real question? Must a Minister of the Government, an elected member of the People always obey a civil servant (the Attorney General who is a civil servant). Who is governing Vanuatu: the elected of the People who govern Vanuatu and take their decision or the civil servants?[54]

This response indicates that degree to which the Big Man syndrome appears to play a role in the politics of the country. Big Man is an expression, usually used disparagingly, that derives from the customary power of chiefly authority. It is used in the countries of Melanesia to refer to a person whose power, although not necessarily derived from chiefly source, is nevertheless exercised as if it is. It has been asserted that the expression as it has been applied and understood in a political context is not authentic but is the result of a process that 'manufactures' custom. Politicians are accorded the same status as chiefs to reflect their importance and contributions. Because of this perceived status they are reluctant to accept criticism and consider it as contrary to custom. However, it has been pointed out that there is really nothing in custom which prevents criticism or sanctioning of inappropriate behaviour by leaders.[55]

Political appointments of unqualified people

A number of reports have disclosed the appointment of people to senior positions, either within the public service, onto the board of a public enterprise or as an employee of a public enterprise. A typical case is that of the hiring of a Deputy General Manager of the Vanuatu National Provident Fund (VNPF).[56] The VNPF received a number of applications from qualified candidates for this position. However, no appointment was made by the VNPF Board until consultations took place with the Finance Minister. The Finance Minister strongly "recommended" an unqualified politician who had recently lost his seat in Parliament. An application was submitted by this person after the closing date, his application was considered and he was "hired" by the Board at a meeting without a quorum. The report on the VNPF matter publicised the political hiring of an unqualified person and identified the lack of independence and relevant knowledge on the part of Board members of the VNPF.

Other examples of this type of conduct are revealed in the <u>Public Report on the Appointment of Senior Public Works Staff</u>[57] where the Prime Minister, in breach of procedure, directly appointed persons, based on the political affiliations of the persons, without consultation with the Public Service Commission or the Department of Public Works and despite the appointees' lack of proper qualifications. The <u>Public Report on Mismanagement of the Vanuatu Livestock Development Ltd</u>,[58] reveals that an unqualified political appointee (the brother in law of the Agriculture Minister) with a criminal record for misappropriation was hired, in preference to a qualified candidate as Manager of Vanuatu Livestock Development Ltd, a government owned enterprise. The company suffered disastrous financial consequences as a result of highly incompetent mismanagement by the appointee.

Conflict of interest

A number of reports also reveal instances of improper conduct that involves conflict of interest. In the Nambawan Bottle Shop case[59] the Ombudsman found that the Minister of Finance, as a partner in a private business enterprise, used his influence to bypass a number of statutory prerequisites to establish a retail liquor outlet. A license (on unprecedented terms) was granted for the operation of this outlet on a 24-hour basis, contrary to the terms of legislation governing the sale of alcohol and contrary to the legal opinion of the Attorney General. The report discloses various other instances of improper behaviour or inaction by officials in relation to this scheme.

Conflict of interest is also illustrated in two public reports involving the lease of government land. In the first case, the Minister of Lands used his power to grant 15 leases in favour of himself, his wife, wantoks, driver and house girl. Proper procedures, including the valuation of the leases, approvals, application fees and other requirements were not followed.[60] Four of the 5 leases that the Minister granted to himself were granted free of any premium (purchase price) and the remaining leases were granted at less than the market value. The Ombudsman's report concluded that the Minister, using his position, had misappropriated property. In the second case, the same Minister again leased a number of properties using an improperly constituted tenders board, one member of which submitted a bid which he subsequently considered as a member of the tenders board (his bid was successful).[61] The leases were fraught with other irregularities and were granted contrary to the advice of the Department of Finance and the Solicitor General.

The <u>Public Report on the Sale of the M. V. Yasur</u>[62] revealed a further instance of conflict of interest. The vessel M.V. Yasur, owned by the government, was leased to a private company. The Secretary General of the Council of Ministers (the cabinet) made arrangements relating to the leased vessel, including the release of two public servants to work on the vessel. At the time he was also an active partner of the company leasing the vessel.

Perhaps the most notorious instance of conflict of interest is revealed in the <u>Public Report on the Vanuatu National Provident Fund Housing Loan Scheme</u>.[63] Many politicians, senior public servants and members of the VNPF Board used their positions to gain preferential treatment in a low interest housing loan scheme from which they benefited at the expense of the 33,000 members of the VNPF whose trust fund was being used to finance the scheme.

Bad business deals

Several public reports show how politicians have, ostensibly acting in the best interests of Vanuatu, become involved in business schemes with foreign interests. The conduct which has been involved in these schemes has been found to be improper in a number of respects. These business arrangements were all entered into in breach of proper procedures which, if followed, would have prevented the risk of unfortunate results.

One notable example of such conduct involves the Bank Guarantee case.[64] The Prime Minister, the Minister of Finance and the Governor of the Reserve Bank arranged for bank guarantees to be drawn up in the sum of US$100,000,000 and provided to an expatriate businessman, together with a diplomatic passport and A$50,000. There was no apparent consideration for these benefits except for the apparently naïve expectation that the guarantees could be invested and return a profit in the order of US$250,000,000 in two years.

Another example of this type of conduct is revealed in the case of the transfer by the Finance Minister of ownership of all of Vanuatu's assets to a secret trust established in Mauritius, contrary to the advice of the Attorney General. The reason for the ministerial order giving effect to this transfer is not clear. Fortunately it was made without the necessary authority and was cancelled by the incoming government.[65]

The Cybank venture provides another example of an improvident business deal with foreigners.[66] The Minister of Finance entered into negotiations with an Australian businessman for the Republic of Vanuatu to invest in an online internet bank and casino. The arrangements were hastily finalised without the necessary approval of the Council of Ministers. The funds for the investment were to come from the VNPF. Cybank was to receive preferential license fees, tax rates and priority access to telecommunication facilities in Vanuatu. Neither Telecom Vanuatu Ltd (which was obliged to provide some of these concessions) nor the VNPF (which was to provide the financial investment) took part in the negotiations. No independent evaluation was obtained before the Finance Minister committed to the investment and a number of necessary procedural prerequisites for such an investment by the government were not followed.

These reports and the matters they reveal demonstrate the extent to which naïveté and corruption are sometimes difficult to distinguish. It should be stressed that the Ombudsman made no finding that there had been bribery in either case. The need to stress this fact stems from the ease with which one might make an unwarranted assumption that it was.

FURTHER OBSERVATIONS AND CONCLUSIONS

The work of the Ombudsman in Vanuatu is largely concerned with the advancement of good governance. It is difficult to accurately assess the effectiveness of the Ombudsman in bringing about good governance within Vanuatu. Many of the matters inquired into by the Vanuatu Ombudsman are themselves of an order of significance that are unlikely to be tackled on a regular basis by ombudsmen of most other jurisdictions. Further, the police and prosecution branches of law enforcement in Vanuatu are relatively weak and unable or unwilling to follow up with prosecutions as recommended by the Ombudsman.

Many of the recommendations arising from the Ombudsman's reports call for the non-reappointment or dismissal of appointed board members, employees of the government or publicly owned companies and the resignation or dismissal of politicians. Others call for the prosecution of those whose conduct has either been concluded or suspected to be criminal. However, few, if any, prosecutions have been initiated on the basis of an Ombudsman's report. A number of politicians have been found to have been in breach of the Leadership Code (some on several occasions) and yet have gone on to further leadership positions contrary to the Ombudsman's recommendations. No politician has resigned over revelations of misconduct and although several charges have been laid, no conviction has, to date resulted from any of revelations of wrongdoing alleged in any Ombudsman report.[67]

Other recommendations call for new or amended laws and procedures to correct deficiencies or fill gaps. Some of these recommendations have been adopted. The passing of the *Leadership Code Act* in August 1998 is one example. However, it is questionable whether the Ombudsman's recommendations were instrumental in getting the laws amended. The move to amend or create the laws in relation to the Leadership Code predated the Ombudsman's office, and new laws may well have been created regardless of her recommendations.

However, although there may have been few formal actions arising from the recommendations in the Ombudman's reports, the Office has had an impact on politicians and society. As has been indicated, the powerful have felt threatened by the Ombudsman's power. The former Minister of Finance, Willie Jimmy, in response to a preliminary report in the Nambawan Bottle Shop case stated that "[the] Ombudsman does not know that the law does not give her the power to act as a Policeman, Judge, Jury and Executioner."[68] While there may be an element of hyperbole in this statement, in a sense it is true that the first Ombudsman assumed the role of a judge. The many conclusions of criminal conduct, the illegality of particular actions and the invalidity of others read like judicial pronouncements. This quality is highlighted in the paucity of judicial pronouncements on the type of conduct that the Ombudsman has investigated and reported on. In respect of the allegation of the Ombudsman being an executioner, it can be said that on at least one occasion, the first Ombudsman did, inadvertently and indirectly, assume this role. The public reaction to revelations contained in the <u>Public Report on the Vanuatu</u>

Provident Fund Housing Loan Scheme included rioting and extensive damage to the office building housing the VNPF and to private property thought to belong to some individuals whose conduct was judged wrongful in the report. Figuratively therefore, one might consider the first Ombudsman to have indirectly wielded the authority of the Old Testament passages which are included in the prefaces of the public reports and to have been indirectly associated with the retributive moral consequences to which they refer.

It may be argued that, compared to many countries with an Ombudsman, the importance of the Vanuatu Ombudsman is greater, given the relative lack of civic awareness and no established tradition of independent investigative journalism. It might also be argued that the lack of these features has increased the difficulty that the Ombudsman encounters in discharging his or her responsibility and gaining the confidence and respect of the political class.

Just as there is very little in the model of the Ombudsman that has been adopted by Vanuatu which is adapted to the specific circumstances of Vanuatu, so there is nothing in any of the reports which addresses the cultural differences of the nation or takes into account how these might provide an understanding of the conduct of the leaders and public servants whose actions are being investigated. It is also notable that the National Council of Chiefs, which is specifically entitled to make a complaint and thereby launch an inquiry has yet to avail itself of this opportunity.

However this does not lead to the conclusion that the reports of the Ombudsman have been without effect. Although it is not possible to conclude that the behaviour of leaders of the country has changed as a result of the presence of the Office of the Ombudsman, it is clear that the Ombudsman has raised the level of consciousness among both the general population and the political class. It is also clear that, even under the new *Ombudsman Act*, there is sufficient power for the wrongdoings of politicians and other government and public officials to be investigated and made public. The challenge now is for the Ombudsman to remain effective in revealing misconduct but, at the same time, to induce those who have power to do so to make changes in accordance with the Ombudsman's recommendations. Ideally, this process will incorporate more consultation and cooperation between the Ombudsman and the powerful than has been evident to date.

ENDNOTES

1   *Ombudsman Act* No. 14 of 1995 (Vanuatu) and *Ombudsman Act* No. 27 of 1998 (Vanuatu).

2   Ferris, C. Goodman, B. and Mayer, G. 1980. *Brief on the Office of the Ombudsman* Ombudsman Committee of the International Bar Association. p 2.

3   This is not universally the case. In the Philippines, the Ombudsman is able to inquire into the judicial branch of the government: see September 14 1999. Hon. Aniano A. Desierto. Republic of Philippines Ombudsman Briefs Sydney business on fight against corruption. *Emanila News.* September 14 1999 www.emanila.com/news/community/desierto.htm (Accessed 30/10/01). In Finland it is also the case that actions of the head of state and judiciary are within the jurisdiction of the ombudsman. See http://www.eduskunta.fi (Accessed 6/11/01).

4   However, an exception to this is found in the Philippines where the Ombudsman does have the power to prosecute. See *Emanila News* above n 3.

5   Lundvik, U. 1981. The New Zealand Ombudsman. *Occasional Paper #7.* Alberta: International Ombudsman Institute.

6   International Ombudsman Institute. 1982. *Ombudsman Office Profiles* Alberta: International Ombudsman Institute.

7   Luteru, P. 1994. *Aid and Development in Relation to Customary Land Tenure: Some Social and Educational Implications in Land Issues it the Pacific.* Suva: Institute of Pacific Studies.

8   Huffer, E. and Molisa, G. 1999. Governance in Vanuatu: In Search of the Nakamal Way. State, Society and Governance in Melanesia Project *Discussion Paper 99/4.* Canberra: Research School of Pacific and Asian Studies, Australian National University.

9   The National Council of Chiefs is a consultative body established under Chapter 5 of the *Constitution* of Vanuatu that is concerned with the use and preservation of custom and may make recommendations for the preservation and promotion of ni-Vanuatu culture and languages.

10 Any limitation period that applies to the complainant's right to a legal remedy is delayed until such a reply is made.

11 These languages are English French and Bislama.

12 This is a feature is not unique to Vanuatu. Canada, a country with more than one official language, safeguards their status in part by the *Official Languages Act* RSC 1985 c. 31. It provides for a Commissioner of Official Languages whose duties include the investigation of complaints regarding the use of official languages and reporting to Parliament.

13 The Ombudsman was the last Constitutional position in Vanuatu to be filled; Vanuatu Ombudsman. 1995. Annual Report. p 14.

14 These aspects can be considered to be the sword and the shield of the Ombudsman. Both are necessary for the effective discharge of duties by any Ombudsman, see de Jonge, A. 1998. The Pacific Ombudsman's Complaints Function: Comparative Perspectives on Fiji, Papua New Guinea and Vanuatu. Delivered at Corruption and Accountability in the Pacific Workshop, State, Society and Governance in Melanesia Project, Australian National University 6–9 November 1998.

15 Dismissal must result from the deliberations of a tribunal comprising 3 persons including the Chief Justice; section 9, *Ombudsman Act* 1995 (Vanuatu).

16 *Ombudsman Act* 1995 (Vanuatu) s.35.

17 The Leadership Code forms Chapter 10 of the *Constitution* and is set out below:

66. (1) Any person defined as a leader in Article 67 has a duty to conduct himself in such a way, both in his public and private life, so as not to:

(a) place himself in a position in which he has or could have a conflict of interests or in which the fair exercise of his public or official duties might be compromised;

(b) demean his office or position;

(c) allow his integrity to be called into question; or

(d) endanger or diminish respect for and confidence in the integrity of the Government of the Republic of Vanuatu.

(2) In particular, a leader shall not use his office for personal gain or enter into any transaction or engage in any enterprise or activity that might be expected to give rise to doubt in the public mind as to whether he is carrying out or has carried out the duty imposed by sub-article (1)

67. For the purposes of this Chapter, a leader means the President of the Republic, the Prime Minister and other Ministers, members of Parliament, and such public servants, officers of Government agencies and other officers as may be prescribed by law.

68. Parliament shall by law give effect to the principles of this Chapter.

18 *Ombudsman Act* 1995 (Vanuatu) sections 17 and 21 respectively.

19 Section 22(2)(c).

20 Section 25(2).

21 An application pursuant to this section was made in connection with the investigation and ensuing report recommending that illegal ex gratia payments made to politicians be repaid to the government. Vanuatu Ombudsman, 1996. Public Report on Ex Gratia Payments. June 4, 1996. Although the Ombudsman is given standing to apply to the court for orders enforcing recommendations, it was not clear who the "responsible person" mentioned in section 30 is and therefore is unclear who, if anyone, an order should be directed to. Further difficulties could arise in relation to such applications where the recommendations are too general to be framed as an enforceable order of the court.

22 Pakistan's Office of the Ombudsman has similar deviations from the generic model. Crossland, K. 1998. Interpretation of the Ombudsmsn role by Vanuatu's first Ombudsman. Presented at Corruption and Accountability in the Pacific. Workshop: State, Society and Governance in Melanesia Project, Australian National University. 6–9 November 1998. http://rspas.anu.edu.au/melanesia/crossland.html (Accessed 6/11/01)

23 Vanuatu Ombudsman. 1999. Annual Report of the Office of the Ombudsman. Table 3.4, page 23.

24 Vanuatu Ombudsman. 1995. Annual Report. p 7, 11.

25 "What occurred in this situation was a first-hand example of maladministration of the very type my Office is repeatedly called upon to investigate by complainants" Vanuatu Ombudsman. 1995. Annual Report. p 12.

26 *Constitution of the Republic of Vanuatu*, Article 56.

27 Direct contributions in the form of money, manpower or other resources have been made to the Ombudsman by the governments of Australia, Canada, Denmark, France, New Zealand and Papua New Guinea. In addition, the Association des Ombudmans et Mediateurs de la Francophonie, the Commonwealth Secretariat, the European Union, the United Nations Development Program and the Economic and Social Commission for Asia and the Pacific (ESCAP) have also made contributions to the Ombudsman. See Vanuatu Ombudsman. 1996, 1998 and 1999. Annual Reports.

28 Vanuatu Ombudsman. 1996. Annual Report. p 5.

29 As quoted in Crossland, K. 1998. Above, note 22.

30 As cited by Crossland, K. 1998. Above, note 22.

31 See for instance, Vanuatu Ombudsman. 1997. Public Report on the Improper interference with a Land Lease by the Former Minister of Foreign Affairs, Mr. Amos Bangabiti. July, 17, 1997, at p 2. In this report, the Ombudsman refers to a major recurring problem, that of expatriates wrongfully becoming the victims of envy and persecution by indigenous ni-Vanuatu.

32 Anti Corruption Ombudsman under attack from Parliament. *Pacific Islands Monthly* Jan 1998 Vol 68 (1) p 14–15.

33 There is really nothing in custom that prevents criticism or sanctioning of inappropriate behavior by leaders. Rather, it is the manufacturing of a *second class* of custom that is used to consolidate the power of the ruling elite. Huffer, E. and Molisa, G. 1999. Above, n 8 at p 7.

34 Dozens of examples abound. For example: "It has been depressing for the Ombudsman's Office to see repeated again and again the selfish and greedy actions of those who put personal gain before public service with such regularity that it is with heavy hearts that the growing pile of complaints is surveyed. Cause for sadness, too, in that those charged with offences have chosen not to follow the path of confession and potential forgiveness but of denial or silence." Preamble to Vanuatu Ombudsman. 1998. Final Report on the Purchase, Repair, Management and Operation of the Prince II. December 2, 1998. Another example is taken from the preamble from Vanuatu Ombudsman. 1998. Public Report on the Multiple Breaches of the Leadership Code by Barak Sope. Once more the Ombudsman Office finds itself reporting yet another clear example of contempt for legal and honest procedures by a leader so desperate to hold on to power that he was prepared to intervene and interfere in the vital matter provision of food.

35 Three random selections serve as an illustration: How long will ye judge unjustly and accept the persons of the wicked? Defend the poor and fatherless do justice to the afflicted and needy: rid them out of the hand of the wicked", Psalm 82 v 2; Vanuatu Ombudsman. 1997. Public Report on the Sale of the M.V. Savin Fana. June 26, 1997; "Do ye thank that the Scripture saith in vain "The spirit that dwelleth in us lusteth to envy" James 4 v 5; Vanuatu Ombudsman. 1997. Public report on the Improper Interference with a Land Lease by the Former Minister of Foreign Affairs Mr. Amos Bangabiti; [t]he getting of treasures by a lying tongue is a vanity tossed to and from then that seek death." Proverbs 21 v 6; Vanuatu Ombudsman. 1997. Public Report on Illegal Passport Scheme and Resort Las Vegas. December 3, 1997.

36 Van den Bergh, N. I. C. 1998. An Analysis of Some Preambles to the Reports From the

Ombudsman's Office, Vanuatu. University of the South Pacific School of Law staff seminar. October 21, 1998. In this paper, it is argued that the quotes are taken out of context and that they imply to the reader that the leaders of Vanuatu act against Gods will and laws, that they are sinful, debased and corrupt. Professor Van den Bergh points out that nowhere in the quotes which form part of the preambles does one find "words of encouragement, of reconciliation, of forgiveness, concepts which form the heart of Chrisianity."

37 *Ombudsman v Fr. Gerard Leymang*, Unreported, Supreme Court of the Republic of Vanuatu, Civil Case No. 3 of 1997 25 August 1997. http://www.vanuatu.usp.ac.fj/paclawmat/Vanuatu_cases/Volume_O-Q/Ombudsman_v_Leymang.html (Accessed 7/11/01)

38 *Ombudsman V Willie Jimmy, Maxime Carlot Korman et al*, Unreported, Supreme Court of the Republic of Vanuatu, Constitutional Case no. 104 of 1997 4 May 2001. http://www.vanuatu.usp.ac.fj/paclawmat/Vanuatu_cases/Volume_OQ/Ombudsman_v_Batick.html (accessed 7/11/01)

39 *Ombudsman v The Attorney General & anor*, Unreported, Supreme Court of the Republic of Vanuatu, Constitutional Case No 114 of 1997, 30 Oct 1997.

40 Although those implicated have an opportunity to respond to a preliminary report before a public report is released and, although their response is included in the public report, the first Ombudsman typically responded to the responses, often in a dismissive or incredulous manner and thereby maintained a position of having the last word.

41 It was strongly recommended by the advisor from Ombudsman Commission of Papua New Guinea that the hiring of Ombudsman's employees be separate from the Public Service in order to avoid this very possibility. Vanuatu Ombudsman. 1995. Annual Report. p 12.

42 Section 6 (1).

43 For example, in the Vanuatu Ombudsman. 2002. Public Report on the Failure of Some Leaders to File Annual Returns to the Clerk of Parliament, the facts revealed that 24 leaders had failed to file an annual return. Sections 19 and 31 of the *Leadership Code Act* No. 2 of 1998 make failure to file a return by March 1 each year. Despite these clear and undisputed facts, the factual finding of the Ombudsman was that the Leadership Code "may have" been breached.

44 Section 21.

45 In Fiji, in the early 1980's at a time when the Fiji Ombudsman had been in operation for roughly the same length of time as the Vanuatu Ombudsman now has, there was an informal initiative to engage in a process which was described as mediation. See Scott, I. 1982. The Ombudsman in Fiji, Patterns of Mediation and Institutionalization. *The Ombudsman Journal* No.2: p. 1.

46 Section 13.

47 The Ombudman has indicated to the writer on several occasions that the use of mediation will expand in the work of the Ombudsman.

48 Crossland, K. 1998. Above note 22, at pp 9 to 11.

49 Vanuatu Ombudsman. 1999. <u>Report on Prison Conditions and Mismanagment of Prison Budget</u>. September 16, 1999 and Vanuatu Ombudsman. 2000. <u>Public Report on the Unlawful Solitary Confinement of Three Prisoners by Prison Authorities</u>. March 13, 2000.

50 Vanuatu Ombudsman. 1999. <u>Public Report on the Vanuatu Fire Service Failure to put out the fire on 6 1998 at Paris Shopping, Snoopy's, Au Peche Mignon and Frank King Tours</u>. May 12, 1999.

51 Vanuatu Ombudsman. 1999. <u>Public Report on the Illegal and Unconstitutional Discrimination in the Citizenshop Act</u>. May 18, 1999.

52 Vanuatu Ombudsman. 1999. <u>Public Report on Conversion Into Anglophone School of French Speaking Public Primary School at Mangliiu (North West Efate)</u>. September 9, 1999.

53 Vanuatu Ombudsman. 1999. <u>Public Report on the Discriminatory Crieteria of the Vanuatu National Examinations Board for Admission to Year 7</u>. August 13, 1999.

54 Vanuatu Ombudsman. 1998. <u>Public Report on Illegal Creation of CVDC SA and the People of Vanuatu Trust and breach of the Leadership Code by Hon. Vincent Boulekone, Minister of Finance</u>. March 13, 1998.

55 Huffer, C. and Molisa, M. 1998. Above, note 8, at p 7.

56 Vanuatu Ombudsman. 1996. <u>Public Report on the Appointment of the Deputy General Manager of the Vanuatu National Provident Fund</u>. November 15, 1996.

57 Vanuatu Ombudsman. 1999. <u>Public Report on the Improper Appointment of Senior Public Works Department Staff</u>. March 11, 1999.

58 Vanuatu Ombudsman. 1999. <u>Public Report on the Mismanagement of the Vanuatu Livestock Development Ltd. By the Former Manager Selwyn Leodoro in 1992–1993 and Illegal Conduct of the Former Chairman of the Board Tom Kalorib</u>. July 23, 1999.

59 Vanuatu Ombudsman. 1996. <u>Public Report on the Numbawan Bottle Shop Case</u>. August 20, 1996.

60 Vanuatu Ombudsman. 1999. <u>Public Report on the Granting of Leases by the Former Minister of Lands Mr. Paul Barthelemy Telukluk to Himself, Family Members and Wantoks</u>. April 22, 1999.

61 Vanuatu Ombudsman. 1999. <u>Public Report on the Mismanagement of the Tender Sale of Ten Deportees' Properties by the Former Minister of Lands Mr. Paul Telukluk</u>. May 28, 1999.

62 Vanuatu Ombudsman. 1996. <u>Public Report on the Sale of M. V. Yasur</u>. September 23, 1996.

63 Vanuatu Ombudsman. 1997. <u>Public Report on the National Provident Fund Housing Loan Scheme</u>. December 17, 1997.

64 Vanuatu Ombudsman. <u>Public Report on the Provision of Bank Guarantees Given in the Sum of US$100,000,000, in Breach of the Leadership Code and Section 14 (f) the Ombudsman Act and Related Matters Thereto</u>. July 3, 1996.

65 Vanuatu Ombudsman. 1998. <u>Public Report on Illegal Creation of CVDC SA and the People of Vanuatu Trust</u>. March 28, 1998.

66 Vanuatu Ombudsman. 1996. <u>Public Report on the Conduct of Barak Sope and the VNPF Board in a Proposed Investment in the Internet Bank "Cybank" Venture</u>. October 16, 1996.

67 Information provided by former Ombudsman, Marie Noelle Ferrieux-Patterson, July 2001.

68 As quoted by Crossland K. 1998. above, n 22.

Review questions

1. Do you think that corrupt activities can be justified in some situations?
2. Do you think that what is corrupt in one country is not necessarily corrupt in another due to cultural differences?
3. In what ways do you see constitutional legitimacy compromised or challenged in your country? What do you think can or should be done to improve constitutional legitimacy?
4. What do you think is the relationship between constitutional legitimacy and corruption?
5. Do you think that the generic model of the Ombudsman, as developed in European and other western countries, is effective in a developing country like Vanuatu?
6. What powers or duties do you think an Ombudsman would need in order to be effective in reducing corruption within PICs?
7. Do you think that combating corruption is a good use of limited resources in PICs?

Further readings

Botchwey, K. (ed) 2001. *Fighting Corruption, Promoting Good Governance: Commonwealth expert group on good governance and the elimination of corruption.* London: Commonwealth Publications.

Habermas, J. 1996. *Between Facts and Norms: Contributions to a Discourse Theory of Law and Democracy.* Cambridge: Polity Press.

Hassall, G. & Saunders, C. 2002. *Asia Pacific Constitutional Systems.* Melbourne: Cambridge University Press.

Larmour, P. & Wolanin, N. (eds) 2001. *Corruption and Anti-Corruption.* Canberra: Asia Pacific Press.

Regan, A. Jessep, O. & Kwa, E. (eds) 2001. *Twenty Years of the Papua New Guinea Constitution.* Sydney, Law Book Company.

Reif, L. Marshall, M. & Ferris C. (eds) 1993. *The Ombudsman: Diversity and Development.* Edmonton, Canada: International Ombudsman Institute.

SECTION 3
CUSTOMARY LAW

5. CUSTOM THEN AND NOW:
THE CHANGING MELANESIAN FAMILY
Jean G. Zorn

6. ISSUES IN CONTEMPORARY CUSTOMARY LAW:
WOMEN AND THE LAW
Jean G. Zorn

7. RITES, WHITES & MIGHT: A CRITIQUE OF
THE EFFECT OF THE REVIVAL OF CUTOMARY LAW
ON THE AUTONOMY OF INDIGENOUS WOMEN
Susan Bothmann

8. THE INCORPORATION OF CUSTOMARY LAW
AND PRINCIPLE INTO SENTENCING DECISIONS IN
THE SOUTH PACIFIC REGION
Tess Newton Cain

It would be possible to produce a whole collection of pieces that were concerned with each of the themes that are considered in this volume. Such is certainly the case in respect of this section. The place of custom in modern and modernising Pacific island societies is a question of ongoing debate in all sectors and at all levels. These debates have political, economic, legal and social aspects to them. These debates can be wide-ranging or narrow in focus. They are conducted in a wide variety of locations and in numerous languages. Some aspects of those debates are identified and explored here. Our authors are sufficiently well versed in the complexities of Pacific legal discourse to avoid oversimplifications of the 'all custom good, all law bad' variety. They are not so presumptuous as to offer solutions to problems or answers to questions that have been vexatious and will continue to be so for many years to come. Rather, they offer their observations and thoughts as part of an ongoing and dynamic dialogue whose aim is to identify the most useful questions, to accurately define the problems before moving on to the next step, the formulation of responses.

The first two chapters are written by Professor Jean Zorn. Her exposition of customary law is one that exemplifies the organic and changing nature of custom, of law and the inter-relationship between the two. The third chapter, by Susan Bothmann, further broadens the theoretical discussions by considering the implications of (re)constituting custom for women. Her chapter draws on concepts established by feminist theorists and those who have written in the field of aboriginal studies in Australia. Dr Tess Newton Cain provides a narrower focus in her chapter. She examines the nature of the inter-relationship between law and custom within a very specific field, that of sentencing decisions in the criminal courts of the region.

One of the most controversial aspects of customary law is its interrelationship with human rights. Several of the issues that the authors raise in this section will be examined further in the following section, which is concerned with human rights.

5. CUSTOM THEN AND NOW: THE CHANGING MELANESIAN FAMILY*

By: Jean G. Zorn

KEY TERMS AND PHRASES

Agnates

Relatives by marriage (cognates are relatives by birth). So, an agnatic relationship is a relationship with an in-law or other relative by marriage.

Kula

This is a Papuan word for the circle trade in precious shells that Hula, Trobriand, Motu and other Papuan people engaged in.

---

*Professor Zorn would like to thank the people without whose help and support, insight and understanding this chapter could never have been accomplished. That list includes Tess Newton Cain, Jennifer Corrin Care, Miranda Dickenson, Kristin Booth Glen, Christine Stewart, Pamela Goldberg, Ellen Mosen James, Simon Fuo'o, the students in Professor Zorn's family law course at the University of the South Pacific, and, especially, Steve, Heather and Christopher.

INTRODUCTION

All times are changing times, but ours is one of massive, rapid moral and mental transformation. Archetypes turn into millstones, large simplicities get complicated, chaos becomes elegant, and what everybody knows is true turns out to be what some people used to think.[1]

One of the difficulties faced by state courts when they try to recognise and apply custom in their decisions is the ever-changing nature of custom.[2] Customs change faster than the law changes, and the rate at which customs are changing probably has accelerated, even since the colonial period, due to the technological, economic and political changes that the Pacific island nations are undergoing.

This chapter looks at a number of questions that are important for courts, clients and counsel. What is custom?[3] What has caused custom to change, and what kinds of changes have occurred since the pre-colonial era? If custom is constantly changing, how do courts assure themselves that what they are applying is custom? In looking at that last question, the chapter will analyse some recent cases that deal with changing customs.[4] The three cases illustrate different reactions to changes in custom. In *Thesia Maip's* case, a Papua New Guinea court refuses to recognise and apply the new practice, determining that it has not yet become widely used enough to qualify as a custom. In *To'ofilu v Oimae*, a Solomon Islands court accepts changed practices, but treats them as if they were rules of the common law rather than customary rules. Finally, in *Molu v Molu*, the Vanuatu court applies new and old customs in a very customary style. We must ask ourselves what prompted these very distinct responses and which is best?

CUSTOM THEN

In pre-colonial times, each of the indigenous societies of the Pacific had its own customs.[5] While there were similarities in the customs of all societies of the Pacific islands, based primarily on broad similarities in their economics and technology,[6] there were also differences from one society to another — some the result of differences in the means of production (fishing versus gardening, for example), some more likely the result of history (chiefly societies versus 'big man' cultures, perhaps). It was through these distinctive customs that each such society defined itself as unique. With only a few exceptions, each of the small village societies of the pre-colonial Pacific was an independent, mono-cultural entity.

Customs are the norms (the rules) of the group. As such, they perform a function within the group similar to the function that law performs within a nation. Without complicated state mechanisms — without legislatures or courts or police forces — the pre-colonial societies of the Pacific nevertheless had functioning legal systems. They had complex sets of (unwritten) rules governing all aspects of social, political and economic behaviour.[7] They had effective methods for ensuring that the rules would be followed, and they also had workable procedures for settling disputes. The same customary legal systems continue to function today in most Pacific villages.[8]

CUSTOMS CHANGING

Colonialism and its aftermath produced many changes in the cultures of the Pacific. Of greatest importance to our study, perhaps, was the introduction into the Pacific of the colonisers' laws and legal systems, which were superimposed upon existing customs and customary dispute settlement methods.

At independence the new Pacific nations might have done away with the legal systems that the colonisers had imported and returned to an indigenous legal system made up entirely of custom. They did not. Instead they kept the structure of the imposed legal system: its courts and legislature. They also kept much of the content of the imposed legal system: the constitutions, statutes and common law imported from or based upon foreign models. But they tried to find a meaningful place for custom within this formal framework.

The constitutions or statutes of most Pacific nations provided that, in addition to statutes and common law, the formal courts[9] should recognise and apply the customs of the indigenous peoples of the nation.[10] But the courts have been reluctant to use custom. One reason may be that the colonisers' disdain for custom has carried over to inform the beliefs and values of judges in the post-colonial period. Another may be that judges who are trained in the common law find it difficult to work with norms that are uncodified and unwritten. Expatriate judges, in particular, unfamiliar with indigenous cultures, may worry that they could be led to choose norms that do not really exist or to apply them incorrectly.[11]

One of the major reasons for the state courts' hesitation to recognise and apply custom may be the tendency of custom to change without warning. The customs of a group are no more than the accumulated beliefs, values and habits of the members of the group. Over time beliefs, values and habitual ways of acting change and, because custom is not written down, the changes go unrecorded. As Ursula LeGuin said, gradually, over time, hardly without our noticing, "what everybody knows is true turns out to be what some people used to think."[12]

During the colonial period courts, for the most part, avoided the problems caused by changes to custom by recognising and applying only those customs that had "existed from time immemorial".[13] At independence, however, the definition of custom was redrawn in a number of jurisdictions to require of courts that they apply such customs as exist at the time of the court action.[14] This has raised problems for courts in ascertaining just what the applicable custom is and in figuring out what to do, once a court has adopted a custom, if that custom later changes.

What makes customs change?

Every society is changing all the time. The societies of the Pacific were always changing, even before the colonial intervention.[15] Drought, excess rain, tribal wars or the lure of the unknown caused whole societies to move to new villages, even to new islands far across the sea. Pigs and sweet potato changed people's diets, their gardening and hunting patterns, and even their feasts and ceremonial exchanges.

Styles of dress and ornament, tattooing and body painting changed over time. Different verses and steps to ritual dances went in and out of fashion, or altered over time as generations forgot old verses or invented new ones. Without written records many changes went unrecorded and unremembered.

Although the societies of the Pacific have always been changing, colonialism brought change of a kind probably never before experienced in the Pacific. Some of the changes were intentional on the part of the colonisers. Others were the unplanned result of changes to the political system, to technology, and to the economy. Whichever the cause, the rate of change was more rapid than ever before, and the political, economic, technological, religious and social leaps probably greater than anyone in the Pacific had ever experienced.[16]

The ways in which customs have changed

The economic, social and political changes that began in the colonial era, and that have continued to occur, changed custom in many important respects. Customary norms have changed to embrace these economic, social and political changes. For example, the settlements to many disputes now include the payment of money, something that did not exist in pre-colonial times. Customary processes have also changed, adopting some of the formalities that characterise the formal courts of the introduced legal system.

The most far-reaching change is probably the one most overlooked. The villages of the Pacific went from being separate, sovereign entities to being lesser parts of larger political entities. Similarly, in the colonial period, custom ceased to be the sole legal system operating in Pacific villages. At best, in territories where the colonial power recognised the legitimacy of custom, it became the lesser of two different legal systems. At worst, even if villagers still utilised custom, in many Pacific colonies, it had no official sanction as a legal system.[17]

The existence of a competing, and more powerful, legal system had a number of effects on custom. Villagers dissatisfied with the results of a customary meeting now knew they could go to one of the formal courts where a different outcome might be obtainable. Once villagers knew that there were courts where one party could win everything, instead of having to agree to a compromise, some were even tempted to try the formal courts without first exhausting customary remedies. Moreover, villagers who disagreed with customary rules of behaviour now knew they could ignore those norms if the introduced legal system had different rules.

CUSTOM NOW

Recent cases illustrate both the nature of the changes that have occurred in the cultures of indigenous peoples and the difficulties that these changes pose for the courts. The cases also show that judges in the Pacific are actively engaging with the problems raised by changing customs, attempting to sort out current custom from bygone tradition, to fashion legal rules that will assist the courts in recognising and applying custom and to treat custom as a viable part of the state legal system. Precisely how they are doing it is the topic of this chapter.

The chapter will focus on cases having to do with marriage and divorce. I have chosen cases from this area of law not because marital customs are any more changed than other customs or because courts handle changing custom in this area either particularly well or particularly badly, but only because the examination of three cases that happen all to be within the same area of the law affords a clearer picture of the ways in which courts react to changes in custom. For the same reason the three cases chosen were all from Melanesia. The continuity of culture from one of these cases to the other makes the nature of cultural change, and the ways in which courts react to it, stand out all the more clearly.

This part of the chapter will begin with a brief overview of marriage law for those who wish to be reminded of the key doctrinal principles. At the same time, the chapter will discuss the kinds of changes that have occurred in customs relating to marriage, divorce and the custody of children. The chapter will then analyse three cases about customary marriage, divorce and custody practices.

MARRIAGE THEN AND NOW

One of the reasons that is often given for the continuing recognition of customary marriages is that people most resist changing those customs — such as marriage and divorce — that are the most personal.[18] Moreover, almost every one gets married so, if marriages performed according to custom were unlawful, a great many people would be in violation of the law. Rather than have that happen the drafters of the marriage and divorce statutes in many Pacific jurisdictions thought it would be better to recognise the validity of customary marriage.[19]

Contrary to prediction, practices related to marriage and divorce have changed considerably over the years, making it more and more difficult for the courts to decide what custom is or was. The changes have been both large and small. One of the larger is the intrusion of Christianity into the marriage ceremony. These days, many couples who believe that they are entering into a customary marriage have a church ceremony, in addition to all the customary feasts, exchanges and rituals. However, if the member of the clergy who performed the church ceremony saw to it that the couple complied with the statutory formalities, and he or she probably did, then they are now married under the statute, regardless of whether they may also be married under custom.[20]

What makes a customary marriage

The first of the cases in this chapter is concerned with whether there can be a customary marriage between people from different parts of the country, places with different customs.[21] One of the many changes that have occurred in the relations between men and women in the Pacific is the growth of relationships between people from different cultures. Some of these relations are between Pacific islanders and people from other countries, both within and outside the Pacific islands. In more diverse countries, such as Papua New Guinea, relationships develop between people from different parts of the country with different matrimonial customs. If the parties live together without going through the statutory form of marriage ceremony, the courts may question whether they are married at all, even under custom. *Application of Thesia Maip* is such a case.[22]

Thesia Maip came from a village in the Western Highlands of Papua New Guinea, Jude Sioni came from Bougainville, another Papua New Guinea province but far from the Highlands, and different in many ways. This is how the judge of the National Court describes the relationship between Thesia and Jude:[23]

> ... they met at Mendi [which is in the Southern Highlands] and started living together. He suggested that if she behaved well they would get married in a church. However there was no formal marriage in a church or under the *Marriage Act* nor was there any public ceremony involving brideprice in the village. They lived together at Mendi and it appears that at no time did Jude Sioni ever visit Thesia's village namely Balk village in the Western Highlands. I am sure that he would have spent some money on her and he states in his evidence he did give her some money at different times. However, this would be expected when two people are living together. And also perhaps relatives did visit and cost him some money. After living together at Mendi for two years, he was apparently arrested and taken to Bougainville for some problems and was locked up for some months. He escaped some time in 1990 and came to the Western Highlands to Balk village to look for Thesia. It would appear that this was his first visit to the village. At that time she had taken up with another man so he then took her to the village court.[24]

Jude's complaint to the Village Court was that Thesia "was his wife and had left him and gone off with another man." Hearing this plea, the Balk Village Court ordered Thesia to pay K700 compensation "which was later reduced to K300 by the Local Court Magistrate" who reviewed the case.[25] Since Thesia was unable to pay that amount, she was imprisoned for 30 weeks. Mr Justice Woods of the National Court on a tour of Highlands prisons discovered Thesia in prison and ordered her release.[26]

But J. Woods could not have ordered Thesia released from prison unless the law gave him a reason to do so. He found that reason in the rules about marriage and adultery.[27] According to the common law that Papua New Guinea imported from England, 'adultery' consists of sexual relations between two persons only if one or both of them is married to someone else.[28] Sexual relations between unmarried persons do not constitute adultery.[29]

The Village Court found that Thesia and Jude were married under customary law, which made her an adulteress. The National Court held that they weren't. The differences between the two courts illustrate two opposite responses towards defining, finding and applying custom when social mores and behaviour are changing. The Village Court took the position that custom changes with the times, and that courts should change along with it:

> The Chairman of the village court has confirmed that according to the traditional custom if two people marry and they both are from the Highlands then they pay brideprice in the village and that is witnessed by the village people. He then stated that in modern times due to the interaction that takes place between the different provinces people from coastal [province]s are marrying people from the Highlands and are not following the traditional procedures. However, even though they are not following the traditional procedures people today are recognizing it as a marriage.

The Village Court was willing to adopt and apply new customs provided that they met two criteria. First, the Village Court required that the new activity be fairly widespread. Thesia and Jude were not the only couple from different provinces to have formed a relationship: "people from coastals" generally, the Village Court chairman said, "are marrying people from the Highlands". Secondly, the Village Court required that there be general acceptance of the new activity among other members of the community: "people" generally, the chairman added, "are recognising it as a marriage."

In understanding that customs change as circumstances change the Village Court chairman was accurate, both as a social scientist[30] and in his application of Papua New Guinea law.[31] But was he correct in stating that marriage practices had changed to the point where the Village Courts ought to recognise liaisons like that of Jude and Thesia's as a new kind of customary marriage? In social terms he probably was. Anthropologists would say that a new way of thinking and behaving becomes a custom when it is fairly regularly practised by more than just a few people in a community and when a large segment of the community, including those who might not themselves engage in the activity, view it as normative.[32]

The National Court judge, however, held that the chairman was incorrect in stating that relationships such as the one between Jude and Thesia met the *legal* definition of custom:

> Whilst one must accept that custom must develop in Papua New Guinea to meet the many changes within the country one must be very careful in accepting that such developments in custom are clearly recognised by everyone and that they do not leave the way open for far reaching consequences.

The judge gave several reasons for deciding that a relationship such as that between Thesia and Jude could not be a customary marriage. These reasons may become guidelines for Village and Local Court magistrates, lawyers, and legal scholars in their attempts to determine which new activities are customs that the state courts will adopt and which are not. It is therefore important that we explore the judge's reasoning.

First, he said that in order for a belief or activity to become a custom, it must be "clearly recognised by everyone". Secondly, he said that the courts must consider what "far-reaching consequences" their adoption of a new custom might have.[33]

What did the judge mean when he said that the custom must be "clearly recognised by everyone"?[34] There are, he said, "three clearly recognisable ways of getting married" in Papua New Guinea:

> Firstly by the traditional custom as has always been. Secondly through the church under the Marriage Act and thirdly by a civil marriage registrar under the Marriage Act.

Since there are already three ways to get married, a fourth is hardly needed. If there is to be a fourth way, it must be as widely recognised as the three that already exist.

That is a very high standard to meet. But the judge had a reason for setting the bar so high. He did not want the courts adopting customs that "might have far-reaching consequences" without first thinking through those consequences. Marriage, he pointed out, creates many rights and obligations. The courts ought not to uphold the rights — or, in this case, enforce the obligations — unless they are quite sure that the parties intended to take on those rights and obligations. The only way to be sure of that is to require that people go through a well-recognised form of marriage:

> In view of the fact that imprisonment can result from the breakdown of marriages at the village court, great care must be taken to ensure that such marriages are firstly properly recognised and comply with either custom or the formal law... Because of the legal implications and responsibilities that arise in a marriage and if imprisonment can be used as a sanction if there is a breakdown, the law cannot recognise anything but a properly arranged or certified marriage whether properly done according to the custom of the place or under the formal law, the Marriage Act.

The judge believed that the law should not easily assume a marriage has occurred because marriage has important consequences for a couple, for their families, for society as a whole. He pointed out that the laws about adultery are not the only ones that operate only if a couple is married. Other important rights that arise only within the context of marriage include the right to receive maintenance, the right to inherit a share of a spouse's property and the right to petition for custody of one's children.[35]

Applying these principles and policies to the relationship between Thesia and Jude, the judge held that they were not married. Their relationship did not meet Judge Woods' test of a custom that the courts should apply; it is not "clearly recognisable by everyone" as a marriage. Indeed, the judge says, relationships like that of Thesia and Jude are "clearly recognisable" by most people as casual liaisons:

> In the modern world two people living away from their homes living together is quite a common occurrence. Often it is just for the convenience of the time. However, sometimes it is a serious trial to see if the two people are seriously interested in getting married.

Moreover, he noted, Thesia and Jude themselves had not thought they were married. Jude had said "when they were living together in Mendi that if she behaved herself he was considering getting married in a church". Their arrangement seems to have been, like the others the judge has described, "no more than a casual arrangement... which suited them both at the time".[36]

Even if one agrees with the outcome of the case, one can quarrel with the tests that Judge Woods devised for ascertaining whether a new practice has become a custom. The test is very hard to meet. That may be appropriate when marriage is at issue, but the bar may be set too high for most other purposes. Can we think of any custom that is recognised by *everyone*? In every society, there are likely to be a few people at least who are unaware of recent changes.

Moreover, the test is vague and will therefore present definitional problems as later courts try to apply it. Just what, for example, is meant by 'recognised'? Does this mean that everyone must now be willing to *act* in accordance with the custom, that they must *agree* with it, or merely that they know of its existence? If the former, then the courts are even less likely to adopt and apply new customs, because, in most societies, there are people who dissent to even the most widely shared customs. Murder, for example, is fairly widely condemned, but there is no society in which murder never occurs. Are we to conclude that respect for life is not customary? And what, precisely, is meant by the adverb 'clearly'?

However, even if we disagree with Judge Woods about the details of his test for recognising changes to custom, I think most of us would agree with him about two things. First, I think we would agree that, whatever our attitude towards Thesia's behaviour, we do not condone putting women, or anyone for that matter, into prison for acts that are not criminal.[37] Secondly, I think we would agree that the courts need a test that lays out rules to recognise new customs and adopt them as customary law. Without such a test, generally accepted by all the courts, each magistrate or judge will have to make up his or her own tests. There will be no uniformity. More likely, in the absence of helpful standards or guidelines, most courts will refuse to adopt and apply any new customs.

Brideprice

The second case looks at the ways in which the exchange of marital gifts has been altered by the addition of cash as part of the brideprice.[38] The intrusion of money into the process has altered the custom in many ways, giving rise perhaps to those "unforeseen consequences" that Judge Woods worried about. The major difference is summed up in the adoption of that unfortunate English term 'brideprice' to describe a custom that originally involved an exchange of gifts, not a sale and purchase.[39] 'Price' suggests that something — or someone — is being bought and sold, and that is the way it has come to be viewed, both by local people, who now talk of 'buying' a bride,[40] and by feminist anthropologists, who argue that the custom of 'buying' wives demeans and dehumanises the women involved.[41] When the husband's family views the bride as a purchase, not as a person, they expect her to redeem the brideprice by working for the family and by bearing children, who are also seen as property that the husband's clan has purchased. This is probably an oversimplified view. Nor does it exist universally.[42] But it does highlight the kinds of new social relations and problems that develop when brideprice is transformed by the infusion of money into the transaction.

Traditionally, brideprice marked the beginning of a relationship not just of the bride with her new in-laws, but also of the two families. The marriage was a key to the many relations — social, political and economic — that would now exist between the bride's clan or extended family and the groom's clan or extended family. Aspects of the complex inter-family relationships that begin with the exchange of brideprice still exist, but the relationships between agnatic families have undergone many changes.[43] Not all of those changes have occurred because money has become a significant part of bridewealth, but, as the case of *John To'ofilu v Oimae*[44] illustrates, money is a potent symbol of the ways in which traditional exchange relationships have been transformed into market economy transactions.

In the *To'ofilu* case, for example, representatives of two families negotiated a brideprice that included six *tafuliae*,[45] $1,000 (SI) in cash, three pigs and four bags of rice. It turned out, however, that, before the marriage, the bride had been made pregnant by another man. She and her new husband lived together as man and wife for only a month and a half before he sent her away. His father sued her father in the Local Court for return of the brideprice.[46]

The Local Court held for the groom's father (the plaintiff). The bride's father (the defendant) admitted that he had known, even before the brideprice negotiations began, that his daughter was pregnant.[47] The Local Court decided the case according to the customary law of the region, which expects both parties to divulge all the important facts during the negotiation for the brideprice.[48] Moreover, "according to Malaita custom only virgins are paid with high price". Therefore, the Local Court "found Oimae… not honest in telling John To'ofilu the truth… [so] according to Malaita custom [Oimae] must refund full brideprice and expenses".[49]

The Magistrate's Court, to which the case was appealed, disagreed with the Local Court not only about how much brideprice should be returned, but also about what the customary rules were that determine the quantum to be paid back. The Magistrate's Court discussed two rules of customary law that seem not to have been mentioned in the Local Court. First, the Magistrates' Court mentioned that the amount of the brideprice might have been high because of the groom's intense desire for this woman, and not because she was presumed to be a virgin. The magistrate, however, decided that this was not a reason in customary law for determining how much brideprice should be returned.[50] The magistrate was swayed, however, by the defendant's argument that less brideprice is to be returned "where the groom rejects the bride."[51] Taking these customary norms into account, the magistrate decided that the bride's family need return only half the brideprice. This decision respected Malaitan custom in a number of ways. Not only did the magistrate make an effort to discover exactly what customary rules govern brideprice, but he also handled the rules in a customary way. In customary dispute settlement, it is common for two or three or even more rules to be mentioned, all potentially applicable to the same case. Here, for example, the parties brought up at least four rules:

- That both sides must tell the whole truth during brideprice negotiations;
- That a virgin deserves a high brideprice;
- That the returned brideprice will be halved if the husband sends his wife away; and
- That the party who shows 'first sight love' has to pay a higher brideprice.

The magistrate refused to accept the last of those rules, but he recognised the other three. He handled the situation very much like an elder or clan leader would handle a customary dispute settlement mediation.[52] He used the rules as markers, as principles, as reminders to all the parties of what their rights and obligations were, not as the guidelines by which he would decide the case. He looked for a way, within the general bounds set by the rules, to get the parties to stop arguing, to give something to each, perhaps, in the hope that he would thereby restore harmony and good relations. Thus, he said that the bride's family acted wrongly, so that some brideprice should be returned. But he made them return only half of it. A very customary solution. Unfortunately for the magistrate's hopes for settlement, however, times — and customs — have changed. A great deal of money was involved, and a court system that allowed for appeals was in place. The plaintiffs promptly did.

The High Court judge, Palmer J., overruled the magistrate, reinstating the Local Court's decision requiring the bride's family to return the entire brideprice. Palmer J. did apply a rule of customary law — he agreed with the Local Court that the bride's father ought to have disclosed her pregnancy during the brideprice discussions — but he applied that rule in a very common law way. First, he made it clear that there could be only one rule operating in this case. Common law adjudication requires that the court find just one rule for every issue, because the judge is supposed to decide the case by applying that rule to the facts, not by exhorting the parties to remember the rules generally and to re-establish good relations in light of the rules.

The High Court determined that of the various customary norms that the parties had suggested the courts should use only the rule that dishonesty about a "material fact" during brideprice negotiations will require the return of all the brideprice.[53] The court chose this norm over the others for a number of reasons. The other rules had not been discussed in the Local Court, and it is a principle of common law adjudication that any issue not raised at trial may not be raised on appeal. Given the adversarial nature of common law adjudication, this is a useful procedural standard because it ensures that all the evidence needed to prove each issue will have been presented in a timely manner. It is not, however, the procedure that customary forums would naturally adopt. There the goal is not to be sure that the truth of all contentions has been tested but to permit everyone to say all they feel like saying so the parties (and their friends, family and supporters) are free to raise whatever seems important, whenever.[54]

A second (and related) reason for the High Court's refusal of the other customary rules was that counsel had not presented sufficient evidence proving the existence of these rules:

> The... issue [concerning the groom's love at first sight] had never been raised in the Local Court as a matter relevant to the question of calculating the quantum of compensation. It was only raised for the first time it seems in the Magistrates' Court but with no evidentiary backing in custom. The learned Magistrate accordingly had no basis in custom to allow that submission to be taken into account in calculating the quantum of compensation.... The Magistrates' Court... was [also] wrong in [taking into account that the groom had sent his wife away].... It had no evidentiary basis in customary law to find that because there had been a rejection of the would-be wife by the husband, that the quantum of the brideprice to be refunded should be halved.[55]

One might ask why evidence was needed to prove the existence of either of these two rules when evidence seems not to have been required to support the Local Court's adoption of the rule that the parties must disclose all material facts during brideprice negotiations.[56] First, the High Court may have been presuming that evidence about the existence of that rule was presented in the Local Court. Secondly, the High Court suggested that it trusted Local Court magistrates not to need evidence, since they are chosen because of their knowledge of custom. Thirdly, the High Court may have been holding that magistrates do not need to produce evidence in support of every custom they intend to apply, but only when they disagree with the Local Court.

The High Court treated the rejected rules differently. In regards to the rule that only half the brideprice should be returned if the husband has rejected his wife, the Court implied that, had the defendant raised it in the proper court and supported it with evidence, then perhaps the case would have been decided on that ground. The High Court had a very different reaction to the rule that the amount of brideprice would be higher if the prospective groom had fallen in love with the bride at first sight. The Court stated that the rule most definitely did not exist. If neither party presented any evidence about the existence of the rule, how could the High Court know this? And if the High Court did know which customary rules exist and which do not, then why did it require evidence of their existence? Why did it criticise the magistrate for adopting customary rules without evidence when it was willing to reject customary rules without evidence?

The answer may be that Judge Palmer, who is a Solomon Islander himself, may have known from his own experience that there was no 'first sight' rule in customary law. Indeed, Judge Palmer may have known from experience about all the rules, but did not want the case decided on that basis. Looking beyond this case to others that will arise in future, he may have wanted to instruct magistrates and other judges about how to deal with custom. To that end he was at pains to announce, and to illustrate, a general rule of procedure, pointing out, first, that the Local Courts are best able to decide what the rules of customary law are, and, secondly, that a Local Court's holdings about custom may be challenged in the Magistrates' Court only if evidence is presented to confirm that the Local Court erred.[57]

The *To'ofilu* case illustrates some of the ways in which the presence of money has changed custom. The High Court looked upon the pre-marital discussions between To'ofilu and Oimae as if they were common law contract negotiations. I do not think the Court was mistaking the nature of their meetings. I am sure that, today, in many parts of the Pacific, brideprice has become subject to negotiated agreement, similar to the negotiations that take place over any other monetary transaction. Moreover, because the brideprice transaction involves money — a scarce, valued and, today, highly necessary commodity[58] — people are probably more prone to go to court when the transaction falls apart than to look for an unofficial way of settling their dispute.[59] And, once the dispute is in the courts, it is more likely to be decided by adjudication, leading to a 'winner-take-all' outcome, than by a negotiation or mediation that encourages compromise and consensus. Of course, that might be one of the reasons people go to court. Because money is involved, a winner-take-all solution may be precisely what they want. They don't want a compromise, such as the one proposed in the Magistrates' Court, that gives them only half.[60]

Brideprice has evolved from a mutual exchange of gifts and promises into a one-way transaction centering on the payment of cash. Brideprice has become a contract between two parties, with terms negotiated essentially at arms' length, instead of the start of a lifelong relationship which begins in mutual feasting and celebration. The focus on money has transformed the role of women, significantly lowering their status. Instead of being the key to the relationship between two families, women now are viewed as servants whose work and childbearing capacities have been purchased. Finally, the large amount of money involved in the brideprice transaction has led to disagreements that have sometimes escalated into violence. In his thoughtful decision, Palmer J. demonstrated his awareness of these changes and responded to them by making the High Court a forum in which disputes over brideprice could be safely and surely litigated.

The custody of children

In our third case the custody of children of divorced parents is at issue and we will see in it the ways in which norms from the imported common law system now mingle with customary norms.[61] If a marriage ends in separation or divorce someone must decide who will have custody of the children of the marriage. When the parents (or other family members) cannot agree, the disputants may turn to the courts to resolve the matter for them. For a long time the courts of the Pacific have been concerned about what to do when there is a conflict between the rules of customary law in regard to custody and the rules of the introduced statutory or common law.[62]

The general principle found in treaties, statutes and the common law is that custody should be decided according to the 'best interests of the child'.[63] What this has meant in practice in the common law courts, at least in the last seventy years, is the assumption that small children belong with their mothers.[64] Different cultures make different assessments about what is in a child's interest. Until sometime in the 1920s, the common law rule in England was that the best interest of the child would be served by giving custody to their father because he was the breadwinner, the property owner, and the person whose name they bore.[65] Only in more recent years, under the influence of twentieth century inventions like family therapy, has the common law decided that young children need a mother's care and that it is in their best interests, therefore, to be with her.[66]

Custom usually provides that children in matrilineal societies live with their mother's people and children in patrilineal societies live with their father's.[67] While that may conflict with the common law notion that small children should always be with their mothers it does not, necessarily, conflict with the 'best interest' standard. The customary law of most Pacific societies presumed that children did not live in tiny nuclear households cared for only by their mother or father, but in villages, surrounded and cared for by grandparents, aunts, uncles, cousins, older siblings — by everyone in the extended family. Thus, customary law did not make a choice between father and mother at all, but between the father's clan and the mother's clan. Customary law held that it was in the best interest of children to remain with their own clan. They were, in a phrase commonly used in societies in which kinship ties are important, 'born for that clan'.[68] Their land, all their inheritance rights, their adult place in the world, sprang from that clan. The members of that clan would love them best and care for them most responsibly.

The contemporary Pacific has changed in many respects that have a bearing on the interests of children. For example, though many children still live with the extended family in relatively traditional village settings, many others have migrated with their parents to urban areas, where they live in nuclear family units, or, at most, in households in which, in addition to their mother, father, and siblings, there are, at most, one or two other adult, or near-adult, relatives. One might ask how the courts should deal with custody issues in these circumstances. Should customary law be applied to everyone, even when it might not be in the best interest of an urban child? Should the common law be applied to everyone, ignoring the interests of village children in patrilineal societies? Should the choice of law depend upon the type of family unit — that is, urban or rural, nuclear or extended — or ought courts attempt to ascertain what the parties, including the children, might want?

Acting Chief Justice (as he then was) Vincent Lunabek of the Vanuatu Supreme Court was confronted with such a case recently, and resolved it by fashioning an order that combined the common law and customary law in ways designed to further the interests of the children involved. In *Molu v Molu No.2*,[69] the Acting Chief Justice applied the 'best interest of the child' standard, but did so in ways derived from the wisdom of customary law.

Patricia Molu was from Pentecost, her husband Cidie Molu from Santo. They married in 1992 in Port Vila,[70] were separated in 1996, and divorced in Port Vila in 1998.[71] They had three children — Yannick, who was born in 1988, ten years old at the time of the divorce; Annie-Rose, born in 1992, six years old at the time of the divorce; and Ian, born in 1994, four at the time of the divorce. Cidie and Patricia did not have a happy marriage. He had spent most of it getting drunk and beating her, allegations that he denied during the divorce hearing when he wasn't blaming it all on Patricia. The Court found his testimony utterly lacking in credibility.[72]

Of the three children only Annie-Rose, the middle child and only girl, was living with her mother at the time of the divorce. Yannick, the eldest child, had been sent to Pentecost to live with Patricia's family when he was four years old, partly because his parents both thought "the general environment... would be better on the island" than in Port Vila.[73] When Patricia and Cidie separated, Cidie's brothers came to Port Vila and, against Patricia's wishes, took Ian, who was then two years old, back to Santo with them. At the time of the custody hearing he was still living with Cidie's family in Santo. Patricia had not seen him in two years.

The divorce was acrimonious and the custody dispute no less so. Each parent sued for sole custody of all three children. The Acting Chief Justice stated that, in making his custody decision, he was bound by the statutory standard.[74] Therefore, the best interests of the children had to be his primary consideration.[75] That requirement, he noted, is contained in the Convention on the Rights of the Child, which was ratified by the Vanuatu Parliament, making it a statute binding upon the courts:

> In all actions concerning children, whether undertaken by public or private social welfare institutions, courts of law, administrative authorities or legislative bodies, *the best interests of the child shall be a primary consideration*.[76]

Using that guideline, the Court decided that Annie-Rose should be in her mother's custody, because, "It is a matter of common sense and human experience that she will be better with her mother than her father.... I am of the view that it will be in her best interest that her custody be awarded to her mother and she will be under the care and control of the Petitioner/mother".[77] The Court's determination about the custody of Annie-Rose was in line with the common law and statutory rules regarding custody. Like countless common law judges before him, the Acting Chief Justice decided that a child of tender years belongs with her mother.[78]

However, the Court did not follow the 'tender years' doctrine in determining the custody of the two Molu boys, even though Yannick, at ten, was probably still a child of tender years, and Ian, only four, was well within the 'tender years' range. The Court applied the statutory 'best interest' standard to them, but did so in a way that departed from common law practice. His holdings in regards to the two boys were infused with the sensibility of customary law. The Court decided that, at least for the time being, both boys should stay where they were—Yannick with his mother's family on the island of Pentecost, and Ian with his father's family in Santo.

The Court's reasoning in regard to Ian was a mixture of common sense, common law precedent and, most importantly, customary law. Using common sense, the Court pointed out that the boy has been with his father's family for quite a while and there had been no reports that he was unhappy or that the family was not caring for him properly.[79] Using common law precedent, the Court quoted a 75-year-old English case, whose holding seemed to be that, given enough time, the child would forget his mother.[80] The customary aspects of the Court's reasoning were not stated so obviously, but were nonetheless present. The father's "intention appeared to be that Ian will be raised by his family rather than the child's mother or father" the Court said, adding, "such an arrangement is not uncommon in Vanuatu".[81] Santo is a patrilineal community. The boys, the Court agreed, belong to their father's clan. Elsewhere, the Court phrased it as "the children are for them".[82] Moreover, the Court seemed, like Cidie's eldest brother, to give 'brideprice' its contemporary connotation. By 'paying' brideprice (earned by their hard work) to Patricia and her family, Cidie's clan has 'paid' for her children. The Court decided that it was in the best interests of this little boy that he be raised in the clan of his fathers. In so doing, the Court brought the common law and customary law together.

The decision partook of the customary legal process in another way as well. To the extent possible, the Court gave something to every party, compromised, looked for a resolution that would restore peace and harmony, even if custom and the common law had both to be bent a little in order to do so. It is a patrilineal world, but, nevertheless, Yannick will stay with his mother's family, at least through primary school. Ian, though of tender years, will stay with his father's family. Annie-Rose will stay with her mother. Even Cidie gets something. Though he does not have physical custody of Ian, the Court gives him legal custody. And everyone, in good customary consensus-building style, is supposed to put their anger behind them and get together to work out regular visits for both parents with all three children.

CONCLUSIONS AND AFTER THOUGHTS

The three cases that have been discussed in this chapter illustrate the ways in which custom is changing (at least in the area of family law) and the different approaches that courts are developing to deal with the changes. All three cases are very much about the impact of the market economy on marriage and the family. In *Thesia Maip's* case we see that the development of towns and industries has led to the beginnings of a working class, of people who move away from home, and who leave the subsistence economy (perhaps forever, perhaps only for a time) to find work and a new style of living. When they meet and form attachments to people from other regions, they are breaking out of the customary framework in which marriages are arranged by parents and other family members and attested to by a series of ceremonial events that take place in the village. But they are still people in-between, they have not broken entirely from village ways. They still expect the marriage to be customary.

Judge Woods is trying also, it seems, to fashion rules that will suit a world in which custom and common law are both undergoing changes. He recognises that norms that were effective within a village setting can have different (and for Thesia Maip, exceedingly unhappy) consequences when moved from that setting into the very different life of the towns. He tells the Village Court magistrates that they cannot impose yesterday's values on today's circumstances. He is not calling for an end to custom, but for the recognition that custom has changed. Nor is he refusing to recognise and apply new customs. He is, instead, creating standards that will enable courts to determine when a new custom exists, so that it can be recognised and applied.

The *To'ofilu* case illustrates some of the changes that occur when the brideprice ritual, which used to be performed in a society that got its motive force from kinship ties, mutual help and reciprocity, begins to be performed in a society characterised by the existence of a market economy. Brideprice is no longer infused with the notion that life is a series of mutual exchanges and that the gifts given by the groom's family are symbolic of the future relations between the two families. Instead, the focus is now on the money and other valuable commodities that are being handed over in payment for a bride and her children.

The court decides to treat brideprice in the same way that the parties do. If the transaction is, indeed, payment for services to be rendered, then the parties must have negotiated a contract about that payment, if not explicitly, then implicitly. The court applies the common law of contracts to the brideprice transaction, assessing whether the contract negotiations were carried out in good faith and with full disclosure of material facts so that there could be the requisite meeting of the minds. Finding that the negotiation did not meet this standard, the court, in effect, holds that the contract was not duly entered into. The money and other valuables given in payment must therefore be returned.

In the third case, a couple living in town, but with ties still to their home villages, cannot agree on which of them should have custody of their children. One child lives in town; the other two are living with the extended family in what is probably a relatively traditional lifestyle. She wants the common law principle applied, so that the children will be with her. He and his brothers prefer custom, at least in regards to their youngest son.

The Court adopts a mixture of approaches, borrowing freely and flexibly, in a very customary way, from statute, common law and custom. Utilising the common law doctrine of 'tender years', the judge decides that the girl should stay in town with her mother. Using custom, he decides that the youngest son should remain in the village with his paternal kin. Using common sense, which may be what underpins both the common law and custom, he decides that the eldest son should remain in another village with his maternal kin.

The customs of Pacific islanders will continue to change and the pace of those changes will continue to be rapid. Nothing in these three cases suggests any attempt on the part of the courts to stifle change. On the contrary the courts have shown, so far, much creativity in keeping up with the changes at the same time that they are trying to make sure that no one is unduly harmed by the application of old rules in new settings. Nevertheless, the decisions raise a number of critical questions. Although the three decisions differ in the balance that they strike between custom and the common law, nevertheless all three courts do seem to presume that the common law is here to stay and that the role of judges is to fit customs, whether old or new, into a common law scheme. It is not too late, but it is time, for judges and lawyers in the Pacific islands to think about the relationship that ought to exist between custom and the common law. And, in contemplating that relationship, we need to think not only about the substantive rules but also, as the judges did in these cases, about the differences in the styles and goals of decision-making between the two legal systems.

The great issue that is raised by all of these cases, though, is the relationship that the people should have to their law, and that the law should have to the people. In no society with a formal governmental structure and legal system is law a direct match for the customs of the people. But, for a society to survive, law and customs must be close to one another. In order to feel that their law is just people need to feel that it is familiar, that it relates to their moral sense and to their values. To the extent that the courts privilege common law principles and processes over customary law, the law diverges from the felt experience of the people. Moreover, to the extent that courts cling to outmoded customs or otherwise refuse to recognise and adopt new customs, the law just as surely diverges from the culture. However, if the law goes too far too fast, if it adopts and enforces practices that are not accepted as customary by most people, then it will just as surely be seen as out of step with contemporary norms and values. The question that these cases raise, that these judges have tried to answer, and that we must continue to consider, is how the law can maintain that delicate, but necessary balance.

ENDNOTES

1   LeGuin, U.K. 2000 *Tales from Earthsea*. New York: Harcourt Inc, at p xiii.

2   For complete and detailed discussions of the role assigned to custom in the legal systems of the Pacific island nations see Ntumy, M. (ed.) 1993. *South Pacific Islands Legal Systems*. University of Hawaii Press: Honolulu (which devotes a chapter to the legal system of each Pacific island country or territory); Zorn, J.G. 1994. *Custom and Customary Law*. Course Book for University Extension Course SEC16, Pacific Law Unit, School of Social and Economic Development, University of the South Pacific, Suva, Fiji, especially Book 2, pp 1–53 and Corrin Care, J., Newton, T. and Paterson, D. 1999. *Introduction to South Pacific Law*. London: Cavendish.

3   Some writers on Pacific and other traditional legal systems distinguish between 'custom' and 'customary law'. Unfortunately for consistency, however, they do so in different ways and for different reasons. There are at least four main differentiations made: (a) Some use 'custom' to mean rules or norms of the indigenous peoples, while 'customary law' is saved for those customary rules that have been recognised and applied by the state courts, thereby becoming part of the formal law. This distinction is useful because readers can easily tell which the writer is referring to. Also, it points out that the adoption of custom by state courts changes the customs into something different. They cease to be the flexible and ever-changing, mostly unwritten, mostly unconsidered, norms of a culture and become rules that courts treat as precedent. See, for example, Woodman, G.R. 1969. Some Realism about Customary Law – the West African Experience. *Wisconsin Law Review* 1969:128–152. (b) Some legal scholars don't like to make that distinction between 'custom' and 'customary law' because it is the distinction that the colonial rulers made, and they meant by it that the 'customs' of indigenous people were not 'law' in any sense and, indeed, were inferior to the 'laws' that the colonisers brought with them or imposed on their subjects. For discussions of colonial approaches to custom, see Zorn, J.G. 1992. Common Law Jurisprudence and Customary Law. In James, R.W. and Fraser, I. (eds.) *Legal Issues in a Developing Society*. Port Moresby: University of Papua New Guinea and Ottley, B.L. 1995. Looking Back to the Future: The Colonial Origins of Current Attitudes toward Customary Law. In Aleck, J. and Rannells, J. *Custom at the Crossroads*. Port Moresby: University of Papua New Guinea. In opposition to that colonial view, many scholars purposely use the phrase 'customary law' to refer to the unwritten norms, usages, rules and values of the indigenous peoples of the Pacific. Another example of this political use of the terms 'custom' and 'customary law' occurs in the laws of Papua New Guinea. The older PNG *Customs Recognition Act* 1963 (now Cap 19), which requires courts to treat the unwritten norms of the peoples of PNG as facts, not as laws, refers to those norms as 'custom'. The more recently enacted PNG *Underlying Law Act* 2000, which provides that these norms and usages are to be the primary and major source of Papua New Guinea's own common law, refers to them as 'customary law'. (c) Colonial (and even some post-colonial) legislation and court-made laws used the term 'custom' to refer only to those norms and usages of the indigenous peoples of the Pacific that had existed since long before colonial times, since 'time immemorial'. Thus spoke the PNG *Customs Recognition Act*, enacted during the colonial period. At Independence, the *Constitution*, s 20, redefined 'custom' to mean the "customs and usages of the indigenous inhabitants of

the country … regardless of whether … the custom or usage has existed from time immemorial". After Independence, the *Customs Recognition Act* 1963 was revised to adopt the new definition of custom. (d) Finally, many lawyers, judges, legislators and scholars use the two terms — 'custom' and 'customary law' — interchangeably, without paying much attention to shades of meaning.

4   The cases discussed in this chapter are *Application of Thesia Maip; In the Matter of the Constitution, s 42(5)* [1991] PNGLR 80; *To'ofilu v Oimae*, Unreported, High Court of Solomon Islands, Civil Appeal Case No. 5 of 1996, 19th June, 1997. and *Molu v Molu No. 2*, Unreported, Supreme Court of the Republic of Vanuatu, Civil Case No. 30 of 1996, Matrimonial Case No. 130 of 1996, 15th May, 1998 (http://www.vanuatu.usp.ac.fj/paclawmat/Vanuatu_cases/Volume_G–N/Molu_v_Molu2.html. Accessed 19/8/02).

5   Many anthropology texts try to describe the pre-colonial cultures of the Pacific. For useful reviews, and a bibliography, of these ethnographies, see Foerstel, L. and Gilliam, A. (eds.) 1992. *Confronting the Margaret Mead Legacy: Scholarship, Empire and the South Pacific.* Philadelphia: Temple University Press. Although, by definition, no anthropologist was in a position to observe Pacific cultures prior to the colonial period, most of the early ethnographies pretend to write as if colonisation had not occurred. Excellent critiques of this ethnographic method can be found in Marcus, G.E. and Fischer, M.M.J. 1986. *Anthropology as Cultural Critique.* Chicago: University of Chicago Press and Kuper, A. 1998. *The Invention of Primitive Society.* London: Routledge.

6   Pre-colonial Pacific islands societies were, for the most part, small, autonomous communities. Membership and status in the community depended primarily on kinship and marriage. Technology was simple (the primary occupations related to food-getting, through swithin or 'slash and burn' gardening, fishing and hunting), producing a subsistence economy, in which each household was expected to produce enough for its own members' survival, leaving insufficient surplus to support a leisure class or to allow for much division of labour in to specialised categories. Even in Polynesia, with its chiefly and royal castes, there was little status differentiation. Members of the community interacted on the basis of relative equality. Most communities partook of a rich and textured social, religious and spiritual life.

7   Customary norms were seldom reduced to writing. They were certainly not written down in pre-colonial times. Nor do most non-governmental groups today write down many of their most important norms. The faculty of a law school, for example, has many norms — who gets which office, when to gather for morning coffee, whether to attend one another's social events — none of which are written.

8   All non-governmental groups have effective means of teaching and enforcing norms. Although there are in every group a few dissidents (just as there are those who refuse to obey some or all of the laws of state societies), most members obey most of the norms most of the time — either because they believe in the values of the group because they need to remain in good repute with other members or the group, or because they fear the adverse consequences of misbehaviour. See, further, Moore, S.F. 1983. *Law as Process: An Anthropological Approach.* London: Routledge at pp 54–81; Rheinstein, M. (ed.) 1967. *Max Weber on Law in Economy and Society.* New York: Simon & Schuster at pp 20–33.

9   I use the phrase 'formal court' or 'state court' to distinguish the official courts of the state legal system from the informal customary dispute-settlement meetings described in the text accompanying n 8 above.

10 For descriptions of the relevant constitutional and statutory provisions, see above n 2.

11 See the cases discussed in Zorn, J.G. and Corrin Care, J. 2002. Proving Customary Law in the Common Law Courts of the South Pacific. *Occasional Paper No. 2*. London: British Institute of International and Comparative Law.

12 See above, n 1.

13 This phrase is taken from the colonial version of the Papua New Guinea *Customs Recognition Ordinance* 1963, though the phrase was used elsewhere in the Pacific as well. The refusal of the colonial courts to apply anything other than long-established customs did avoid the problems associated with change, but that was not the major reason for the rule. Colonial courts were, for the most part, intended to wean Pacific islanders from custom, and to head them towards acceptance of the imposed legal system in place of custom. The courts continued to apply customs only because they believed it unfair to impose western law on people not yet sufficiently acquainted with it, but the general view during the colonial period was that custom would gradually wither away, at which point courts would no longer need to apply it. See, further, the cases cited in Ottley, B.L. and Zorn, J.G. 1983. Criminal Law in Papua New Guinea: Code, Custom and the Courts in Conflict. *American Journal of Comparative Law* Vol 31: 251–300.

14 See, for example, the *Constitution* (Papua New Guinea), s 20, the Papua New Guinea *Customs Recognition Act* [Cap. 19], as it was revised after Independence, and the Papua New Guinea *Underlying Law Act* 2000.

15 Bellwood, P. 1979. *Man's Conquest of the Pacific: The Prehistory of Southeast Asia and Oceania*. New York: Oxford University Press.

16 Howe, K. R. 1984. *Where the Waves Fall: A New South Seas History from First Settlement to Colonial Rule*. Sydney: Allen & Unwin.

17 There are too few articles or books about law in the colonial period. Until the definitive text is written, see the articles collected in Starr, J. and Collier, J.F. (eds.) 1989. *History and Power in the Study of Law: New Directions in Legal Anthropology*. London: Cornell University Press.

18 The countries and territories that recognise both statutory and customary marriages are Papua New Guinea, Vanuatu, Solomon Islands, the Federated States of Micronesia, Palau, the Commonwealth of the Northern Mariana Islands, and the Republic of the Marshall Islands. Zorn, J. G. 1994. Above, n 2, at pp 88–89.

19 Zorn, J. G., 1994. Above, n 2, at pp 95–98. For informative discussions of the relationship between customary and statutory marriage laws, see McCrae, H. 1981. *Cases and Materials on Family Law – Part I: Marriage*. University of Papua New Guinea: Port Moresby at pp 2–7 and McCrae, H. 1982. Reform of Family Law in Papua New Guinea. In Weisbrot, D., Paliwala, A. and Sawyer, A. (eds.) *Law and Social Change in Papua New Guinea*. Sydney: Butterworths.

20 *Islanders' Marriage Act* [Cap. 171] (Solomon Islands) ss 4–9; *Control of Marriage Act* [Cap. 45] (Vanuatu).

21 *Application of Thesia Maip; In the Matter of the Constitution s 42(5)* [1991] PNGLR 80.

22 Readers who wish to read the decision in conjunction with reading this chapter, will find the Papua New Guinea Law Reports at the University of the South Pacific law library and at many other libraries. See, also, Zorn, J.G. 1996. Custom and/or Law in Papua New Guinea. *Political and Legal Anthropology Review* 19:15–27.

23 In this chapter, I will quote frequently from the National Court decision, using a mimeo version. Since the decision is quite short (3 or 4 pages), I will not use page references to the PNG Law Reports. Unless otherwise referenced quotes in this section come from the National Court decision.

24 The rules about village court jurisdiction, personnel and procedures are contained in the *Village Courts Act* 1973 (PNG).

25 *The Village Courts Act* 1973 (PNG) provides that all decisions of village courts may be reviewed by the Chief Magistrate of the District Court in the district where the village court operates. K700 is approximately USD200 though, for a village woman without a regular cash income, it is a staggeringly huge amount.

26 *Thesia Maip's* case was one of a number that suggested the village courts in the Highlands were discriminating against women and treating them unduly harshly. In 1990, the year that Thesia Maip was imprisoned, more than fifty complaints were made to the national court in the Eastern Highlands about women being imprisoned by village courts for marital matters. Thesia Maip was one of three Highlands women whom Judge Woods freed from prison in a single month. Different village courts had ordered each of them imprisoned all on the same grounds. All three women were charged with adultery, ordered to pay fines, and imprisoned when they could not pay. In large part because of Judge Woods' efforts, which brought these and similar cases to the attention of the press and the higher courts, Village Courts were convinced to abandon this practice. For a more detailed discussion, see Zorn, J.G. 1994–5. Women, Custom and State Law in Papua New Guinea. *Third World Legal Studies* 1994–95: 169–205.

27 Judge Woods found different reasons to release the women in the other cases that he heard that month. One woman was released on the ground that charging her with adultery when her husband had, to all intents and purposes, deserted her several years before, violated her right to equality under s 50 of the *Constitution* (PNG). See *Application of Wagi Non; In the Matter of the Constitution s 42(5)*, Unreported, National Court of PNG, 1991. Judge Woods released another woman on the grounds that it was a violation of natural justice to order her to pay compensation, when the village court knew she was a village wife with no access to cash. See *In the Matter of Kaka Ruk; In the Matter of the Constitution s 42(5)* [1991] PNGLR 105. See, further, Jessep elsewhere in this volume.

28 There is no definition in the statutes. The standard treatise defines adultery as 'voluntary or consensual sexual intercourse between a married person and a person (whether married or unmarried) of the opposite sex not being the other's spouse.' Cretney, S.M. & Masson, J.M. 1976. *Cretney's Principles of Family Law* (2ⁿᵈ ed.). Sweet & Maxwell: London. At p 102.

29 It seems that the customary law of the Balk villagers, as interpreted by the Balk Village Court, was the same. Judge Woods does not quote the customary rule, but he does say

that Jude told the Village Court magistrate that he and Thesia were married and Thesia told the court they were not, implying that the Village Court's decision about adultery under customary law turned on whether Thesia and Jude were married.

30 Customs are not written down in the way that laws are written down, so customs can, and do, change more easily than laws can. Customs are nothing more than beliefs, values and habitual activities. Beliefs, values and habitual activities change constantly, to meet new circumstances or just because everything in human behaviour changes over time. Rheinstein, M. (ed) 1967. Above, n 8, at pp 11–20.

31 *Constitution* (PNG), s 20, defines custom as 'customs and usages'.

32 Nanda, S. and Warms, R.L. 1997. *Cultural Anthropology* (6ᵗʰ ed.) Columbus: Wadsworth at p 43.

33 The judge also raises a jurisdictional issue: "My initial confusion is how can a man from Bougainville come to a village court in the Western Highlands and seek what is in effect an order for restitution of conjugal rights when there has been no contact at all between him and that village apart from his living with a woman from that village elsewhere in Papua New Guinea".

34 Note the subtle, but important difference between the Village Court's standard ("people today are recognising it as a marriage") and the National Court's standard ("clearly recognisable by everyone"). The Village Court, unlike the National Court, does not require that everyone recognise the custom, nor that the recognition be *clearly* recognisable.

35 See for example *John Noel v Obed Toto*, Unreported, Supreme Court of the Republic of Vanuatu, Civil Case No. 18 of 1994, 19ᵗʰ April, 1995 regarding inheritance (http://www.vanuatu.usp.ac.fj/paclawmat/Vanuatu_cases/Volume_g_N/Noel_v_Toto.html Accessed 19/9/02); *Pandosy Jean Charles v Pascaline Thuha*, Unreported, Supreme Court of the Republic of Vanuatu, Matrimonial Case No. 16 of 1996, 10ᵗʰ December, 1997 regarding custody of children (http://www.vanuatu.usp.ac.fj/paclawmat/Vanuatu_cases/Volume_O_Q/Pandosy_v_Thuha.html).

36 The judge also suggests that there may be some hypocrisy on Jude's part: "The thwarted man here had ample opportunity to consider a proper marriage, either by a public ceremony in the village concerned or in the church or registry office under the Marriage Act. He elected not to take any of these procedures". Jude wanted, the judge is suggesting, none of the responsibilities that a real marriage would entail, but all of the rights of marriage.

37 "Jails are for criminals," Judge Woods says, near the conclusion of his decision, "not as a means of revenge on the breakdown of a living together arrangement which discriminates against the female partner".

38 *To'ofilu v Oimae*. Unreported, High Court of solomon Islands, Civil Appeal Case No. 5 of 1996, 19 June 1997. I am grateful to Jennifer Corrin Care for sharing with me her detailed case note on this decision. See Corrin Care, J. 1999. *To'ofilu v Oimae* Case Note in *Journal of South Pacific Law*, case note 4 of Volume 3 (http://www.vanuatu.usp.ac.fj/journal_splaw/Case_Notes/Corrin_Care3.html Accessed 19/9/02).

39   In pre-colonial Melanesia, and in other parts of the Pacific as well, marriages were arranged between the parents of the prospective bride and groom. The marriage was confirmed when the groom's extended family gave a feast for the bride's family and presented them with gifts. The gifts usually included pigs, polished shells, fine mats, carved bowls, boars' teeth, and yam, taro or other foodstuffs. The groom's father tried to get members of his family — his uncles, brothers and sisters — to contribute as much as possible towards the brideprice, as the amount signified the value and status of the family, as well as their respect for the bride and her family. *Pidgin* has been heavily influenced by colonialism, so the Papua New Guinea *pidgin* term for brideprice now is *baim meri* ('buy a woman'). In most of the indigenous languages of Melanesia, however, the concept of a price or purchase is absent. According to Simon Fuo'o, a law student from Kwara'ae region of Solomon Islands, there is no word in Solomon Islands *pidgin* for brideprice. In his own (local) language it is *daurai'ia*, for which there is no accurate English translation. He said, after some thought, that today most people would think of the word as having something to do with an exchange to compensate for the fact that the bride's family were going to lose her services.

40   Many comments posted on a thread about brideprice in April–May 2001 on the Solomon Islands Department of Commerce message board substantiated this, though a number of the e-mail notes also pointed out that the custom did not, at least traditionally, have anything to do with a sale or purchase. See www.commerce.gov.sb

41   Rubin, G. 1975. The Traffic in Women: Notes on the Political Economy of Sex. In Reiter, R.R. (ed.) *Toward an Anthropology of Women*. New York: Monthly Review Press.

42   However, these attitudes do exist, as a number of the comments on the Solomon Islands message board demonstrated. See www.commerce.gov.sb

43   The relationships between inter-married clans and families have been changed by a number of causes. One of the causes can be found in the changed political situation which has limited tribal warfare thereby lessening the need for members of different clans to depend on one other to provide help in times of war. Economic change has also reduced the inter-relationships between in-laws. For example, as traditional inter-island trading, as exemplified by the *kula* ring, disappears, so does the need to create agnates in order to have dependable trading partners. See, further, Malinowski, B. 1984. (original edition 1922) *Argonauts of the Western Pacific*. Waveland Press: New York. The development of a market economy, in which buying and selling carries no traces of reciprocity or other relationship between the purchaser and seller has also lessened the need for people to extend their family ties.

44   *To'ofilu v Oimae*, above, n 38.

45   These are shells so special that they are referred to in English as 'shell money'. They differ from cash, however, in that they are supposed to be exchanged only at ceremonial occasions. They cannot be used to buy goods or services the way cash is used. They are valuables in and of themselves, not, like money a means to enable actors in the marketplace to buy and sell.

46   In addition to the return of the full value of the shell money, rice, pigs and cash, the To'ofilu family also asked to be compensated for the money they had spent traveling to the brideprice ceremony. The Local Court ordered the defendants to pay for these expenses,

the Magistrates' Court denied them these expenses, and the High Court reinstated the Local Court's order.

47 See above, n 28 at p 2.

48 "...in the circumstances, the Defendant owed a duty in custom to disclose this material fact to the Plaintiff during the course of discussions and negotiations for the amount of brideprice to be fixed... [but] the Defendant did not disclose this fact;... the Plaintiff thereby was deprived of the opportunity to either re-negotiate the amount of the brideprice fixed or to decline to pay the amount asked for... in the circumstances, the Plaintiff must be compensated in custom for this breach of customary duty or obligation, the quantum being the refund of the brideprice in its entirety." See above, n 44 at p 2.

49 See above, n 38 at p 3.

50 "...brideprice should not be taken as a yardstick to measure the man's love for his wife. In this case clearly it was the man Ronny who showed first sight love for Fiona. Whether the woman Fiona was pregnant before the marriage or not is a matter for negotiation so as to determine the amount of the brideprice to be paid to the girl's family."
See above, n 44 at p 5.

51 See above, n 38 at p 4.

52 One of the purposes of a legal system is to resolve disputes between members of the group so that the dispute does not result in violence and so that the interdependent activities of group members can continue. In state societies the courts assume this function also, applying the rules of tort, contract or property law to disputes between citizens, and resolving the disputes according to these rules. The aim of these court proceedings is to reach a definitive conclusion, based upon the applicable rules, both so that the parties to the dispute will feel that a resolution in accord with their beliefs and values has been attained and so that participants in the market economy generally can act in the confidence that, so long as they are acting in accordance with the rules, their expectations will be rewarded. In the non-state societies of the pre-colonial Pacific, there were customary means of resolving disputes. One method consisted of meetings, attended by everyone with a concern for the parties to the dispute, often by everyone in the village, in which the grounds of the disagreement would be discussed, commented upon, and discussed again, until all those at the meeting had reached a consensus about how to resolve the dispute. Often a chief or elder presided at these meetings but the outcome was not his to dictate. He acted as a mediator not as a judge because without the threat or reality of police at his command, he had no means to enforce his orders. He had to depend upon the willingness of both parties to the dispute to enforce the outcome upon themselves. The aim of these customary meetings, therefore, was to restore peace and harmony between the disputants and within the group as a whole, so that the members of the small community could go back to living and working together.

53 See above, n 38 at p 2. The use of the phrase "material fact" is itself an indication that the High Court is treating custom as if it were common law. That phrase is part of common law jurisprudence, not part of customary dispute settlement. Another common law motif occurs in the way in which the High Court judge views the brideprice negotiation. He describes it as a judge would describe any negotiation over a contract, not necessarily as one would the more free-flowing, open-ended negotiations that occur in customary environments.

54 The High Court also noted that the Local Court, being closer to the parties and their village, and made up of magistrates who are chosen for their knowledge of custom, is better equipped to decide what the customary rule governing each case is than are magistrates, who live farther away and whose training has been, for the most part, in the common law.

55 See above, n 38 at p 6.

56 The *Customs Recognition Act* 2000 (No. 7 of 2000) (Solomon Islands) provides, at s 3, that the courts must have evidence of the existence of any customary law that a court intends to use, and that, for this purpose, customary law is to be treated as a fact. The Act did not exist at the time *To'ofilu v Oimae* was decided, and the Solomon Islands courts did not seem to believe that evidence of custom was always required.

57 This is a carefully, and purposefully, limited decision. The High Court has said here only that evidence must be presented to overturn a Local Court's decision about custom. The High Court has not said that evidence must be presented every time a party wishes custom to be adopted by a state court.

58 This is particularly the case in today's world where people need (or want) many things that they cannot grow or make for themselves. Cash is needed today for every thing from store-bought clothes and canned goods, airplane flights, television sets, trucks and other tools to a primary school education. In the early 1970s, when I observed brideprice ceremonies in the Papua New Guinea Highlands, cash was included amongst the gifts, but cash was not as necessary a part of people's lives at that time as it has become since. It tended more to show the prestige of the donor — 'I'm one of those few with access to the western world and its paper money' — than to be of real use to those who received it.

59 Of course, people having arguments over brideprice did not have the ability to go to a formal court in pre-colonial times, because no state courts existed. Even during the colonial period, few disagreements of this sort would have been heard in state courts, because those courts tended to be forums primarily for criminal cases and for disputes between expatriates. Ottley, B. L. 1995. Above, n 3, at pp 97–107.

60 Another reason people probably prefer the courts to customary mediation, especially where a large amount of money is involved, is because of the perceived finality of a court solution. Even in a civil suit brought in a local court, courts have the power of the state behind them, enforcing every judgment. And the magistrates and judges speak so definitively. However, despite their desire for an absolutist verdict (or, perhaps, because of it), people are led by the hierarchal nature of the court system into continuing appeals, making resolution of the dispute ever more elusive. The High Court decision in *To'ofilu v Oimae* was handed down more than four years after the matter first came before the Local Court.

61 *Molu v Molu No. 2*. Unreported, Supreme Court of the Republic of Vanuatu, Civil Case No. 30 of 1996, Matrimonial Case No. 130 of 1996, 15 May 1998.

62 The leading case, holding that custom may be applied in determining custody so long as custom does not conflict with the common law 'best interests of the child' standard, is from Solomon Islands. See *Sukutaona v Houanihou* [1982] SILR 12.

63 The United Nations Convention on the Rights of the Child (CRC), art. 3(1), adopted by the General Assembly of the United Nations, 20th November, 1989, provides that "in all

actions concerning children... the best interests of the child shall be a primary consideration." The Convention is self-executing. It is binding on every country that has ratified it and all the Pacific island nations, including Solomon Islands, have ratified it. (The only nations not to ratify it are the United States and Somalia.) An example of a Pacific Islands statute mandating that custody decisions be based solely upon the best interests of the child is the *Custody of Children Act* [Cap 20] (Tuvalu), s 3(3): "...the court shall regard the welfare of the child as the first and paramount consideration and shall not take into consideration whether from any other point of view the claim of the father is superior to that of the mother or the claim of the mother is superior to that of the father". In other Pacific jurisdictions — for example, in Solomon Islands — the 'best interests of the child' standard has been established by the courts, rather than directly by statute. See, for example, *Sukutaona v Houanihou* [1982] SILR 12. In some jurisdictions, the statutory standard also takes the interests of other family members into account. In Marshall Islands, for example, the statute requires the courts to take into account the interests of everyone involved. See *Domestic Relations Law* [26 Revised Statutes, Cap 1] (Marshall Islands). Section 4 of the *Matrimonial Causes Act* [Cap 282] (PNG) stipulates that the courts should take into account equally the welfare of the child, the conduct of the parents, and the wishes of each parent. Section 3 of the *Custody of Children Act* [Cap. 20] (Tuvalu) also permits the court to take the conduct and wishes of the parents into account, but specifies (as quoted above) that they be secondary to the child's welfare.

64 See, for example, the discussion of this point in *Sukutaona v Houanihou* [1982] SILR 12.

65 Yes, the major common law countries (England, Australia, the United States) were patrilineal and patriarchal, and this was reflected in the common law. See Cott, N.F. 2001. *Public Vows: A History of Marriage and the Nation*. Harvard University Press: Cambridge; Hartog, H. 2000. *Man and Wife in America: A History* Harvard University Press: Cambridge and Yalom, M. 2001. *History of the Wife*. Harper Collins: New York.

66 I do have to point out that, despite the certainty of judges, there is no certainty in the psychological, sociological or medical literature as to whether children of 'tender years' are invariably best served by being in their mother's custody, even when their mother is in all respects fit to care for them. The consensus amongst professionals seems to be: 'It depends on the mother, the father, and the children'. See Baris, M.A. and Garrity, C.B. 1988. *Children of Divorce*. Psytec: New York.

67 An excellent discussion of customary and statutory custody rules can be found in McCrae, H. 1981. *Cases and Materials on Family Law – Part III: Custody, Maintenance, DeFacto Relationships and Ex-Nuptial Children*. University of Papua New Guinea: Port Moresby at pp 2–7.

68 A phrase used in many kin-based societies to signify the inter-dependence of clan members. For descriptions of the important role played in a child's life by the extended family in kin-based societies, see Glasse, R.M. and Meggitt, M.J. 1969. *Pigs, Pearlshells and Women. Marriage in the New Guinea Highlands*. New York: Prentice Hall; Hutter, M. 1959. *The Family Experience: A Reader in Cultural Diversity*. London: Allyn & Bacon; Mead, M. 1959. *Coming of Age in Samoa*. New York: Mentor; and Pulea, M. 1986. *The Family, Law and Population in the Pacific Islands*. Suva: University of the South Pacific.

69 *Molu v Molu No. 2*, Above, n 61.

70 It was a statutory marriage, performed in a church, although Cidie and his family also gave brideprice to Patricia's family. To his mind, therefore, they also had a customary marriage. The Court points out, however, that, under the *Marriage Act* [Cap 60] (Vanuatu), if one is married with all the proper formalities in a church, the law recognises it as a statutory marriage, and only a statutory marriage, regardless of what additional customary ceremonies may have been performed. Therefore, the Court must apply the statutory standards, not the customary rules, to all aspects of the marriage, including divorce, child custody and property division. See above, n 61 at p 12. But what if, in addition to observing the statutory formalities, the couple had gone through all the aspects of a customary marriage, rather than just giving brideprice? The Court does not say whether it would, then, be willing to apply customary law, rather than the statute, in determining custody or the division of property. It does say, "There is no evidence that the marriage between the Petitioner and the Respondent was a custom marriage performed in a place and according to the form laid down by local custom of the parties". See above, n 61 at p 12. This suggests that the Court *might* apply customary law, at least within the bounds permitted by the statute in such a circumstance.

71 See *Molu v Molu No. 1*, Unreported, Supreme Court of the Republic of Vanuatu, Civil Case No. 130 of 1996, Matrimonial Case No. 2 of 1996, 21st April, 1998. (http://www.vanuatu.usp.ac.fj/paclawmat/Vanuatu_cases/Volume_G–N/Molu_v_Molu1.html Accessed 19/9/02).

72 See above, n 71 at pp 4–8.

73 See above, n 61 at p 5: "I accept the general environment which both the Petitioner and Respondent thought would be better on the island. But I reject the evidence that Yannick wanted to go to Pentecost to escape the behaviour of his father since he was just a little boy (4 years) when he was sent there, even if the Respondent admitted he slapped him on one occasion".

74 The Vanuatu *Constitution* provides, at Art 72, that 'the rules of custom' are part of Vanuatu law, and, again, at Art 93(3), that 'customary law shall have effect as part of the law of the Republic". The *Constitution* does not, however, stipulate amongst statutes, custom and the common law, as to which takes precedence. The Acting Chief Justice ruled, in this case, that he had to follow the dictates of the *Matrimonial Causes Act* [Cap 192] (Vanuatu) in relation to matters arising out of marriages performed under the *Marriage Act* [Cap 60] (Vanuatu).

75 *Matrimonial Causes Act* [Cap 192] (Vanuatu), s 15. The *Matrimonial Causes Act* [Cap 192] (Vanuatu) itself does not expressly mention the 'best interests' standard. It provides only that "the Court may... make such provision as appears just with respect to custody..."

76 Convention on the Rights of the Child, Art 3(1), adopted by the General Assembly of the U.N., 20th November, 1989; ratified by Vanuatu Parliament, *Ratification Act* 1992 (Vanuatu). The emphasis in the quotation was added by the Acting Chief Justice. See above, n 61 at p 6.

77 See above, n 61 at p 7.

78 See text at n 66 above.

79   It should be noted that, though the Court gave formal custody to Cidie, the father, the Court intended that the boy live not with the father in Port Vila, but with the paternal family in Santo — an important distinction, since Cidie Molu had spent most of Ian's life drunk and beating up Ian's mother.

80   The Court quotes from the decision of *Re Thain* [1926] All E.R.384: "one knows from experience how mercifully transient are the effect of parting and other sorrows [for young children]; and how soon the novelty of fresh surroundings and new associations effaces the recollection of former days and kind friends". The quotation, it seems to me, could just as well mean that, if Ian were returned to his mother, he would soon stop missing the people in Santo. Today, as opposed to 1925, most childcare and child psychology professionals would agree that children have very long memories, that they do not soon get over parting and other sorrows, and that the novelty of fresh surroundings do not diminish their longing for former days, especially if those former days included their parents. Baris, M. A. & Garrity, C. B. 1988. Above, n 66. However, those studies were done, for the most part, in the United States, Australia and the United Kingdom. It is altogether possible that children in other cultures, especially those cultures in which most children live in extended families, rather than in nuclear families react differently.

81   See above, n 61 at p 5. However, the Court notes, it is unusual for such an arrangement to occur over the objections of one of the parents.

82   This is a phrase found, in one version or another, in all clan-based societies, to mean that the children belong to the clan. The clan is for them, and they are for the clan. See above, n 68.

6. ISSUES IN CONTEMPORARY CUSTOMARY LAW: WOMEN AND THE LAW*

By: Jean G. Zorn

KEY TERMS AND PHRASES

Discourse

A conversation or dialogue, usually of a formal kind or in a formal setting.

Dualism

A condition in which a single entity is made up of two, sometimes conflicting, parts.

Ultra vires

A Latin phrase meaning an action that ought not to be taken because it is beyond one's power or authority, most often used in reference to government officials or company directors.

---

* The list of people who deserve thanks for their contributions to this chapter includes Bruce Ottley, Pamela Goldberg, Jennifer Corrin Care, Christine Stewart, Tess Newton Cain, Heather McCrae and Imrana Jalal. Some of you have actually read drafts of the chapter; every one of you has written or said things that made me think — and think again. Thanks to you all. And to the women of CUNY School of Law, who have taught me the value of a woman's approach to legal issues. And, especially, to Steve, Heather and Christopher.

Many people argue that the law does not discriminate against women. Certainly, many laws have been changed in their written form so that they seem gender-neutral, seeming to treat men and women equally. However, the legislation may have bad effects on women because women are not socially and economically equal to men. The law is produced by social, economic and political forces. It does not of itself make women unequal, but it does influence their situation. Patriarchal interpretations of written and unwritten laws combine with local social, cultural and political forces to keep the status of women inferior to that of men.[1]

INTRODUCTION

One of the criticisms of custom frequently heard these days is that it discriminates against women.[2] Many of the critics believe that customary gender discrimination will end whenever women can get their cases into the formal courts, where judges will use the constitutions, statutes and the common law to defeat custom.[3] Imrana Jalal has provided us with an excellent definition of gender discrimination:

> Discrimination means treating people in different ways, depending on their sex, race, religion, political opinions, creed, sexual preference and so on. We may discriminate against a particular group of people, just as we may discriminate in favour of that particular group of people. Here we are concerned with sex discrimination. This is often called "gender discrimination" because it focuses on whether a person is male or female.[4]

Jalal differentiates between two kinds of gender discrimination — direct and indirect. She defines direct discrimination first:

> Discrimination takes many forms, both direct and indirect. In law, direct discrimination against a woman means that something happens to a woman because she is a woman and not because she is an individual. The discrimination may be based on a particular characteristic applying generally to women (for example, being able to have babies) or it may be based on a particular characteristic that people may think women have (for example, being "emotional"). Direct legal discrimination may be obvious in the legislation or legal practices specifically permitting certain rights to men but not to women.[5]

When people say that custom discriminates against women, it is usually direct discrimination that they have in mind. Polygamy is often cited as an example of direct discrimination because in most societies that practice polygamy men are allowed to have several wives but women are not permitted more than one husband.[6] Brideprice has also been criticised as an example of gender discrimination,[7] as has the customary political process in that it tends to place women in an inferior position and to shut them out of public discourse.[8]

It is the thesis of this chapter that whether or not indigenous cultures are discriminatory their critics are wrong — or, at least, have been wrong up to now — in presuming that the state courts will redress the balance. To the extent that gender discrimination does exist under customary law, the rules and agencies of state law do little, or nothing, to correct it. State law fails to address customary examples of direct sex discrimination because, in Jalal's phrase, the instrumentalities of state law are 'indirect discrimination'. She notes that indirect discrimination can occur in three ways:

[1] Most legislation is written in gender-neutral form. It may seem not to favour men over women, but it indirectly discriminates against women, because the courts and law agencies that apply, interpret or enforce the written laws do not consider the disadvantages of women.

[2] Indirect discrimination occurs also when social and cultural attitudes cause officers of the courts, law enforcement agencies and associated agencies to interpret laws and procedures in ways that discriminate against women.

[3] The law may also be indirectly discriminatory where it fails to correct discrimination. Here, discrimination occurs not because the law does something, or does it badly, but because it omits to correct something.[9]

We will see examples of all three kinds of indirect discrimination in the cases to be discussed in this chapter.

In recent years, a number of instances have arisen in which customary law has discriminated against women. For example, many people in Vanuatu, especially in the Port Vila expatriate community, were shocked when four custom chiefs forced a woman to return from Port Vila to her home in Tanna because she refused to be reunited with the husband who had beaten her.[10] Another example of customary discrimination against women had arisen a few years earlier in Solomon Islands, when village men refused to enter a voting booth on the grounds that its prior use by women contaminated it.[11] In yet a third incident, which occurred in Papua New Guinea, a man who had killed a young girl promised to give his own daughter to the girl's parents in compensation for her death.[12]

All three of these incidents prompted much discussion in their respective countries and most people probably assumed that the state courts would deal with all three by voiding the relevant customary norms since they conflicted with state laws prohibiting sex discrimination. As the following discussion demonstrates, however, those expectations were proven wrong. In each instance, the case was decided on entirely other grounds. The Courts barely noted the existence of discrimination and certainly did not base their decisions on it. As such, the decisions are examples of Jalal's third definition of indirect discrimination: failures by officers of the law to correct discrimination. As the following discussion will demonstrate, the cases provide us with examples of Jalal's other forms of indirect gender discrimination as well.

WOMEN AND THE POWERS OF CHIEFS

In Vanuatu, in 1993, four "very important chiefs"[13] from the southern part of Tanna held a meeting in Port Vila in an attempt to resolve the problems that had caused their kinswoman Marie Kota to leave her husband Walter.[14] Marie and Walter were from Tanna, both subjects of the Tanna chiefs but, like many other rural villagers, they had been drawn to the capital city and had been living there for a while. A number of other Tannese, mostly friends and kin of the couple, attended the meeting. Walter was happy to attend. Marie did not want to but the chiefs sent two officers from the Vanuatu Police to her house to compel her attendance.

> At the meeting the Chiefs and a number of other people suggested that Marie and her husband should get back together. Marie said that she did not wish to go back to her husband, as he had beaten her, and that she wanted a divorce. The meeting was then adjourned for 15 minutes, so that she could decide whether she really wanted the divorce or not. After that period, she said that she did want the divorce, and then it was the Chief Andrew who announced the decision of the Chiefs, that she must go back to Tanna. This decision appears to have been a consensual decision made by all the chiefs present.[15]

Marie told the chiefs she did not want to go back to Tanna so men were sent with her to her home, while she packed, and then to the wharf where she was put aboard a boat bound for Tanna.[16] She cried all the way. She thought about jumping off the boat before it left Port Vila harbour, but was sure that, if she did, the men would find her, beat her and put her on the boat again. With help from the Vanuatu Association of Women against Violence against Women she returned to Port Vila the following week and, a few weeks later, filed a criminal complaint.[17]

Walter Kota, the chiefs and the other participants in the meeting were charged, some with kidnapping, some with inciting to kidnap.[18] The Supreme Court had little trouble, on these facts, finding several of them guilty. Their major defence seems to have been that they did not use force but the Court noted that a conviction for kidnapping does not require the use of force. It requires merely that force be threatened[19] and the Court had no trouble deducing from Marie Kota's testimony that threats had occurred:

> I believe the Complainant when she said that she was crying, and that she was fearful [as] to what would happen to her, she believes that the situation she was in was such that if she had jumped off the vessel, she would have been beaten up and put back on it, and that if the ship had left the wharf and she had swam to shore, she would have been beaten.[20]

The defendants also raised the defence of mistake of fact.[21] The Supreme Court was not sure what the defendants meant by this, as there did not seem to be any facts that they had misunderstood. The Court concluded that the defendants must be arguing that they had mistakenly believed that custom controlled the matter and that they would not be held liable under state law for actions governed by Tanna custom. The Court held there was no mistake of fact, stating: "If anything there was a mistake of law and the effective custom, but not facts".[22]

The judgment could have stopped there. No more was needed to dismiss the defendants' arguments, but the Court went on to discuss the role that custom had played in the matter — and the role that custom should play. One must ask why the

Court did this, knowing, when it did so, that its pronouncements on custom were, at best, *dicta*. The judge, Downing J., an expatriate, was very upset at what the chiefs had done, and particularly upset that they had invoked custom to support their actions.[23] And there are suggestions in the decision that this was not the only example of chiefs overstepping the legal bounds of their role.[24] It may be that the Court took advantage of this case to lay down general rules for chiefly behaviour. That would explain the Court's insistence that the case did not raise a conflict between custom and the laws introduced by the colonisers, but between custom and the laws enacted by the defendants' own Parliament and people.[25]

Although custom is part of the law of Vanuatu it is secondary to the *Constitution* and statutory law and therefore cannot be invoked to excuse actions that are in conflict with the *Constitution* or with statutes.[26] In this case, the Court found that the chiefs' actions violated several different constitutional and statutory provisions. In forcing Marie Kota to go back to Tanna, the chiefs had violated her constitutional rights to liberty and to freedom of movement, as well as her statutory right to be free from coercion.[27] Their behaviour also violated Marie Kota's right to equal treatment:

> Article 5 of the Constitution makes it quite clear that men are to be treated the same as women, and women are to be treated the same as men. All people in Vanuatu are equal and whilst the Custom may have been that women were to be treated or could be treated as property, and could be directed to do things by men, whether those men be their husbands or chiefs, they cannot be discriminated against under the Constitution.[28]

Gender equality is one of the Court's major concerns, one of the primary reasons for the lengthy discussion of custom that concludes the judgment. But it is not the Court's only concern about custom and the behaviour of the chiefs. It may not even be the Court's primary concern.

The Court is also very much concerned about the chiefs' attempt to give themselves greater powers than they actually have in a parliamentary system of government:

> ...the Chiefs must realise that any powers they wish to exercise in Custom is subject to the Constitution of the Republic of Vanuatu, and also subject to the Statutory Law of Vanuatu.[29]

The Court is speaking here in particular about the chiefs' use of the police to compel Marie Kota to attend the meeting. The Court is so upset about this abuse of police authority that it mentions the police twice. The subject comes up first when the Court is describing the facts of the case. At that point, the Court criticises only the police themselves:

> The police were consulted at the Police Station, and 2 police in a police truck... went to the house where Marie Kota was living and forced Marie to go to the meeting. I find it most astonishing and abhorrent that Vanuatu Police had anything to do with this matter.... The Vanuatu Police had no authority in the legislation of this country to act as they did in this case, to bully and force a person

to attend a meeting, and I propose to take this matter up to the Chief Commissioner of the Police.[30]

The Court brings up the topic a second time and this time focuses on the role of the chiefs in telling the police what to do:

> ...it is most unfortunate that the meeting was called in the circumstances in which it was called. It is also extraordinary as I have said, that the police were used to bully the Complainant, and this has risen again from the fundamental misunderstanding of the constitutional rights by the Chiefs, together with those around the Chiefs, whether they be assistants or members of committees of the community.[31]

Like everyone else in Vanuatu, the Court said, chiefs must learn to abide by the *Constitution*. It did bother the Court that the chiefs discriminated against Marie Kota. But the method they used to discriminate bothered the Court more. The chiefs assumed they had the power to command the nation's police — and the police agreed. It was the chiefs' assumption of the powers of modern government that most upset the Court.[32]

For centuries, chiefs were the supreme leaders of many of the traditional societies of the Pacific. The colonial authorities usurped much of their power, subsumed their chiefdoms into larger political entities, and changed many of the norms under which the chiefs had governed.[33] At independence a number of Pacific island nations attempted to create a new balance, making a place for chiefs in the constitutional scheme of government. But the role created for the chiefs tends to be small and very different from the authority they enjoyed prior to the colonial period.

In Vanuatu, for example, Chapter 5 of the *Constitution* establishes a National Council of Chiefs composed of custom chiefs elected by their peers, but the Council is not a true legislative body. Its powers are limited to discussion, recommendation and consultation about matters relating to custom.[34] Moreover, the constitutional provisions are merely permissive. Nothing in the *Constitution* requires the Council to hold discussions or make recommendations, nor, except in relation to land laws, does it require Parliament to consult with the Council. When the Council does choose to make recommendations, the *Constitution* does not require Parliament to follow them. Indeed, except in relation to land, the *Constitution* does not mention Parliament in relation to the Council. The *Constitution* does not specify which governmental body the Council is supposed to make recommendations to.

Despite the limitations on their powers at the national level, chiefs continue to play an important role in the political life of Pacific villages. No village is likely to do anything as a corporate body or community group without the chiefs' leadership or approval. Chiefs still maintain a measure of control over the allocation of the clan's customary land. And, as in Marie Kota's case, villagers still expect their chiefs to chair village meetings, to resolve disputes between villagers, and to punish villagers who offend against the social order.[35]

It can be said that in Vanuatu — as in many other Pacific nations — two separate but occasionally interlinking spheres of government have developed. There is the post-colonial sector, characterised by the practices, and to some extent the ideologies, of democracy, to which people belong according to the rules of citizenship and nationality. And there is also the traditional sector, characterised by chiefly (or 'big man') rule, by reciprocity and exchange, to which people belong according to kinship. Some people in Vanuatu live in only one of these worlds, either the post-colonial or the village sphere. Most people, however, have to find a way to function in both worlds.

To an expatriate judge — perhaps to anyone trained in the parliamentary system of government or the common law system of law; certainly to anyone who lives primarily, if not wholly, in the post-colonial sphere — the distinctions between the post-colonial and traditional systems probably seem too obvious even to need explaining. To their way of thinking, except as granted by the *Constitution*, chiefly power is confined to the traditional sphere; to the extent that chiefs have any authority at all in the post-colonial sphere, it is limited to that given by the *Constitution*; and, since the *Constitution* gives to chiefs no authority over the police, it is *ultra vires* for chiefs to try to exercise power over the police. Similarly, to the minds of those living in the post-colonial sector, the police are purely a product of that sector, ought to take orders only from officials within that sector, and have no business doing what someone in the traditional sector has told them to do.

However, to chiefs and other villagers, and to persons (members of the police force, for example) who are attempting to negotiate a life that spans both spheres, the distinctions may appear very different. Chiefs are used to commanding their men to do their bidding, especially when the chiefs think they are doing right. Chiefs see themselves as political leaders, equal, if not superior to, the members of parliament from their districts. Villagers have the same dualistic perspective and most police officers come from, still live in, villages. So it is not surprising for chiefs to assume that, on a visit to the capital city, they can ask those who enforce the rules, at the behest of political leaders, to act for them in the same capacity. Nor is it surprising that the police would do so.

Out of the dualism that characterises Vanuatu politics today, something new will evolve. It is from crossovers of this sort that a new political system will gradually emerge. The expatriate judge who decided *Public Prosecutor v Kota* believed that he knew what the future should be. Chiefs, he believed, should stay in their sphere, police in theirs. But he will leave, and Vanuatu will go on. Ni-Vanuatu chiefs, police, villagers, town-dwellers, judges, magistrates, lawyers, members of parliament, husbands and wives will all have a say, whether or not they intend to, in the political system that is to come. We cannot know today precisely what it will be like, but we can make some guesses. Will it treat women with more respect and less discrimination? That is greatly to be hoped. Will it find creative and functional ways to merge the post-colonial and the traditional, introduced law and custom? That, too, is to be hoped — and, I think, expected.

WOMEN AND THE VOTE

In Solomon Islands in 1986 twenty-two men came to a polling station intending to vote in an election for the Malaita Provincial Assembly but left without voting.[36] Since the successful candidate won by only three votes it is evident that the votes of the twenty-two might have changed the outcome of the election. The men did not vote because:

> Men who follow the old religion believe they will be ritually contaminated if they enter a room that contains a menstruating woman or which has contained a menstruating woman that same day. The presiding officer refused to make special arrangements for these men such as allowing them to vote first; bringing the ballot box outside the voting compartment; or voting on their behalf.[37]

The High Court was asked to overturn the election on the grounds that "the voting was so conducted by the Returning and Presiding Officers as to be discriminatory against" these twenty-two voters.[38] The Court let the results of the election stand. In doing so, it noted that if the election officials had made any special provisions for the men so that they could vote — allowing them to vote first, for example, or building them a separate polling booth — that might have constituted discrimination against women.[39] But, despite the fact that the Court said this, women's right to equal treatment under the law was not the legal basis on which the decision turned, nor was gender equality the value that the Court seemed most interested in protecting.

The legal argument that swayed the Court was a narrowly literal reading of the applicable regulations which provide that voting is to take place in a "screened compartment in the polling station".[40] And, the Court held, "it was no part of the duty of the presiding officer to make any alternative arrangement".[41] The regulations did provide an exception to the requirement that voters cast their ballots in a closed room, but the exception applied only to voters unable to cast their votes "by reason of blindness or other physical disability."[42] "In the instant case", the Court pointed out, "the twenty-two pagan voters had no physical disability whatever and there was nothing to prevent them from voting other than their fear and respect for their custom".[43]

If the Court had wanted to, it could have interpreted the regulations more broadly, in a way that would have allowed the twenty-two disenfranchised men to vote. For example, the Court could have looked to the purpose of the regulation[44] which, so the Court itself finds, is to protect the secrecy of the voter's choice.[45] The Court could have pointed out that this purpose is intended to benefit voters and could then have held that the persons that a regulation is intended to benefit can waive the benefit, especially if they do not experience it as benefiting them.[46]

Counsel for the election officials gave the Court another argument that the Court might have used to avoid the strict application of the regulation. Counsel pointed out that government was currently considering new regulations that "would expressly enable anyone prohibited by any customary rule from entering the polling station… to be able to require the presiding officer to cast his vote for him".[47] The Court turned down the opportunity to fashion relief for the voters from this for two reasons. First, the Court said that the revised regulation was not yet in force and "I can only look at the law as it stands at the present time".[48] Secondly, the Court questioned whether the men's distaste for entering the voting booth after women had been in it actually was "a point of customary law" — or was it, the Court asks, "merely a religious tenet or belief"?[49]

If the men were motivated solely by religion and not by customary rule, the Court seemed to be holding, then their actions would not be protected by the regulation, even if the revised version were in force, because it refers to "customary rules" and not to "religious tenets or beliefs". No one seems to have brought to the Court's attention s 5(1)(f) of the *Constitution* (Solomon Islands), which guarantees freedom of worship and belief. We cannot know, once the new regulation came into force, whether a Court might hold that it could not stand because it violated this Constitutional guarantee.[50]

We must wonder, because the Court's distaste for the religion practised by the twenty-two men seems to have been the core value driving the Court to the decision it reached on the law. The Court mentioned the fact that the men's actions discriminated against women only once, and only in the course of quoting the arguments made by counsel for the election officials.[51] The Court dwelt, however, on the fact that the men were, in its words, "non-christian".[52] They are, the Court noted more than once, "pagan".[53] They practise "the old religion"[54] which has rules that out of "fear" they will not disobey.[55] These are not words that a disinterested party would use to describe a religion other than her own. These are the words and concepts Christianity uses to impugn non-Christian religions. The Court's choice of words is evidence that the Court's dislike for the traditional religious beliefs of Solomon Islanders had little to do with their attitudes toward women and everything to do with the fact that they dared to be non-Christian.

The case was resolved (at least until the new regulations were in force) in favour of women, but the reasons for that resolution did not involve women's equality. It involved the inferiority, in the minds of a Christian judge, of all religions except Christianity. This is not an unusual viewpoint to find in Melanesia. Although the Pacific was colonised primarily for economic and political reasons, the colonisers often justified their brutal mission on the grounds that they were bringing the benefits of civilisation, law and religion in particular, to the savage pagans of the Pacific.[56] But if the colonisers were to convince themselves, let alone Pacific islanders, of the truth of this justification, they had to remain convinced at any cost, that Christianity was superior in all respects to the homegrown religions of the Pacific.[57] It is sad, but not surprising, therefore, to find that contemporary carriers of the colonial banner still believe it imperative to trumpet the merits of the Christian religion at the expense of other belief systems.

WOMEN AND COMPENSATION

In a 1991 case in Papua New Guinea a defendant pleaded guilty to the unlawful killing of his sister-in-law.[58] At the sentencing hearing the defendant argued that he should receive a light sentence because he would have to comply with the "customary obligation… to hand over one of his daughters for the deceased's family" to compensate them for the loss of their daughter.[59] As an example of gender discrimination the case is problematic. The defendant's willingness to give away a daughter seemed to the expatriate and urban communities, who read about the case over their morning newspapers, to mean that he and the customary rules he was following were treating a young woman with no more regard than they would treat a pig or a shell or any other kind of property that is normally given as part of a compensation agreement. However, the Court did not treat the matter as gender-related. Instead, the Court seemed to presume that the custom might apply to children of either sex. As such, the Court held that the custom was wrongful, not because it discriminated against women but because, to the Court's mind, it failed to care properly for children.

The Court was probably correct in finding that the custom of giving children in compensation applies to boys as well as to girls.[60] Nevertheless, the Court's analysis of the issues in the case would have benefited from a gendered approach. It is particularly ironic that the Court did not do so in this case because the judge, Doherty J., is a woman. Feminist jurisprudence teaches us to pay attention to the particularities of litigants' stories, to the context of their cases and to the narrative that gave rise to the issues.[61] Had the Court done this, it might have found a way to resolve the matter that affirmed the dignity and selfhood of the individuals involved without denying the integrity and value of their customs.

The Court, however, approached the case as if every instance in which a child is given in compensation to grieving parents is the same. There is nothing in the decision about the particular facts of this case, about how the defendant felt at giving up his child, about how the foster parents would treat the child. The Court held that the custom violated both the *Customs Recognition Act* [Cap 19] (PNG) and the *Constitution* (PNG). It would violate s 3 of the *Customs Recognition Act* because, to the Court's mind, it would be:

> contrary to the welfare of [a] child under sixteen years… and… contrary to the public interest to… reduce sentence where it was shown that a child or young person or even an adult was handed over by one group of people to another family or group in payment of obligations of some member of the child's clan or customary group.[62]

But, is it necessarily contrary to the welfare of a child to give her (or him) to grieving parents who will welcome a child to replace their lost daughter or son? The judge's words suggest that she believes it is never in 'the welfare of a child' to use the child in payment of an obligation. But, if the welfare of the child is at issue, ought not the inquiry to be into whether the child has been placed in a good and proper home rather than into the motivations that prompted the placement?

The Court's second reason for refusing to recognise and apply the custom was that the custom violated s 253 of the *Constitution* (PNG), which prohibits "slavery and the slave trade in all its forms, and all similar institutions and practices".[63] The Court reasoned that the custom of giving a child to replace the child one has killed is a practice similar to slavery:

> I am unable to trace any case law in our jurisdiction on the interpretation of this section [of the *Constitution*] and the word 'slavery' is not defined in our legislation... [but]... The International Convention on the Abolition of Slavery and the Slave Trade... refers to slavery as "the status or condition of a person over whom all or any other powers attaching to the right of ownership are exercised."[64]

Using this definition, the Court found that the defendant's obligation to part with his daughter was, in the words of s 253 of the *Constitution*, an institution or practice similar to slavery in two ways. First, the child had no say in the transaction. Secondondly, the defendant was "handing over... a child, or an adult, to another family or group in payment or recompense for the misdeeds of a third person".[65]

Despite the Court's care to find a definition of slavery, whether a practice is like slavery may be in the eye of the beholder. If it is slavery to place a child with a family without the child's consent then almost all foster placements and adoptions, wherever they happen, are practices similar to slavery, because the consent of the child is seldom sought. And if it is wrong to give a child in compensation for one that has been lost, then many common, and quite legal, practices are wrong. That reasoning would make it wrong for a poor woman to give up her child so that wealthier parents can raise the child. It would make it wrong for couples to pay surrogate mothers, to invest in fertility clinics or otherwise to compensate anyone for helping them to adopt or give birth to a child.[66] All these practices involve, either directly or indirectly, payment in connection with obtaining a child, the practice that seems to most anger the Court in this case.

Whether the gift of the child was in the child's welfare, whether it forced the child into slavery, depends upon the particular facts of the story. If the adopting family were intending actually to treat her as a daughter then it might not be against her welfare. It might not be slavery. If the child and her new family were from the same village the child's circumstances might not even change appreciably, despite the normative change in parents. In most Pacific villages children move freely around the village, cared for by every adult.[67] If, on the other hand, the adopting family were forever to hold her father's crime against the child, if she were made to work ceaselessly to pay his debt, then it would not be in her welfare. It would be slavery. We cannot decide this, however, without knowing more of the story behind the case.

In the end, the Court did not even decide the case on these grounds. Instead, the Court decided the case on the basis of evidentiary rules, holding that the existence and application of the custom had not been proved, and although "customary compliance is a matter that can be considered in mitigation" of sentence, "customs must be proved as a fact, that is by sworn evidence or affidavit evidence".[68] The Court was even aware that the custom did indeed exist, but nonetheless refused to recognise or apply it in the absence of sworn evidence put into the record by the defendant's counsel:

> I am aware of this Custom in that part of the Sepik from other cases but I consider in this situation before me where a submission by Counsel only is put forward is insufficient evidence that a custom exists, what the custom exactly is and whether the defendant has complied with it.[69]

In choosing to decide the case on this basis the Court may here have been reacting to other cases in which counsel had failed to prove custom as the statute required.[70] The Court may have been trying to send a message to counsel that courts would not apply customary law unless counsel did the work of presenting that law to them. It seems more likely, however, given the extensive *dicta* on the Court's view that this custom is unlawful and unconstitutional, that the Court wanted to be as certain as possible that no appeal would enable the defendant to get a mitigated sentence on account of this practice.

The people in every culture believe that they know what is in the welfare of their children. And they do. At least, they know what is in the welfare of the children of their culture. But cultures differ, and what may be in the welfare of the children of one culture is not necessarily good for the children of another culture. A child taught to honour the clan, to raise healthy pigs and to fight with bravery would do very well in the Highlands of Papua New Guinea but not so well in London. However, a child taught to find his station on the London Underground, to buy his lunch from the fish and chip shop and to conjugate Latin verbs would not survive for long in a Highlands village, no matter how well-prepared he was for English life.

In deciding *State v Kule*, Doherty J. seems to have confused the values, needs, interests and beliefs of Papua New Guinea culture with those of her own. In her culture, with its nuclear families and its consequent emphasis on the parent-child relationship, it might well be against the welfare of the child to be adopted for any reason other than that its adoptive parents intend to cherish it. In Papua New Guinea's villages, however, it may be less necessary for the state to put its efforts into strengthening the parent-child bond, because children are loved and cared for by every adult in their extended family or clan. In Papua New Guinea, it may well be in the best interests of this child to move from one village household to another, so long as she will be loved in both, and especially as she will know that, in doing so, she is helping to preserve her father's honour and the good relations of everyone in the village.

CONCLUSIONS AND AFTERTHOUGHTS

We have looked at three cases that might have been about custom's treatment of women, but turned out to be about other things entirely. *Public Prosecutor v Kota* was about the powers of chiefs in Vanuatu's dual political system. *Talusui v Tone-ewane* was about religion in Solomon Islands. And *The State v Joseph Kule* was about the welfare of children. In at least two of the cases the judges recognised that women were being made the subjects of discrimination but in none of them did the courts see it as their job to put an end to gender discrimination. This blindness on the part of the state legal system, these examples of indirect discrimination, permitted the direct discrimination of customary law to continue unchecked.

The cases demonstrate the varieties of indirect discrimination that Imrana Jalal has identified.[71] The proposed regulation described in *Talusui v Tone-ewane* was gender-neutral on its face but would have had a discriminatory impact on women, a result the Court failed to consider. In *The State v Joseph Kule* the judge's social and cultural attitudes blinded her to the possible realities of the situation. And, in *Public Prosecutor v Kota* the judgment did not necessarily correct the discrimination created by custom.

These cases raise a number of questions and issues about custom, state law and gender. In particular they make us realise that women are the subjects of double discrimination. They are directly discriminated against by custom — at least by custom as it operates today — and they are indirectly discriminated against by a state legal system that fails to redress the problems caused by custom. How might women's lives differ if judges recognised and redressed gender imbalances? How differently might these cases have been decided if the judges focused on gender? The decisions raise issues for the lawyers who represent women as well. The discriminatory nature of certain customary norms and practices must be carefully spelled out to the courts by counsel if we expect the courts to act in favour of women's rights to equality at all.

Finally, the cases raise questions about the treatment in the courts of custom and customary law. In each of these cases, state courts refused to recognise and apply a customary norm. And, in each case, the court did so for a different reason. In one case, the customary practice conflicted with the Court's notion of proper religious expression. In another, the customary norm was at odds with the Court's view of the separation that ought to be maintained between the chiefly and parliamentary spheres of government. In the third the Court believed that custom did not take due regard of the welfare of children.

Whether custom or the state courts is correct in each of these instances is not the most important question. The more important inquiry is why customary law and the law of courts and constitutions continue, more than a quarter-century after most Pacific nations came into being, to be so far apart. What can be done to bring them into better conjunction with one another so that citizens do not feel themselves torn between two legal systems placing conflicting duties and obligations upon them?

We who would like to do better are faced with a problem. We want to respect the integrity of the indigenous cultures of the Pacific, but we also want those cultures to act in ways that affirm the integrity and dignity of all persons. How do we accomplish both these goals? The state courts have so far failed to find the proper balance. In the cases we have discussed in this chapter, the courts have interfered with indigenous cultures without creating laws that improve the lives of women. How do we, and the courts, do better?

ENDNOTES

1   Jalal, P.I. 1998. *Law for Pacific Women: A Legal Rights Handbook*. Suva: Fiji Women's Rights Movement at p15.

2   Counts, D.A. Brown, J.K. and Campbell, J.C. (eds.) 1999. *To Have and to Hit: Cultural Perspectives on Wife Beating* (2nd Edition). Chicago: University of Illinois Press; Toft, S. (ed.) 1985. *Domestic Violence in Papua New Guinea (Monograph No. 3)*. Boroko: Papua New Guinea Law Reform Commission; Zorn, J.G. 1994–95. Women, Custom and State Law in Papua New Guinea. *Third World Legal Studies*. 1994–95: 169–205.

3   See, for example, the references collected in Counts, D.A. Brown, J.K. and Campbell, 1999. Above n 2, pp 299–301; Papua New Guinea Supreme Court. 1991. *Annual Report of the Judges 1990*. Port Moresby: Government Printing Office, p 7.

4   See above, n 1 at p 16.

5   See above, n 1 at p 16.

6   Kaganis, F. and Murray, C. 1991. Law, Women and the Family: The Question of Polygyny in a New South Africa. *Acta Juridica* 1991: 116–132; Jessep, O. 1992. The Governor General's Wives – Polygamy and the Recognition of Customary Marriage in Papua New Guinea. *Australian Journal of Family Law* 1992: 29–49.

7   See Zorn elsewhere in this section and the cases and articles on brideprice discussed and cited therein.

8   Gailey, C.W. 1987. *Kinship to Kingship: Gender Hierarchy and State Formation in the Tongan Islands*. Austin: University of Texas Press; Berndt, R.M. and Lawrence, P. (eds.) 1971. *Politics in New Guinea*. Nedlands, W.A.: University of Western Australia Press.

9   See above, n 1 at p 16.

10 The case, discussed below, is *Public Prosecutor v Kota*, Unreported, Supreme Court of the Republic of Vanuatu, Criminal Case No. 58 of 1993, 31st August 1993.

11 That case, also discussed below, is *Talusui v Tone-ewane* [1986] S.I.L.R. 140. The Solomon Island Law Reports are available at many court and university libraries throughout the Pacific.

12 *The State v Joseph Kule*, Unreported, The National Court of Justice of Papua New Guinea, N1034 of 1991. The case is on file at the University of Papua New Guinea and the University of the South Pacific Law School libraries.

13 So they are described by the court in *Public Prosecutor v Kota*, above n 10 at p 2.

14 Throughout Melanesia village meetings are the customary proceedings through which disputes are resolved. The meetings are usually called by one of the parties to the dispute, though sometimes friends, kinspeople or chiefs organise the meeting. Everyone in the village, everyone related to the parties, anyone with an interest in the dispute, is encouraged to attend and to speak at the meeting. Unlike a trial in a state court which follows strict rules of evidence and procedure, and at which discussion is limited to the particular issue that brought the parties to the trial, village meetings range broadly over all the issues that have arisen between the parties. The aim of the meeting is not to declare that one party has won and the other lost, but to resolve the dispute between them through compromise or consensus. To that end, chiefs or other leaders of the meeting do

not act as judges, issuing rulings and deciding the case. Instead, they tend to act as mediators, trying to bring the parties to a conclusion that both can agree upon. A chief may state his opinion about what the parties should do. A chief may remind the parties of the values of their society. But the chief will not force an outcome. Thus, while the chiefs in this case ordered Marie to go back to Tanna, they did not order her to go back to her husband. They believed she should, they said she should, they obviously hoped that, once in Tanna, she would decide to do it. But they did not order it. They refrained from making that order, just as chiefs involved in village meetings have always refrained from making orders, because, in traditional Melanesia, there were no police to enforce the orders of chiefs. Chiefs could depend upon being obeyed only when people agreed with what the chief had said so chiefs did not go beyond what people would do. The chiefs could use their power to get Marie back to Tanna, but they did not have the power to make her stay with Walter. For further information on the village meeting as a cornerstone of customary legal procedure, see Epstein, A.L. (ed.) 1974. *Contention and Dispute: Aspects of Law and Social Control in Melanesia.* Canberra: Australian National University; Nader, L. and Todd, H.F. (eds.) 1978. *The Disputing Process – Law in Ten Societies.* New York: Columbia University Press; Adamson Hoebel, E. 1979. *The Law of Primitive Man.* New York: Atheneum.

15 See above, n 10 at p 2.

16 Plane flights between Port Vila and Tanna take under an hour but they are expensive. Ni-Vanuatu villagers are more likely to travel on one of the many small cargo and passenger boats that are a major means of commercial transportation amongst the several islands that make up the archipelago. Even though the boat trip between Port Vila and Tanna takes two days it is considerably less expensive than a plane trip. Nonetheless it is costly enough so that the average villager would not do it often.

17 The decision does not say so but she probably would not have been able to afford the fare to return without the assistance of the Association.

18 See *Penal Code* [Cap. 135] (Vanuatu), ss 35 (incitement) and 105(b) (kidnapping).

19 See above, n 10 at p 4.

20 See above, n 10 at p 3.

21 *Penal Code* [Cap 135] (Vanuatu).

22 See above, n 10 at p 4. Counsel for the defendants might also have intended to raise custom as a mitigating factor at the sentencing stage, but I doubt they did so after the court's decision on the merits.

23 The case was a subject for much discussion in the expatriate community at the time and for several years after, mostly as an example of the misogyny of custom.

24 See, for example, the Court's comment near the end of the decision: "It is up to the Parliament of this Nation to consider whether any amendments need to be made with the Constitution or other Legislation to clarify what is the role of the Chiefs" above, n 10 at p 4.

25 See above, n 10 at p 4.

26 See above, n 10 at p 4.

27 See *Constitution* (Vanuatu) Art. 5(1)(b) (liberty) and Art. 5(1)(i) (freedom of movement); *Penal Code* [Cap 135] (Vanuatu) s 105(b).

28 See above, n 10 at p 4.

29 See above, n 10 at p 4.

30 See above, n 10 at p 2.

31 See above, n 10 at p 4.

32 To be fair, the Court is also concerned that chiefs act in ways that do not discriminate against women: "I think it is very important that if the role of the Chiefs is clarified by legislation, the fundamental rights of women in Vanuatu must be protected", above n 10 at p 4.

33 The discussion of chiefly powers in this and the following paragraphs of the text is taken from Zorn, J.G. 1994. *Custom and Customary Law (Book Two)*. Suva: University of the South Pacific Extension.

34 The Council of Chiefs "has a general competence to discuss all matters relating to custom and tradition", may make recommendations for the preservation and promotion of ni-Vanuatu culture and languages, and may be consulted on any matter in any bill before Parliament, particularly on bills relating to tradition and custom. See *Constitution* (Vanuatu), Art 29. In addition, Article 74 provides that Parliament may, after consultation with the Council of Chiefs, enact a national land law.

35 See, for example, *Kaliopa v Silao*, Unreported, High Court of American Samoa, Land and Title Division, 1983; *Mose v Masame*, [1930–49] WSLR 140; *McMoore et al. v Popoali'i et al.*, Unreported, High Court of American Samoa, Land and Title Division, LT No. 20–88, 1989.

36 *Talusui v Tone-ewane* Above, n 11.

37 See above, n 11 at p 141.

38 See above, n 11 at p 141.

39 Actually, it was counsel for the election officials who mentioned the possibly discriminatory impact of requiring women to wait until the men had voted, but the Court approved of counsel's submission, calling it a reasonable argument. See above, n 11 at p 142.

40 *Local Government (Elections) Regulations* (Solomon Islands), s 20(d) paraphrased in *Talusui v Tone-ewane* above, n 11, at p 142.

41 *Local Government (Elections) Regulations* (Solomon Islands), s 20(d).

42 *Local Government (Elections) Regulations* (Solomon Islands), s 20(g).

43 See above, n 11 at p 142.

44 Courts have available a variety of methods to help them interpret statutes. This court chose to look only at the 'plain meaning' of the statute — what the words, on their face, seem to say. A positivist court (a court that prefers to apply the rules as written, rather to look at the policies or purposes behind the rules) would probably insist that, in interpreting a statute, it is limited to the statute's 'plain meaning' unless that meaning is not plain. Unless, that is, the statute is itself confusing or ambiguous. Most courts today, however, will look to the purpose that the statute is intended to serve, regardless of whether there is an ambiguity on the face of the statute, because most judges today would prefer to enforce the law that was actually intended, rather than some typographical error

that has crept into the law and made it into a mockery of itself. Courts that interpret statutes by looking to the policies and purposes they are meant to serve can find those policies and purposes in three ways — by reading the preamble or other purposive language contained in the statute, by looking to the legislative history for clues as to what Parliament intended when it enacted the bill, or by drawing the purpose from the general language and effect of the statute.

45 See above, n 11 at p 142.

46 The Court might have decided not to use this argument because the case was not actually brought by the disenfranchised men themselves, but by the losing candidate for elected office, who claimed he might have won had they voted for him.

47 See above, n 11 at p 143.

48 Yes, but: If it had wanted an outcome that supported the 22 non-voters, the Court could have taken the proposed change in the legislation, especially since it was close to coming into force, as a signal that government policy favoured a broad interpretation of the regulation so as not to disenfranchise voters. See above, n 11 at p 143.

49 See above, n 11 at p 143.

50 The Court could hardly be unaware of the existence of Sec. 5(1)(f) of the *Constitution*. It is possible that the Court felt unable to use it because it had not been brought to the Court's attention by counsel. It is also possible that the Court was unwilling to use it for the reasons discussed in this chapter.

51 See above, n 11 at p 142.

52 See above, n 11 at p 141.

53 See above, n 11 at, p142 (three times), p143 (once) and p144 (once).

54 See above, n 11 at p 141.

55 See above, n 11 at p 142.

56 See Moorehead, N. 1966. *The Fatal Impact: The Invasion of the South Pacific 1767–1840*. London: Hamish Hamilton at pp 79–85; Howe, K.R. 1984. *Where the Waves Fall: A New South Sea Islands History From First Settlement to Colonial Rule*. Sydney and London: Allen & Unwin at pp 288–318.

57 In the event, Christianity was spread so successfully that it could now be considered the new custom of the islands.

58 *The State v Joseph Kule*. Above, n 12.

59 See above, n 12 at p 4.

60 Freedman, M.P. 1970. Social Organization of a Siassi Community. In Harding. T.G. and Wallace. B.J. (eds.) *Cultures of the Pacific*. London: Collier Macmillan. 159–179, at p 166.

61 Weisberg, D.K. (ed.) 1993. F*eminist Jurisprudence: Foundations*. Philadelphia: Temple University Press.

62 See above, n 12 at pp 4–5. Section 3(1)(b) of the *Customs Recognition Act* [Cap. 19] forbids the recognition by state courts of customs that are contrary to the best interests of a child under sixteen years, and s 3(1)(a) forbids the recognition of customs that are contrary to the public interest. For an excellent discussion of customary law as it relates to the best interests of children, see McCrae, H. 1981. *Cases and Materials on Family Law –*

Part III: Custody, Maintenance, De Facto Relationships and Ex-Nuptial Children. Port Moresby: University of Papua New Guinea. At pp. 2–7 and McCrae, H. 1982. Reform of Family Law in Papua New Guinea. In Weisbrot, D. Paliwala, A. and Sawyer, A. (eds.) *Law and Social Change in Papua New Guinea.* Sydney: Butterworths. 127–148.

63 I do not know of a Papua New Guinean society that had a slave class. I am therefore left to wonder where this constitutional provision came from. Usually, fundamental rights provisions refer to wrongs that the government itself (or a previous government) has committed.

64 See above, n 12 at p 5.

65 See above, n 12 at p 5.

66 All of these practices have been held legal by courts in various jurisdictions. See Areen, J.K. 1999. *Family Law* (4th ed.) Westbury, New York: Foundation Press and Saban, C. 1999. *Miracle Child: Genetic Mother, Surrogate Womb.* New York: New Horizon Press.

67 Mead, M. 1930. *Growing Up in New Guinea.* New York: Mentor.

68 See above, n 12 at p 4, citing *Henry Aisi v Malaita Hoala* [1981] PNGLR 199, at p 203.

69 See above, n 12 at p 4.

70 The *Customs Recognition Act*, s 2(1), required custom to be proven as a fact. It has been superceded recently by the *Underlying Law Act* 2000, which provides that custom is law and can be found by judicial notice. So, under the new Act, the fact that the custom was notorious enough for the judge to know about it would probably have meant that the judge could not refuse to recognise it, at least not on evidentiary grounds.

71 See above, n 9 and accompanying text.

7. RITES, WHITES AND MIGHT: A CRITIQUE OF THE EFFECT OF THE REVIVAL OF CUSTOMARY LAW UPON THE AUTONOMY OF INDIGENOUS WOMEN

By: Susan Bothmann

KEY TERMS AND PHRASES

Aboriginal

Generally of people, animals or plants existing in a place from the earliest time or from before the arrival of colonists. The initial inhabitants of Australia were once most commonly called **Aborigines** but this term has been replaced more recently by the term Aboriginal(s).

Assimilation

To absorb and integrate people, ideas or cultures into a wider or more dominant society or culture. To remove the differences exhibited by one nation or group by having it swallowed up into the mainstream. This concept was a deliberate policy of white politicians in Australia for a time, in order to get the Aboriginal population to disappear.

Critique

A detailed analysis and assessment of something, especially a literary, philosophical, artistic or political theory. The process of discussing critically.

Essentialism

A view that things have a certain set of characteristics, or an essence, that makes them what they are. In the context of categories of people, the idea that there exist defining characteristics that make, for example, all women, women; or all Aboriginals, Aboriginals and that members of those groups always contain those characteristics.

Exponential

Originally a mathematical term. Describes the expansion of a thing at a rate where each item increases the capacity for further increases (like population growth). Used generally to describe ever faster growth.

Governance

The actions taken by a governing body or the manner in which a government governs.

Indigenous

Originating or occurring naturally in a particular place. Native. Describes plants, animals and groups of people that are known to hail from a specific area before any other similar stock could have been introduced there.

Lores

A body of traditions and knowledge held by some particular group. Typically passed from person to person by word of mouth. Often used to describe the rules governing the behaviour of indigenous peoples to contrast them from western style laws.

Mores (Pronouced mor-ays).

The essential or characteristic customs or conventions exhibited by a social group. Acceptable habits and modes of behaviour particularly identifying a specific group of people. Always expressed as a plural noun.

Patriarchal

A patriarch is the male head of a family or tribe. A patriarchal situation is any situation where men dominate or have power by virtue of being male.

Postmodernism

A late 20th century style and concept originating in the visual arts and extending into criticism and philosophical debate. It represents a departure from the ideas of modernism. It consists of a general distrust of grand theories and ideologies. Postmodernists try to break down concepts into smaller bits or peel back the layers of notions inherent in any one notion to highlight the invalidity of general overarching claims or ideas.

Poststructuralism

An extension and critique of structuralism. (Structuralism is the idea that a thing's structure is more important than what it is used for, its function.) Both structuralism and its aftermath are largely French approaches to interpreting language. Jacques Derrida is the most well known exponent. He started writing in the 1960's about deconstructing ideas. His ideas were developed further by departing from structuralism's idea of objectivity. Poststructuralism argues that all things have pluralities and deferred meanings.

INTRODUCTION

> *I always say that I'm Aboriginal first… Then I'm a mother, daughter, sister, aunt, cousin, woman, historian, etc.*[1]

> *I find it difficult to say I'm black first and a woman second or vice versa. I can't make that kind of distinction.*[2]

Why should these two Australian Aboriginal women be confronted by an apparent identity conflict? The first question, I suggest, is not how they choose between these hierarchical notions of self, but why they should feel an inclination to do so at all.

This notion of dissecting oneself and parcelling pieces of one's identity up into special categories is a practice that comes from western models of thought and theory[3] and has had no place in some other social constructs, including the traditional backgrounds from which these two women come. Many traditional indigenous communities do not share western conceptualisations of themselves or their societies. Rather, life is an holistic and integrated experience. This different approach to living has been recognised by western outsiders and sometimes idealised,[4] sometimes derided.

Customary social structures, customary law, and pre-colonial behavioural norms continue to exert influence upon the lives of most indigenous communities to some extent, both practically and theoretically. Now some indigenous communities are seeking to renew their customary ideas and practices as an overt political project.

In examining the *concept* of Custom[5] one must ask whether a return to a customary legal system (which may resolve the quest for identity) will be helpful in achieving political autonomy[6] for indigenous women of colour. Or may Custom become a vehicle for *indigenous men* to further disempower and oppress indigenous women?

Adopting customary law as part of the legal system applicable to indigenous people in post-colonial circumstances may increase the oppression experienced by indigenous women unless those women are awake to the structures and interpretations that are placed on Custom by men, indigenous and non-indigenous.

In analysing whether indigenous women's quest for cultural identity is theoretically inconsistent with a desire for autonomy (where such identity is based upon a return to traditional social and legal mores) it will be assumed that indigenous women want both a special identity and autonomy for themselves.[7]

"One cannot claim to be either impartial or comprehensive, nor can one claim to speak for everyone, to everyone, nor about everything."[8] Speaking from the position of 'outsider' one can hope nevertheless to be seen as a sympathetic outsider with some claims to insight into the dilemma faced by the women in the particular communities referred to here.

POSITIONING FEMINIST DISCOURSE IN THE DEBATE ABOUT CUSTOM

Recent developments in jurisprudence have been rapid, exponential and diverse. Critical Legal Studies (CLS), Feminist Legal Theor(ies) and Critical Race Theory (CRT) have been launched, extended, inter-related and critiqued. Postmodernism has infiltrated legal philosophy. Generally these discourses have tended to focus on western style legal systems.

The political implications of feminism have been widely explored, for example:

> Feminism challenges the construction of knowledge about ourselves and the Other, and is not confined to the critique of a particular discipline. It is also an engaged political project — it seeks knowledge in order to change the 'condition of women'.[9]

Feminist legal scholarship has burgeoned in the past two decades. The most recent developments in feminist legal theory have tended towards "fragmentation, individuation and uncertainty":

> This postmodernist approach challenges the notion that women can be encapsulated within some single theory of society and law; denies that the interests of all women are the same, as if there is some 'essential women' (*sic*) imbued with the characteristics and needs of every woman, irrespective of age, race or class.[10]

Women of colour have played a vital role in highlighting the limitations of thinking about 'woman' as 'essential'.[11] Non-white female scholars and commentators have berated white feminists for contributing to the plight of women of colour.[12] They argue that throughout any colonial period of interaction between white western colonisers and indigenous populations, white women have participated actively in the oppression of the coloured minority, including and often, in particular, its women.

White women, whilst undoubtedly victims of oppression themselves, are clearly not innocent victims free from implication in the dominating and controlling of women of colour.[13] Women of colour argue that today's white middle class feminists cannot appreciate the needs of, cannot represent and cannot incorporate the struggle of non-white women.[14]

Some women of colour recognise a 'collective otherness' based on being non-white but they also insist that their particular circumstances set them apart from each other as well.[15] Some women of colour who feel marginalised or excluded from mainstream feminism identify one version of difference.[16] Their emphasis on difference is to deny essentialism. Their scholarship highlights their personal experiences. Racism is as great or greater a form of oppression against them, participated in by white women, than sexism. Because this is the reality they experience, they know they must consider the practical and theoretical implications of supporting the views of and seeking solidarity with their own menfolk against whites of both sexes.[17] Such theoretical considerations also link difference with identity.

It has become very important for 'post-colonial' indigenous communities to regain their traditions and customs. Indigenous people themselves perceive this return to their own ways as a casting off of the western imposed yoke. It becomes a way of re-establishing their particular identity in the world. A global movement towards recognising and incorporating elements of customary legal systems into 'mainstream' systems in countries that have indigenous populations has emerged. This trend is evident in Australia particularly in relation to Aboriginal land claims,[18] and is manifest in Vanuatu where it has been specifically provided for in the *Constitution*.[19]

'Difference' is also a theoretical construct behind the desire to return to or renew customary systems. Western democratic, capitalistic legal systems are held to be inappropriate to indigenous populations who crave a social system based on norms which accord with their cultural aspirations. They seek self-determination or the right to be different. This issue of the role, if any, for traditional lores in women's lives is a current concern for indigenous women. It has been raised in relation to Australian Aboriginal women,[20] Canadian first nation peoples, American native peoples[21] and peoples of the Pacific.[22]

An extensive body of knowledge has accumulated to establish what customary rules really are.[23] There continues to be controversy about the fact that *general knowledge of particular* customs is often based on evidence gathered by white anthropologists about certain indigenous rites and social regulations. Beyond the elements of any one customary system the general or non-specific idea of Custom is a fluid concept. In some places there remains a lively and vital tradition. In other places it has been absorbed and must be actively reconstructed by indigenous people. The trend towards a revival of Custom has raised two issues directly important to women.

First, it is perceived by some that traditional mechanisms of social control may be more oppressive towards the women in those societies and more limiting of women's scope for equal rights and humane treatment than a western human rights perspective.[24] This can be seen, for example, in those countries where there has been a (re)turning to fundamentalism.[25] 'Oppression' itself is a complex concept:

> Actually a family of concepts, oppression has five aspects... exploitation, marginalisation, powerlessness, cultural imperialism, and violence.[26]

From the perspective of indigenous women of colour, while they may endorse the reaffirmation of traditional and cultural mores as a way of asserting their own cultural or racial identity within the larger social environment, they are mindful that this approach can be a means of reducing or taking away some of their hard won 'rights'. It can also create an environment in which the struggle for further rights is made more difficult.[27] Consider, for example, a ni-Vanuatu woman trying to reconcile her individual right to cast a secret ballot in general elections with her husband's expectation that she will vote as he directs.

Secondly, there has emerged a body of scholarship driven by indigenous women themselves which posits the notion that Custom has been 'bastardised' by exposure to white western legal theories and it is now impossible or dangerous to revert to those systems. This thinking starts from the premise that interaction between the indigenous population and the colonial force has been conducted within a framework of western patriarchal power. Even at its most friendly, interest shown in indigenous ways has been by men about 'men's business'.[28] Where in traditional cultures there was or is a parallel, respected and 'equal' stream of 'women's business' this has been given no attention and has been overshadowed.[29]

Implementation of a political theory encompassing a revival of customary lores could therefore have the negative effect of doubly oppressing indigenous women because indigenous men may take advantage of the imbalance created by an exclusively male perspective that already taints Custom. Indigenous women were indisputably oppressed during colonialism, now they face the prospect of further oppression by having any traditional autonomy reduced. Further, indigenous men may use Custom as a vehicle to shame women into submission by suggesting that any opposition to Custom would be a disloyalty to the collective identity.[30]

Postmodern/poststructural feminists and race/ethnicity feminists recognise that there are diverse forms of power and identity. They share hostility to the ideas of a singular conception of power, and of women as a group. The former deconstruct universalising "procedures in modes of thought"[31] by showing that these procedures are not neutral but are connected with dominance. In other words, they break down or unpack the elements that lie behind universal concepts and show that in fact they are loaded with value laden assumptions. Those unstated assumptions can allow notions of domination to be continued, implicitly. By contrast, race/ethnicity feminists typically interpret diversity in relation to power and identity in a more cautious way.[32] They note that supposedly recognised differences between ethnic groups are often perceived as different because of different power positions between the observer and the observed.

It is possible to engage in a deconstruction of the *notion* of Custom (to show that it is not a neutral concept) without *threatening* the utility of any customary system as a political vehicle and without denying the fundamental importance of Custom as a sign or indication of identity.

The indigenous women at the Fourth World Conference of Women, held in Beijing, argued for a global strategy that the women's movement struggle be in terms of self-determination, rather than gender equality. This is because self-determination is an inclusive concept, incorporating women's right to determine their political status, and economic and social development.[33] This quest by indigenous women for self-determination in the context of gender may have arisen as an ideological offshoot from the postcolonial movements by indigenous peoples to establish their rights to reassert their cultural identities.[34]

Invariably, indigenous people have experienced and are experiencing cultural schizophrenia as a result of colonialisation. That is not to say the experience of every indigenous person is the same but there is no indigenous community that has not been put upon to some extent by another culture. One solution adopted to overcome this psychological and political dislocation has been for indigenous communities of colour to look to reaffirming their own cultural mores and re-establishing personal and collective identities from within the refreshed elements of their unique cultures.

> It is hard to walk the lines between the two cultures... We do not want to adopt the whiteness of the dominant culture. We want to preserve our brownness... We are happy to be who we are and we are fighting to protect that identity... to allow our culture to continue to live.[35]

The political framework for this quest for indigenous identity arises in part as a reaction to broad based policies of assimilation practised in many places until fairly recently, including Australia and Canada. These policies and practices are perceived by the victims of this approach as a nearly effective form of genocide. Women of colour have also argued that, in theoretical terms, white feminist essentialising of women is another aspect of an assimilationist approach.

Indigenous women of colour acknowledge that they experience being outsiders in relation to their own communities as a product of their gender but they focus more on describing the overwhelming experience and greater sense of 'outsiderhood' in the context of their race and colonised status. Yet the 'corrosive psychic effects'[36] of discrimination as a form of 'spirit murder'[37] is not something that every woman experiences in the same way. For indigenous women seeking their own identities through Custom that process itself can constitute further spirit murder if they find their own spiritual needs being denied. Since the role of Custom is theoretically relevant only as it applies *within its own community*, the element of otherness arises in a purely gender context. In other words, women can feel excluded from the source of their spiritual heritage by being rendered 'outsiders' in their own world solely because of their gender.

WHAT IS CUSTOM? SOME MODELS CONSIDERED

> True 'tribal law' is probably dead everywhere.[38]

> [H]uman communities are living beings that continue to change; while there may be a concept of the 'traditional Indian'... no such being has ever existed. All along there have been changes.[39]

The western model or paradigm of distinguishing our 'legal system' from other spheres of human activity and defining 'laws' specifically as rules for correct behaviour has little place in those social constructs described (from the perspective of the western paradigm) as customary legal systems. Whilst indigenous peoples invariably have (or in some cases, had) modes for organising social governance, these 'systems' might differ widely in content. It is nevertheless possible to identify some common features.

> Traditional societies have no culture of individual rights. They maintain their structure and coherence through a culture of duties.[40]

No thorough or systematic study of customs and traditions in Melanesia[41] has been carried out but it is clear that throughout the area "law is not quantifiable as an autonomous institution, but is an aspect of the total way of life of the people".[42] In the Vanuatu island communities, for example, there is no traditional body of laws that is only understood and applied by specific operatives with special knowledge, such as judges, lawmakers or specifically trained chiefs. There is social order, discipline and control, and many of the languages[43] include terms that recognise the concepts of codes of conduct, ethics and values, but not the 'rule of law'.[44]

In Melanesian communities there is no 'law' as a definable, isolated concept, but there is a way of life combining the present with the future. The nearest term to describe the concept is the expression *pasin*[45] a pidgin rendering of 'fashion'. The notion of law must include "the ways of the people in their total environment, both physical and metaphysical, tangible and intangible, concrete and abstract".[46]

Similarly, when Australian Aboriginal Hobbles Danayarri says "[m]y law only one"[47] he is referring to the concept of the Dreaming which is a set of principles governing all human behaviour and indeed the laws of the universe.[48]

A recurring feature of indigenous cultures is a heavy emphasis on the relationship between the community and the land and some form of collective responsibility towards land.[49] These concepts clearly pre-date any contact with the later colonising powers.

The Australian Aboriginal people have suffered a 200-year period of oppression at the hands of the colonisers and during that time have had their own traditions badly damaged, and in many cases wholly destroyed. This has not been a uniform process. Some communities of people, now described as 'urban aborigines', have been completely dispossessed from their lands and the framework of their cultures by forced separations from their families and by numerous other means.[50] Other groups, sometimes geographically distinguished as those still living in the desert areas and the 'outback', have retained substantial elements of their older lifestyles and belief systems. These people have struggled to maintain their identities as members of their Aboriginal communities.

The Melanesian experience in Vanuatu is unique. The colonisers there were French and English planters and pastoralists, Catholic and Protestant missionaries, government administrators from both colonising powers and stray 'rascals' who came in numbers to exploit first the whales, then the sandalwood[51] and other prized timbers, and finally the human economic resource. Hundreds of men were stolen away or 'blackbirded' to work virtually as slaves in Queensland cane fields.[52]

In both places the litany of introduced diseases, rape and pillage, Christianisation and the removal of people to missions, development of farms, stations and plantations and outright murder of the local populations has been the legacy of colonisation for the indigenous communities. It is only fairly recently that the colonisers and others in the west have come to understand the extent of the damage inflicted and the continued struggle by the local people to retain their heritage. The process of cultural disintegration was not a simple, straightforward one. Some Aboriginal men 'joined' the outback stations as stockmen whilst others did not. Some Melanesian men and women went to Queensland more than once and some never returned home. Cargo cults[53] were born as a way of explaining and making sense of why whites seemed to be so much better off materially than the local people. Whatever the impetus the result was inevitably disruption to an existing way of life. In neither Australia nor Vanuatu did the indigenous populations have a tradition of writing as it is known in the west. Customs are recorded through usage and oral accounts.

'Returning' to Custom is more than a symbolic strategy for many groups. In Australia the notion of incorporating aboriginal customary law into the municipal laws has been extensively examined.[54] Whilst in general there is little move to recognise customary law, in the context of native title it is the basis upon which decisions determining ownership will be made.[55] Similarly in Vanuatu 'Kastom' has been legislated into the legal system and in land matters it is the determining factor.[56]

In Vanuatu the adoption of Custom is a conscious ideology initiated by those who pushed for independence. It is a clear example of a community wanting to give credence and value to its own creeds and codes of social control as a means of re-establishing a unique identity.[57] In Australia, colonialism, which continues to exist, has governed the context in which customary rules are allowed to be determinative within the traditional environment because the colonial power (the Australian government) has made the rules about that. The Aboriginal people themselves have virtually no power to determine how effective their own 'laws' can be. If they follow their own laws they are sometimes breaking 'white-man's law.'

The great difficulty in the implementation of Custom as a matter of practice is the problem of deciding what Custom is. Where do genuine precepts come from after there has been so much disruption? Custom changes, even without traumatic interventions. Dynamic systems respond to new situations. Despite the common western misconception that customs are somehow 'written in stone',[58] they are neither ageless nor immovable. Whilst communities understand that there has been a profound impact during the colonising years on their means of social organisation they nevertheless crave a returning to something genuine and wholly their own. This is as true for indigenous women as it is for the men.

WHERE ARE THE WOMEN'S VOICES?

In Melanesian communities the division of labour is generally drawn on gender lines.[59] This is not uncommon in traditional indigenous societies. Only recently have we come to see that throughout the pre-colonial period there existed in traditions a body of knowledge that was exclusively female.

'Women's business' is also emerging as an ongoing vital tradition among Australian Aboriginals. Pat O'Shane refers to three specific anthropological re-examinations and notes:

[A]ltogether, then it would appear that far from being 'abject pawns in the games of male political power' Aboriginal women enjoyed a greater degree of economic, social and political power than did women in Western society.[60]

Yet one needs to look very deeply into the literature generated by western academics and anthropologists to find any mention of aspects of traditional lore that might spring from and be fostered by women predominantly, or exclusively.

In 1955 Colin Simpson wrote a book of "vivid studies of Melanesia"[61] called *Islands of Men*.[62] It commences with an "Author's Note: Why Islands of Men" in which he writes:

> Melanesia *seems to me* to be *characteristically* male, and Polynesia female... in the 'Black Islands' to the west [of Polynesia] the women are *less attractive* than their Polynesian sisters. The *warrior male* is, dramatically and even savagely, the figure *dominant* in *our* Melanesian image. (The emphasis is mine).

One could write a whole essay unpacking that snippet, but there is more. Later in the book Simpson relates a story told to him by one Tom Harrisson who had come to the New Hebrides as a biologist with the Oxford Expedition. Harrisson describes ridgetop Santo villages "where the menstruating women are kept in cages at one end and fed through the bars with bananas".[63] Simpson further reports Harrisson as saying "[L]ife was good in those [communal] houses. In the night, if you were careful, you could get anywhere. In most parts one does not see enough of the ordinary life of the women. Here one saw more than enough".[64]

Simpson is described on the dust jacket as a "trained observer" but no other qualifications are revealed. He wrote three other books entitled respectively, *Adam in Orche: Inside Aboriginal Australia*, *Adam with Arrows: Inside New Guinea* and *Adam in Plumes*. One is left to wonder about Eve.

In 1965 P. Lawrence and M. J. Meggitt edited a book containing articles about Melanesian religions.[65] In it R. B. Lane[66] wrote a piece about the people of South Pentecost[67]. He[68] describes a situation illustrating a decision making process:

> In the evening around the cooking fire in the communal men's house where every event of the day is brought forth, re-created, and dissected for the edification and pleasure of the group, he presented his experiences... The discussion went on through most of the night... The ultimate consensus of opinion was that W. had actually had an encounter with a spirit-being.[69]

He talks about analysis taking place in group discussions and notes that "individual conclusions are not necessarily disclosed in public".[70] The analysis he describes takes place in the absence of the women who are presumably having similar conversations in their own communal house from which the writer is excluded. 'Public' presumably means the collective of men, women and children of the village. Perhaps women also decline to disclose their discussions in public. The notion that every event of the day is discussed by the men begs serious questions about what the women experience all day long.

Later in the article we find a subheading, "Graded Society".[71] This section runs for four pages. Having given three full paragraphs of explanation about the men's grading system, the fourth small paragraph states:

> Associated with the men's graded society is a less elaborate women's graded society. There are three basic grades with subdivisions and each of the grades may be repeated at different times in different ways. The taking of these women's grades is sometimes linked with the achievements in the men's society by a woman's son or husband.[72]

So much for that, now let's get back to eight more paragraphs about the important stuff of men's grades. Even the scant material about the women's system is relevant only in so far as it arises from achievements of the woman's male kin.

This selectivity mechanism is frequently repeated and has been increasingly identified by feminist writers.[73] Its effect is to rub out matters of interest and concern to indigenous women and thereby render the women completely devoid of any political voice for themselves. Deborah Bird Rose discusses this phenomenon of erasure[74] in the context of Aboriginal native title land claims. Indigenous knowledge systems include boundaries of exclusion and silence across gender lines. She argues that colonisation has had the effect of importing western European notions of gender into the Australian consciousness and land claims are squeezed into that framework. Aboriginals must substantiate their links to their land by giving oral evidence. The process excludes women in two ways. The available bodies of learning have made men the central players and men's business the prime focus. Women's concerns are seen to be merely peripheral to those of men. This is the consequence of a white male anthropological construct such as the one described above. Further, the need for women to protect their traditions requires silence. If they speak their secrets to men they break their lores, if they do not their silence is interpreted as "absence of knowledge".[75]

Serious consequences of erasure arise when the learning and understanding accumulated in these texts is relied upon today by indigenous people themselves to help reconstruct their customs. Another factor is the disproportionate growth and development that might take place in the two gendered streams of custom and tradition following contact with whites. Women's business may not make dynamic strides to keep up with modernising influences. Equally the division of labour and power between the sexes is likely to widen.

Margaret Jolly has identified examples of both these phenomena.[76] In her study about the relationship between men and women in food production in South Pentecost she notes the influences of colonialism. Among the traditional people (those less influenced by having been Christianised)[77] men's leaving home to work temporarily on other islands is a preferred strategy for raising cash. This pattern of migration has had the effect of increasing the work load for women while the men are away and reducing the power women have to influence what happens to the product of labour.

The men exercise greater control over the cash and what it buys than they did over the food grown collectively.

Jolly identifies two other interesting spin-offs. Firstly, since the men tend to travel in groups:

> They thus secure themselves against the depredations of European bosses, and the more ethereal ravages of alien sorcerers. This time together... [is] like an extended experience of the *mal*.[78] Thus it tends to heighten male solidarity, vis-à-vis women.[79]

Possibly the same male bonding took place amongst young men from different traditional villages who were sent away to do their secondary schooling overseas in the pre-independence years. Several of these men returned to Vanuatu and established the various independence movements. This is a further illustration of how western influence can tip the balance between the traditional sex roles so that women's traditional role loses value.

Second, "[m]ales also monopolize contact with European ideas and values. They *quite consciously* inhibit the contact which women have with the outside world."[80] Through greater 'sophistication' in the ways of the west and with material goods (for example firearms) the men further exclude women from exercising power in the community.

The interweaving complexity of the influences that contact with western cultures has had on indigenous groups like the Australian Aboriginals and the ni-Vanuatu is too profound to describe in all its detail. What can be said is that it has had a major impact on those parts of traditional systems that are devised and operated by women. How does it impact on indigenous communities now? How does it affect the position of indigenous women struggling to establish *their* right to self-determination *within their own communities*?

DEFINING THE MASCULINIST RHETORIC OF NOSTALGIA.

Nostalgia is a sentimental longing or wistful affection for the past. It is a desire for a return to a period or place with happy personal associations. This is one of the theoretical underpinnings of the political project for re-establishing Custom. Why then 'rhetoric', with its negative connotation of insincerity?[81] Is it not as Ati George Sokomanu past President of Vanuatu has written:

> The political demand is to reconstitute, reclaim, revive and reinvent, because of what has been destroyed or lost under colonial rule. It is an urge simply to attain political power and freedom not only from colonial domination and oppression, but also from Christian ethics. It constitutes a process of santification (*sic*) of a new creation for a common cultural identity.[82]

This is passionate language that speaks of a *common* struggle for rebirth. But Sokomanu goes on to state that the "real past must be argued with proof, perhaps genealogically and ritually... for Pacific Islanders, their history is in the form of a story that is passed from the great-grandfather to grandfather to father to son".[83] Here is proof that the 'proof' used to reconstitute, reclaim, revive and reinvent will be men's stories about men.

Women must be vigilant in analysing seemingly laudable propositions so as not to be swept up in the male rhetoric of Custom. When the Acting Chief Justice of Vanuatu (as he then was) stated in a judgment,[84] "it is clear from the lessons of history that the price to be paid for failure to cherish and uphold the customs and traditions of Vanuatu, is a heavy one: the loss forever of a national identity and way of life" he is engaging in one form of rhetorical nostalgia. The price has been a heavy one; almost certainly heavier for women,[85] but the loss was not of a *national identity* as that never existed in the first place.[86]

Indigenous men wittingly and unwittingly conspire in reducing the perceived importance of women's business for their own ends.[87] Indigenous men may wish to exploit the position of women in the light of their own exploitation by colonisers and consequent feelings of alienation, and repress women as a means of overcoming their own 'castration'[88] feelings at the hands of their colonial masters,[89] but (whilst this process might be expected, accepted and understood) its outcome is the oppression of women.

The overwhelming male rhetoric of Custom is often a lie that can be used to foster greater gender power of men in the indigenous communities. At several levels men may use the impact of colonialism to reinterpret Custom to suit themselves. At its highest level, a whole stream of Custom has ceased to exist through a combination of anthropological inputs largely of the Simpson variety and great disturbances in and movement away from traditional life styles. This can lead to complete annihilation of women's business. Of course it has a substantial impact on the culture as a whole. In Vanuatu there has been surprisingly little academic study of Custom[90] with substantial gaps in time between studies. Fairly isolated communities are selected for fieldwork but, inevitably, general conclusions are drawn and encompassing findings are made from these data. In the communities nearest to urban centres the de-Customising is often greatest because of the impact of western churches and missionaries and exposure to expatriate labour roles. There may be no collusion by indigenous men with the colonisers in the prime process but neither are the men unaware of the benefits they alone derive from these dislocations. It was the 'big-men', (selected by the colonisers usually) who got the privileges available from the dominant culture.[91] Having thus gained standing, that power base has been developed to gain rank recognised in Custom.[92]

The second level operates because outsiders (anthropologists, settlers, historians, tourists, whoever) have misinterpreted the place of men and women in indigenous culture and have put everything into a western patriarchal framework. We shall never know what the traditional mode of living was for many Australian Aboriginal communities. Larissa Behrendt is an urban Aboriginal woman of the Eualeyai[93] and she explains that her remarks about her culture are based on generalisations and what she has been told of her language group's customs and values. She maintains that there did not exist a concept of men being generally dominant to women, in her traditional culture.[94]

> Because the spirit of creation was a female energy, there is respect for women and nurturing is valued in our traditional community. We, as women, had and still have spiritual rituals, dances, songs and stories that are for women only. We are respectful of elders. We know that with age and experience come wisdom and powers. Women in our community are given as much respect as men. A female elder can be as influential in a community as a male elder.[95]

But she acknowledges that "[s]exist oppression by [black] men started when the white invaders arrived".[96] We have already noted how women's grades in Vanuatu have been glossed over and substantially ignored in the western literature. In Vanuatu, pig-killing is a widespread ritual, significant for many purposes including cementing friendships, inaugurating chiefs and taking grades. One can still attend pig-killing ceremonies conducted by and for men. Ceremonies involving women being engaged in pig-killing are never discussed. Yet Margaret Rodman has documented women's pig killing rituals on East Aoba.[97]

These days in order to establish and maintain a political presence Aboriginal people are required to organise into committees and lobby groups. This mechanism has been picked up and developed by indigenous men.[98] Invariably, one sees the same imbalance of gender representation in these bodies as one does with non-indigenous activities. Deborah Bird Rose[99] notes the importance of the written record in Aboriginal claims and the fact that this record becomes a permanent structure for describing the 'truth' about ownership. The Land Councils (Aboriginal bodies) have a "tunnel vision approach... which asserts that as long as people get their land, it does not matter who gives evidence... gender equity appears to be classed as an optional extra... The idea is that people present their case, get their land, and get on with their lives".[100] She notes the fallacy of this notion. In fact people do incorporate the elements utilised in the claim procedure into their lives.[101] Thereafter, "[e]ven junior men... are treated as if they know more than the most senior women."[102]

Thirdly, the situation arises where women are denied a vehicle for their traditions to be recognised. In Helen Stacy's analysis of the Hindmarsh Island case[103] she outlines how women of the Ngarrindjeri tribe, who were opposed to the construction of a bridge to the island for reasons that were based on secret women's business, were subject to allegations that their lore was a fabrication:[104]

> Doug Milera, a senior Ngarrindjeri man and the husband of one of the women claiming to be a custodian of the secret women's business, claimed that the beliefs had been fabricated in an effort to stop the bridge. He subsequently withdrew his allegations of fabrication, saying that he had been drunk at the time of making the claim.[105]

Because he is a man his view was initially given greater credence in the public arena than the word of the women, and this doubtful credibility *about this issue* lingered despite his later discrediting of himself.[106]

On a fourth level, in the situation where an existing custom becomes substantially modified because of a change in circumstances, men again reinvent and thereby gain greater control over women. For example, in Vanuatu where custom owners of land or family members obliged to pay value would once have settled the obligation with mats (produced by women) or pigs (tended by women) the trend is now to operate a cash economy. The payment with money changes the nature of the mutual obligations significantly, because women generally have less access to cash and therefore relatively less power. Alternatively, other women's greater access to cash wealth can operate to increase traditional penalties. *Waiwo v Waiwo and Banga*[107] concerned a petition for divorce on the grounds of adultery also the plaintiff wife sought damages from the co-respondent.[108] Coincidentally, all three parties came from the same area and were governed by the same *Kastom*. A decision had already been made by their chiefs that the co-respondent (who was a financially independent woman) should pay the plaintiff 10,000 vatu.[109] They also ordered the respondent to pay the co-respondent's husband 20,000 vatu. The co-respondent argued that any further claim would amount to punitive damages. The Senior Magistrate[110] held that damages should be awarded *in accordance with customary law*. He noted the seriousness with which adultery is regarded in *Kastom* and ruled "that there is a common basis throughout Vanuatu that adulterers must be customarily penalized... [thus] damages [for adultery] should be considered as punitive damages on the basis of custom".[111] He then ordered the payment of 100,000 vatu.[112] Interestingly, he made no reference to the discussion about adultery in the document prepared by the *Malvatumauri*[113] (the paramount council of chiefs) which would seem to have been a good source for the customary position on the matter. In any event that document offers no indication of the appropriate penalty.[114] This case highlights brilliantly the difficulty of reconciling imported concepts with traditional ones. If damages for adultery were to be payable *as a matter of custom* (rather than as a surviving anachronism from English property law) then surely the most suitable assessors of the quantum of those damages would be the parties' own area chiefs and the principles for determining that quantum should also stem from custom.

Fifthly, where the power paradigm has become entirely patriarchal men become the sole arbiters of what custom was and so what it is to be. This level involves more direct gender oppression. At its most overt it is a bald assertion of gender dominance and the least subtle employment of the rhetoric of nostalgia. For example in Vanuatu a white female citizen was appointed as the first Ombudsman.[115] Certain indigenous men in authority came under scrutiny and the Ombudsman published a number of reports outlining quite serious allegations of misconduct against senior politicians. One Member of Parliament[116] stated publicly that he did not have to take any notice of the allegations because a woman issued them and they were therefore contrary to *Kastom*. Upon this rationale he did not feel obliged to address the question of the validity or otherwise, of the allegations.

Finally there are circumstances where men simply tell lies about Custom. In land claims in Vanuatu this situation is not infrequent[117] where competing male disputants will adduce evidence about apparent customary rules but all will neglect to explain the matrilineal aspects of their customary succession.

CONCLUSION

Dissecting the psyche and categorising personal planes of self in some perceived hierarchy is a western theoretical device. If western women have become discomforted by being analysed and analysing themselves in such splintered terms, how much more must that be true for indigenous women of colour whose cultural outlook is integrative rather than segregationalist.

Indigenous women of colour feel they are different from other people and want to be different in pursuing their individual identities and their unique collective identity. The collective identity involves a connection with the men of the group and the women do not want to deny this part of their identity. To be comfortable in that place given that as colonised people they experience 'spirit murder' in other places, they want to embrace the vitality of their Custom/*Kastom*/Country. Internally, solidarity requires consensus. That means that to be able to feel connected to each other within a customary framework, men and women need to agree upon the general principles that will govern them. Equally, externally the political agenda proscribes divisiveness. To strengthen the collective claim for the validity of custom indigenous men and women do not want to be seen as being at loggerheads.

Neither do women want to criticise traditional mores and customs because that may stimulate outsider scorn that Custom is primitive and uncivilised. The drive for a reinvigoration of Custom thereby potentially casts women into another form of schizophrenia because the loyalty to a customary ideology comes up against the masculinist interpretations that erase their gender perspective. Indigenous men know 'spirit murder' too. While indigenous men struggle to overcome the past they must not be allowed to redefine it so as to spirit murder their women anew.

ENDNOTES

1 Huggins, J. 1998. *Sister Girl*. Queensland Australia: University of Queensland Press, p 120.

2 Pat O'Shane in Mitchell, S. 1984. *Tall Poppies*. Australia: Penguin Books, p 153.

3 One of the underpinnings of the western philosophical model as compared to less linear, less categorical systems, is a difference in concepts of 'time'. See, e.g., Herman, A. 1997. *The Idea of Decline in Western History*. New York: The Free Press, p 13.

4 As in the concept of the 'noble savage' being the idealised representative of primitive mankind of Romantic literature symbolising the innate goodness of humanity when free from the corrupting influence of civilisation. See too Rolls, M. 1998. Cultural Colonisation: Monica Furlong and the Quest for Fulfilment. *The Australian Feminist Law Journal* 11: 46–64.

5 Capitalised 'Custom' is used to denote the concept at its widest which encompasses traditions, norms, rites and practices, religious concepts and observances, rituals and art.

6 'Autonomy' here is meant in a somewhat restrictive sense, as a freedom from oppression rather than freedom from external control or influence.

7 Nelson, C./UN/ESCAP. 1999. <u>Promoting CEDAW Through NGO Networks in the Pacific: Project Implementation Report</u>.

8 Young, I. M. 1990. *Justice and the Politics of Difference*. Princeton: Princeton University Press, p 13.

9 Pettman, J. 1993. Gendered Knowledges: Aboriginal Women and the Politics of Feminism. *Journal of Australian Studies* 35:120–131.

10 See above, n 8 at p 8.

11 Hooks, B. *Ain't I a Woman*. 1981. USA: South End Press; Harris, A. 1994. Foreword: The Jurisprudence of Reconstruction. *California Law Review* 82:741–785; Williams, J. 1991. Dissolving the Sameness/Difference Debate: A Post-Modern Path Beyond Essentialism in Feminist and Critical Race Theory. *Duke Law Journal* 296–347.

12 See, for example, O'Shane, P. 1976. Is There any Relevance in the Women's Movement for Aboriginal Women? *Refractory Girl* 31–32 Huggins, J. 1998. Above, n1.

13 For an alternative view, see Haggis, J. 1990. Gendering Colonialism or Colonizing Gender? Recent Women's Studies Approaches to White Women and the History of British Colonialism. *Women's Studies International Forum* 13:105–115.

14 Mohanty, C. 1998. Under Western Eyes: Feminist Scholarship and Colonial Discourses. *Feminist Review* 30:64–81. She uses the term 'women of colour' interchangeably with 'Third World women'.

15 Huggins, J. 1998. Above, n8 at p 65.

16 Threlfall, M. 1996. *Mapping the Women's Movement* London: New Left Books at p 48; Behrendt, L. 1993. Aboriginal Women and the White Lies of the Feminist Movement: Implications for Aboriginal Women in Rights Discourse. *The Australian Feminist Law Journal* 1:27–51 at p 27.

17 See above, n 12 and n 16, Behrendt, L. 1993 at p 32: O'Shane, P 1976. Above, 12 and Behrendt, L. Above, n 16 at p 32: "Aboriginal women feel that to turn against Aboriginal men and start treating them as the enemy is divisive and denies the strong cultural and political ties between Aboriginal people of both sexes."

18 *Native Title Act* (Cth) 1993 (Australia).

19 *Constitution* (Vanuatu) article 95(3): "Customary law shall continue to have effect as part of the law of the Republic of Vanuatu".

20 Bell, D. 1993. *Daughters of the Dreaming*. Sydney: Allen & Unwin.

21 Dussias, A. 1999. Squaw Drudges, Farm Wives, and the Dann Sister's Last Stand: American Indian Women's Resistance to Domestication and the Denial of Their Property Rights. *North Carolina Law Review* 77:637–729.

22 Jolly, M. 1991. The politics of difference: feminism, colonialism and decolonisation in Vanuatu. In Bottomley, S. (ed.) *Intersexions: Gender/Class/Culture/Ethnicity*. Sydney: Allen & Unwin, p 57.

23 See, for example. Speiser, F. 1990. *Ethnology of Vanuatu: An early Twentieth Century Study*. Bathurst, Australia: Crawford House Press; Berndt, R. & Berndt, C. 1996. *The World of the First Australians: Aboriginal Traditional Life Past and Present*. Canberra: Aboriginal Studies Press.

24 The elements of this interesting debate now raging in feminist international law circles raise questions beyond the scope of this paper. A human rights perspective tends to be based on individual interests and a discussion about Custom requires an examination of collective interests. But see Howe, A. 1994. White Western Feminism Meets International Law: Challenges/Complicity, Erasures/Encounters. *The Australian Feminist Law Journal* 4: 63–91.

25 The plight of the women in Afghanistan subject to the Taliban is an obvious example.

26 Young, I.M. 1990. Above, n 8 at 9.

27 The difficulties in reconciling customs and culture with eliminating discrimination against women is highlighted in countries like Vanuatu that have acceded to CEDAW. See above, n 7.

28 Gale, F. (ed.) 1974. *Woman's Role in Aboriginal Society*. Canberra: Australian Institute of Aboriginal Studies, p 1.

29 Bell, D. 1993. Above, n 20 at p 3.

30 Huggins, J. 1998. Above, n 1 at p 65: "Our men, are starting to get a bit agitated with seeing Black women in this country gravitating towards feminism rather than back to the Black environment, the Black community if you will. The whole problem of where one is disloyal to their people or appears to be disloyal to their people is something that I, certainly as a Black woman, have had to grapple with".

31 Huggins, J. 1998. Above, n 1 at p 65

32 Huggins, J. 1998. Above, n 1 at p 103

33 Watson, I. 1998. Power of the Muldarbi, The Road to its Demise. *The Australian Feminist Law Journal* 11: 28–45 at p 38.

34 See, for example, Draft Declaration on the Rights of Indigenous Peoples United Nations Doc E/CN.4/SUB.2/1994/2/Add. 1.

35 Behrendt, L. 1994. Aboriginal Urban Identity: Preserving the Spirit, Protecting the Traditional in Non-Traditional Settings. *The Australian Feminist Law Journal* 4: 55–61, p 61.

36 Williams, S. 1991. Above n 11.

37 Williams, P. 1987. Spirit-Murdering the Messenger: The Discourse of Fingerpointing as the Law's Response to Racism. *University of Miami Law Review* 42: 127–347.

38 Strethlow, T. J. H. 1986. Submission 33. Australian Law Reform Commission Report 31: The Recognition of Aboriginal Customary Laws.

39 Silko, L. M. 1996. *Yellow Woman and a Beauty of the Spirit: Essays on Native American Life Today*. New York: Simon & Schuster, p 200.

40 Brown, K. 1997. Customary Law in the Pacific – An Endangered Species. *Journal of South Pacific Law*, article 2 of Vol. 3.
   (http://www.vanuatu.usp.ac.fj/journal_splaw/articles/Brown1.htm Accessed 19/9/02).

41 Melanesia is usually taken to include the island of New Guinea and its lesser islands, Solomon Islands, Vanuatu, New Caledonia and Fiji Islands.

42 Brown, K. 1997. Above, n 40.

43 Note that it is estimated that Vanuatu has 108 different languages with each language community being associated with different elements of custom and culture. See Sokomanu, A. G. 1992. Government in Vanuatu: The Place of Culture and Tradition. In Crocombe, R. *et al* (eds.) *Culture and Democracy in the South Pacific*. Suva: Institute of Pacific Studies, p 52.

44 Sokomanu, A.G. 1992. Above, n 43.

45 Sokomanu, A.G. 1992. Above, n 43 at p 19. The term comes from New Guinea tok pisin. In the Bislama of Vanuatu, the term is *"fasin"* meaning "fashion, method, manner or way". See Crowley, T. 1995. *A New Bislama Dictionary*. Suva: Institute of Pacific Studies, p 72.

46 Sokomanu, A.G. 1992. Above, n 43 at p 19.

47 Hobbles Danayarri quoted in Rose, D.B. 1984. The Saga of Captain Cook: Morality in Aboriginal and European Law. *Australian Aboriginal Studies* 2: 24–42 at p 31.

48 See Bottomley, S. & Parker, S. 1997. *Law in Context (2nd ed.)*. Canberra: The Federation Press, chapter 10.

49 See, for example, Rose, D. B. 1996. Land Rights and Deep Colonising: The Erasure of Women. *Aboriginal Law Bulletin* 3: 6–13.

50 See, for example, Behrendt, L. 1993. Above, n 16; and Behrendt, L. 1994. Above, n 35.

51 See Shineberg, D. 1967. *They Came For Sandalwood*. Carlton, Victoria: Melbourne University Press.

52 See Docker, E. W. 1981. *The Blackbirders: A Brutal Story of the Kanaka Slave-trade*. Australia: Angus & Robertson.

53 See, for example, Worsley, P. 1974. *The Trumpet Shall Sound: A Study of 'Cargo' Cults in Melanesia*. New York: Schocken Books.

54 See Australian Law Reform Commission. 1986. <u>Report 31: The Recognition of Aboriginal Customary Laws</u>.

55 *Native Title Act* 1993 (Cth).

56 *Constitution* (Vanuatu) article 74. In the last two years, work has been done towards establishing a customary system of determining issues of land ownership throughout Vanuatu.

57 In practice the implementation of customary law has been limited. See, for example, Brown, K. 1997. Above, n 40.

58 See Bottomley, S & Parker, S. 1997. Above, n 48.

59 See, for example, Speiser, F. 1990. Above, n 23.

60 See O'Shane, P. 1976. Above, n 12, at p 32.

61 This is a quote from the dust jacket summary.

62 Simpson, C. 1955. *Islands of Men: Inside Melanesia*. Sydney: Angus & Robertson.

63 See Simpson, C. 1955. Above, n 62 at p 118.

64 See Simpson, C. 1955. Above, n 62 at p 118. Harrisson himself published a book entitled *Savage Civilisation*.

65 Lawrence, P. & Meggitt, M.J. (eds.) 1965. *Gods, Ghosts and Men in Melanesia: Some Religions of Australian New Guinea and the New Hebrides*. Melbourne: Oxford University Press.

66 Lane R.B. 1965. The Melanesians of South Pentecost, New Hebrides. In Lawrence, P. & Meggitt, M.J. (eds.) *Gods, Ghosts and Men in Melanesia: Some Religions of Australian New Guinea and the New Hebrides*. Melbourne: Oxford University Press at p 250.

67 Pentecost is an island of Vanuatu.

68 Presumably the author is male. None of the authors are identified anywhere with their first names. R.B. Lane notes that he collected the data for the article in field trips funded by a Fulbright grant and the Carnegie Corporation of New York. Margaret Jolly, in a later work, notes that American anthropologists Bob and Barbara Lane did field trips in 1953–4 and 1957–8. See Jolly M. 1981. People and Their Products in South Pentecost. In Allen, M. (ed.) *Vanuatu: Politics, Economics and Ritual in Island Melanesia*. Sydney: Academic Press, at p 290.

69 Lane, R.B. 1965. Above, n 66 at p 252.

70 Lane, R.B. 1965. Above, n 66 at p 252.

71 Lane, R.B. 1965. Above, n 66 at p 270.

72 Lane, R.B. 1965. Above, n 66 at p 271.

73 See, for example, above, n 12, at p 31 and above, n 16, Behrendt, L. 1993 at p 29.

74 Rose, D. B. 1996. Above, n 49.

75 See above, n 74.

76 Jolly, M. 1981. Above, n 68, at p 269. Interestingly, Jolly is studying the same region as Lane, the South Pentecost area.

77 Jolly, M. 1981. Above, n 68, at p 289. The people of Bunlap and Pohurur have retained their traditions and largely rejected christianising.

78 The *mal* is literally the 'men's house' but the concept encompasses 'men's business'.

79 Jolly, M. 1981. Above, n 68, at p 288.

80 Jolly, M. 1981. Above, n 68, at p 289. (My emphasis.)

81 Note the definition in The New Oxford Dictionary of English "language designed to have a persuasive or impressive effect on its audience but which is often regarded as lacking in sincerity or meaningful content". For an interesting discussion about the role of language in the law and two sides of rhetoric see Meehan, M. 1994. An Anatomy of Australian Law or The Human Element in Legal Argument. In *The Happy Couple: Law and Literature*. Sydney: The Federation Press, at p 376.

82 Sokomanu, A.G. 1992. Above n 43 at p 52.

83 Sokomanu, A.G. 1992. Above n 43 at p 53.

84 *Peter Salemalo v Paul Ren Tari and the Electoral Commission*, Unreported, Supreme Court of the Republic of Vanuatu, Election Petition No. 30 of 98 28th August, 1998 (http://www.vanuatu.usp.ac.fj/paclawmat/Vanuatu_cases/Volume_R–Z/Salemalo_v_Tari .html Accessed 19/9/02).

85 See, for example, Behrendt, L. 1993. Above, n 16 at p 28: "The culture and spirituality of Aboriginal women is being destroyed at a faster rate than that of Aboriginal men."

86 Vanuatu's pre-contact history is one of isolated communities existing throughout the islands each having little contact with the others. Even today ni-Vanuatu identify themselves first by the village or island community from which they come. The creation of Vanuatu as a nation state is a post-colonial contrivance.

87 I am indebted to Prof. Jean Zorn for her insightful comments about these issues.

88 This seems an appropriate metaphor for indigenous men's own feelings of powerlessness in the face of white domination and it may help to explain the apparent attraction of an extreme macho image to indigenous men that can be observed. Having said that one must also be very mindful of the dangers in stereotyping their behaviour.

89 In Vanuatu today there are still some elderly ni-Vanuatu men who refer to white men as '*masta*' more than twenty years after independence.

90 Brown, K. 1997. Above, n 40 at p 1 where he notes the paucity of reliable and detailed anthropological information.

91 Van Trease, H. 1987. *The Politics of Land In Vanuatu*. Suva: Institute of Pacific Studies. He cites the case of Peter Milne, missionary on Nguna who sought to suppress the matrilineal tradition because it appeared to him to be contrary to the Scriptures (p 9).

92 Kalsakau, G. 1978. *History of the Three Flags*. Vanuatu: I.P.V, in which he outlines the history of his own powerful chiefly family.

93 Behrendt, L. 1993. Above, n 16 and Behrendt, L. 1994. No One Can Own the Land. *Australian Journal of Human Rights* 1(1): 43–56.

94 Behrendt, L. 1994. Above, n 93, at p 55.

95 Behrendt, L. 1994. Above, n 93, at p 56.

96 Behrendt, L. 1993. Above, n 16, at p 33.

97 Rodman, M. 1981. A Boundary and a Bridge: Women's Pig Killing as a Border-Crossing Between Spheres of Exchange in East Aoba. In Allen, M. (ed.) *Vanuatu: Politics, Economics and Ritual in Island Melanesia* Academic Press: Sydney. Either the practice has ceased or it is not generally referred to, in either case its erasure is instructive.

98 Berndt, R. & Berndt, C. 1996. Above, n 23 at p 542: "Many Aboriginal communities now have their own councils of management, with responsibility for controlling socio-economic projects."

99 Rose, D.B. 1996. Above, n 49.

100 Rose, D.B. 1996. Above, n 49 at p 9.

101 Rose, D.B. 1996. Above, n 49 at p 9.

102 Rose, D.B. 1996. Above, n 49 at p 9.

103 Stacy, H. 1996. Lacan's Split Subjects: Raced and Gendered Transformations. *The Legal Studies Forum* XX(3):277–293.

104 Stacey, H. 1996. Above, n 103 at p 283; Rose, D.B. 1996. Above, n 49.

105 Stacey, H. 1996. Above, n 103 at p 284. A group of women from the same community also disputed the existence of the special knowledge but that does not affect the argument that women's business is often systematically belittled or denied by those having no knowledge of it.

106 As Stacy points out, his later loss of credibility is explained in racist terms as a component of his black unreliability.

107 Unreported, Senior Magistrate's Court of the Republic of Vanuatu, civil case No. 324 of 1995 28th February, 1996 (http://www.vanuatu.usp.ac.fj/paclawmat/Vanuatu_cases/Volume_R–Z/Waiwo_v_Waiwo.html Accessed 19/9/02).

108 Damages for adultery are provided for in the *Matrimonial Causes Act* [Cap 192] (Vanuatu) s 17.

109 The equivalent of approximately 120 AUD.

110 Mr. Lunabek has since been appointed Chief Justice.

111 See above, n 107 at p 9.

112 This case went to appeal. See *Banga v Waiwo*, Unreported, Supreme Court of the Republic of Vanuatu (appellate jurisdiction), Appeal Case No. 1 of 1996 17th June, 1996 (http://www.vanuatu.usp.ac.fj/paclawmat/Vanuatu_cases/Volume_A–F/Banga_v_Waiwo.html Accessed 19/9/02).

113 *Custom Policy of the Malvatumauri* issued by the (Vanuatu) National Council of Custom Chiefs.

114 See above, n 113, article 24.

115 This is a constitutional position provided for in Part II Article 61 of the *Constitution* of Vanuatu.

116 Barak Sope. Mr Sope held the position of Minister for Finance and has also been Prime Minister in Vanuatu.

117 See, for example, the discussion in *John Noel v Obed Toto*, Unreported, Supreme Court of the Republic of Vanuatu, Civil Case No 18 of 1994 19th April 1995 (http://www.vanuatu.usp.ac.fj/paclawmat/Vanuatu_cases/Volume_G–N/Noel_v_Toto.html Accessed 19/9/02).

8. THE INCORPORATION OF CUSTOMARY LAW & PRINCIPLE INTO SENTENCING DECISIONS IN THE SOUTH PACIFIC REGION

By: Dr Tess Newton Cain

KEY TERMS AND PHRASES

Mitigation

Mitigation is the reduction of the severity or the effect of a wrongful act. A 'plea in mitigation' is the submission of certain facts by an offender in the hope of receiving a more lenient sentence than the court would otherwise impose.

Restitution

Resitution involves making good a loss to a wronged person whether by actual replacement of a lost good or providing recompense in monetary or other terms. Restitution is similar to reparation which involves a wronged person being compensated for loss that has been caused by an offender.

INTRODUCTION

Within the South Pacific region[1] there are fewer instances of having to reconcile customary law and 'introduced' law within the realm of criminal law and procedure than is the case in other areas of law such as family law or land law. By this I mean that when we look to the available sources of law in relation to criminal matters, it is evident that this is an area that has been extensively codified, either during the colonial period or since then.[2] A reading of these codes indicates that reference to issues of customary law and principle occur rarely and are very limited in nature.

Once a matter is reported to the police and the issue is brought within the scope of the 'introduced' (or 'adopted') criminal justice system, the relevant statutory provisions relating to offences, defences and procedure make very few references to customary concerns. This is despite the fact that within many Pacific island communities there is a great deal of evidence (although it is largely undocumented) that people who feel themselves to have been wronged by another person or group of persons[3] seek resolution of this type of dispute by reference to customary law and practice as declared and/or interpreted by chiefs or other community elders. These processes are commenced, conducted and concluded without any recourse to the police, the Office of the Public Prosecutor or the 'formal' court system. There is also evidence of some communities refusing to recognise the authority of the police or other agents of the criminal justice system.[4] In some areas the courts have not attempted to close this gap between statute and social reality. Instead the courts have, in several areas, taken an exclusionary approach to the introduction of issues of custom prior to the sentencing stages of criminal matters. For example, we may refer to the case of *Public Prosecutor v Iata Tangitom*.[5] This concerned a charge of indecent assault contrary to s 98(2) of the *Penal Code* [Cap 135] (Vanuatu). There was some dispute as to the age of the victim but this was determined to be 13 by Marum J, who then went on to make the following comment:

> In mitigation, the counsel submitted that in custom, this is recognized and accepted and further, age is irrelevant. In my view, if there is a conflict between custom and public law, that is criminal law, then the law must prevail and that is provided for under section 11 of the Penal Code Act (*sic*) where it expresses that ignorance is no defense.

When we turn to the particular issue of sentencing, the situation is markedly different. At this stage of the criminal justice process the impact of customary principles, most notably reconciliation and compensation, is much more visible. It is also at the sentencing stage that the potential ideological conflicts between the underlying rationales of customary socio-legal structures and the introduced legal system are highlighted:

> The potential for paradox where such a notion of justice[6] comes up against customary penalty with very keen communal and collective investments is clear. For instance, with traditional community shaming the whole village is co-opted into the process and the offender's family may take collective responsibility not

only for the harm but also for his (*sic*) rehabilitation. Common law liability, on the other hand, tends to isolate the offender from the community at all stages of the penalty process. While requiring the individual to restore the social balance through his guilt and shame.[7]

This chapter examines the question of how, if at all, the law as enacted and subsequently applied by the courts attempts to reconcile such paradoxes. There are three parts to this chapter. The first part is an examination of the written law to identify what provision is made for the recognition of customary law in relation to sentencing decisions of the courts.[8] The second is a consideration of some of the sentencing decisions of the courts of the region. The third is a brief overview of law and procedure in other jurisdictions to provide some points of comparison with the situation in the USP region.

THE WRITTEN LAW

Here, we shall examine the written law both in the form of constitutional provisions and in the form of enacted legislation related specifically to sentencing and customary law. In examining the relevant legislation the statutes constituting courts are considered, as it is sometimes the case that courts are given broad powers to take customary matters into account when making decisions.

Constitutional Recognition of Custom and Customary Law

There are many examples in Pacific constitutional documents of statements as to the significance of customary law. These statements are often framed in very broad terms. There are two main types of this sort of statement.

The first is the kind of statement that does not expressly refer to customary law in relation to the particular jurisdiction but instead refers to the concept of 'existing law', which could (and possibly should) be interpreted as including customary law. An example of such a statement is Art 71 of the *Constitution* 1974 (Niue) which should be read in conjunction with Art 82 where 'existing law':

> ...means any law in force in Niue immediately before Constitution Day; and includes any enactment passed or made before Constitution Day and coming into force on or after Constitution Day.

However, the *Constitution* of Niue makes no specific reference to the significance of customary law other than in relation to land issues. Similar statements appear in the *Tokelau Act* 1948 (NZ)[9] and the *Constitution* (Cook Islands).[10]

The second form of constitutional statement that is found in the region in relation to the significance of customary law is the type that makes express reference to the status of custom, again in fairly broad terms. An example of this type of provision appears in the Preamble to the *Constitution* [Cap 1] (Tuvalu):

> And whereas the people of Tuvalu desire to constitute themselves an Independent State based on Christian principles, the Rule of Law, and Tuvaluan custom and tradition.

The status of custom is reiterated in s 85, which is concerned with the jurisdiction of the courts:

> ...provided that in the exercise of their jurisdiction the courts shall, to the extent that circumstances and the justice of any particular case may permit, modify or adapt such rules as to take account of Tuvalu custom and tradition.[11]

In addition, it is possible to identify constitutional provisions that make reference to issues of punishment. Again, these tend to be framed in very broad terms rather than being detailed as to how the courts should sentence criminal offenders. An example of such a provision is Cl 10 of the *Constitution* (Tonga):

> No one shall be imprisoned because of any offence he (*sic*) may have committed until he has been sentenced according to law before a Court having jurisdiction in the case.[12]

It is evident that these provisions, and the constitutional documents of the region more generally, do not make specific reference to the role that customary law should play in relation to sentencing decisions made by the criminal courts. A possible partial exception is s 186 of the *Constitution Amendment Act* 1997 (Fiji Islands) which does make specific reference to the recognition of "traditional Fijian processes" within the context of "dispute resolution". It is therefore necessary to examine the legislation that is relevant within the sphere of criminal law and procedure to ascertain if and how the written law defines the role of customary law and principle at this stage of the criminal justice process.

Legislative Provisions Concerned with Sentencing and Customary Law

In this section, we shall examine some of the legislative provisions that are concerned with the relationship between sentencing decisions of the courts and customary law. More particularly, we will be looking at how the relevant legislation seeks to incorporate issues of reconciliation and compensation into sentencing decisions.

First, it is possible to identify provisions that give guidance as to the applicability of custom and customary law within the whole of the criminal sphere, including the specific issue of sentencing in the criminal courts. One of the most comprehensive examples of such a provision is para 3 of Schedule 1 of the *Laws of Kiribati Act* 1989 (Kiribati):[13]

> 3. Subject to this Act and any other enactment, customary law may be taken into account in a criminal case only for the purpose of:
>
> > (a) ascertaining the existence or otherwise of a state of mind of a person; or
> >
> > (b) deciding the reasonableness or otherwise of an act, default or omission by a person; or
> >
> > (c) deciding the reasonableness or otherwise of an excuse; or
> >
> > (d) deciding, in accordance with any other enactment whether to proceed to the conviction of a guilty party; or
> >
> > (e) determining the penalty (if any) to be imposed on a guilty party,

or where the court thinks that by not taking the customary law into account injustice will or may be done to a person.

A provision of this type has the potential to be very wide-ranging in scope and effect. However, it is important to bear in mind that the application of customary law in any or all of the identified circumstances is not mandatory in this provision. This is indicated by the use of the word 'may' rather than 'shall' in the first line of the paragraph.

In addition to general provisions of this type the different levels of courts may be subject to particular legislative provisions that define or shape the relationship between customary law and principle and sentencing decisions.

Magistrates' courts and 'custom' courts created by statute

In some jurisdictions, courts in these categories[14] are empowered by statute to take custom and customary law into account when dealing with criminal cases. For example, s 10 of the *Island Courts Act* [Cap 167] (Vanuatu) reads as follows:

> Subject to the provision of this Act an island court shall administer the customary law prevailing within the territorial jurisdiction of the court so far as the same is not in conflict with any written law and is not contrary to justice, morality and good order.[15]

Section 16 of the *Local Courts Act* [Cap 19] (Solomon Islands) bears a close resemblance to this provision. However, in this case the only limiting factor on the application of custom by the local court is that "the same has not been modified by any Act". Similarly, in Samoa the operation and jurisdiction of the *fono*[16] has been placed on a statutory basis by the *Village Fono Act* 1990 (Samoa). The incorporation and application of custom is central to the functions of the *fono* as envisaged by the Act. This is clearly demonstrated in those sections that are concerned with the handing down of sentences in criminal cases. For example, s 6 pertains to "Punishments" and grants the *fono* the power to "impose punishment in accordance with the custom and usage of its village" and deems that such power includes the imposing of the following forms of punishment:

(a) The power to impose a fine in money, fine mats, animals or food; or partly in one or partly in others of those things;

(b) The power to order the offender to undertake any work on village land.

It is also interesting to note that s 8 of this Act indicates how these customary punishments or penalties are to be viewed by other courts (such as the district courts[17]) when making subsequent sentencing decisions:

> Where punishment has been imposed by a Village *Fono* in respect of village misconduct by any person and that person is convicted by a Court of a crime or offence in respect of the same matter the Court shall take into account in mitigation of the sentence the punishment by that Village *Fono*.

Superior courts

In the field of criminal procedure, including sentencing, the primary piece of legislation that governs the courts is a criminal procedure Code or Act. Some examples of this type of legislation are *Criminal Procedure Act* 1980–81 (Cook Islands); *Criminal Procedure Code* [Cap 21] (Fiji Islands); *Criminal Procedure Code* [Cap 17] (Kiribati); *Criminal Procedure Act* 1972 (Samoa); *Criminal Procedure Code* [Cap 7] (Solomon Islands); *Police Act* [Cap 35] (Tonga); and the *Criminal Procedure Code* [Cap 136] (Vanuatu). These are the laws that form the legislative framework within which the courts of the region make sentencing decisions in relation to criminal matters. Of particular interest here is what, if anything, these pieces of legislation say about how the courts should approach customary issues when making these decisions.

The relevant provisions of the legislation of Vanuatu[18] provide a good starting point for this consideration. This is because they make explicit reference to customary forms of dispute resolution, namely reconciliation and compensation. Section 118 is concerned with the promotion of reconciliation. It reads as follows:

> Notwithstanding the provisions of the Code or of any other law, the Supreme Court and the Magistrate's Court may in criminal causes promote reconciliation and encourage and facilitate the settlement in an amicable way, *according to custom* or otherwise, of any proceedings for an offence of a *personal and private nature* punishable by imprisonment for less than 7 years or by a fine only, on terms of payment of compensation or other terms approved by such Court, and may thereupon order the proceedings to be stayed or terminated. (Emphasis added).

This provision leaves several things unclear. Words and phrases such as "reconciliation" and "amicable way" are not defined. Therefore, it is difficult to know how they should be applied in practical terms. Similarly, no guidance is provided as to the meaning of "offences of a personal or private nature". In addition, the use of a phrase such as this seems to be in conflict with the notion that criminal offences have an inherently *public* nature or aspect as reflected elsewhere in the criminal law.

A further significant point regarding this provision is one that arises in relation to similar provisions in other jurisdictions of the region:[19]

> ...where these provisions exist, they do not make any references to offences that would qualify for settlement by way of reconciliation in terms of the nature of the offences and/or the sentences they attract but which should be excluded from the ambit of such provisions by virtue of their social significance. Incidents of 'domestic violence' are very clearly in this category.[20]

Whilst incidents of "domestic violence" may qualify under a provision such as s 118 referred to above as examples of the sort of offence that may be resolved through reconciliation, it may be that to do so leads to an absence of a meaningful sanction for this type of offence:

...because of the unequal power positions of persons negotiating domestic reconciliations, the private nature of their terms, and the application of expectations that may go well beyond the immediate issue of the assault or future threats of violence, reconciliation may become more of an avoidance of penalty. For instance, where a complainant withdraws her allegation of assault as a result of reconciliation, this may be the consequence of threats from the husband[21] to throw a wife out into the street if she does not 'reconcile', rather than any genuine rapprochement. The court would not become aware of this by simply seeking an assurance of reconciliation from the accused and the complainant may not be examined by the court in this regard. The community, the traditional witness and enforcer of reconciliation, also has no voice in the court hearing.[22]

Concerns of this nature indicate that in some situations the promotion of reconciliation requires very careful consideration by the courts. It may also require that the reconciliation process is supervised and monitored either by the courts or by some other appropriate agency.

To return to the provisions that apply in Vanuatu, s 119 of the *Criminal Procedure Code* [Cap 136] (Vanuatu) is concerned specifically with issues that relate to sentencing decisions. This provision of the Code states:

Upon the conviction of any person for a criminal offence, the court shall, in assessing the quantum of penalty to be imposed, take account of any compensation or reparation made or due by the offender under custom and if such has not yet been determined, may if he (*sic*) is satisfied that undue delay is unlikely to be thereby occasioned, postpone for such purpose.

Again, a provision such as this one may be ambiguous or even problematic. The use of the word "shall" in the first line indicates that it is mandatory that the court take customary "compensation or reparation" into account. However, there is no guidance as to what principles the courts should follow in so doing. There is nothing in this provision that stipulates that the effect of having already complied with or undertaken to comply in the future with some form of customary settlement should be to mitigate the sentence. However, as is evident from the judgments of the courts,[23] such settlements are considered within the context of reducing a sentence rather than increasing it. Of particular significance within a jurisdiction such as Vanuatu is the absence of any guidance as to which (or whose) custom should apply in determining practical issues such as the means by which reparation should be made or the amount or type of compensation that is due.

In relation to issues of procedure, these provisions do not make reference to any timescale for the envisaged reconciliation processes. Neither does the legislation indicate what should happen in the event that the relevant parties agree to undertake some form of reconciliation when they are before the court but subsequently fail to go ahead with it. However, it is recognised that in many cases customary reconciliation may have been initiated and, indeed, concluded before the case ever comes before the court. Elsewhere in the region similar issues arise as it is generally the case that where such legislative provisions appear the processes for implementing them are not clearly defined.

AN EXAMINATION OF SENTENCING DECISIONS OF THE COURTS WITH REFERENCE TO THE INCORPORATION OF CUSTOMARY LAW AND/OR PRINCIPLES.

It is reasonable to assume that the decisions of the subordinate and lower subordinate courts are more likely to refer to issues of custom than would be the case in the sentencing decisions of the superior courts. However, it is extremely difficult to get access to the decisions of the magistrates' courts and courts that operate at the lower subordinate level (e.g. island courts or local courts). In many cases the judgments of these courts are not fully transcribed unless they are requested by one of the parties. Therefore, in this section I will focus on examples of how sentencing decisions of the superior courts take account of custom and customary law. This will provide only a partial picture of this area of criminal law and procedure. However, it will illustrate some significant issues and questions that are important to this type of decision-making throughout court structures at all levels, whether those structures are 'formal' or 'informal' in nature.

The questions of when and to what extent customary settlement and/or punishment should be taken into account by the courts when passing sentences in criminal cases has been considered in many of the jurisdictions of the region. There are first instance decisions and appellate decisions that are relevant to this consideration. An examination of judgments from a number of jurisdictions of the region reveals a number of issues. They are identified and discussed here. The order in which the issues are discussed does not necessarily reflect their order of importance.

The first issue is that in many cases the customary settlement, whether by means of formal apology, payment of compensation or some other process, occurs prior to the case coming before the court for sentencing purposes. This means that it is the most likely scenario that the issue of the customary settlement is raised within the context of a plea in mitigation. Further to this, it is evident from some of the judgments that the perception of the victims and offenders is that it is the customary settlement that is the final resolution of the situation with the court case being considered superfluous and, sometimes, unwelcome. This type of perception is referred to in the judgment of the Court of Appeal of Tonga in *Hala v R*.[24] In this case, part of the appeal was based on the fact that the trial judge had given insufficient weight to the fact that the offender had helped the victim's family financially, had made his peace with them and that there was reason to believe that the family "did not wish the case to go to a hearing".

However, a situation may arise in which the court hands down a sentence that has been reduced on the basis that there will be some form of customary settlement process at some point subsequent to the conclusion of the proceedings. This raises the problem of what should happen in the event that an undertaking to pay compensation or undertake some other form of customary settlement is not fulfilled. A very similar issue to this was considered in the appellate case of *Rainer Gilmete v Federated States of Micronesia.*[25] In this case the appellant was initially sentenced to imprisonment (partly suspended) and to pay restitution. The restitution was not paid within the time that the Court had prescribed and the appellant was sentenced to a further year's imprisonment. He appealed against the modified sentence. The modified sentencing order had been made on the basis that where a convicted person was unable to pay restitution, his or her family was obliged in custom to do so. The Supreme Court of FSM held that:

> If the defendant is incapable himself (*sic*) of paying restitution and he has made a request for assistance to his family, the family's bad faith in not paying cannot be imputed to the defendant and result in increased imprisonment (*per* Benson AJ)

It is not clear from the judgment in this case whether the original sentence was one that had been mitigated or reduced by virtue of the accompanying order to pay restitution. It may be preferable that where the plea in mitigation is based on an undertaking to go through a customary form of settlement rather than evidence that such settlement has already been reached, that the court should defer final sentencing until such time as is considered reasonable for the resolution to have been achieved. However, a reading of a number of cases from the region concerning this issue indicates that, in practice, it is usual that customary reconciliation and/or compensation has already been undertaken before the sentencing stage of the 'formal' proceedings is reached. This can be seen from explicit and implicit comments that appear in many of the cases that are considered in this chapter.

Second, a reading of the cases makes it clear that the courts' approach is one of limiting the scope of the effect of customary settlement to mitigation. In the Solomon Islands case of *R. v Nelson Funifaika and others*[26] Palmer J made the following statement as to the effect of payment of customary compensation by the offenders and their relatives to the victims and their communities:

> The significance of compensation in custom however should not be over-emphasized. It does have its part to play in the communities where the parties reside, in particular it makes way or allows the accused to re-enter society without fear of reprisals from the victims (*sic*) relatives. Also it should curb any ill-feelings that any other members of their families might have against them or even between the two communities to which the parties come from. *The payment of compensation or settlements in custom do not extinguish or obliterate the offence. They only go to mitigation. The accused still must be punished and expiate their crime.* (Emphasis added).

This limiting approach has been demonstrated elsewhere in the reluctance of the courts to accept customary obligations or beliefs as defences to serious criminal offences. Reference has already been made to the Vanuatu case of *Public Prosecutor v Iata Tangaitom.* Another striking example is the Solomon Islands Court of Appeal case of *R. v Loumia.*[27] This case highlighted the potential for conflicts between customary law and constitutional principles and between customary law and primary legislation. The appellant sought to persuade the Court that the customary requirement to 'pay back' a killing should afford him a defence to a charge of murder (and a reduced charge of manslaughter) under s 204(c) of the *Penal Code* [Cap 26] (Solomon Islands) which states that a defence exists if the accused:

> ...in causing the death... acted in the belief in good faith and on reasonable grounds that he was under a legal duty to cause the death or do the act which he did.

The defence was not recognised by the Court on the basis that it was inconsistent with constitutional protections of the life of the individual.[28] In addition, the Court made the following statement as to the relationship between the customary duty to 'pay back' a killing and s 204(c) of the *Penal Code*:

> The matters of extenuation which will reduce the offence from murder to manslaughter are set out in ss.196, 197 and 199 of the Code[29] and it is sufficient to say that the desire to avenge the death of another or exact retribution are not matters of defence or extenuation either under the Code or at Common Law. Clearly therefore, in my judgement, custom which calls for action which is a criminal offence by the statute law of Solomon Islands is inconsistent with statute.[30]

The legislative provisions discussed in the previous section do not preclude the court imposing a heavier sentence as a result of taking custom into account than might otherwise be the case. However, the cases demonstrate that the usual result of reference to customary settlement between victim and offender (and their respective family or community groups) is that of a reduced sentence. A similar trend has been identified in the neighbouring jurisdiction of Papua New Guinea.[31]

Third, it can be seen that the courts adopt different approaches to the significance of customary reconciliation and/or compensation depending on the circumstances of the case. The most significant factor appears to be the seriousness of the offence in question. This is illustrated in the contrasting decisions of the Supreme Court of Fiji in two cases dating from 1977.[32] In *Eernale Cagiliba v R*.[33] the Court, on receiving evidence that the appellant was reconciled with the complainant, quashed the original sentence of two years' imprisonment and substituted one of 12 months' imprisonment. The offence in question was that of robbery with violence contrary to s 326(1)(b) of the *Penal Code* [Cap 17] (Fiji Islands). However, the sum stolen was $7 and the victim and offender were cousins. In *Suliasi Nalanilawa v R*.[34] the appellant had once again been sentenced to two years' imprisonment. In this instance, the offence was that of assault with intent to commit rape. The Court refused to accept an argument that the sentence should be reduced because the complainant's family had forgiven the appellant "in accordance with Fijian custom". It would seem that both of these cases could come within the scope of the Fiji Islands' legislative provisions relating to the promotion of reconciliation that were discussed previously. However, it is evident that the exercise of discretion by the courts allows judges to differentiate between situations in accordance with broader policy issues.

In other jurisdictions, such as Vanuatu, reference to the role of customary settlement in sentencing is not restricted by reference to the nature or seriousness of the offence involved. However, it remains the case that the courts do make differentiation between when reconciliation and/or payment of compensation should and should not operate to mitigate sentence. Again, the seriousness of the offence is a significant factor in this regard. Recent comments made by the Supreme Court of Vanuatu indicate a marked reluctance to accept customary settlement as a significant mitigating factor in cases of serious violence, especially where death results. In the case of *Public Prosecutor v Peter Thomas*,[35] Marum J identified that the "normal" penalty he would impose in such a case was one of nine years' imprisonment. He then made, *inter alia*, the following comment:

> The Court under Section 119 of the CPC[36] is also to take into consideration any customary settlement into determining what is an appropriate penalty. I have stated earlier in some of my sentencing on violence causing death that compensation in compensating the life of a dead person is totally useless to the dead person, because it cannot compensate him (*sic*) by putting him back to life, and that is why I say that compensation is useless, when death occurs. However, the Court does take into consideration compensation but of less significant (*sic*).

> After consideration of everything in this matter I consider that the appropriate penalty to impose by the Court on the Defendant is to sentence him of 7 years and 6 months.[37]

LAW AND POLICY ELSEWHERE.

The issues and questions that have been identified here in relation to USP jurisdictions have also arisen and been considered elsewhere in the world. Here, we shall briefly examine some of the approaches that have been advocated and/or adopted in Papua New Guinea, South Africa and Australia. It is intended that this brief overview will identify questions and concerns that currently require or will require consideration by legislators and judges of the countries of the USP region as this area of criminal law and procedure develops.

Papua New Guinea

In Papua New Guinea, issues of customary compensation have been 'elevated' to a statutory basis in the *Criminal Law (Compensation) Act* 1991 (PNG), as amended. It is a significant piece of legislation in the Pacific as it provides a legislative framework outlining the detail of judicial and magisterial powers and duties when making compensation orders. This Act operates on the basis of the courts imposing orders to pay compensation "in addition to any other punishments imposed".[38] Section 3 of the Act identifies those factors that are to be taken into account when making compensation orders. The section makes specific reference to "custom" as a factor that may affect compensation orders in s 3(1)(d). These customs include:

> any relevant custom regarding compensation, including but not limited to:

(i) any custom regarding the nature, the amount, the method of payment and the appropriate person or persons to be paid the compensation; and

(ii) any custom which relates the amount of compensation to the age or life expectancy of the person suffering injury or loss;

Thus, this legislation recognises that compensation may be in something other than monetary form and that recognition of the dictates of custom in relation to compensation may lead to *compensation* being paid to a person or persons other than the victim of the crime in question. This makes this statutory framework quite distinct from those that govern the imposing of compensation orders in jurisdictions such as the United Kingdom.[39] The PNG Act is silent on how the courts should deal with cases where customary compensation is negotiated between the relevant individuals and/or groups outside the formal court process prior to the making of any orders as to sentence, including orders that may be made under this legislation. In subsequent commentary, it has been argued that "any compensation payments outside of the prevailing criminal compensation regime must be disregarded and discounted in sentencing."[40] Just as was noted previously, the courts in this jurisdiction have sometimes indicated that the imposition of a compensation order may not be appropriate.[41]

South Africa

In a recent publication,[42] the Law Commission of South Africa has raised several issues of significance in this area. Of particular interest are the comments and recommendations that were made highlighting the possible areas of conflict between the rationale, structure and operation of 'traditional courts' and the supreme law of constitutional provisions. One of the most complicated aspects of attempting to incorporate customary law and principle into sentencing procedures (or indeed into any other aspect of law) is how conflicts between customary law and other sources of law should be resolved, if indeed they can be. The issues and resolutions that arose in the case of *Loumia* discussed previously are relatively clear cut in this regard. However, other considerations are more complex and ambiguous. A pertinent example is that of the place of women in customary systems of dispute resolution whether as victims, offenders or adjudicators. The South African Law Commission has made the following recommendation; its careful wording is indicative of the potential problems in this area:

5.6 The traditional element of popular participation whereby every adult was allowed to question litigants and give his (*sic*) opinion on the case should be maintained and encouraged as this boosts the legitimacy of the court. However, to comply with s.9 of the Constitution, *consideration should be given to the full participation of women members of the community.*[43]

Similarly, the Commission also considered the question of corporal punishment, which is another issue with constitutional implications. The Commission's report notes that previously a chiefs' court could administer corporal punishment on "unmarried males under the apparent age of 30."[44] This, however, was determined to be in breach of s 12(1)(e) of the *Constitution* by the Constitutional Court in the case of *S. v Williams*.[45] Further to this decision, the *Abolition of Corporal Punishment Act 1997* (South Africa) was passed. Thus the Commission has recommended that:

> 6.7.3 The traditional courts therefore need to be alerted that a sentence of corporal punishment is contrary to the law.[46]

This type of consideration provides a very good illustration of the difficulty of attempting to 'blend' introduced or adopted legal and democratic concepts such as gender equality and constitutional individual rights with the longstanding beliefs and values of traditional societies.

Australia

Many significant questions and concerns regarding the place of customary law in relation to sentencing decisions of the criminal courts have been debated in Australia with particular reference to how the criminal justice system does or should impact upon members of the Aboriginal and Torres Strait Islander communities.

The legislative framework for sentencing of Aboriginal offenders and the attendant recognition of Aboriginal customary law differs between the Australian States and Territories. In Victoria, the 1988 Sentencing Committee concluded that "[A]borigines should not be given preferential treatment in sentencing; *that customary laws not be recognised*; and that no special sentencing options be developed for Aboriginal offenders."[47] In other parts of the country, where there are larger rural Aboriginal populations and less assimilation of Aborigines with the non-Aboriginal community,[48] the courts have adopted a somewhat different approach.

One of the most problematic aspects of giving recognition to Aboriginal customary law in sentencing decisions stems from the fact that in many instances, a system of ritualised physical punishment (such as being speared in the leg) is used by the community group.[49] It would be very surprising to find the courts expressly recommending or condoning a form of customary punishment that constitutes a criminal offence (assault or wounding). Indeed, the courts have had to tread a very careful path in this area. In the 1992 case of *R. v Minor*[50] the Court of Criminal Appeal of the Northern Territory held that where tribal payback punishment had already been carried out or was to be carried out in the future, the Court should have regard to this fact when passing sentence:

> As I understand it, payback, in certain cases, which must be carefully delineated and clearly understood, can be a healing process... It would be a serious and impermissible abrogation of the court's duty to reduce a sentence on any person of whatever race or creed because of assurances that friends or relatives of the victim were preparing their own vengeance for the assailant. If payback is no more than this it is nothing to the sentencing process. If, however, it transcends vengeance and can be shown to be of positive benefit to the peace and welfare of a particular community it may be taken into account; though even then I do not believe the court could countenance any really serious bodily harm.[51]

Elsewhere in that judgment, the following points were made about the nature and purpose of payback in the Aboriginal communities of the Northern Territory. It is significant to note the highlighting of the relationship between this form of customary resolution and the written law of the Territory:

> ...there was no evidence upon which his Honour could have concluded that the form of punishment proposed was unlawful. An assault is not unlawful if authorised by the 'victim' unless the person committing the assault intends to kill or to cause grievous harm: *Criminal Code* (NT), s.26(3). 'Grievous harm' is defined to mean 'any physical or mental injury of such a nature as to endanger life or to cause or be likely to cause permanent injury to health': Code, s.1... In my opinion... there was no evidence that the injury caused by the proposed spearing must or even was likely to cause grievous bodily harm... However that may be, I wish to make it clear that it is one thing for a court to take into account the likelihood of future retribution to be visited upon the accused, whether lawful or unlawful; it is yet another for a court to actually facilitate the imposition of an unlawful punishment.[52]

CONCLUSION

In this chapter, we have examined constitutional, statutory and case law relating to the recognition of customary law and principle within the context of sentencing decisions handed down by the criminal courts. It has been demonstrated that the rather scant provisions of the written law can raise ambiguities and complexities when the courts seek to give practical effect to them. A brief examination of other jurisdictions has demonstrated further issues that the jurisdictions of the South Pacific region may have to consider if this area of law and procedure is to develop in a coherent and principled fashion.

Increasingly in the region an interest is growing in the use of 'restorative justice' techniques in the field of criminal justice generally and, more particularly, to deal with juvenile crime. In the context of this debate tensions may arise between traditional dispute resolution principles and practice and ideas, such as constitutional rights, that are associated with introduced or adopted laws. Some of these tensions have been identified in this chapter, particularly in relation to crimes that occur within relationships that are characterised by an imbalance of power, whether perceived or actual.

If communities continue to feel dissatisfied with the 'formal' mechanisms for dealing with 'rising crime' (the police, prosecuting agencies and courts)[53] then we are likely to see increasing interest in a (re)turn to structures and processes that are more 'traditional' in nature. However, as the discussion in this chapter has indicated, a complete (re)acceptance of customary norms and practices can lead to ambiguities and concerns that are reflections of the impacts of colonial and post-colonial modernisation in the South Pacific region. At present, it is not possible to accurately gauge the thoughts and views of 'the community' on these issues. Do the people of the region want the issue of punishment for criminal offences to be determined according to the principles of custom, the principles of introduced or adopted law or some combination of the two? This question has not been subject to rigorous research here or elsewhere. It is likely that in this socio-legal environment, as in most others, that the answer would be a version of 'it depends'.

The questions and concerns that have been raised here illustrate wider political issues that are associated with the continuing place of custom in the legal systems of the region, whether as part of the criminal law or any other part of the law. The tensions associated with the reconciliation of modern living and the role of customary law and practice in sub-national, national and regional identities are ones that will continue to be played out in this area as in many others in the years ahead.

ENDNOTES

1   This is taken to comprise the countries that are served by the University of the South Pacific: Cook Islands, Fiji Islands, Kiribati, Marshall Islands, Nauru, Niue, Samoa (formerly Western Samoa), Solomon Islands, Tokelau, Tonga and Vanuatu. In addition in this chapter I will also make reference to other jurisdictions in the region such as Papua New Guinea, Federated States of Micronesia (FSM) and American Samoa.

2   For example, see the *Penal Code* [Cap 17] (Fiji Islands) and the *Criminal Procedure Code* [Cap 21] (Fiji Islands). The Fiji legislation is largely indicative of the colonial legislation that has been continued in force in many of the countries of the region. Examples of post-colonial legislation include the *Electable Offences Decree* 1998 (Fiji Islands) and the *Probation of Offenders Act* [Cap 28] (Solomon Islands).

3   It should be borne in mind that within customary systems of law, the distinction between criminal and civil wrongs is not distinct.

4   See Brown, K. 1986. Criminal Law and Custom in Solomon Islands. *Queensland Institute of Technology Law Journal* 2: 133–139; Newton, T. 1998. Policing in the South Pacific Islands. *Police Journal* LXXI (4): 349–352; Newton, T. 2000. Policing in the South Pacific Region. *Occasional Paper No. 1* School of Law, USP.

5   Unreported, Supreme Court of the Republic of Vanuatu, CR No. 14 of 1998, 3rd August 1998 (http://www.vanuatu.usp.ac.fj/paclawmat/Vanuatu_cases/Volume_O–Q/PP_v_Tangaito m.html Accessed 19/9/02).

6   Here 'justice' is used to refer to the 'introduced' common law notion.

7   Findlay, M. 1997. Crime, community penalty and integration with legal formalism in the South Pacific. *Journal of Pacific Studies* 21: 145–160 at pp 148–9.

8   It is not my intention to explore at length the question of the relationship between customary law and 'introduced' law other than within the specific context of sentencing decisions. This issue has been explored elsewhere. See, for example, Corrin Care, J., Newton, T. & Paterson, D. 1999. *Introduction to South Pacific Law*. London: Cavendish, at chap. 3.

9   See s 5 as amended by the *Tokelau Amendment Act* 1976 (NZ). It is recognised that this Act is not a constitution. However, it contains many 'constitution type' provisions and thus resembles other constitutional documents that exist in the region.

10 See Art 77.

11 For further examples of this type of constitutional provision, see s 75 and para 2(1) of Schedule 3 of the *Constitution* (Solomon Islands).

12 See, also, Art 5(2)(g) of the *Constitution* (Vanuatu) which states that persons cannot be punished with a greater penalty than that which existed at the time the offence in question was committed and s 5(1)(b) of the *Constitution* (Solomon Islands) which is framed in terms of a custodial sentence being an exception to the right to personal liberty.

13 Para 3 of Schedule 1 of the *Laws of Tuvalu Act* 1987 (Tuvalu) is almost identical to this provision.

14 For more detail on the structure and jurisdiction of the courts of the region, see above, n 8 at chapter 11.

15 For more detail on the structure and functions of the island courts of Vanuatu see Jowitt, A. 2000. Island Courts in Vanuatu. *Occasional Paper No. 2* School of Law, USP.

16 Village assembly or council.

17 District courts were created under the *District Courts Act* 1969 (Samoa). However, in this piece of legislation, as elsewhere, the courts are sometimes referred to as magistrates' courts.

18 *Criminal Procedure Code* [Cap 136] (Vanuatu), ss 118 & 119.

19 *E.g. Criminal Procedure Code* [Cap 21] (Fiji Islands), s 163.

20 Newton, T. 2000. The differential impact of criminal law on males and females in Pacific Island jurisdictions. *Development Bulletin* 51: 13–16 at p 15.

21 It could also be as a result of pressure applied by the husband's family or the family of the wife. Such pressure may well include expressed or implied disapproval of the wife's complaints about the husband's behaviour.

22 Findlay, M. 1997. Above, n 7 at p 157.

23 See below for further discussion.

24 [1992] Tonga LR 7.

25 Unreported, Supreme Court of the Federated States of Micronesia (Appellate Division), FSM Appeal Case No. P4–1988, 1st November 1989. (http://www.vanuatu.usp.ac.fj/paclawmat/Micronesia_cases/Volume_G–N/Gilmete_v_FSM.html Accessed 19/9/02).

26 Unreported, High Court of Solomon Islands, Crim. Case No. 33, of 1996, 6th June 1997(sentencing) (http://www.vanuatu.usp.ac.fj/paclawmat/Solomon_Islands_cases/Volume_R–Z/R_v_Funifaka.html Accessed 19/9/02).

27 [1985/86] SILR 158.

28 *Per* Connolly J.A. at p 163.

29 The section numbers are revised in the 1996 consolidation of the legislation of Solomon Islands.

30 Above, n 27.

31 See Banks, C. 1998. Custom in the Courts: Criminal Law (Compensation) Act of Papua New Guinea. *British Journal of Criminology* 38(2): 299–316.

32 In 1977, the 'Supreme Court' fulfilled the role of today's High Court.

33 Unreported, Supreme Court of Fiji Islands (Appellate Jurisdiction), Criminal Appeal No 30 of 1977, 13th May 1977.

34 Unreported, Supreme Court of Fiji Islands (Appellate Division), Criminal appeal No. 30 of 1977, 13th May 1977.

35 Unreported, Supreme Court of the Republic of Vanuatu, CR No. 4 of 1998, 22nd March 1999 (http://www.vanuatu.usp.ac.fj/paclawmat/Vanuatu_cases/Volume_O–Q/ PP_v_Thomas.html Accessed 19/9/02).

36 *Criminal Procedure Code* [Cap 136] (Vanuatu).

37 See also *Public Prosecutor v Lissy Kalip*, Unreported, Supreme Court of the Republic of Vanuatu, CR No. 54 of 1997, 6th October 1998 (http://www.vanuatu.usp.ac.fj/paclawmat/Vanuatu_cases/Volume_O–Q/PP_v_Kalip%20 (Sentence).html Accessed 19/9/02).

38 Section 2(1).

39 See ss 35–38 of the *Powers of Criminal Courts Act* 1973 (UK) as amended.

40 Kalinoe, L. and Twivey, T. 1996. Compensation Payment Outside Court By Perpetrators of Crime: *The State v. William Muma. Melanesian Law Journal* 24: 117–121 at p 121.

41 Banks, C. 1998. Above, n 31.

42 South African Law Commission. 1999. *The Harmonisation of the Common Law and Indigenous Law: Traditional Courts and the Judicial Function of Traditional Leaders.* Discussion Paper 82.

43 South African Law Reform Commission. 1999. Above, n 42, at p 17. Emphasis added.

44 South African Law Reform Commission. 1999. Above, n 42, at p 31. Emphasis added.

45 (1995) 7 BCLR 861.

46 South African Law Reform Commission. 1999. Above, n 42, at p 31. Emphasis added.

47 Tomaino, T. 1999. Punishment practice. In Sarre, R. & Tomaino, J. (eds). *Exploring Criminal Justice: Contemporary Australian Themes.* Adelaide: South Australian Institute of Justice Studies Inc., at p 213. Emphasis added.

48 These states are Northern Territory, Queensland and Western Australia.

49 However, it should be remembered that it is not possible to make sweeping generalisations about Aboriginal customary law and practice. As in the South Pacific region, different communities have different customs.

50 (1992) 79 NTR 1.

51 *Per* Asche CJ.

52 *Per* Mildren J.

53 For examples of expressed dissatisfaction with the (in)activities of police forces in the region see Newton, T. 2000. Above, n 4.

Review Questions

1. Of all the differences between state law and customary law, which do you think are the most significant and why?

2. Do you think that customary law and introduced law can co-exist in a single legal system? Why/why not?

3. What policies or principles should the courts follow when incorporating customary issues (such as reconciliation and compensation) into sentencing decisions? Can these policies and principles be applied to other areas of law?

4. What would be the advantages and disadvantages of establishing 'custom criminal courts' in the countries of the region? Could such courts be usefully used in other areas of law?

5. Do you think that custom discriminates against women? If so, how? Do you think that introduced law can usefully be used to correct any discrimination?

Further readings

Allen, M. (ed) 1981. *Vanuatu: Politics, Economics and Ritual in Island Melanesia.* Sydney: Academic Press.

Findlay, M. 1997. Crime, community penalty and integration with legal formalism in the South Pacific. *Journal of Pacific Studies* 21: 145 – 160.

Jalal, P.I. 1998. Law for Pacific Women: A Legal Rights Handbook. Suva: Fiji Women's Rights Movement.

Rose, D.B. 1996. Land Rights and Deep Colonising: The Erasure of Women. *Aboriginal Law Bulletin* Vol 3 No. 85: 6 – 13.

Zorn, J.G. & Corrin Care, J. 2002. *Proving Customary Law in the Common Law Courts of the South Pacific.* London: British Institute of International and Comparative Law.

SECTION 4
HUMAN RIGHTS

People who live in the South Pacific would seem to know a lot about human rights. That is, they hear a lot about human rights. Issues of human rights loom large on a daily basis, whether in the context of constitutional reform, the place of women in public life, the roles and functions of policing organisations or clashes between landowners and migrant settlers. The concept of human rights appears to have established and entrenched itself very securely in the consciousness of the region. In this section our authors present some timely and provocative critiques of the orthodoxy of human rights discussions as they are usually presented in the region.

The first two chapters go some way to filling gaps that are often present when human rights are discussed. First, Anita Jowitt grounds the concept of 'universal' human rights in an exposition of historical and jurisprudential development. Second, Ian Fraser examines the political and pragmatic aspects of the development of human rights and the extent to which they are accepted in Pacific island societies. Finally Owen Jessep considers the particular tensions that arise between customary family law and laws that seek to act to prevent or counter gender discrimination. His more practical consideration serves to reiterate and exemplify further the broader questions that were raised in the preceding chapters.

9. THE NOTION OF HUMAN RIGHTS

By Anita Jowitt

KEY TERMS AND PHRASES

Rhetoric

Whilst rhetoric has particular meaning in reference to classical Greek principles and rules of composition, it more popularly is used to indicate the art of, or a body of, persuasive (although not necessarily well reasoned) writing.

Jurisprudence/jurisprudential

Jurisprudence can be thought of as the philosophy of law, and jurisprudential thought as philosophical thought about law.

Discourse

The word discourse is used to represent a body of thought and writing on a particular topic or idea. As such it represents a collection of works. Whilst there will be a plurality of views within this body of ideas, a dominant strand of argument will usually come to represent the whole body of discourse. As such the notion of discourse can be perceived as an implicitly ideological device for referring to a body of ideas.

Hegemony/hegemonic

Hegemony is used to refer to a system in which control is maintained not by force but by influence over others. This influence is gained through use of social institutions to portray and reinforce a particular ideology.

Ideology

A system of beliefs that cannot be established as being true about the way that things are or should be.

INTRODUCTION

Human rights appear to be an incontrovertible part of the modern legal and political world. The Universal Declaration of Human Rights 1948,[1] which purports to affirm a number of universal inalienable rights, is probably the United Nations' best known document. In the Pacific the constitutions of almost all USP member countries enshrine human rights.[2] Powerful political organisations, including women's rights and minority rights movements form around human rights and are a prominent part of political discourse in most modern Western or Western influenced democracies including Pacific island countries. For example, the human right of self-determination provided a focal point for Pacific decolonisation movements.[3] Globally a number of large international organisations, including the United Nations, have the protection and promotion of human rights as central goals. It seems that all right thinking people agree with human rights.

Although there seems to be international agreement with a core number of universal inalienable human rights, in recent years the use of human rights throughout the Pacific has proved to be one of the most contentious legal issues. Clashes between customary norms and human rights, particularly in relation to the issue of equality for women, have resulted in a number of judicial interventions.[4] Such clashes mean that the idea of universal inalienable rights is thrown into question. After all, if such rights really were universal and inalienable then they would exist within all cultures and surely customary norms would have developed in accordance with them. Additionally, on a socio-political level the rhetoric of human rights has been used for objectionable, or at least inequitable, ends. For instance, George Speight justified the May 2000 coup in Fiji Islands on the grounds that it was necessary to protect the indigenous peoples' rights. Whilst this is an extreme example, and possibly not a good one as it is widely acknowledged that indigenous peoples' rights were a mere front for the underlying political power plays, human rights are used in this way to favour one group of people at the expense of others. How can this be right?

This chapter examines the following questions: What are human rights? Where do they come from? Can anyone prove that they exist? Who decides what human rights are right? Why do most people seem to accept the idea of human rights? In examining these questions the chapter will consider the philosophical and political history of human rights. As the history of human rights in Western political thought stretches back to the early Greek philosophers this chapter is necessarily an introduction that only touches on the broad themes that underpin the concept of human rights. It is hoped that this introduction will also provide a background to some major strands of jurisprudential thought that can be used to examine not only human rights, but other aspects of law and policy as well.

WHERE DO HUMAN RIGHTS COME FROM: NATURAL LAW THEORY

If asked what human rights are or where they come from many people will say that human rights arise because they are a natural part of being a human being. They are something that you are born with, an innate part of being human. Such a rationale is present in the United Nations Universal Declaration of Human Rights 1948. Both the preamble and the articles emphasise that the rights come from the inherent dignity or innate nature of humankind as the excerpts below indicate (italics added):

Preamble

Whereas recognition of the *inherent dignity and of the equal and inalienable rights of all members of the human family* is the foundation of freedom, justice and peace in the world...

Whereas the peoples of the United Nations have in the Charter reaffirmed their faith in *fundamental human rights, in the dignity and worth of the human person* and in the equal rights of men and women and have determined to promote social progress and better standards of life in larger freedom...

Article I

All human beings are born free and equal in dignity and rights. They are endowed with reason and conscience and should act towards one another in a spirit of brotherhood.

We can also see the concept that human rights are an innate part of being a person reflected in constitutions within the Pacific. For example, the Preamble of the Marshall Islands *Constitution* 1979 states:

WE, THE PEOPLE OF THE MARSHALL ISLANDS, trusting God, the Giver of our life, liberty, identity and our *inherent rights*, do hereby exercise these rights and establish for ourselves and generations to come this Constitution, setting forth the legitimate legal framework for the governance of the Marshall Islands. (Italics added)

The concept of human rights being a natural part of being a human being is part of the jurisprudential tradition of natural law theory. Put simply, natural law theory is the idea that the whole universe is governed by overarching natural laws. Because the physical reality of the universe is unchanging and applies everywhere this natural law is also unchanging and applies everywhere. To Aristotle's illustration that "a law of nature is immutable and has the same validity everywhere, as fire burns both here and in Persia..."[5] we can add that fire burns both now and in ancient Greece. This natural law is the source of innate rights. The Roman lawyer and statesman Cicero described natural law, which he referred to as "true" law, in the following way:

True law is right reason in agreement with nature; it is of universal application; unchanging and everlasting... And there will not be different laws at Rome or at

Athens, or different laws now and in the future, but one eternal and unchangeable law will be valid for all nations and for all times...[6]

Natural law is conceived of as law derived from the higher order of nature that exists independently of laws made by people. It provides natural moral or ethical criteria from which the rules for correct living can be derived. It should be noted that although human made law should accord with these natural moral and ethical criteria it is not necessarily true that human made law will comply with the natural law. Bad laws, or laws not in accordance with nature, can be made by human institutions and will be recognised as valid in accordance with the rules of recognition created by those institutions, regardless of their *complilance* with natural law.

How can we identify what is natural?

The first belief as to how natural law can be identified is through the belief that natural law can be revealed by a higher source that has knowledge of the natural order of things. This higher source is often believed to be a god who has knowledge of the natural order of things because he or she is also the creator of things or has divine knowledge of the natural order. We can see evidence of the provision of natural law through divine revelation in the very earliest laws. The Sumerian king Hammurabi, who wrote the oldest known code of laws around 2000 B.C., claimed to receive these laws from the Sun-god Shamash. Islamic law, which today provides the basic legal system for a considerable number of countries, is based on the Koran, a recording of divine revelations made to the Prophet Mohammed.[7] Within Judaism and Christianity probably the best-known example of law through divine revelation is the ten Commandments that were handed to Moses. In the modern English common law tradition we can continue to see the influence of the divine revelations recorded in the Bible even though law is meant to be secular. Most law students will be familiar with Lord Atkins's statement in *Donoghue v Stevenson* that "[t]he rule that you are to love your neighbour becomes in law, you must not injure your neighbour".[8] This principle is the basis for the modern law of negligence although the rule can be found in both the Old and New Testaments.[9] Laws found in divine revelations also affect the legislature within modern common law systems. For example, the fourth of the ten commandments, that the Sabbath should be kept as a day of rest,[10] has influenced some employment contracts legislation. For example, Vanuatu's *Employment Act* [Cap 160] states that "no employee shall be required to work on a Sunday"[11] and that "every employee shall be entitled to a weekly rest of 24 consecutive hours which shall normally fall on a Sunday".[12]

The second main belief as to how natural law can be identified is the belief that, as nature is rational, the rational observation of human beings and society will enable these criteria to be logically deduced. Such an approach to the identification of natural law can be found in the works of the classical Greek philosophers. Of these, Plato and Aristotle have had the most influence on modern legal and political thought.

Plato's view of nature was that the world we live in is merely an imperfect reflection of reality. Reality consists of ideal forms. These ideal forms are true to nature and the appearances that we see are only imperfect copies of these real forms. Plato's conception of nature is explained in *The Republic* in the allegory of the cave. In a dialogue Socrates explains to Glaucon that the appearances we perceive are a mere shadow of reality.[13] He creates an allegory of people chained in an underground den and unable to turn around with a fire behind them and a wall in front of them. All they can see is shadows of people and objects passing behind them in front of the fire. As this is all they know, they presume the shadows that they see to be reality. This story represents people in the ordinary world, who only see imperfect shadows of reality and mistake these shadows for reality. In Plato's conception of the state only very few people have sufficient reasoning capacity to comprehend reality. Given a high degree of training, these "philosopher kings" would be placed to rule the everyday world according to nature as found in the reality of ideal forms.

Aristotle sees nature, or the correct order of things, as being determined by a thing's end purpose. Aristotle's belief is that all things have a particular potential, and this is their nature. For example, the potential of a coconut is to grow into a coconut tree. This is the coconut's natural end. By observation and reason a thing's end can be determined. Natural laws are the laws that allow things to achieve their ends. As nature, for Aristotle, is determined by the *telos* or end purpose of a thing, his analysis is said to be teleological.[14] In respect of people, government and laws should be created to allow individuals to fulfil their *telos*, which is *eudaimonia*, a word usually translated as meaning happiness. *Eudaimonia* includes a sense of success and of material, mental and physical well being over time and is achieved by allowing people to fulfil their social and political natures.

In modern times the idea that reason can be used to discover truths about nature has become particularly important. The rise of science[15] has greatly influenced philosophy and in particular has led to the development of the social sciences. These social sciences include disciplines such as sociology, psychology and economics. Just as sciences such as chemistry, physics and biology rely upon observation, experimentation and experience to discover the natural laws of the physical universe, so too do these disciplines aim to apply scientific methods to discover truths about the behaviour of society and human beings. Whilst we may now take such a methodological approach for granted, such an approach has only been developed and systematised fairly recently. The word sociology was only coined in the early nineteenth century by Auguste Comte, who attempted to apply scientific method to the study of society.

It should be noted that a belief in the existence of a god and divine revelations can coexist with a belief that natural laws can also be ascertained through the use of reason. This was demonstrated most eloquently by the medieval Christian theologian St Thomas Aquinas. In Thomist philosophy God's eternal plan or reason for the universe provides the eternal law. This eternal law provides the correct ordering of things. Humanity can know of the eternal law in two ways. The first is through revelation by God, primarily through the scriptures. Such revelations form the divine law. The second way that humanity can come to know of the eternal law is through rational observation of the order of things. In identifying the eternal order St Thomas Aquinas adopts Aristotle's teleological analysis and looks to the ends or purposes of things. As everything is ordered according to the eternal law rational inquiry will reveal part of the eternal law. The parts of the eternal law that come to be known to humanity through reasoned observation form the natural law. Finally, there is the law made by humankind.[16]

The challenge to natural law theory

The difficulty with natural law theory is the question of how the existence of some kind of higher natural order can be proved or conclusively identified. St Thomas Aquinas finds his source of natural order in God, a belief that cannot be proved but requires faith. 'Scientific' approaches relying upon rational observation also require that assumptions about the natural order or human nature be made. For instance, Aristotle believed that you could identify the natural order through rational observation of the telos of things, but deciding on what the telos of humanity is requires the making of assumptions about human nature. What human nature is cannot be proved but is also a matter of faith or belief, so such reasoning becomes somewhat circular. It can also be noted that slavery is part of Aristotle's natural order. These days most people consider slavery to be abhorrent, but it was an accepted part of Greek society in Aristotle's time. Its inclusion in Aristotle's concept of natural order indicates that assumptions about what is natural are influenced by one's society and environment. There are also philosophical challenges to the question of how far we are able to accurately observe nature.[17] Whilst natural law theories contribute significantly to the idea of human rights, the problem that remains with such an approach is that the question 'what is natural?' cannot be objectively answered, but is always reduced to a matter of faith or belief. Just as people have faith in different religions so do people have differing views about what natural order is, whether these ideas come from different religious faiths or some other source.

ARE HUMAN RIGHTS SIMPLY MAN MADE LAWS?

If, then, we are unable to identify the source of natural order from which human rights seem to spring, does this mean that human rights are nothing more or less than human made laws? The legal positivist answer to this would be yes. Legal positivism takes the view that the law, including human rights, is simply a product of human institutions. Whether something is a law is a matter of fact. There are rules of recognition, including parliamentary rules about what must be done in order to validly enact a statute and the doctrine of judicial precedent, that assist in determining this fact.[18] Law, then, is identified by its pedigree, or the way it was made, and not its content. Ideas of what is natural still retain a place in society and may influence the content of the law, but are not law. Law is what actually exists in conventions, on the statute books and within cases. Belief about what is natural provides people with morals from which come beliefs about what law ought to be. Human rights have force, then, not because they are natural, or somehow morally correct, but because they are validly passed laws.

The positivist approach answers the question 'what are human rights?' satisfactorily from the perspective of a practising lawyer who does not have to examine why laws get made but only has to identify what is law in order to be able to apply it. However, on a philosophical level the positivist answer to what human rights are is quite unsatisfactory. It does not help to explain why human rights seem to be special, or why the rhetoric of human rights is so pervasive within modern Western legal and popular thought. It also does not tell us much about how perceptions of morality influence the law.

THE PERVASIVENESS OF HUMAN RIGHTS

Perhaps we can go beyond the positivist approach to human rights by saying that they represent the most commonly shared beliefs about what is natural and right. Because human rights represent the common ideal they assume higher status than other laws that are concerned with the regulation of human lives rather than the upholding of ideals. Such a conception of human rights subtly shifts away from natural law theories. A natural law conception of human rights would hold that human rights are rights that are in accordance with the innate nature of humankind. This conception holds that human rights are rights that are in accordance with what the majority of people believe to be the innate nature of humankind. As such, human rights are human made laws, but they gain their authority from a widespread belief about what is right.

If one accepts that human rights are based on beliefs about what is natural then human rights become disputable. Whilst one cannot argue with a concrete, provable, natural order one can argue about beliefs about what this order is. Indeed, in the Pacific, where human rights were received as part of the Western-style constitution making, we are well placed to question the dominant belief about natural order. The post-colonial discourse that challenges the cultural imperialism of the colonisers who believed that their way of life was the right way and saw part of their role as 'civilising' islanders is challenging beliefs about the natural order. In terms of human rights, we sometimes see challenges to human rights because of their focus on individual equality and freedoms rather than communitarian values that are part of traditional Pacific island lifestyles.[19]

However, human rights were generally adopted into Pacific constitutions and are widely accepted both in the Pacific and internationally. Although if one stops to think about human rights one may come to realise that they are only *beliefs* and therefore open to challenge, challenges do not often occur with any success. Why is this?

The place of ideology

The answer to this question may be that most people do accept, or at least not question, the current concept of human rights as being natural or somehow fundamental. We can say that they are the dominant ideology, or belief system about the way the world is ordered. As a belief system about natural order this ideology will support the beliefs of some people whilst rejecting the beliefs of others. As such, ideology is not neutral. It supports the interests, as reflected in the beliefs, of one group, whilst rejecting the views of others. Remember that Aristotle believed that slavery was part of the natural order. Whilst this belief obviously suited the slave owners, who could justify their behaviour as upholding nature, one wonders what the slaves thought of this.

Karl Marx was one of the most significant philosophers to pick up on the idea that the way in which society was organised is not neutral. His view was that all of society is organised around its means of production and relations of production. In a capitalist society things are therefore organised around class lines, with the people who own the factories and other means of production, the capitalists, exploiting the workers. These exploitative relationships are maintained by ideology, a widespread belief amongst all members of society that this is the natural order, or the only order that society can take. Marx's analysis of ideology has contributed significantly to much modern political discourse. Within the field of law, schools of jurisprudence such as critical legal studies and feminist legal studies rely upon this ideological analysis. Their aim is to look behind the law to see what power structures are being upheld by the supposedly neutral laws before which every person is meant to be treated equally.[20] Some of the key beliefs of such analyses are that:

- Institutions, or the ways in which society is organised, are not neutral. Instead they are designed to maintain particular relationships and power structures.

- Ideology maintains these power structures. Ideology is a belief system, something people believe to be true even though it cannot be proven to be objectively 'true'. This belief system is often unconscious, or taken for granted without conscious thought.

- Hegemonic control is used to maintain ideologies/power relations without the need to use force. In other words, the 'oppressed' themselves consent to the system of oppression because they believe it to be 'natural'. Education, media, the political system, the legal system, religion, family structures and other social structures all help to maintain control without force. This is why ideology becomes so powerful. Although it is only an idea or belief, through hegemonic control people come to accept that the ideology is actually real, and therefore do not question it.[21]

Examining the ideology of the law therefore involves looking at the power structures behind the law and who they benefit. One cannot presume that law is neutral. An analytical approach that expressly acknowledges the place of ideology is powerful because it makes seemingly unassailable ideas more open to challenge. If something like human rights has ideological support it will be accepted as natural. It will seem to be more than simply a man made law and therefore will be difficult to challenge.

However, using an ideological analysis one can challenge the idea that things are 'natural' on the grounds that this is just a belief representing a particular ideology.

Ideology within human rights

Liberalism is the conservative politics linked to both to the rise of capitalism and, frequently, to the rise of modern formulations of human rights. Capitalism operates on the idea of free market (or *laissez faire*) economics. Freedom to do anything that will not impinge upon other people's freedoms is one of the cornerstones of human rights. *Laissez faire* economics relies upon individuals acting competitively in self-interest in order for the free market to operate efficiently. Again we see this in the individualistic nature of human rights formulations which stress the rights of the individual and balance the rights of one individual again other individuals. Capitalism also relies on the idea that an individual's private property will be protected from arbitrary interference, something that is protected within human rights documents.[22] Indeed liberalism is behind many other things in the common law legal system, such as the notion of freedom of contract, the shift from strict liability to fault based liability in negligence and the arrangement of Western land tenure systems. Even the things that the State says are crimes protect the liberal ideology or capitalist order (one can at least argue).

This argument that human rights uphold liberal ideology is further strengthened when one looks at the history of modern human rights documents. The modern conception of human rights was first drafted into constitutional significance at the time of the events of the American and French Revolutions. The first draft of the American *Constitution* was presented in 1787 and came into effect in 1791. The French Declaration of the Rights of Man and the Citizen was produced in 1789. Both share similar philosophical roots.[23] The principles enshrined in these documents provided the basis for the UN Declaration of Human Rights, 1948, which has in turn fed into modern constitutions and bills of rights in the Pacific region and elsewhere. The French revolution has been labelled a middle class revolution in that it aimed to free a newly emerging class of capitalists from the oppressive rule and taxation regime of the monarchy.[24] Similarly progressive interpretations of the American Revolution was largely fuelled by dissatisfaction with British taxation of the colony and its exports and aimed to accomplish political, economic and social ends favourable to the development of free enterprise.[25]

Human rights were also the product of Western societies and thinkers. As such they may be criticised for being ethnocentric, or focussed on upholding the beliefs and social structures of particular ethnicities at the expense of the beliefs and social structures in other cultures.[26]

However, although human rights may be linked to an ethnocentric liberal ideology, they can be used to support other peoples' ideological agendas. Here, for example, we can look to the events of May 2000 in Fiji Islands, during which George Speight and his supporters used the notion of indigenous people's rights to gain legitimacy for their actions. Here human rights were used to justify underlying political power plays. I said in the introduction that Speight's actions are possibly not a good example of how human rights can be used for inequitable ends because they were a mere front for the underlying political power plays driving the attempted coup. However, I tend to think that this is an excellent example of how rights discourse can be manipulated to meet particular agendas. We can also look at women's rights movements both throughout the Pacific and internationally, that have used the notion of human rights to fight patriarchal (or male dominated) social structures within various cultures and economic systems.[27]

CONCLUSION

In this chapter we have looked behind that idea that human rights are 'natural' and therefore that they hold special moral force. We have seen that, rather than actually being part of the natural order, they only represent beliefs about this natural order. We have also seen how through the ideological device of hegemonic control, this belief is accepted as really representing the natural order. I have also briefly linked the concept of human rights to ethnocentric liberalism. Whilst liberalism is probably the dominant ideology (or world order) in Western societies today there are many other ideologies or belief systems that either work in parallel or aim to refute liberalism. Patriarchy, the belief that men are inherently superior to women, is an ideology. Modernisation, or the belief in the organic evolution of society towards a higher goal, is an ideology (often closely linked to liberalism through various development programmes that see capitalist economic development as being the ultimate development agenda). The idea of the 'Melanesian Way'[28] is an ideology. The belief that white people (or black people or any other kind of people) are inherently superior to others is an ideology. All of these things affect the power structures in society. Some of them are very pervasive. People tend to accept them because they are 'natural'.

Analysis that challenges or critiques ideologies is useful for questioning human rights and opening up debates about what the place of the current concept of human rights should be in relation to other rights such as community, cultural and religious rights. It is also useful for looking behind other aspects of law and social order to see what power structures are supported by seemingly neutral social institutions.

The final question I want to pose is how important is it that human rights merely represent beliefs about what is right? It seems to be part of the human condition that we do not actually know what it is that nature has ordained for us. Maybe the best that we can do is to create beliefs and ideals for the collective humanity to strive for. Human rights, so long as they are recognised as being a statement of belief about ideals, and not an unchanging statement of natural order, can provide governments and peoples with aspiration and goals. Maybe this is sufficient justification for them to retain their central place within current legal and political thinking.

ENDNOTES

1   General Assembly resolution 217 A (III) of 10th December 1948.

2   USP is the University of the South Pacific. The member countries are Vanuatu, Solomon Islands, Fiji Islands, Samoa, Tokelau, Tuvalu, Marshall Islands, Niue, Cook Islands, Kiribati, Tonga and Nauru. The only USP member countries that do not enshrine human rights in their constitutions are Niue (Niue *Constitution Act* 1974) and Tokelau (*Tokelau Act* 1948 (NZ)).

3   On a global level the United Nations also framed decolonisation in the language of human rights. The Declaration on the Granting of Independence to Colonial Countries and Peoples – resolution 1514 (XV) made on 14th December 1960 states that "the subjection of peoples to alien subjugation, domination and exploitation constitutes a *denial of fundamental human rights*, is contrary to the United Nations Charter, and is an impediment to the promotion of world peace and cooperation, and that steps should be taken to transfer, unconditionally, all powers to the Trust and Non-Self-Governing Territories so that they might enjoy complete freedom and independence" (italics added).

4   Chapters in this collection that provide further detail on clashes between human rights and custom include chapter 6, by Zorn, J.G.; chapter 7, by Bothmann, S.; and chapter 11, by Jessep, O.

5   Aristotle *Nichomeachean Ethics* as quoted in Weeramantry, C. G. 1982. A*n Invitation to the Law*. Butterworths: Australia, at pp 262–263.

6   Cicero *The Republic* quoted in Davis, M. 1994. *Asking the Law Question*. Sydney: Law Book Company, at p 61.

7   See Weeramantry, C.C. 1982. Above, n 5, chapter 1, for further discussion of Sumerian law, Islamic law and other legal systems.

8   [1932] AC 562 at p 580.

9   See, for example, Luke 10: 27–29, which also provides Lord Atkins's lawyer's question of 'who is my neighbour?'

10 Exodus 20: 8–10.

11 Section 23(1).

12 Section 25. It should be noted that the Sabbath was originally recognised as being Saturday. It still is recogised as such within the Jewish tradition. However, because of the influence of Catholicism and other forms of Christianity the Sabbath is now widely recognised to fall on Sunday.

13 Plato *The Republic* Book VII. (http://www.wsu.edu/~dee/GREECE/ALLEGORY.HTM#A Accessed 26/9/01).

14 Most jurisprudence textbooks will provide a general discussion of the contributions of Plato and Aristotle to jurisprudence. See, for example, McCourbrey, H. & White, N. 1996. *Textbook on Jurisprudence (2nd ed)*. London: Blackstone Press Ltd; Davis, M. 1994. Above, n 5.

15 The rise of science is linked in particular to the scientific revolution, which occurred in the late 1500s–1600s, and the Enlightenment, otherwise known as the Age of Reason, an era from the late 1600s–1700s. For an overview of these periods and the changes that took

place in thinking at these times see Spenser, L. & Krauze, A. 1997. *The Enlightenment for Beginners*. Cambridge: Icon Books Ltd; Hankins, T. 1985. *Science and the Enlightenment*. Cambridge: Cambridge University Press; Henry, J. 1997. *The Scientific Revolution and the Origins of Modern Science*. London: Macmillan Press.

16 For more on the legal philosophy of Aquinas see Sigmund, P. 1993. Law and Politics. In Kretzmann, N. & Stump, E. (eds.) *The Cambridge Companion to Aquinas*. Cambridge: Cambridge University Press, at pp 217–231.

17 See, for example, Kuhn, T. 1970. *The Structure of Scientific Revolutions* (2nd ed). Chicago: Chicago University Press; Newton-Smith, W. H. 1981. *The Rationality of Science*. London: Routledge.

18 Most jurisprudence texts will contain further discussion of legal positivism. See, for example, McCourbey, H. & White, N. 1996. Above n 14; Harris, J. W. 1997. *Legal Philosophies* (2nd ed). UK: Butterworths.

19 For other chapters in this collection that discuss the clash in communitarian and individual values see above, n 4.

20 For further discussion of ideological analysis of law see Grigg-Spall, I. & Ireland, P. 1992. *The Critical Lawyers' Handbook*. London: Pluto Press.

21 Antonio Gramsci initially developed the concept of hegemony. For an introduction to his work see Ransome, P. 1992. *Antonio Gramsci A New Introduction*. London: Harvester Wheatsheaf. For later applications of hegemonic analysis and extensions of theory relating to the analysis of ideology see Young, M. 1971. *Knowledge and Control*. London: Collier-Macmillan; R. Harker, C. Mahar and C. Wilkes. 1990. *An Introduction to the Work of Pierre Bourdieu*. London: Macmillan.

22 See, for example, Article 17 of the Universal Declaration of Human Rights.

23 See Dunn, S. 1999. *Sister Revolutions: French Lightning, American Light*. New York: Faber and Faber Inc.

24 Such an interpretation of the French Revolution is found in Marxist commentary on the Revolution. Georges Lefebvre, in summarising such interpretations states "Another criticism [of the Revolution]... is that it favoured one class at the expense of the others, namely the bourgeoisie that drew it up... economic liberty, though not mentioned, is very much in [the Declaration of the Rights of Man and the Citizen's] spirit... The Declaration, in short, is blamed for having allowed capitalism to develop without control..." Lefebvre, G. 1964. Declaration of the Rights of Man as the Essence of the Enlightenment. In Church, W.F. (ed.) *The Influence of the Enlightenment on the French Revolution: Creative, Disastrous or Non Existent*. Boston: Heath and Company. For more recent commentary on Marxist interpretations and contemporary revisions of the Revolution see Temple, N. 1992. *The Road to 1789: From Reform to Revolution in France*. Cardiff: University of Wales Press.

25 For an overview of different historical interpretations of the American Revolution see Greene, J. (ed.) 1968. *The Reinterpretation of the American Revolution 1763–1789*. New York, Evanston & London: Harper and Row Publishers; Webking, R. 1988. *The American Revolution and the Politics of Liberty*. Baton Rouge & London: Louisiana State University Press.

26 For further discussion of these criticisms see Weeramantry, C.G. 1982. Above, n 5 at pp 210–211.

27 Wide ranging discussion of the role of ideology in human rights and the uses to which rights discourse has been put can be found in Dunne, T. and Wheeler, N. 1999. *Human Rights in Global Politics*. Cambridge: Cambridge University Press.

28 'The Melanesian Way' has been used by a number of Melanesian politicians as device for creating identity around a supposedly homogeneous Melanesian culture. See, for example, Sokomanu, G. 1992. Government in Vanuatu: The Place of Culture and Tradition. In Crocombe, R. Neemia, U. Ravuvu, A. and von Busch, W. (eds.) *Culture and Democracy in the South Pacific*. Suva: Institute of Pacific Studies.

10. HUMAN RIGHTS VS. CUSTOM IN THE PACIFIC: STRUGGLE, ADAPTATION, OR GAME?

By: Ian Fraser

KEY TERMS AND PHRASES

Analogy

The comparison of one item with another, suggesting that they are alike in some relevant way. In the common law analagous reasoning is the extension of a rule derived from a precedent to a different factual situation, by arguing that the new situation is relevantly similar to that of the precedent.

Aspiration

An aspiration is a wish to achieve, or attain, some state or condition. A constitution's aspirational element may be a unified, prosperous, and orderly society.

Discrimination

To discriminate is to differentiate among things, or people, in order to treat different categories of those things or people differently. Every statute and every legal decision does this, of course, but as normally used in the law the meaning of the term is more specific. It describes discrimination which is unjustified or unlawful. (A government does not discriminate when it issues passports only to its citizens, but it is discriminating when it issues passports only to male citizens.)

Globalisation

The growing standardisation of any of a number of activities and values across countries and cultures. Most commonly, the expansion of developed world, especially American, economic practices to the rest of the world.

Idealisation

The conception that for every phenomenon in the world there is a perfect model, or archetype, of which the actual phenomena are merely imperfect examples. One could say marriage is often idealised as a loving, complete, and permanent union, even by people who have never known a real couple who lived so. This way of conceiving of reality has great power in Western philosophy.

Ideology

A set of beliefs which is internally consistent, forming the basis of a person's outlook on life or some aspect of life. (The term is usually used to refer to beliefs about politics and political issues.)

INTRODUCTION

I propose here a scheme for considering what is going on when, in argument about a government policy or decision, some people invoke 'human rights' (or 'constitutional rights') to justify their views and other people, opposing them, invoke 'custom' (or 'tradition'). Such arguments may be political contests within a government's own bureaucracy, or in Parliament, or academic debates in pages like these or in university cafeterias, or legal submissions to courts of law or law reform bodies, or popular disputes in editorial pages, over kitchen tables or under village trees. I propose a scheme, a set of models, for thinking about the patterns that these arguments assume whatever their setting.

The models emphasise what is distinctive about the different views one can take. This will accurately reflect what is going on in some instances of the arguments. For others, it might seem to be exaggeration, a most un-Pacific focus on difference, on the implications or assumptions of what a person says, or believes. But the aim here is clarity in observation, not viable tactics for resolving disputes. (Those, one hopes, are fostered by clear perception.) We, as students of the South Pacific, are observing events, and observers need categories to make sense of what they see — it helps to have lobsters and true crabs in mind when studying coconut crabs — and what follows, I think, helps understand this field of study.

The scheme: struggle, adaptation, game

This is not a purely legal view. From a legal point of view, the issue is simple if considered in the abstract — yet in any concrete case it is complex, too complex to yield even a narrowly legal answer.

The simplicity lies in the hierarchy of laws, the first thing any student of law learns, in the Pacific or elsewhere. The constitution is above all other law in the sense that if any conflict arises between it and what some other 'law', or source of law, seems to say then the constitution prevails. At the same time it is below all law, in the sense that all lawful acts and decisions must, however indirectly, be based on it. It is the foundation of law, the only set of rules and principles whose validity does not depend upon some other set of legal rules and principles. It just is: it is *that* it is, to invoke a Biblical, and so quite apt, analogy (as I shall argue). So, 'in principle', legal principle, the answer to any question involving the legal powers, disabilities, rights, privileges, or prohibitions of anyone or any authority is simple. The law's answer is whatever the constitution says. If that accords with the 'rights' side, that side wins; if it accords with the 'tradition' side, that side wins. This marvellously straightforward approach to otherwise thorny issues is the very point of the movement for — originally an idealistic dream of — written constitutions.[1]

The complexity, of course, lies in the second thing any student of law learns. The same set of words may quite legitimately mean different things to different people. That is, one can disagree with someone else about what a set of words, including a provision of the constitution, should mean (should be 'held' by a court to mean), while admitting that the other interpretation is a possible, or plausible, one. It is just that more than one plausible interpretation exists, especially as the words are applied to any particular set of circumstances. Further, in any given set of circumstances, one finds that others do not necessarily share the interpretation one would prefer. At that point everyone is agreed that the constitution should prevail: yet there is no agreement on what should actually be done. Should the constitution mean what the words it uses are held to mean in foreign jurisdictions? Should it mean what one thinks 'the people' would read it to mean? If it reiterates rights in terms shared by international and foreign bills of rights, as all the Pacific constitutions do, but also expresses an adherence to the traditional values of its place — as all Pacific constitutions also do[2] — can its true meaning be that one prevails over the other?

An example is the recurring issue in Melanesian jurisdictions of migrants settling on land to which they have no title, near capital cities, who become perceived by more secure residents of those cities as labour pools for criminal gangs. Since before independence in Papua New Guinea, since the early 1980s in Solomon Islands, and by the end of last century in Vanuatu, proposals have been regularly thrown up by the press and politicians to 'send the squatters back home'. Just as regularly they are met by the objection that this would violate the squatters' rights. The legitimacy of kicking the miscreants off rightful owners' land lies in custom. Village leaders in the squatters' home areas should take responsibility for their people and *make* them return. The legitimacy of letting the citizens stay where the opportunities are lies in the rights granted by the constitution: they share everyone's right of movement within their country, they share everyone's liberty from arbitrary seizure. The debate assumes that form, and then it freezes. (If action does follow, it is a matter of sheer force: bulldozers in PNG, militias in Solomon Islands.)

Should we regard this suspended argument as the legal aspect of a political struggle, in which the concept of rights is a weapon, whose wielders face opponents armed with the concept of custom? I shall consider this view first; it is the closest to what would seem to be the orthodox or mainstream analysis. Legal argument is imagined litigation, which is politics by other means. Like Clausewitz' view of war, this is an idealisation of law — in his terms, 'true' law — law as the pursuit of judicial orders in accordance with correct norms.[3] In this model, what is going on is a struggle (or set of struggles) to accomplish some social or economic end(s), in which the struggling parties attempt to use legal concepts against each other. As observers we should examine the actual use and effectiveness of these concepts, imagine how they might be used and applied, and consider how they could be improved.

But perhaps that model assumes too much rationality in the people, and groups of people, we are observing. Perhaps they are not so calculating and goal-oriented. Law, like war, is not always resorted to as a rationally chosen means to an end. It could be that the concept of rights is attractive to people for reasons other than practical utility: that they are drawn to it not because they have decided that it will help them achieve some goal, but because of some less rational kind of attraction. Perhaps the attractive quality is not so tangible. Perhaps it represents a moral good to them. Perhaps they do not really choose to invoke it at all. Perhaps the concept of rights, in a sense, chooses them — the sense being that the concept, in a way more familiar when we are observing fashions, religions, or consumer preferences, spreads and 'catches on' as though it were alive and people were its environment.

In this model, my second, what is going on is competition between ideologies, 'rights' representing one and 'custom' another. The competition may be conscious, played out in the hearts and minds of the people observed, the subject of deliberate debate; this is the first version of the model. I shall call it the moral version. Or it may be more like natural selection in an ecosystem, played out indeed in hearts and minds but not by those hearts and minds. It could be that the competition is of the attractiveness of concepts, without people being conscious of what attracts them. This is the second version. I shall call this the evolution version. Both versions emphasise the ways a concept can be *adapted* to its environment.

Finally, perhaps both the above models involve being misled by appearances. Perhaps, in the reality the models are intended to describe, rights are *not* 'taken seriously' — any more than communism and anti-communism were in, say, 1980s Africa. It could be that 'human rights' is a mask, a rhetorical device to conceal manoeuvres and motivations quite unconnected to the concept itself — the playing of a *game*. One could see it as a misleading label, stuck onto legal policies which really amount to no more than a continuation of the colonial heritage — the commercially-oriented individualism and freely-alienable property rights that were once labelled 'civilisation' or 'progress'. A corporation, for example, could resist regulation of advertising in the name of 'freedom of expression'.

In this third model what is going on is forces for Western-style development making the associated legal policies more palatable to local people. But one could also see the intended audience as external. This generates another version of the third model. In it, what is going on is local people, especially in government, putting on 'human rights' as a team uniform, showing the international sources of aid, loans, and legitimacy that they are on the same side. What the real manoeuvres and motivations are is arbitrary in relation to the concepts of 'rights' and 'custom'. Those concepts, as in the version described in the paragraph above, are used as labels, but the labels have no relation to the policies they label — like the colours of sports-team uniforms.

What follows, then, is the consideration of several different ways of observing, and thinking about, the significance and relative success of rhetoric about rights and rhetoric about custom in the modern South Pacific. Note that although the rights concept is generally associated with the former colonial powers, it includes notions of collective rights, especially national self-determination and the importance of indigenous status, which are not necessarily of the colonial heritage. Note too that although the custom concept is associated with the quality of being indigenous, its rhetorical deployment generally borrows a great deal from foreign example and non-indigenous institutions (within the region and beyond it). Legal and academic writers advocating the use of custom borrow freely from African literature and Colonial authorities created major custom institutions like the Land and Titles Court in Samoa and the (Great) Council of Chiefs in Fiji Islands. There is no purity in culture. Human affairs are rarely simple. Clarity can only be relative.

STRUGGLE? THE MANA OF HUMAN RIGHTS

It is beyond question that as interpreted in developed world bills of rights a right of movement means that people may not be 'sent back' to their home areas, even if ejecting them from others' land is permissible. Likewise, even the bare right of liberty is incompatible with a chief, or village authority however constituted, ordering a person to live in one place rather than another. The point is simply not arguable — such an order would not be valid even if authorised by a duly enacted statute. It is equally beyond question that village authorities could, in custom, order people of their village to live here or there.[4] This too is not an arguable point — in its context. But in the developed world context land is only property and any association between kinship and locality means very little, and in the customary context people of the village lived in the village. (Because people lived with their leaders, the leaders' power was less autocratic than it might seem when described abstractly.) But the context of modern 'settlements', whether in Port Moresby, Honiara, or Port Vila, is neither of these. This is what leads to the stalemate in argument. Each side is grasping at a branch that has no tree.

Yet each side, if skillful enough advocacy is employed, has a perfectly good legal argument. Each truly does rest on constitutional principle. The constitutions themselves are sufficiently 'flexible' (that is, vague) to support either side in any such issue. This is, notoriously, a feature of constitutions generally. It is crystallised in the Pacific by the explicit recognition of custom as a source of law. Beyond the Pacific, and in particular in the jurisdictions from which Pacific law is derived, a similar complication is expressed, in courts and in popular debate, by appeals to 'common sense', 'community values', or 'the ordinary person'. Within the Pacific courts lump those things together as a distinct source of law called 'custom'. Here too, of course, they really *are* law for all practical purposes, for the majority of the population.[5]

Here in the Pacific, that is, constitutional rights are not the 'trump' they are seen to be in Western jurisdictions: the top-value card that beats any card drawn from ordinary statute or common law. Nonetheless they are, in law, strong bases of argument. Is that status, their force as the basis of argument in law, the reason that people use them in argument generally? Are they attractive because they are seen to carry *mana*, the quality of someone whom others choose to obey (or, time before, a victorious warrior)?

If one thought so then one would have to say that people do intend to achieve ends 'in the real world', outside the courtroom, by invoking rights. In the squatter example it would mean those who advocate letting the squatters stay think that that is what the government will do if they can persuade it, or the courts, that that is what the squatters' rights entail. The power of rights may be restricted to actual litigation, or it may be more general, a *mana* to which public or elite opinion responds, even outside courts of law. If it is that kind of general *mana* then it would follow that if the public or the elite is persuaded that the law requires a course of action there will be support for that course of action. In other words, this model of rights as weapons entails the belief that the law itself is *effective* in causing events outside the legal system — or at least that rights-advocates believe this. Is that justified?

We could consider it justified if there were examples of such impact, comparable to the history of rights-advocacy in other jurisdictions. In America successful rights arguments contributed crucially to ending official racial segregation and enabling access to legal abortion. In Canada they changed the procedures by which refugees are recognised and criminal suspects are investigated. In the UK they cut down the government's immunity to negligence suits. The legal sources of the rights arguments varied, from constitutional bills of rights in North America to common law in Australia and treaties in New Zealand and the UK. But in each jurisdiction it is the legal force of claims of right that created these changes. One should not exaggerate. One should note, especially, that all of these changes are most clearly changes *within* the legal system, whose precise effects on action outside it are much less obvious. But that there are actual effects, often as dramatic as legitimising 'settlements' would be, is indisputable.

Are there such stories in the Pacific jurisdictions? The rights are there in a legal sense. The issues are there in society, including, rather prominently, ones of discrimination, women's security and police powers. Rights arguments have been addressed to courts about political and religious discrimination in Samoa and about police powers in PNG, to take two examples. In deciding that *matai* were not accorded a constitutionally-entrenched preferential franchise, however, the Samoan court relied on interpreting the constitutional provisions relating to the franchise, avoiding decision on the relevance of a right to vote among non-*matai*.[6] Papua New Guinean courts did create a line of decisions excluding evidence from criminal trials for police violation of suspects' rights, although they relied on the common law as much as the rights per se. They created another line awarding damages to village people illegally raided by the police, although these decisions emphasise the common law even more.[7] In neither area, however, is there much sign that police conduct has been affected.

As one can question the precise reality of the rule of law in the Pacific, especially in the large Melanesian countries with their shrinking public services, so one can doubt this first model. Certainly courts of law are not the preferred forum for debating, much less settling, issues which seem to concern human rights — indeed, courts are rarely so used at all. In Fiji Islands and Solomon Islands the effective installation of unconstitutional governments in 2000–2001 has left the notion of a rule of law with only a precarious role in public affairs.

Is this then a likely model? It may describe what some people mean, although probably not many who are not lawyers. As a general view it does seem strained.[8]

ADAPTATION? THE FITNESS OF HUMAN RIGHTS

The inspiration for this model is the inevitable analogy between human rights and Christianity. Both are originally foreign notions. The potential local applicability and actual local incompatibility with existing practices of human rights, today, are both obvious — but three to six generations ago the same could have been said of Christianity. Christianity undeniably 'succeeded'. Did it succeed because it could be used effectively by people who wanted to accomplish something — because, when people worshipped in the appropriate way, things happened 'in the real world' which otherwise would not have happened? Christianity is strikingly dominant in Pacific culture, popular and official. Is this due to God responding to Christian prayers, as one might say the equally striking prevalence of rights-talk in the West is due to courts responding to rights-arguments and other institutions responding to courts?

The question cannot be answered precisely as put, of course. And there are many who would say it is not even the kind of question appropriate to a text examining legal and political affairs, especially if the approach is critical or sceptical. But then there are many, too, who would say the same of questions about human rights ideals. These too have their believers, people who consider human rights ideals beyond criticism (whatever arguments one may have about implementation). Both sets of people, insofar as they exist in the Pacific, are among those we are observing here; as observers we should ask not just whether we agree with them but also why they believe what they do.

In this model, the answer is 'no' (at least to the question precisely as put). Even if one reason why Christianity was so widely and thoroughly adopted was that it worked, in an instrumental sense, that does not seem to explain why the concept of human rights is as attractive as it is. This is the conclusion reached about the first model. The analogy is rather with another reason Christianity succeeded. In this model, human rights and Christianity are indeed analogous, and understanding the appeal of one helps understand the appeal of the other, but the analogy is in features of the ideas — 'human rights', and 'Christianity' — rather than their *instrumental* effectiveness in making things happen in politics.

Why was Christianity so attractive when it arrived? It was not instantly successful, of course. On many islands besides one near that from which I write, Erromango in Vanuatu, it was not the ideas of the very first missionaries that were first swallowed. In some places it only took real root once the local leadership decided, on personal and, quite likely, instrumental grounds, that people would have to adopt it, while in others missionaries struggled for a time with local authorities. But, fairly rapidly everywhere, Melanesian and Polynesian people found in Christianity some quality or feature which made it 'applicable and appropriate' to their lives (in the phrase used by constitutional drafters as a test for adopting foreign law), despite the fairly radical adjustment to behaviours that it meant.[9]

It was a great variety of particular doctrines of Christianity that were adopted, although in the usual particular village there was a consensus as to what sort of 'Christianity' the people would adopt. There seems to have been no great theological, as opposed to political, debate concerning the choices. One could conclude that it was some general quality or feature of Christianity as such which was attractive, rather than anything specific enough to distinguish, say, Catholicism from Lutheranism.

These points suggest two things for the model being proposed here. One is that it is something in the general idea of human rights, too, rather than any particular application of it that is attractive.[10] This is a strong point and, I argue, a valid analogy, to which I shall return. It is at the base of the evolution version of this model. The other is the relation of the imported idea to other changes. Christianity, of course, did not arrive anywhere alone; it came in association with other things — especially material improvements and opportunities which threatened tradition, disaster in the form of new diseases and the sheer fact of dramatic change, largely out of the people's control, in itself. People were not entirely passive, of course, but many of the changes must have felt like impositions. Becoming Christian would have meant many things, but one of them, and surely one of the more significant, was joining 'the modern world' in a way that was *chosen*.

And why chosen with such enthusiasm? Perhaps because in Christianity people saw a form of modernisation which promised something good in itself. The *other* forms of modernisation — material change and dependence and overturned political order — were to be reluctantly accepted either to avoid worse, like submission to new political powers, or to try to obtain something desirable while minimising the cost, like selling labour or land (or sending children to school).

In the moral version of this model, what is attractive about human rights now is the same thing that was attractive about Christianity then. The concept offers a morally good quality to modernisation. The worth of modernisation is ambiguous, and in any event largely instrumental, whether it is called 'civilisation', 'development', or '*globalisation*'. Development, now that the distribution of wealth following political independence is over, can seem as threatening as the disease and arbitrary rule that modernisation first brought a century ago. Religion gave a moral face to that first globalisation, which presaged colonialisation. Perhaps human rights represent the moral face of the current globalisation, which replaces government largesse with economic 'discipline'. Championing human rights finds in this process something to welcome precisely *not* because of what it can accomplish, but because it is good in itself.

This requires accepting that people do see something morally good in human rights and that they saw something morally good in Christianity. As it would have been several generations ago, it still is today a valid argument in the Pacific to say squatters should not be abused because that would be un-Christian: we are equally God's children, called to love all our fellows. Is there something similar going on when people say squatters should be better treated because they have a human right (or a constitutional one) to such better treatment? Do people affirm this because it affirms the moral equality of human beings (or of citizens)?

Perhaps they do. Perhaps the concept of rights has come to symbolise a modern morality, appropriate to this post-independence era of constitutions and globalisation, just as Christianity did during its initial era here. But *why* this would be is not obvious. Of course Christianity includes love for fellow human beings, an account of why we exist and a promise to reward virtue: but so do other religions, including the traditional ones it replaced.[11] Likewise, the concept of human rights includes many very strong notions of the morally good, but so do the traditional concepts making up custom. The second, evolution, version of this model focusses one's view on why human rights would be seen to *be* 'good'.

Ideas are often said to 'have a life of their own', and in a useful sense this is more than a figure of speech. The useful sense is that they can spread, and evolve, in a way closely analogous to living species; and sometimes considering them in this way can explain their adoption better than an assumption that people consciously and rationally choose what to believe. It is not necessarily a radically different point of view. It is an emphasis on ideas themselves, when considering their relation to the people holding them. Religion has been the usual object of this view; few religious people, after all, choose their religion — the overwhelming majority of human beings, including those who believe very devoutly, profess the religion their parents professed. Having secured a niche in one generation's minds, the ideas of the particular faith spread naturally through parental authority to the next generation. Likewise, naturally, the great majority on the global scale of those who support the idea of human rights are offspring of parents who supported that idea. It is the *changes* that require explanation — why is there sometimes a pattern of people adopting a set of ideas that come to them horizontally, so to speak, from beyond their community?

In the case of religions, such patterns coincide with social upheaval. Faced with a greatly disruptive force, people tend to shift their adherence to a faith compatible with a way of dealing socially with that force.[12] This is consistent with the account above of Christianity's reception in the Pacific: it seemed a *good* morality because it was a morality *compatible with* accepting the disruptions of modernisation. Naturally enough, given its long residence in Europe, Christianity was better adapted to the 'modernising' environment than were the old beliefs; and this was true of all the particular denominations of Christianity that Pacific islanders embraced.

Do we see something similar going on with the appeal to human rights today? Consider our example. Do people find it easier to acknowledge the unpleasant side of modernisation, in our example the slum-like settlements, by asserting a more benevolent side of that same modernisation — the notion of rights based policies? Do these go together as aspects of the same times? Given the way so many of the changes in Pacific society are provoked by events and decisions occurring outside the region, modernisation could seem a matter of space as well as of time. Could we say, even on matters of morality and social policy: as foreign problems take root here, so we treat them with foreign tools? This does seem plausible. Human rights, today, could seem morally good because as a set of values it is compatible with the disruptive forces of today. Human rights, that is, as a species of idea competing with custom for the same ecological niche, is naturally better adapted to the ways society is changing in the Pacific.

One can trace the compatibility — the adaptive features of this species of ideology — more specifically. Especially as compared to custom, the human rights concept opens up several useful ways of thinking to its adherents. It allows one to accept change, to justify subjection to the market and government rather than to chief and family, to welcome the 'westernising' element of modernisation and to accept identity as citizen (or even just human) rather than as member of a personally known group. Most importantly in the Pacific, it can allow one to experience individualism as liberty rather than as isolation, as independence rather than selfishness.[13]

GAME? HUMAN RIGHTS AS TEAM COLOURS

Finally, there is a model that notices a significance of human rights different from both their legal utility and their content. This is their symbolic value. By attaching human rights labels to them one can justify policies, and even judicial rulings, which are no departure from colonial policies and judgments. They thus seem modern, even progressive, without changing. Similarly, but more shallowly, one can invoke human rights as a general flag of convenience, indicating to the outside world that the government is on side — part of the human rights team of nations.

There was a project, in the independence era, to generate a new kind of law, a combination of the colonial heritage and indigenous tradition — Melanesian, or Pacific, rule of law.[14] Much of it was included in independence constitutions, in the aspirational invocations of tradition with Christianity (as discussed above at note 2). It has not been seriously pursued since those times, despite the constitutional mandates. When 'the law' notices custom, it does so as something other than true law — either as fact, like 'compensation' treated as part-payment of damages or as a factor in sentencing,[15] or as foreign law, like customary marriages. Custom is objectified and so kept out of the development of local common law.

The human rights label could justify this rejection of custom as a source of legal norms. Fault in negligence, say, or *mens rea* in criminal law, could be justified as manifestations of liberty rights. The general individualism of common law doctrine could be justified as reflecting the same philosophy in human rights. One would then be rejecting custom because it did not adequately protect liberty, or because its sense of 'liberty' was insufficiently individualistic. The new label could be better received than the old one, which was the 'civilisation' of the metropolitan country. After all, it amounts to no more than a simple claim to cultural superiority. There seems little sign of this thinking, however, even where the colonial era 'civilisation' mission is doubted. It does not seem to be what is going on, although an observer might look for it in the future.

The other version of this model is the most obvious, and the most cynical. Declared to an audience of foreign donors or development partners, a governmental or NGO commitment to human rights signifies willingness to join the team — like anti-communism 20 years ago or 'good governance' in our day. There is obvious advantage to this and it would not necessarily be illegitimate for any such body to seek that advantage. It must then be considered whether at least some of the talk of human rights we witness actually means very little, in itself — like a sports team's choice of colours.

What does matter is how easily the audience is satisfied that the government, or NGO, is indeed on the human rights team. Are such declarations of policy (including the signing of treaties and enactment of legislation, on the part of governments) perceived as sufficient? As a case to observe on this point, consider, as it develops, the various governments' commitment in the Biketawa Declaration to supporting human rights in each other's jurisdictions, declared at the October 2000 Pacific Islands Forum meeting in Kiribati. Have governments issued any public comments on the human rights situations in other island countries? Has there been resentment of such comments? Are there any signs that diplomatic, trade, or other inter-governmental relationships are affected by human rights concerns?

CONCLUSION

The models proposed here are meant to assist observation, as tools of description. But does their consideration lead to any *prescriptive* conclusions about how we should react to the ways human rights are invoked?

In the jurisdictions most familiar with rhetoric about rights (notably, the United States of America) there has been much debate about the political and ideological effects of 'rights-talk'. After all, claiming a right to do something, or to resist someone doing something to one, is not the only way to those ends in any political or legal context.

The rights-claim appeals to law, but it is not the only source of standards of behaviour. Within law it appeals to a particular set of legal standards, usually constitutional ones. The common law and the statutory law offer other legal standards. The differences are not just in content but also in the form of the argument: emphasising analogy and authority in common law claims, textual sense in statutory ones, and broad statements of value in constitutional ones. Religion, tradition, professional ethics and a community's morality, in contrast, offer non-legal standards.

When I claim a right to freedom of expression to justify my writing something critical of a government I have chosen a particular form of justification. Instead of appealing to the heritage of open debate in village councils, the Bible, the idea of academic freedom or a community's tradition of tolerating such criticism, I have invoked the law. And within law I have appealed to rights, constitutional or human rights, as opposed to the common law civil liberties (or some particular authoritative decision) and to applicable legislation.

Noticing that invoking 'rights' involves such a choice, and asking why it is made, has led many thinkers to conclude that people often — and perhaps usually — do not realise just what choice they have made, or its implications. And the implications are not necessarily — are perhaps not even usually — favourable to the people who invoke rights. Rights become 'reified' in people's thinking: they distract them from what is occurring in the real world. They commit people to the legal system as opposed to political struggle. In litigating claims in the legal system the advantage is always with the already privileged who have the money for lawyers and the education to use them. And democracy does not rule in a courtroom. Rights direct a political movement's resources to managing and paying for lawyers, rather than organising and leading people. These points are known as 'the rights critique', associated with leftist white academics in the 1980s.[16]

On the other hand, invoking rights can serve as a rallying point around which to organise popular movements. Succeeding in a rights-claim, even just in the courtroom, can be experienced as empowering. And for some people, small or nearly powerless minorities, political struggle is simply not a viable option. Rights (that is, legal struggle) offer them their only hope of improvement. People likely to become criminal accused are the ones most likely to benefit from rights-arguments in court as opposed to political pressure, since they do not constitute any politician's constituency; squatters are in a similar position. These points are known as 'the critique of the rights-critique', associated with a later (1990s) generation of racial- and sexual-minority academics.[17] The debate has not noticeably moved beyond these platforms, although, as a cause, human rights have certainly advanced: most notably, for Pacific jurisdictions, in New Zealand and the UK.[18]

That debate is premised on the potency of rights as a weapon in litigation, the first of my models here. It is premised too on a Western social context, where community feeling is elusive, individualism is embedded in popular ideology, and government is experienced as an all-powerful professional bureaucracy. Does this limit the debate's relevance in the South Pacific? The obvious relevance is limited to the point, in the rights-critique, of reliance on rights draining resources to lawyers and, on the other side, the point that a right can be an effective rallying cry (as it is used in Pacific women's movements).

Perhaps, however, the basic ideas of the critique could acquire relevance as — or if — human rights gain momentum as a cause. Rights are a distraction from other means to achieve political ends. To the extent that people trying to achieve political ends by invoking rights assume that custom is something they must overcome, they allow the impression that they oppose the values associated with community and tradition. This is a drastic, even fatal, concession to make; few people want to see themselves as throwing away tradition. In the West, this was an argument of the rights-critics: if in using rights-claims to achieve progressive ends we give the impression that we oppose tradition and community, then our conservative opponents will be able to portray themselves as the defenders of these values. We may, for example, support more rights for women, in order to achieve safer and healthier family life, but if this is seen as an attack on all the traditional roles of women the conservatives will be able to say *they* are the guardians of 'family values'.[19]

Reliance on rights to justify one's claims involves reliance on law, immediately or by logical entailment, displacing perhaps a more appropriate reliance on garnering popular support. This can be an error even where, legally, rights really are 'trumps'. Observing a gathering responsiveness to human rights talk, if that is what we see in the future, we should not necessarily be congratulatory of the rights proponents.

But all of the above, again, takes rights as weapons, a particular kind of tool, rationally (if not necessarily wisely) chosen to suit the job. If my second model is valid, however, these observations miss the point. Rights-talk will gain in power whether it is rationally effective or not — rhetorical power, in public discussion (which may or may not move courts of law). It will be swept along as the current form of modernisation gathers force.

If we see the third model gain plausibility, governments and NGOs associating themselves with rights purely as team colours, will that affect the attractiveness, or adaptiveness, of rights-talk among people? And if so, what sort of *custom*-talk will that development favour?

It may be a combination of the second and third models that proves most apt. If, on the custom side, one focusses on the role of 'chiefs', the rights side can be seen as an alternative. To some extent this is co-evolution of the very old dichotomy — or dualism, in legal terms — of traditional/modern, indigenous/introduced. Those terms are losing cogency as chiefhood develops, and indeed as originally-foreign legal and political influences are internalised in Pacific societies (as religious ones were so long ago).

It seems clear now that the role of chiefs is in large part to mediate modernisation.[20] The independent state appeared previously to almost all of its people, in most of the Pacific, as a source of largesse. This significance is passing. In its wake, the phenomenon of chiefly power represents a mobilisation of local solidarity. Rights-talk, seen in this light, constitutes an alternative way to try to integrate the realities of modernisation: mobilising international solidarity.

ENDNOTES

1   See the chapter on the Civil Tradition in Glenn, H. P. 2000. *Legal Traditions of the World*. Oxford: Oxford University Press.

2   As examples, consider the earliest constitution, that of (Western) Samoa: "WHEREAS the Leaders of Western Samoa have declared that Western Samoa should be an Independent State based on Christian principles and Samoan custom and tradition;" (Preamble), and that of the most recently independent among the larger states, Vanuatu: "WE the people of Vanuatu... HEREBY proclaim the establishment of the united and free Republic of Vanuatu founded on traditional Melanesian values, faith in God, and Christian principles..." (Preamble). There is of course much more to constitutional interpretation than Preambles; the point here is the inspirational role of these two basic aspirations. Note the difference in the very recent (1997) *Constitution* of Fiji Islands: it protects, in an elaborate way, indigenous Fijian *'interests'* rather than *values*, within a multicultural framework (Section 6: Compact).

3   Von Clausewitz wrote of the theory of war, at the turn of the 19th century, urging that war be considered 'the continuation of politics by other means'. This was 'true war', what soldiers should train for and armies be prepared for. 'Real war' — looting, raiding, massacres, and so on, what today is called irregular warfare — should be abandoned by civilised military traditions. See Keegan, J. 1993. *The Transformation of Warfare*. Toronto: Key Porter Books.

4   The village authority could be a 'chief', as in Micronesia, Polynesia, and Vanuatu, most of Solomon Islands, and the coastal and island regions of PNG, or the 'big men' or something like a council, in the rest of Melanesia. I do not mean to imply that identifying exactly who has the requisite authority is easy, even where chiefly status is recognised. Nor indeed is the 'recognition' of chiefly status always unproblematic. In Vanuatu the status appears to have evolved in response to the need to interact formally with outsiders, and now to have specialised in adjudication (as opposed to leadership more generally). Bolton, L. 1999. Chief Willie Bongmatur Maldo and the Incorporation of Chiefs into the Vanuatu State. *Discussion Paper No. 99/2 of the State, Society, and Governance in Melanesia Project*. Canberra: Australian National University, pp 4, 8 & 11.

5   Note that the operation of custom is nonetheless subject to the influence of men whose local power is sometimes due to legal form — like being police officers, civil servants, or members of Parliament (and, in a nice demonstration of how custom and that form influence each other, they are men rather than women).

6   *Le Tagaloa Pita et al v Attorney-General*, Unreported, Court of Appeal of Western Samoa CA 7/95, December 1995.

7   For examples of the first, invoking the common law of confessions, see *State v Joseph Maino* [1977] PNGLR 216 and *State v Evertius and Kundi* [1985] PNGLR 109. For the second, where 'negligence' is the cause of action despite the nature of the police acts complained of, see, for example, *Helen Jack v Karani and Papua New Guinea* [1992] PNGLR 391 (assassination) and *Komaip Trading v Waugulo and Papua New Guinea* [1995] PNGLR 165 (shop-burning).

8 I discuss some implications of this strain in Fraser, I. 2000. Legal Theory in Melanesia: Pluralism? Dualism? Pluralism long Dualism? *Journal of South Pacific Law* Vol. 3 (http://www.vanuatu.usp.ac.fj/journal_splaw/articles/Fraser1.htm Accessed 19/9/02).

9 See, for an overview, Garrett, J. 1982. *To Live Among The Stars: Christian Origins in Oceania*. Geneva & Suva: World Council of Churches & USP. In particular, see pp 72–78 (Tonga), pp 102–114 (Fiji), pp 121–129 (Samoa), pp 171–185 (Vanuatu), pp 241–243 (Papua) and pp 298–300 (Solomon Islands).

10 What Ronald Dworkin calls a concept, rather than a conception: the expression in a particular context of a principle, rather than the precise term with which the appropriate ruling is expressed. He had in mind contrasts like a right to liberty in one's private life (the concept) and the deregulation of condom sales (the conception). See, for example, Dworkin, R. 1977. *Taking Rights Seriously*. Cambridge, Mass: Harvard University Press.

11 One can — of course! — debate issues of emphasis here; traditional beliefs, for example, would usually have to redefine who counts as 'one of us' before they could be said to feature love of one's neighbours. Suffice it to say that Christianity is as capable as any other religion of supporting xenophobia. The faithful interpret their own religions fairly freely — as lawyers do their constitutions. Not one word of the US Bill of Rights was changed, for instance, between when segregation was 'constitutional' and when it became 'unconstitutional'.

12 That way could be opposition and resistance, of course, as long as these seem viable options. Consider the spread of 'fundamentalist' versions of Christianity, Islam, Judaism, and Hinduism, as well as the Pacific movements, perhaps precursors to cargo cults, which featured the destruction of goods, animals, and homes, in the expectation of a messianic deliverance to the intact old ways. (There were such movements in North America and South Africa as well.)

13 In other words, it can thus allow 'a new politics', characterising the current post-modern era, in which one's personal identity becomes identified with one's political convictions. This is as contrasted to the distinction of personality and politics characterising modernity, and to the tying of personality to politics through kinship characterising traditional times. One factor promoting it is a focus on issues rather than ethnic or personal association. See, further, Larmour, P. 1994. Is there a 'New' Politics in the South Pacific? In vom Busch, W. *et al*, (eds.) *New Politics in the South Pacific*. Raratonga & Suva: Institute for Pacific Studies. 3–15 at pp 4–6.

14 The best-known example of this thinking — though expressed long after constitution-framing — is Narakobi, B. 1989. *Lo Bilong Yumi Yet*. Papua New Guinea: Melanesian Institute.

15 See Newton Cain, T. elsewhere in this volume.

16 For a contemporary overview, see the special issue of *Stanford Law Review*, Vol 36, 1984. For a more recent version in the British tradition, see Waldron, J. 1993. A Rights-Based Critique of Constitutional Rights. *Oxford Journal of Legal Studies* 13:18–51.

17 See, for the instigation of this reaction, Delgado, R. 1987. The Ethereal Scholar: Does Critical Legal Studies Have What Minorities Want? *Harvard Civil Rights-Civil Liberties Review* 22:301.

18   I discuss the potentially great ramifications of the UK's effective adoption of the European Convention on Human Rights as domestic legislation in Fraser, I. 2000. The Cradle Will Rock: The South Pacific and the Coming Revolution in English Common Law. Paper presented at ALTA Conference, July 2000 (Canberra). It will soon be impossible for Pacific courts to invoke contemporary English case law without discussing human rights.

19   This could mirror what seems to be the distinction already established in popular thinking: that 'politics' is national and 'custom' is local; and only the political power gained in the latter sphere is wholly legitimate. Huffer, E. and Molisa, G. 1999. Governance in Vanuatu: In Search of the Nakamal Way. *Discussion Paper No. 99/4 of the State, Society, and Governance in Melanesia Project*. Canberra: Australian National University.
This work was based on a survey of people conducted in November 1997. There is a maxim in American politics: 'all politics is local' — the political issues that actually motivate voters are the local issues.

20   "[P]aramount chiefs are good to Westernise with," quote Lindstrom, L. and White,G. 1997. Chiefs Today. In Lindstrom, L. and White,G. (eds.) *Chiefs Today: Traditional Pacific Leadership and the Postcolonial State* Stanford, California: Stanford University Press at p 18. Their point is the importance of not seeing 'chiefs' as simply the rearguard of retreating tradition. See also White, G. The Discourse of Chiefs: Notes on a Melanesian Society in the same volume, with reference to Solomon Islands.

11. CUSTOMARY FAMILY LAW AND GENDER DISCRIMINATION IN PAPUA NEW GUINEA

By: Owen Jessep

KEY TERMS AND PHRASES

(Gender) discrimination

Discrimination is the act of treating things differently. Popularly discrimination is often used to refer to 'unfair' treatment, or treating people differently because of prejudice or irrelevant reasons. Gender discrimination specifically refers to treating men and women differently because of their gender and no other reason.

Monogamy

A condition or practice during which a person only has or is permitted one mate at any time.

Patriarchal

A patriarchal society popularly means a society in which men control a disproportionately large share of the power. When used in an anthropological sense patriarchy refers to a social organisation marked by the supremacy of the father in the clan or family, the legal dependence of wives and children, and the determination of descent and inheritance by the male line.

Polygamy

A situation in which a person may be married to more than one mate at the same time. It is not a gender specific term — a polygamous realtionship can be one in which a woman has more than one husband or a man has more than one wife. However, polygamy is often popularly used only to refer to a situation of polygyny, which is a situation in which a man can have more than one wife.

INTRODUCTION

One of the continuing legal debates in Papua New Guinea in the years since Independence in 1975 has been the proper weight to be accorded to custom in the national legal system. At first glance, custom assumes a prominent position among the sources of law set out in the *Constitution*, as one of the two principal sources (together with common law) of what is called the 'underlying law'.[1] Despite this there has been no shortage of complaints since 1975 as to the lack of progress in establishing and developing an appropriate "indigenous jurisprudence", that is, a body of legal doctrine which reflects Melanesian ideas and principles.[2] The reasons for this situation are complex and the topic has been approached from different points of view. One persistent strand in the discussion has been the continued reliance of courts and lawyers on the imported common law. Relevant explanations for this phenomenon include the apparent ignorance or laziness or antipathy of expatriate lawyers and judges towards custom,[3] the nature of education and training given to Papua New Guinean lawyers,[4] and limitations relating to the adversarial trial process and judicial methodology.[5]

Another side to the debate, even in cases where the common law has not been directly involved, has been the tension and possible conflict between elements of custom and other legal principles, such as the human rights provisions set out in the *Constitution*.[6] That is to say, the recognition of custom in a particular case is never automatic but is made subject to a number of constitutional or statutory restrictions and qualifications. In the field of customary family law, for example, these 'screening mechanisms' have assumed particular importance in the last decade, as Papua New Guinean courts have taken the initiative in challenging and refusing to recognise aspects of custom in individual cases relating to things such as marriage, divorce, and custody of children.

It is not possible in this chapter to consider all of these recent developments. Instead, I will focus on one matter in particular, which is also receiving attention in other parts of the Pacific and in numerous African jurisdictions;[7] the conflict and interaction between customary family law, on the one hand, and constitutional or other legal provisions dealing with gender equality, on the other.

OUTLINE OF CONSTITUTIONAL AND STATUTORY PROVISIONS

By virtue of s 9 of the *Constitution* of Papua New Guinea, the laws of the country include the *Constitution* itself, various categories of legislation, and the 'underlying law'. According to s 20, until such time as an Act of Parliament provides otherwise, the underlying law is to be understood as set out in Schedule 2 of the *Constitution*. According to that Schedule, the two principal sources of the underlying law are custom[8] and the common law.[9] In relation to custom, Sch 2.1(1), so far as relevant, states that 'custom is adopted, and shall be applied and enforced, as part of the underlying law'. This is however made subject to subsection 2, which requires that the custom not be inconsistent with any constitutional law inconsistent with a statute or "repugnant to the general principles of humanity".

Another important statute dealing with custom is the *Customs Recognition Act* [Cap 19] (PNG). According to s 3(1) of this Act, custom may not be recognised or enforced in a particular case or context if to do so would result in injustice, would not be in the public interest, or would not be in the best interests of a child under the age of 16 years. The same statute, in s 5, provides (so far as relevant) that in a civil case, custom may be taken into account in relation to:

(f) marriage, divorce or the right to the custody or guardianship of infants, in a case arising out of or in connexion with a marriage entered into in accordance with custom.

In relation to customary marriage, it may also be noted that by virtue of s 3(1) of the *Marriage Act* [Cap 280] (PNG), a Papua New Guinean[10] who is not already a party to a statutory marriage may enter a customary marriage in accordance with the custom of either of the parties. In this case, s 3(2) states that the customary marriage "will be valid and effectual for all purposes".

Section 55 of the *Constitution*

It follows from the constitutional and statutory provisions outlined above that there are a range of requirements that represent potential obstacles to the recognition and enforcement of family law and custom in a particular case. In practice these requirements may often overlap and the same arguments be used in relation to several of the grounds at the same time. For instance, the same considerations that are claimed to make a custom inconsistent with a provision of the *Constitution* or repugnant to the "general principles of humanity" may simultaneously found an argument that to enforce the custom would cause "injustice" "not be in the public interest" and so on.[11] Examples of such alternative forms of argument will appear below. In what follows, however, I will concentrate on the ground of inconsistency with the *Constitution*, and in particular those provisions dealing with gender equality.

To begin with, there are relevant references in the 'National Goals and Directive Principles' (NGDP) in the Preamble to the *Constitution*, such as NGDP 2(5) which refers to "equal participation by women citizens in all political, economic, social and religious activities", and NGDP 2(12), to the effect that "a complete relationship in marriage rests on equality of rights and duties of the partners". Nevertheless, these NGDPs are made "non-justiciable" (which in effect means not directly enforceable by a court or tribunal)[12] by s 25(1) of the *Constitution*. More directly applicable is s 55, dealing with the equality of citizens. This section reads as follows:

(1) Subject to this Constitution, all citizens have the same rights, privileges, obligations and duties irrespective of race, tribe, place of origin, political opinion, colour, creed, religion or sex.

(2) Subsection (1) does not prevent the making of laws for the special benefit, welfare, protection or advancement of females, children and young persons,

members of under-privileged or less advanced groups or residents of less advanced areas.

(3) Subsection (1) does not affect the operation of a pre-Independence law.

One or two cases in the 1980's made passing references to s 55 in relation to custom, but without any serious discussion of the scope of this provision. For instance, in 1981 the Supreme Court had to consider the legality of sending PNG troops to Vanuatu for a peacekeeping operation. Michael Somare as leader of the Opposition had sought to challenge the constitutional validity of a parliamentary decision and an Act of Parliament approving the commitment of troops to Vanuatu. The Court's decision in *Supreme Court Reference No 4 of 1980*[13] dealt merely with the preliminary issue of the petitioner's standing to challenge the actions of the Parliament. A majority of the Supreme Court held that the petitioner did have standing, based on his status as a Member of Parliament and as a citizen of Papua New Guinea. It is not necessary here to consider the reasoning of the judges, except to note that several of them refused to acknowledge the petitioner's claim to standing based on his position as a 'big man' according to custom. Of interest here is Kidu CJ's statement in response to this argument:

> [Counsel for the petitioner] submitted that in Papua New Guinea 'big men' can speak in any forum. Mr. Somare should be allowed to speak in this forum because he is such a man. If this is so, it goes against s 55(1) of the *Constitution*:
>
>> Subject to this Constitution, all citizens have the same rights, privileges, obligations and duties irrespective of race, tribe, place of origin, political opinion, colour, creed, religion or sex.[14]

This is an intriguing comment, but it is not clear which part of s 55 Kidu CJ had in mind. Since part of the petitioner's evidence was based upon custom in his home province, the Chief Justice may have simply had in mind differences based on "tribe" or "place of origin", that is, that this custom may have been different to those found in other parts of the country. On the other hand, Kidu CJ might have been objecting to a custom pertaining to 'big men' in contrast to women, that is that if men rather than women have a right of public audience this would be an example of discrimination on the basis of "sex". Since there was no real clarification of the point, this brief reference to s 55 unfortunately remains ambiguous.

Another judge in 1989 referred more clearly to s 55 as prohibiting discrimination between the sexes, but again in a context where detailed discussion was not necessary. In *Bore Konia v Daniel Dosinga and the State of PNG*[15] Los J was hearing a claim for damages by a father whose son had been unlawfully shot by a police officer. The claim was based both on breach of the right to life guaranteed by the *Constitution* and on breach of custom. During the trial evidence was given as to the relevant custom in the deceased's area relating to compensation for wrongful death. Referring to this evidence, Los J noted that the claim for customary compensation had now to be considered subject to the requirements of the constitutional framework. Thus:

Killing as pay-back, based on the notion of an eye for an eye, and tooth for a tooth is unconstitutional.... Giving away women as compensation cannot apply now because it is not only repugnant to the general principles of humanity but it is in breach of specific sections of the Constitution. A woman is a person not a property. As a person she has the same rights as a man... Section 55(1) summarizes it all...

I am aware that equality of women does not go down well with a traditional PNG man, but he has to accept that, that is the position that he himself through the Constituent Assembly accepted at Independence...

By our Constitution all lives are equal. They are not graded according to gender, social or official status. See s 55(1) of the Constitution cited earlier. The amount of compensation paid for loss of life must be equal whether a person is a man or woman, big man or little man.[16]

The judge proceeded, without quantifying the damages in his judgment, to find the first defendant liable, and the state of PNG vicariously liable for the wrongful actions of the first defendant.

CUSTOMARY FAMILY LAW CASES AND SECTION 55

In the early 1990's, a number of cases arose in which the National Court felt obliged to intervene to protect women from excessive punishment at the hands of village courts.[17] One such case was the 1991 decision of *Re Wagi Non and the Constitution Section 42(5)*.[18] The husband had left his wife and their four children in the care of his relatives in his village when he travelled to another province for employment. After he had been away for five or six years without making contact with his family or relatives the wife eventually formed a relationship with another man. The husband's relatives then complained in the Village Court that the wife had committed adultery, in breach of customary expectations, and obtained an order for compensation against her. When she failed to pay the amount required, the Village Court ordered her imprisonment. In the National Court, Woods J ordered her release, stating (among other reasons) that the custom relied on by the relatives of the husband should not be recognised, as it infringed s 55 of the *Constitution*. In the opinion of the Court:

I cannot help feeling that the going off and leaving the wife and children without his support and protection yet expecting her to remain bound by custom is a custom that must be denigrating to her status as a woman. It is denying her the equality provided in the *Constitution*, s 55... I am not saying that a man cannot have several wives and cannot travel but if he chooses to have wives and travel elsewhere he must accord them equality in care and participation and she must have the same freedoms that he has... The facts of this case suggest that this woman is bonded, almost in slavery, to the husband even when the husband neglects her. This must clearly be a denigration of the woman's humanness.'[19]

A similar result was reached by Woods J on almost identical facts in *Re Kaka Ruk and the Constitution Section 42(5)*,[20] although, there, the Court preferred to ground the decision on the doctrine of "repugnancy to the general principles of humanity".[21]

Returning to s 55, in *Re Kepo Raramu and the Yowe Village Court*,[22] a Village Court had sentenced a woman to a term of six months' imprisonment for commencing a new relationship after her husband had died. On appeal, the National Court ordered her immediate release. One of the several grounds relied on for this decision by Doherty J appears in the following passage:

> I am well aware of the custom in many areas that says women whose husbands have died are not to go around with another man... I do not know of any equivalent custom that says a man whose wife has died is not allowed to go around with other women, and, as such, I consider this custom strikes against the basis of equality provided in s 55 of the *Constitution*.
>
> It appears to me, to quote the words of [Kidu CJ], 'it is a custom that is oppressive to women', and the Village Court is in error in upholding this custom.[23]

Other village court decisions, such as those concerning the law of customary divorce, have also been the subject of National Court appeal cases. Some of these decisions were made by the judge in the role of prison visitor and the judgments are rather cursory and have not been reported. The former Chief Justice, Kidu CJ, heard several cases in 1991 in which he asserted the freedom of wives to leave their husbands regardless of any rule of custom to the contrary. One example is that of *Re Raima and the Constitution Section 42(5)*.[24] There, a woman had been imprisoned by a Village Court after being unable to pay the 300 kina[25] compensation ordered in favour of her former husband, whom she had left. Kidu CJ upheld several objections to both the compensation order and the sentence of imprisonment. After examining the Village Court records, the Chief Justice stated:

> The order does not say why the compensation was ordered to be paid by her. Was it to be paid because she broke the marriage or was it to be repayment of the bride price paid for her by the husband of 3–4 months? On the face of it, it would appear to be merely for her speaking strongly of breaking her marriage. This is, of course, wrong in law. Whether under introduced law or customary law a woman has the right to break her marriage. It is her right and she should not be penalized for this. If a woman breaks her marriage the village court only has the right to consider the repayment of bride price according to customary law. A village court has no power to penalize her for breaking the marriage.[26]

Although the basis for this decision is not spelt out in the brief judgment, it is likely that considerations of equality between the sexes were in the mind of Kidu CJ. The clear implication of his statement is that any custom which denied the woman the right of divorce would not be recognised and any court order enforcing such a custom would similarly be invalid.

Unlike the cases considered so far, in which National Court judges were responding to what they saw as the excesses and misuse of jurisdiction by village court magistrates, the 1997 case of *Re Willingal*[27] reached the National Court after publicity in one of Papua New Guinea's national newspapers.[28] In response to the newspaper article, National Court proceedings were instituted by a non-governmental human rights organisation, the Individual and Community Rights Advocacy Forum. The proceedings featured a whole battery of legal challenges against a custom requiring a woman's forced marriage. The unfortunate woman was Ms Miriam Willingal, an 18 year old high school student from the Western Highlands area of Papua New Guinea, who was being made the unwilling participant in a complicated compensation settlement between two kin groups.

It is not necessary here to set out the full facts of the case, which began with the death of Miriam's father, who appeared to have been the innocent victim of a police raid on a Highlands village. For various reasons this then led to extended negotiations between the members of his kin group (to which Miriam also belonged) and the kin group of his mother, two clans which had for generations enjoyed a close relationship. At issue was the question of how to restore the balance between the two groups in order to ensure their continued co-existence and alliance in the future.

At the trial there was some disagreement over the details of the customary compensation claim. The broad outlines of the claim referred to 25 pigs, 20,000 kina and two women.[29] Some witnesses said that no particular women were identified in the negotiations, that no woman would be pressured to comply with the arrangement, and that the marriages might not take place until some years in the future. Other witnesses, including Miriam, gave a contrary impression, to the effect that pressure could be or had been brought to bear on individual women by the clan leaders, and that a delay in arranging the marriages would cause aggravation and ill feeling between the two groups. On this crucial point Injia J found that Miriam had already been subjected to pressure, that she did not like the idea of being used as a form of payment and that she was afraid that the men of both clans might become impatient and try to force her to accept the planned marriage.[30]

Turning to the relevant law Injia J had no doubt that Miriam's constitutional rights had been infringed and gave multiple reasons for this conclusion. His general approach to the issue of recognition of custom appears in the following passage:

> The traditional customs of the people of [this area] like the rest of PNG have existed from time immemorial and they serve complex value systems which only they themselves best know. It is not easy for any outsider to fully understand the customs and the underlying values and purposes they serve. Any outsider including the modern courts must not be quick to extract those customs and their values and pass judgments on their soundness or otherwise... But it is clear to me that the framers of our Constitution and modern day legislators were thinking about a modern PNG based on ethnic societies whose welfare and advancement was based on the maintenance and promotion of good traditional customs and the discouragement and elimination of bad customs as seen from the eyes of an ordinary modern Papua New Guinean. No matter how painful it may be to the small ethnic society concerned, such bad custom must give way to the dictates of our modern national laws.[31]

The Court accordingly held that a number of provisions of the *Constitution* and of other statutes would be infringed were the custom to be enforced. These included constitutional guarantees of sexual equality, about which Injia J had this to say:

> It is further submitted that to oblige or pressure a woman to marry someone from another tribe against her will restricts her right to freedom to choose a partner in marriage on equal terms with men. It is submitted that this is contrary to *Constitution, National Goals and Directive Principles* No 2(5) and (12)... I agree with these submissions...

> It is submitted that the same custom infringes Section 55 in that it violates the equal choice that a woman in [this area], in this case Miriam, had of choosing a partner from anywhere in Papua New Guinea just like men from [her] tribe and the [other] tribe. I accept this submission. There is no evidence that the same custom which targets young women from [Miriam's] tribe also targets eligible men from the [other] tribe.[32]

For these and numerous other reasons, the court then proceeded to issue permanent injunctions and restraining orders against the various groups and their members.

DISCUSSION

I have outlined a number of cases arising in the last decade in Papua New Guinea in which the courts have been prepared to strike at aspects of customary family law. These cases have variously concerned differing expectations about spousal behaviour in a customary marriage, parental custody rights, customary divorce, proper behaviour as a widow and forced marriage. Section 55 of the *Constitution*, among other provisions, has been invoked against customs which appeared to the courts to be one-sided, oppressive or patriarchal in their application, and therefore to be unlawful examples of gender discrimination. It is fair to say, however, that the discussion in these cases of the notion of 'discrimination', and of the proper scope and meaning of s 55, remains at a relatively simple and straightforward level.[33]

This is not to say that the judges in these cases should have been expected to engage in a lengthy theoretical analysis. After all, judges obviously respond primarily to the arguments presented to them. In few of the cases has there been much if any attempt to justify or provide supporting arguments for the custom in question. Nor has the court been requested to attempt an overall assessment of the relationship between those parts of the *Constitution* emphasising the importance of custom and the provisions dealing with rights of equality. Is it possible to reconcile these provisions, or should one set of provisions always take precedence over the other? Could a court in a particular case be asked to engage in a balancing exercise, weighing up the benefits and values of the customary principles and concepts, on the one hand, and the equality rights of men and women, on the other?

As to the interpretation of s 55, there has also not been any attempt to date to uphold elements of family law custom by reference to s 55(3), which states that the non-discrimination principle in subsection (1) "does not affect the operation of a pre-

Independence law". The expression "pre-Independence law" is defined in Sch 1.2 of the *Constitution* to have the same meaning as in Sch 2.6 (on the adoption of pre-Independence laws), which defines the term to refer exclusively to statute law. At first glance, therefore, a custom which existed prior to Independence would not gain any special protection from subsection (3). On the other hand, what if the custom in question was recognised and validated by a pre-Independence (that is, pre-1975) statute? Two such provisions relating to customary marriage have been referred to earlier, namely s 5(f) of the *Customs Recognition Act* (first passed in 1963, now Cap 19 of the Revised Laws), and s 3 of the *Marriage Act* (also first passed in 1963, now Cap 280 of the Revised Laws). By virtue of the former, custom may be "taken into account" in relation to a marriage, and the latter provision states more specifically that a marriage entered into in accordance with the relevant custom "is valid and effectual for all purposes". Could it be argued, then, that an otherwise discriminatory feature of customary marriage law would thereby be protected, *via* subsection (3), from challenge under s 55(1)?

Questions of this sort would no doubt arise if it were sought to challenge fundamental elements of the system of customary marriage in Papua New Guinea. In recent years, the most controversial family law topic has been that of polygamous marriage. Even more than the constant controversy over elements of customary brideprice,[34] the practice of polygamy (which in practice means polygyny, that is the right of a man to have more than one customary wife) has produced a constant flow of public debate.[35] While polygamy is virtually unknown in many parts of the country today, it remains a relatively common practice among leaders from the Highlands provinces. One memorable example of the public interest in polygamy is the controversy which erupted when a newly-appointed Governor-General decided to prefer the younger of his two wives to accompany him to England to receive his knighthood, and then to occupy the viceregal residence with him.[36]

In legal terms, a polygamous customary marriage has generally been regarded as valid by virtue of s 3 of the *Marriage Act* [Cap 280] (PNG), referred to earlier. Thus, in the passage previously quoted from *Re Wagi Non and the Constitution Section 42(5)*,[37] Woods J stated plainly: "I am not saying that a man cannot have several wives…", but went on to insist that all the wives must be treated fairly and equally.

Against advocates of the practice, who rely on the *Constitution*'s support for traditional customs, objections have come from community and church groups as well as magistrates and judges dealing with the frequent financial and custody disputes, criminal assaults and murders (whether between spouses, or between co-wives) arising from polygamous arrangements.[38] Since 1996, private members' bills designed to abolish or ban polygamy have been circulated on several occasions in Parliament, so far without any collective governmental response.

In the absence of any legislative initiative it is interesting to speculate on whether a court in Papua New Guinea might be faced with an objection to some aspect of customary polygamous marriage. While an out-and-out constitutional challenge to the custom is theoretically possible, it is far more likely that the issue would arise in the circumstances of an everyday case. Such a claim might be raised in any context in which a party's rights or responsibilities will vary according to whether the marriage is legally valid or not (such as spousal maintenance, property claims, inheritance, compensation in relation to fatal accidents and so on). The contending party, then, could be a husband, a wife, a relative, an insurance company or anyone else with an interest in the result of the litigation.

Some years ago, it should be noted, a Task Force of the PNG Law Reform Commission expressed the view that the custom of polygamy was "unconstitutional", because the freedom to have more than one spouse was only extended to males. Rather than argue for a similar liberty to be extended to females, however, the Task Force concluded that Parliament should insist on monogamy for everyone.[39]

In its claim that polygamy was unconstitutional, the Task Force presumably had in mind the prohibition on discrimination contained in s 55 of the *Constitution*. An alternative form of the same argument might focus on the imbalance in the respective rights and responsibilities expected from each spouse in relation to the other. While it can be argued, as Kaganas and Murray have attempted in the African context,[40] that:

> The treatment of women as property, sexual stereotyping and domination are not limited to polygamy, nor are they practices that can be shown to be inevitable in polygamy...

the approach and judicial logic consistently demonstrated by the National Court judges in the cases outlined earlier, culminating in the 1997 case of *Re Willingal*, would suggest that the customary incidents of a polygamous marriage in Papua New Guinea typically infringe the right to sexual equality in s 55(1). If so, then the court would have to give consideration to s 55(3), as to whether the custom could be saved as depending upon a "pre-Independence law".

Of course, leaving aside these complications surrounding the proper interpretation of s 55, it is clear that some of the other grounds canvassed above could also come to the fore here: for instance, that customary expectations and practices relating to polygamy in a particular Papua New Guinean community might be inconsistent with other rights guaranteed by the *Constitution*, might produce injustice, or might be contrary to the public interest (see *Customs Recognition Act* [Cap 19] (PNG), s 3). A court's decision invalidating, on any of the grounds mentioned, a particular polygamous marriage (that is, by denying recognition and enforcement to the relevant custom) would not automatically spell invalidity for all polygamous marriages, but would obviously have significant implications for other cases. Alternatively, such a decision might prompt further calls for legislative intervention.[41]

CONCLUSION

It has been frequently argued that many aspects of customary family law in Papua New Guinea reflect entrenched gender discrimination against women.[42] Whether referring generally to the law of customary marriage and divorce, or to the extremely high incidence of domestic assaults and sexual violence reported for many parts of the country,[43] these commentators would certainly agree with the views of Los J, expressed in a different context some years ago:

> Although the equality of sexes is now a constitutional principle in Papua New Guinea, at this stage it is more a matter of books, rather than practice. The character of all aspects of life is a male dominance.[44]

In this chapter, I have outlined some of the tensions and possibilities for conflict between constitutional norms that incorporate custom as part of the law of the country, and other constitutional provisions that support the principles of gender equality. In the last decade, National Court judges have begun to take the initiative in challenging aspects of customary family law, by refusing to acknowledge and enforce elements of custom which are found to denigrate or oppress women. This has been especially evident in relation to custom as reflected and purportedly implemented in decisions of village courts in some provinces. In overturning such decisions, the National Court judges have employed a variety of judicial weapons, among them s 55 of the *Constitution*.

Of course, there is no reason to think that orders of the National Court immediately bring about changes in ideas and behaviour among the people concerned,[45] and it is very likely that similar cases will continue to arise in the future. Were such cases to go further and question more fundamental characteristics of the system of customary marriage (such as polygamy or brideprice), the courts would then be faced with the task of analysing the concepts of gender equality and discrimination, and the interpretation of s 55, in a more detailed way than has so far proved to be necessary.

ENDNOTES

1   See *Constitution of Papua New Guinea*, ss 9, 20, and Sch 2. See also *Underlying Law Act* 2000 (PNG).

2   "Indigenous jurisprudence" is the expression used in s 21(1) of the *Constitution*.

3   For an early example, see Weisbrot, D. 1982. The Impact of the Papua New Guinea Constitution on the Recognition and Application of Customary Law. In Sack, P. (ed.) *Pacific Constitutions*. Canberra: Research School of Social Sciences, Australian National University.

4   See, for example, Nonggorr, J. 1993. Development of Customary Law: Replacing the *Customs Recognition Act. Melanesian Law Journal* 21: 49–62.

5   See, for example, Amet, A. 1995. Severing the Umbilical Cord from the Common Law. In Aleck, J. & Rannells, J. (eds.) *Custom at the Crossroads*. Port Moresby: Faculty of Law, University of Papua New Guinea.

6   It may be noted that while Papua New Guinea has ratified certain international human rights instruments such as the Convention on the Elimination of Discrimination against Women (ratified in January 1995) and the Convention on the Rights of the Child (ratified in March 1993), these instruments do not have effect as domestic law within Papua New Guinea. This would only be the case if the Conventions were specifically implemented by national legislation.

7   In relation to current debates in Southern Africa, for example, see Nhlapo, T. 1994–95. Indigenous Law and Gender in South Africa: Taking Human Rights and Cultural Diversity Seriously. *Third World Legal Studies* 1994–95: 49–71; Letuka, P. & Armstrong, A. 1996 Which Law? Which Family? Which Women? – Problems of Enforcing CEDAW in Southern Africa. In Lowe, N. & Douglas, G. (eds.), *Families Across Frontiers*. The Hague: Nijhoff; Fishbayn, L. 1999. Litigating the Right to Culture: Family Law in the New South Africa. *International Journal of Law, Policy and the Family* 13: 147–73.

8   In Sch 1.2 of the *Constitution*, the term 'custom' is defined to mean: "the customs and usages of indigenous inhabitants of the country existing in relation to the matter in question at the time when and the place in relation to which the matter rises, regardless of whether or not the custom or usage has existed from time immemorial".

9   By Sch 2.2 of the *Constitution*, 'common law' here means "the principles and rules of common law and equity in England" as at Independence Day (16th September 1975).

10 As an indication of how little has changed in the years since Independence, the statute in fact still uses the colonial expression 'native', which would today be understood to mean 'automatic citizen' (as defined in the *Constitution*, s 65).

11 The case of *Re Willingal* (1997) N 1506, to be referred to below, provides an excellent example.

12 *Constitution*, Sch 1.7.

13 [1981] PNGLR 265.

14 [1981] PNGLR 265, at 271.

15 (1989) N 745.

16 (1989) N 745, at 8, 14. Similar sentiments were expressed by Kidu CJ, apparently in relation to the 'repugnancy' doctrine, in the case of *State v Nerius and Tingas* (1982) N 397. There, two Baining men (East New Britain Province) charged with rape pleaded as an excuse that they were obliged to commit the rape by their custom of payback. Custom has never been accepted in Papua New Guinea as a complete defence to a criminal charge, although it may be taken into account in determining sentence (*Customs Recognition Act* [Cap 19] (PNG), s 4). Kidu CJ (at 3) was not impressed with the defendants' argument: "If this is a custom of the Baining people then it is repugnant to the dictates of Papua New Guinea's Constitution. Women/girls... are not "things" or "chattels" to be dealt with by men as they wish. Any custom which says that if A rapes B's sister, B is entitled to rape A's sister cannot be condoned by the Courts.... Women are equal to men in Papua New Guinea under our Constitution. They must be so treated by men".

17 See Jessep, O. 1992. Village Courts in Papua New Guinea: Constitutional and Gender Issues. *International Journal of Law and the Family* 6: 401–16.

18 [1991] PNGLR 84. For a thoughtful discussion of this case, see Zorn, J.G. 1994–95. Women, Custom and State Law in Papua New Guinea. *Third World Legal Studies* 1994–95: 169–205.

19 [1991] PNGLR 84, *per* Woods J at 86–87.

20 [1991] PNGLR 105.

21 Another illustration of the use of the 'repugnancy' doctrine is found in the 1994 case of *Ubuk v Darius* [1994] PNGLR 279. This was a dispute over custody of a child aged 20 months, whose parents had lived together in a *de facto* relationship for about two years. When the relationship broke up, the man (who had been previously married by custom) returned to live with his customary wife and their children. He sought custody of the ex-nuptial daughter, and emphasised his wife's apparent willingness to look after her. He relied on evidence of local custom to the effect that if an informal relationship did not progress to the status of a customary marriage, the father was entitled to automatic custody of any child born in the meantime, subject to a payment of compensation to the woman for having borne the child. The Court was not impressed with the argument, and gave custody of the child to the mother, with access rights to the father. In the words of Sevua J (at 283–84): "Whether one views it subjectively or objectively, the woman is a sex object. So where is the morality and value of humanity in this woman?... How does a woman in such a situation free herself from this seemingly sexual domination? I consider [these] customs repugnant to the general principles of humanity and, therefore, inapplicable to the present case. The applicant can gain no assistance from that customary law".

22 [1994] PNGLR 486.

23 [1994] PNGLR 486, *per* Doherty J at 486. Another of the grounds upheld was that there was no such offence prescribed as part of the Village Court's criminal jurisdiction.

24 Unreported, National Court, Mt Hagen Western Highlands Province, 15th April 1991.

25 At this time the kina was approximately equal to AU$1.33.

26 See above, n 24 at p 1.

27 *Re Willingal* (1997) N 1506.

28 As is mentioned in the judgment of Injia J, (1997) N 1506 at 7, the *PNG Post Courier* of 3 May 1996 contained an article with the headline "Girl Sold in Death Compensation". For comment on the case, see Mydans, S. 1997 When the Bartered Bride Opts out of the Bargain. *New York Times*, 6 May 1997, p A4; and Gewertz, D. & Errington, F. 1999. *Emerging Class in Papua New Guinea: The Telling of Difference.* Cambridge: Cambridge University Press, ch 6.

29 (1997) N 1506, at 24. At this time, the value of the kina was approximately equal to AU$0.92.

30 See above, n 27, at p 42.

31 See above, n 27, at pp 51–52, 54–55.

32 See above, n 27, at pp 47–49.

33 Zorn, J.G. 1994–5. Above, n 18 at p 179: "But discrimination means more than merely differential treatment. Feminist theory, for the most part, applauds the recognition of difference. It is only when differences are used to promote inequality, when difference is used as the excuse for permitting one group access to desired goods and statuses and denying access to another group, that discrimination can be said to exist." For some useful treatments of the concept of discrimination in the context of the new South African Constitution, which is of relevance to the Papua New Guinean situation, see Liebenberg, S. (ed) 1995. *The Constitution of South Africa from a Gender Perspective.* Cape Town: Community Law Centre.

34 On brideprice, see Jessep, O. & Luluaki, J. 1994. *Principles of Family Law in Papua New Guinea* (2ⁿᵈ ed). Port Moresby: UPNG Press, ch 2, pp 17–20, 80–85.

35 For discussion, see for example Jessep, O. 1993. The Governor-General's Wives – Polygamy and the Recognition of Customary Marriage in Papua New Guinea. *Australian Journal of Family Law* 7: 29–42. Analogous contemporary discussions in various African jurisdictions are referred to in the articles mentioned at n 6 above, and other papers in Eekelaar, J. and Nhlapo, T. (eds.) 1998. *The Changing Family – Family Forms and Family Law.* Oxford: Hart.

36 Jessep, O. 1993. Above, n 35.

37 [1991] PNGLR 84, *per* Woods J at 86–87.

38 Among the frequent references in the press, the Catholic Church of PNG has recently called for "a total ban on polygamy" (*PNG Post Courier*, 21st April 1999), and a National Court judge has called for legislation to punish husbands when co-wives are led to injure or kill one another (*PNG Post Courier*, 7th May 1999).

39 PNG Law Reform Commission, Task Force on Family Law Reform, Press Release, 20th June 1990.

40 Kaganas, F. Z & Murray, C. 1991. Law, Women and the Family: The Question of Polygyny in a new South Africa. *Acta Juridica* 116–34, at 128. Even so, they go on to say (p 128) that "Nevertheless, it is extremely difficult to disassociate these practices from polygyny or to envisage a polygynous household in which the husband does not dominate".

41 On the difficulties inherent in any legislative attempt to ban or discourage polygamy, see Jessep, O. 1993. Above, n 35 at pp 40–41.

42 See, for example, Johnson, D. 1979. Aspects of the Legal Status of Women in Papua New Guinea in *Melanesian Law Journal* Vol 7: 5–81, at p 33; PNG Law Reform Commission 1992. <u>Final Report on Domestic Violence: Report No 14</u> PNGLRC: Port Moresby, at p 22; Toliman, M., Davani, C. & Passingan, L. 1994. Papua New Guinea in <u>Women and Law in the Pacific – Report of a Regional Seminar</u> International Commission of Jurists: Suva; Doherty, T. 1999. International Standards, Domestic Litigation and the Advancement of Women's Rights: Perspectives and Experiences from the South Pacific. Adams, K. Byrnes, K. & A. (eds.) *Gender Equality and the Judiciary*. London: Commonwealth Secretariat, at pp 135–38. See also Zorn, J.C. 1994–95, Above, n 18 at pp 202–204.

43 See, for example, PNG Law Reform Commission, above n 43; and Dinnen, S. & Ley, A. (eds.) 2000 *Reflections on Violence in Melanesia*. Sydney: Hawkins and Asia Pacific Presses.

44 *State v Kopilyo Kipungi and others* (1983) N 437, at 5.

45 For example, in the year following the decision in *Re Willingal* (1997) N 1506 (the case of Miriam, discussed above), the *PNG Post Courier* carried a front page story with the headline "Clan Gives Girls Away In Compo Settlement" (7th August 1998). The item, by W. Palme, told of a death compensation negotiation between two clans in the Western Highlands. The original claim was for 30 pigs and 30,000 kina, subsequently changed to 30 pigs, 20,000 kina, and two 16-year-old women. A judicial inquiry was ordered into the matter, but the outcome was never reported in the newspaper.

Review questions

1. Do the people of your jurisdiction tend to view 'human rights' as being opposed to 'custom'? Do you?

2. Why do you think that human rights and custom seem to clash so much?

3. What areas other than women's rights do you think create the most clashes between constitutionally enshrined human rights and custom?

4. Human rights are often viewed as being 'natural'. Do you agree with this viewpoint? Why/why not? What other aspects of your countries legal and social systems do people treat as being 'natural? Are they actually natural?

Further readings

Aleck, J. & Rannells, J. (eds) 1995. *Custom at the Crossroads*. Port Moresby: Faculty of Law UPNG.

Barber, B. 1995. *Jihad vs McWorld: How globalism and tribalism are reshaping the world*. New York: Ballantine Books.

Dunne, T. & Wheeler, T. 1999. *Human Rights in Global Politics*. Cambridge: Cambridge University Press.

Ishay, M. (ed) 1997. *The Human Rights Reader: Major political essays, speeches and documents from the Bible to the present*. New York & London: Routledge.

Sheleff, L. 1999. *The Future of Tradition: Customary Law, Common Law and Legal Pluralism*. London: Frank Cass.

Sperber, D. 1996. *Explaining Culture: A naturalistic approach*. Oxford: Blackwell Publishers.

Weeramantry, C.G. 1982. *An Invitation to the Law*. Australia: Butterworths.

SECTION 5
NATURAL RESOURCE ISSUES

12. ENVIRONMENTAL LAW ISSUES IN THE SOUTH PACIFIC AND THE QUEST FOR SUSTAINABLE DEVELOPMENT AND GOOD GOVERNANCE
Laurence Cordonnery

13. LEGAL DEVELOPMENTS IN THE CONSERVATION AND MANAGEMENT OF HIGHLY MIGRATORY AND STRADDLING FISH STOCKS IN THE WESTERN AND CENTRAL PACIFIC OCEAN
Laurence Cordonnery

Consideration of natural resource issues in relation to law in the Pacific islands has tended to focus on land tenure issues. This is unsurprising, given the unique natures of many land tenure systems within the region. These systems, which draw upon custom and, sometimes, blend with introduced systems of land management, provide an area of interest and challenge for legal theorists and policy makers. The central importance of land within Pacific island cultures also means that people from other disciplines such as anthropology, sociology and political science take a keen interest in Pacific land tenure systems and have contributed to the literature on the subject.

This body of literature has resulted in a general awareness of the sensitivity and importance of land issues in the Pacific island region. However the Pacific islands also face a number of pressing issues to do with the use and management of other natural resources that are, maybe, less widely discussed in academic literature. This section aims to introduce readers to some of the natural resource issues other than land tenure that Pacific island societies and legal systems currently have to address.

The first chapter provides an overview of the most common and pressing natural resource issues that are being faced by the countries in the region. This overview particularly focuses on areas in which domestic legal interventions can be used to ensure that natural resources are not squandered. Current 'best practice' approaches to addressing these issues that incorporate the concept of good governance are also described and examples of various legal interventions are provided. An interesting point to note here is that the good governance agenda, which is possibly most commonly linked to combatting corruption, can be seen to be equally relevant in a different setting, that of environmental protection.

The second chapter analyses the particular issue of tuna fishing. As well as providing detailed information on management of tuna resources in this region this analysis provides us with a different angle from which to view resource issues. It focuses our attention on the interplay between international law and domestic responses and stresses the importance of cooperation at both international and regional level in order for many natural resources issues to be addressed.

Together these two chapters indicate the range of legal and social issues and responses relating to natural resource management in the Pacific islands today. Micro level interventions that maybe affect only single communities or areas, national law and policy and international law and policy, particularly at the level of regional cooperation are all shown, indicating the number of different layers of law and policy that have an impact upon natural resource management.

12. ENVIRONMENTAL LAW ISSUES IN THE SOUTH PACIFIC AND THE QUEST FOR SUSTAINABLE DEVELOPMENT AND GOOD GOVERNANCE

By: Laurence Cordonnery

KEY TERMS AND PHRASES

Biodiversity

Also referred to as biological diversity, biodiversity describes the variety and variability of nature. Plant and animal species are the most commonly recognised units of biological diversity.

Sustainable development

In 1987, the World Commission on Environment and Development (the Brundtland Commission) defined sustainable development as "development that meets the needs of the present without compromising the ability of future generations to meet their own needs." It requires an integration of economic, social and environmental considerations in decision making at both government and corporation levels in order to aim for development that does not rely upon the short term exploitaition of any resources.

Environmental impact assessment (EIA)

A critical appraisal of the likely effects of a policy, plan, program, project or activity on the environment. These assessments are usually carried out by independent assessors in order to assist the authority making the decision about whether to proceed with a particular activity.

Good governance

The term refers to a form of democratic governance that assumes legitimacy through accountability, predictability and openness of government formed by consent of the people and in accordance with the rule of law. In terms of resource allocation and acquisition, good governance presupposes consultation and participation of those affected by projects and transparency of decision making and resource allocation.

INTRODUCTION

This chapter will introduce some of the environmental issues that need to be urgently addressed in the South Pacific. It focuses upon the issues that Pacific island countries (PICs) have some leverage in devising solutions for, whether within regional, national and/or local legal and management frameworks. In presenting current approaches to environmental protection and sustainable development the reasons why PICs should depart from a strict transposition of western legal models, the relevance of participatory democracy at the community level and the need for more transparency and accountability of state actions will be emphasised.

THE MOST CRITICAL ENVIRONMENTAL ISSUES FOR THE SOUTH PACIFIC

Climate change

Vulnerability to climate change and the resulting impacts on coastal environments due to sea level rise and coastal erosion, coral bleaching and changes in the productivity of marine ecosystems is certainly the most pressing environmental issue faced by PICs today, particularly for low-lying islands and atolls. Yet, despite general awareness of the issue at regional and governmental levels, any solution to climate change (as opposed to an adaptive reaction) will depend on the outcomes of the global negotiations on the implementation of the Kyoto Protocol to the United Nations Convention on Climate Change. To that extent, climate change remains an external issue for PICs despite them being its first victims. It can only be hoped that further regional solidarity will be demonstrated against the inflexibility of the JUSCAN group of countries (Japan, USA, Canada, Australia, and New Zealand) to effectively tackle the issue by accepting to reduce greenhouse gases emissions at their source. Typically, the example of climate change illustrates the lack of leverage of PICs to address this global issue. Because of the inability of PICs to be proactive in creating a solution to climate change this environmental threat will not be considered further in this chapter.

The loss of biodiversity

The loss of biodiversity, which mostly occurs through land degradation, is another pressing environmental issue of international relevance which has a better potential to be addressed within appropriate regional and national frameworks. This is because biodiversity loss is a direct result of population growth, urbanisation and unsustainable development activities within the region.

The tropical South Pacific is renowned worldwide for its high level of species diversity and endemism[2] (mostly on the high islands of PNG, Solomon Islands, New Caledonia and Vanuatu). The region is also known to have the most extensive coral reef system in the world. Pacific islanders rely heavily on these biological resources for subsistence and for their economic, social and cultural well being. But island environments are some of the areas in which biological diversity is most threatened in the world. For smaller islands of the region, such as atolls, up to 75% of indigenous plant species are in danger of extinction.

Island ecosystems are described as fragile because of their generally small size and endemicity. Given the small land space, endemic species on islands can be lost within a very short time span due to introduction of insect pests, diseases, predators or destruction of critical habitat (often associated with construction activities). The loss of any habitat is likely to mean the extinction of species of plants or animals. Because of size, a large proportion of the land, its inhabitants and the adjacent sea are likely to be affected by disturbances that might be only minor regional events on a larger landmass.

Unsustainable logging

Typically, unsustainable logging describes a situation where the rate of log harvests exceeds sustainable yields, leading to the depletion of a resource. Unsustainable logging practices commonly occur in the region but are of particular concern in Solomon Islands where large scale logging operations are conducted by multinational companies, mostly taking place on customary land. To address this issue both Solomon Islands and Vanuatu have adopted codes of logging practice. However, both countries have experienced implementation difficulties either due to lack of training, monitoring and enforcement capacity, as in the case of Vanuatu, or because of generalised corruption at all levels of the decision making, a process facilitated by a rapid monetarisation of certain sectors of society and the emergence of new elites in villages.[3] In addition, the issue of corruption in Solomon Islands is extremely difficult to address given the economic dependency of the country on log exports. To illustrate the current ineffectiveness of the logging regulation, in 1995 Solomon Islands set a sustainable yield for logging activities at 325,000 cubic metres per year but in that year the log exports reached 748,500 cubic metres.[4]

Unsustainable coastal fishing

Over-exploitation of inshore marine resources combined with the use of damaging fishing practices (using dynamite for example) and coastal pollution has caused declines in the amount of coastal fish stock. This is the case notably for rock cod (*Serranidae*), mullet (*Mugilidae*), scad (*Carangidae*) and mackerel (*Scombridae*), while some species, such as coconut crabs[5] and giant clams, have been driven to extinction in several areas. The question of sustainability in the exploitation of inshore resources can be formulated in terms similar to logging. As stated by King *et. al* "a fish stock may be regarded as over-exploited when the numbers of fish are reduced to such an extent that the remaining adults are unable to produce enough young fish to maintain the stock."[6]

Secondary degradation because of unsustainable land use

Degradation of land and coastal environments is now widespread throughout PICs, typically as a result of development activities that are either unsustainable by nature, as in the case of clearfell logging, or for which no environmental impact assessments (EIAs) were conducted and therefore no monitoring, mitigation or alternative development options were devised. The most common types of impacts from development activities include soil erosion, impacts of sedimentation on coral reefs, mangrove reclamation and degradation and pollution by sewage and industrial effluents.

Erosion

Soil erosion is a common consequence of construction projects, agriculture and forestry activities, especially on steep slopes. Poor land use practice is the most common reason for soil erosion. Soil erosion leads to poorer soil productivity and to sedimentation downstream.

Sedimentation

As mentioned before, sedimentation[7] on coral reefs is usually a consequence of soil erosion and more generally of all coastal developments since almost every project generates suspended sediment (at least during the construction phase) and countries in the region are surrounded by coral. The impacts of sedimentation on coral reefs is to reduce photosynthesis of algae growing as part of their structure. In the best case scenario sedimentation will therefore inhibit coral growth. However, long term exposure to sediment will kill all or part of the coral colony. Even if the exposure does not kill the coral directly, it will reduce coral growth as energy is diverted to clearing sediment. Sediment exposure has led to 'coral bleaching', which occurs because of the loss of the algae.

Mangrove degradation

Mangrove degradation and reclamation is another issue linked to the widespread perception of mangroves as wastelands that can be used as garbage tips or for land reclamation. This view is now being challenged as the ecological role of mangroves is gradually better understood. Mangroves, as a group of trees adapted to living on the boundary of marine and terrestrial environments, play several crucial ecological functions such as slowing down water movement and aiding in sediment deposition, thus reducing sedimentation of reefs. Mangroves provide organic matter (through their leaf litter and from nutrients of river water) that supports communities of micro-organisms that in turn provide food for the young fish living in the mangroves. Finally, they also provide habitats for juvenile fish species (about 60 to 80% of commercial fish species are associated with mangroves at some point in their life cycle) and for wildlife species including birds.

Pollution

Coastal pollution, due to organic and industrial effluents, is localised to urban areas. The impacts of organic effluents (sewage, fish wastes, slaughterhouse wastes and food processing wastes) are to change the receiving ecosystem by stimulating algae growth at the expense of other organisms, coral for example. This phenomenon can lead to eutrophication and ecological death when algae growth reaches such a level that the dissolved oxygen in the water is all used up by the decaying algae. Regarding industrial effluents, concerns can particularly be raised with toxic chemicals concentrated in the food chain, as happens with the insecticide DDT.

As can be seen, a wide range of environmental issues are of concern to the South Pacific region. In addressing these concerns a number of approaches can be taken. Introduced legal methods such as EIAs, the setting of polluting emissions standards and land use planning schemes can be used to great effect in some situations. Traditional environmental management methods in line with the realities of customary land and marine tenure may also be used to address these issues. The various approaches to addressing environmental concerns and their potential benefits and shortcomings must, however, be analysed in the light of good governance prerequisites in order to ensure that effective and appropriate responses to environmental issues are formulated.

THE NATURE AND ROLE OF ENVIRONMENTAL LAW

Environmental law first developed in western countries as a result of parliamentary activity and the adoption of statutes that broadened the scope of administrative control. In this sense, environmental law is almost entirely a product of legislation. The reason for this is that the scope and content of environmental law falls largely within the category of 'public law' rather than 'private law'. Accordingly, the emergence of environmental law in western countries coincides with the recognition by the public and the government of past mistakes and of the necessity of using the Earth's resources in a more sustainable manner. The evolution and gradual recognition of environmental law in a given country will therefore be a function of the public acceptance and awareness of non-economic as well as economic factors that are important in enhancing the quality of life to which we all aspire. In other words, the evolution and expansion of environmental law is dependant upon the extent to which the limits of conventional development models (that do not systematically incorporate non-economic parameters such as the social and environmental impacts of development schemes) are recognised.

This is translated into the incorporation of the concept of sustainable development and sustainability[8] in the exploitation of resources in environmental legislation, which outlines the need to integrate conservation and development so as to ensure that the rights of future generations are not compromised.

At the national level the implementation of the concept of sustainable development raises a number of questions. How should governments change policies and priorities to reflect the concept of sustainability? How will the concept find concrete expression in law so that it is capable of being enforced? In terms of decision making there may also be practical problems in reconciling the policy objective of sustainability with development priorities and objectives. Should governments legislate to give priority to concepts of sustainability and if so how will these be legally defined and what mechanisms will be put in place to ensure coordination, continuity and compliance in decision making? This also raises the question of the relevance of using foreign legislative models in introducing comprehensive environmental legal reform, as the enforcement of foreign models may be of questionable practicality in the context of PICs. As Farrier puts it:

> Symbolic legislation may satisfy the demands of international conventions, but legislation which is not enforced will do little to protect the environment of your South Pacific Countries. Indeed it may lead to a complacency, based on a belief that something is being done, that is positively damaging.[9]

Further, the implementation of environmental legislation presents a number of difficulties due to commonly found reasons, such as:

- the isolation of communities, resulting in lack of awareness of laws created by the central government and lack of enforcement due to travel restrictions;
- the smallness of communities, generating difficulties in getting independent enforcement officers to apply sanctions;
- the inadequacy of penalties for environmental offences (usually relying upon the imposition of fines) and the need to find more culturally appropriate models of communal sanction against environmental offenders;
- cultural traditions of customary landowners which may be opposed to central government implementation of the law, unless a genuine participation of local and landowner in the drafting is ensured; and
- the lack of recognition of traditional methods of resource management and control in the legislation.

Further, one should bear in mind the appropriateness of foreign model legislation for addressing the actual environmental issues of the country in which environmental law reform is under consideration.[10] A simple but striking example of the ineffectiveness of foreign model command and control legislation is the *Anti-Litter Decree* 1992 of Fiji. This decree has never been enforced and, in the absence of public information campaigns, the population remains unaware of its existence. Despite the imposition of severe penalties this piece of legislation has had little effect on curbing the litter problem in Fiji. It shows that in order to be effective, there must be an ongoing commitment to law enforcement and education of the population on the reasons for the law. Without such a commitment any piece of legislation remains largely irrelevant to the population and will therefore be largely ignored.

Another example that illustrates the difficulty of imposing foreign model legislation and institutions is the proposed Environment and Resource Management Bill in Vanuatu. This Bill is intended to facilitate the establishment of relevant institutions and mechanisms for managing the environment (pollution control, mandatory EIAs, protection of natural heritage and biodiversity conservation). A number of modified versions of this Bill have circulated amongst the various stakeholders as a number of legal experts and draftsmen succeeded each other, but after several years the Bill still has not been tabled in Parliament for consideration. Unfortunately none of the legal experts and draftsmen are aware of the issues facing Vanuatu in terms of feasible institutions and enforcement procedures. Therefore their work tends to rely on foreign models of legislation that appear too elaborate to be able to grasp the environmental issues and to address issues of capacity and responses to law enforcement that are specific to Vanuatu. Given the existing financial and human resource constraints to implementing introduced models of law enforcement, traditional conservation and resource management practices have the potential to bring more effective results than western models of law enforcement in the South Pacific.

In fact, one can argue that many of the environmental problems or existing gaps in the law of PICs may be resolved without enacting command and control legislation, but instead by strengthening existing institutions in government (such as the Environment Unit in Vanuatu) as well as local government or village authorities and providing community leaders with the necessary environmental awareness and education.

It is argued here that the implementation of the concept of sustainable development in the South Pacific requires first and foremost the institutional development of a society. That is, good governance and community participation in the development process itself is needed.

GOOD GOVERNANCE AND CAPACITY BUILDING

If governance is defined as the manner in which power is exercised in the management of a country's economic and social resources for development, then the linkage with sustainable development and environmental law is quite obvious, despite having been overlooked to a large extent in the good governance discourse.[11] Good governance presupposes efficient administration and transparent institutions capable of meeting the requirement of accountability. To achieve this, public administration reforms are necessary. In particular priority needs to be given to the establishment of a state governed by law, the development of a judicial system and of local government autonomy and administration.

Strengthening the public sector

Public administrative reforms are leading to institutional changes in the South Pacific as in most developing countries, but whether or not these reflect the objectives of sustainable development can be questioned. One shortcoming can be readily identified in the fact that such reforms are often driven by aid donors without necessarily taking into consideration the cultural factors responsible for most cases of corruption, nor the applicability of the economic model proposed. For example, under Vanuatu's Comprehensive Reform Programme (CRP), whose establishment was part of the conditions set by the World Bank for granting further loans to the Republic of Vanuatu, a reform of the civil service has been undertaken. This reform led to a drastic reduction in the number of civil servants while increasing the salaries of senior officials to provide incentives to productivity and efficiency in the public service and to diminish the risk of corruption. Although these reforms appear necessary to improve the accountability of the executive, the CRP has also been criticised for its focus on privatisation (such as introducing the user pays principle as opposed to provision of essential services by the state) and corporatisation of the public sector. It has been argued that this reform promotes economic development without taking into account the interests of people in sustainable development. Instead, as what constitutes development is largely subjective, development strategies must be determined by the people themselves and adapted to their particular conditions. Similarly, the corporatisation of the public service does not take into consideration the fact that the majority of Ni-Vanuatu people are relying on subsistence agriculture and are therefore unable to pay for the services that used to be provided by the state.

Accountability and the Office of the Ombudsman

Institutional strengthening of bodies whose specific role is to ensure the accountability and transparency of administrative decisions is also an essential component of the good governance agenda that clearly impacts upon environmental policies. For example, the Office of the Ombudsman can play a significant role in assisting environmental protection by way of the complaint procedure. The complaint procedure to the Ombudsman is a way of ensuring that public officials conduct themselves and their administration according to the law. For example, in Solomon Islands, various Ombudsman's reports to Parliament in recent years have demonstrated the inadequacies of present law and practices in the forestry sector, also questioning the legality of logging practices.[12]

Decentralisation

Decentralisation is often referred to as a form of government in line with the agenda of good governance as its aim is to devolve executive and legislative power to local and provincial government entities while relying on a number of good governance assumptions to achieve this goal. The first of these assumptions is that, through decentralisation, greater accountability will be achieved by ensuring public participation in decision making. Secondly, decentralisation assumes that budgeting and planning take place at the local and regional level, giving decisions makers the opportunity to take into account the specificity and aspirations of community groups and to accommodate them, thus promoting greater self-reliance. Thirdly, decision making takes place amongst groups that are more closely integrated with local communities, hence facilitating a more precise knowledge of issues amongst such groups. Fourthly, in countries of great cultural and linguistic diversity such as Solomon Islands and Vanuatu, decentralisation is meant to foster the recognition of the separate identity of groups and regions while at the same time uniting them.

Whilst discrepancies exist between the rhetoric of constitutional and legal autonomy and the actual practice of decentralisation in the South Pacific,[13] the concept of devolving power to communities and allowing self determination is of great relevance in terms of environmental issues. Although devolution of power to community groups has only begun to be used recently in the environmental context, there are now a number of examples of the successful use of community capacity building programmes.

At the regional level, SPREP has initiated a number of projects aiming at building up the capacity of local resource owners and users to sustainably manage and develop their own marine resources (coral reefs, mangroves, seagrasses) while encouraging better coordination between government, NGOs and local communities. For example, SPREP has initiated:

- village level coral reef monitoring programmes and national training courses in coral reef monitoring methods;

- a regional training workshop on developing a permit system for the coral trade in PICs;

- community based marine protected areas workshops; and

- integrated coastal management initiatives to improve the capacity of PICs to respond to changes and threats to coastal areas and resources from urbanisation, land and marine based sources of pollution, inappropriate coastal and port development and land use practices.

COMMUNITY PARTICIPATION AND CO-MANAGEMENT OF RESOURCES

Another approach to good governance through decentralisation is to improve community participation in the allocation and use of resources through planning. An illustration of such a bottom-up approach can be found with the Community Area Resource Management Approach (CARMA) launched at the village level by the Land Use Planning Office (LUPO) (within the Ministry of Lands) in Vanuatu. This project is part of the Vanuatu Land Use Planning Project funded by AusAID to collect information on land use so as to achieve sustainable development and conservation of land resources. The aim is to first gather representatives of several villages in an area to make an inventory of their resources. Development and exploitation options are discussed and optimum areas for specific uses are identified. For example prime agricultural land is zoned across community councils. LUPO's role is to provide advice on the need to ensure sustainability of resources. If preservation is identified as the best option LUPO advises on how people can receive financial compensation. Once agreed amongst the communities involved, the local land use plan is submitted to the local government council and then to national government for approval. Maps are produced using the Vanuatu Resources Information System (VANRIS), a geographic information system containing attribute and statistical data, which combined with maps generated at any desired scale provide an excellent decision support tool for development options and are also relevant to EIAs. LUPO also runs workshops where government and local people are taught how to use VANRIS aiming at building the necessary training capacity for self-reliance in the use and maintenance of VANRIS. Unfortunately, despite the continuing existence of LUPO, funding for the Vanuatu Land Use Planning Project stopped in 2000, without having entirely achieved the level self-reliance that was expected in the time frame set for the completion of the project.

Environmental impact assessments

Community participation in decision making regarding development options, allocation and use of natural resources can take many forms. Whichever forms of community participation are favoured, in order to be truly effective they need to be accommodated within the legal and management tools that are required to address relatively new issues of large scale and potentially damaging and over-exploitative activities brought by technological development. A perfect example of such a legal and management tool devised in western countries for this purpose is the EIAs.[14] This tool has already been adopted for use in some countries in the region and is in the process of becoming mandatory in a number of other Pacific countries. In Solomon Islands, EIA procedures are included in Part III of the 1998 *Environment Act*. In Kiribati, EIA procedures are included in Part III of 1999 *Act to Provide for the Protection, Improvement and Conservation of the Environment of the Republic of Kiribati and for Connected Purposes*. In both Fiji and Vanuatu EIAs appear as guidelines only, but their legal status is likely to change with the enactment of the *Sustainable Development Bill* in Fiji and the *Environment and Resource Management Bill* in Vanuatu, which both detail EIA procedures.

The object of an EIA process is to identify the possible risks to the environment that may result from a proposed action. This information is then used to decide whether to proceed with the action and on what conditions. The ultimate purpose of an EIA is not just to assess impacts; it is to improve the quality of decisions. EIAs not only force environmental knowledge into the policy process but also reveal the inadequacy of the decision making process caused by incomplete information. As a formal process EIAs can only be conceived and developed in societies with an effective system of government administration and where there is enough wealth to support them. This is because they require technical expertise coupled with scientific research in order to determine the nature and extent of potentially adverse environmental impacts.

Applied to the South Pacific, the EIA process necessarily requires a minimum institutional capacity that needs to be located at the appropriate level of government (whether central, provincial or local) where development and sectoral policies, programmes and projects are evaluated. To establish a formal EIA process, SPREP[15] recommends three administrative levels so as to secure a minimum level of impartiality in the decision making process:

- Firstly, an environment unit to carry out the government functions of screening, scoping, reviewing and enforcing EIAs;

- Secondly, a senior body with authority over other departments to require them to adhere to environmental policies is required to make decisions about controversial projects. The suggested structure of this senior body is a commission made up of permanent secretaries or ministers from the major departments that influence the environment. Such a commission would be mandated to review both public and private sector projects;

- Thirdly, SPREP recommends that each government department concerned with natural resources should appoint a middle management person to ensure that the projects initiated by that department follow EIA procedures.

From a good governance perspective the EIA review process must ensure that there is sufficient evidence showing that people affected by the project have been consulted and that members of the local community understand the information contained in the environmental impact statement. In other words, community participation in development decisions must be established as a legally enforceable right.

With respect to the environmental issues described in the first part of this chapter, EIAs could address issues of soil erosion by developing mitigation measures such as erosion control practices like terracing or recommending the use of ponds to control sediment runoff around construction projects involving earth movement/disturbance. Through the EIA process the erodability of soils in areas to be logged could also be determined and sensitive areas could be mapped out. Similarly, it is notable that the impacts of sedimentation on coral reefs can be easily monitored by establishing monitoring sites where the percentage of live cover of coral is measured, and that such a monitoring measure can be incorporated into the EIA process.

Addressing coastal pollution resulting from land based activities is also within the scope of EIAs by determining whether the receiving waters (stream, river and/or bay) can accommodate the additional nutrient load that will result from the proposed activity. The answer will depend on the amount of dilution that can be expected. For example, in the case of a river, the dilution is controlled by the volume of flow. In the case of a marine discharge, dilution will be determined by the amount of flushing, a function of the tidal range and the water currents. If there is insufficient dilution to reduce the nutrient loading to near background levels within 100m of the outfall, then the EIA should recommend a sewage treatment to reduce the nutrients loading. One way of addressing this issue could be to ensure that the EIA for a proposed development that has industrial effluent describes the average chemical content of the waste, and the average and peak volumes.

Finally, the recognition of the ecological importance of mangroves can be incorporated in the scoping of sites subject to EIAs by proposing alternative sites.

The use of customary approaches

Community participation in the management of resources can also be promoted through a legal recognition of customary rules and practices adopted by communities themselves. Most countries in the South Pacific have in fact two legal systems in operation: that of customary law and that established through government legislation.

Although the relative positions of customary law and introduced law vary from country to country, it is fair to say that both systems of law are intended to be complementary, which is why both are generally recognised within countries constitutions. In practice though, the two systems are not always mutually supportive and tend to operate independently of each other. Yet improvements in environmental protection and resource management may be achieved through stronger links between customary practices on one hand and, on the other, processes developed under state law. There are also merits in strengthening customary law with new information and management practices designed to cope with resource options now available due to increased pressures on resources rising from things such as population growth, the introduction of a cash economy and the advent of new technologies.

In most countries in the South Pacific customary land and marine tenure systems have been maintained or restored after independence, with customary landholding being the dominant form of land ownership.[16] Dispute resolution methods that take customary methods into account, including separate customary court structures, have also been established to resolve land disputes at least in the first instance.[17] But despite the importance of customary land tenure, customary land law and customary dispute resolution methods are not fully treated as equal to introduced law as customary courts often remain subordinated to higher courts, which rely on introduced common law. For example, island courts in Vanuatu, which have been established to provide for customary resolution of disputes, are not effective in resolving land issues as most cases are directly appealed to the supreme court due to the lack of training of support staff and low level of competence of Justices over customary law.[18] Indeed, under the *Island Court Act* [Cap 160] of Vanuatu the customary exercise of justice by chiefs is not recognised, despite the fact that the chief's role in maintaining social order remains important in most areas of Vanuatu, particularly where there is little police presence or control. In ensuring regulation of the environment (or, indeed, other areas of social regulation) to fail to utilise a functioning, and largely effective, system of authority seems to be a gross oversight, particularly when governments do not have the resources to commit to creating new systems of authority and regulation. Since chiefly authority is a working system acknowledged by all why treat it as an alternative system of justice and not fully incorporate the chiefly system of justice into the judicial system, at least in so far as land and natural resource issues are concerned?

The option of utilising traditional systems of justice for regulation of the environment has been fully explored in Samoa through the adoption of village by-laws for managing inshore marine resources. It has been such a success that the feasibility of transposing this model to other PICs is currently debated within regional forums and conferences. By-laws for the conservation of inshore fisheries were introduced in Samoa as a result of a drastic decline in catches due to over-exploitation and the use of destructive fishing methods. This situation raised alarm not only within the Fisheries Division but in a number of villages. Village *fono* or councils of chiefs first started to use local media to advertise village rules in order to prevent further decline of fishery resources. Advertisements focused on banning the use of explosives, chemicals and other destructive fishing methods and the prohibition of fishing in designated areas. These advertisements also indicated penalties to be paid to village *fono* for any breach of their village rules by their own residents. Any breach committed by people who were not residents of the village was subject to threats of litigation. However, as some village rules contradicted existing laws, several *fono* could not pursue court action against breaches by neighbouring villages.[19]

While the value of such a campaign to improve the conservation and management of inshore fisheries was acknowledged by the Fisheries Division, the necessity of giving legal recognition to the rules set by the village *fono* in the introduced courts and to ensure that such rules to do not contradict provisions of national fisheries legislation was also realised.[20] A consultation process was then initiated between representatives of village *fonos* and the Fisheries Division on the appropriateness of their proposed rules. This consultation process has now been formalised as the second step in the formulation of any village by-law, followed by a final check and clearance by the Office of the Attorney General. Every by-law is signed by the Director of the Ministry of Agriculture, Forest and Fisheries and Meteorology, and then passed to the Legislative Assembly to be gazetted while also being published by the Fisheries Division in the local newspaper and copies distributed in neighboring villages. As a result, the *Fishery Act* 1988 gives legal recognition to village by-laws and details procedures upon which a village can declare its own rules as by-laws. By-laws apply to all citizens equally, and cover any measure assisting the management and conservation of inshore fishery resources, including:

- restriction on sizes of fish and shellfish that can be taken;
- bans on certain types of fishing gear and methods;
- allocation of fish quotas;
- restriction of mesh sizes for nets and fish traps; and
- closure of fishing seasons or areas to allow fish to reproduce.

The main advantage of village by-laws over the regular laws is that the rules are created by the people with a real interest in the management and the conservation of fishery resources. This means that the village *fono* is more inclined to monitor and enforce such rules. Communities either build watch houses, maintain patrol canoes or employ watchmen to monitor illegal activities in their coastal zones and marine protected areas. Customary fines (the provision of pigs and taro for example) are imposed on residents of villages that own the by-laws while legal action can be taken against any breach by outsiders.

The success of the village by-law model in Samoa is therefore linked to community participation in the management of resources based on customary ownership. This model integrates one of the most important yet easily forgotten aspects of development: culture, as reflected in customary land and marine tenure systems.

The transposability of the Samoan village by-law model will be determined by the extent to which customary law is given legal recognition in the country considered and the extent to which the cultural and social of customary practices have been maintained in society generally. In much the same manner such by-laws should be a success in other PICs, provided that the system of custom is utilised in the same way as in the Samoan context.

Transposing the Samoan village by-law model to Melanesian countries may present additional difficulties due to the greater cultural and linguistic diversity and the erosion, in some parts of Vanuatu and the Solomon Islands, of the chiefly system and the questioning of chiefly decisions and authority. This difference may be explained by the homogenous character of Polynesian societies, both ethnically and geographically, in contrast with Melanesian countries.

A parallel to Samoa's by-laws regime can be made with the *Decentralisation and Local Government Regions Act* adopted by the Vanuatu Parliament in 1994, which allows the introduction of by-laws whose function is to "outline create and draw up regulations governing the environmental protection zones (natural parks, natural reserves or tourist attraction areas in the national interest)" under section 20(9) of the Act. Such by-laws designate protected areas on the basis of custom, amenity and livelihood. Customary tenure is strengthened by making it an offence to contravene the rules governing a protected area while the term of the by-laws is specified by the landowners. In addition amendments may be made by landowners at any time. Finally, under this by-law model, for every declared protected area a committee of management is set up representing both landowner interests and community interests through chiefly representation.[21] However, compared with the Samoan village by-law model now applied in at least 54 villages on Upolu Island, the Vanuatu model has hardly been applied by local governments. One reason may be the focus on protected areas designation as opposed to management of resources. Another reason may be the ineffectiveness of local government structures. In addition, whereas the Samoan legislation was created because communities were already making by-laws and these needed legal recognition, the Vanuatu legislation has been drafted by law makers with little awareness by and little commitment from communities.

With an improved approach to community participation the situation may be different, as demonstrated by the co-management approach recently adopted by the Vanuatu Fisheries Department for the *Trochus Niloticus* combining traditional management methods with fisheries management regulation and wild stock enhancement using hatchery reared *trochus* juveniles. Co-management means a cooperative approach between communities, acting in their local interests, and governments, acting in the national or public interest, in the management of a particular resource. In a co-management context, the central government (in this case the Fisheries Department) acts as the coordinator and provider of technical advice, but the process should be owned by the community and be based on traditional and customary practices.

As Amos notes "customary law in Vanuatu dictates that most near-shore areas especially coral reef flats owned by clans or larger communal groups are not open to access fisheries".[22] Such areas are therefore currently managed through traditional restrictions imposed by the resource owners including limited entry, closed seasons and restricted harvests. Again, as Amos points out, the major feature of customary tenure is that controls are expected at a local level, not from fisheries officers considered as outsiders. This gives rise to the main difficulty of combining traditional management practices and fisheries management regulations — establishing a working relationship between the Fisheries Department (as outsiders) and the resource users and owners. This relationship must necessarily take into account the need to devise income generating alternatives for communities who are depending heavily on the depleted resources concerned. As Amos[23] concludes, if the people are not provided with alternatives that will ensure that their subsistence and financial needs are met, they will continue to over-exploit the resources concerned, regardless of management controls.

The advantage of co-management is that it combines scientific methods of fisheries management when sufficient data exists for it to be workable and when relevant, with traditional practices of resource exploitation. Fishing communities in turn acquire a better understanding of fisheries management principles. The costs of enforcement and management are minimised as well as the social and political conflicts between the government and the community.

CONCLUSION

This chapter explored current environmental issues in the South Pacific and possible ways of addressing them by giving meaning to two concepts commonly found in aid policies: sustainable development and good governance. Strengthening the rule of law and government institutions and introducing environmental law reforms are certainly relevant and necessary to address these issues from a top-down perspective of management. From a bottom-up perspective however, improved community participation in development decisions and the legal recognition of customary resource management practices are the most culturally appropriate and the most cost-efficient ways of addressing the limitations and shortcomings of the state and of promoting greater self-reliance. This approach is extremely relevant today given the increasingly limited powers granted to the state in the context of the globalised economy. Yet, reliance on these elements of a bottom-up approach to sustainable development and good governance necessitate access to education, both formal and vocational, a prerequisite that has received too little attention in the South Pacific beyond the training of future elites who tend to lose connection with the needs of their communities as they become the main beneficiaries of globalisation. Hence, before sustainable development and good governance can become truly meaningful concepts in the Pacific region, environmental education and subsequent wider consciousness of environmental issues needs to be established.

ENDNOTES

2 The term 'endemism' refers to living species whose distribution is to be found within a specific geographical area.

3 For a discussion on the issue of corruption in the Solomon Islands forest industry see Kabutaulaka, T. 2000. Rumble in the jungle: land, culture and (un) sustainable logging in the Solomon Islands. In Hooper, A. ed. *Culture and Sustainable Development in the Pacific*. Canberra: National Centre for Development Studies, Australian National University. p 88–97.

4 Kabutaulaka, T. 2000. above, n 2.

5 Although coconut crabs can be considered as land-based species once they reach mature age, juveniles stay close to the water, and gradually develop their own shell and become more like land animals. As they grow they move further inland away from the coast. This species is omnivorous and forages along beaches and over coral rocks looking for food. Since harvesting takes place along the seashore (during the day coconut crabs hide in holes in the sand or under coconut trees and shrubs) it is relevant to include this species in any discussion on over-exploitation of coastal resources in the Pacific region. For additional information see: http://www.spc.org.nc/coastfish/Countries/CookIslands/ MMR/7Somespecies/Ccrab.htm (Accessed 26/9/01).

6 King, M. Faasili, U. and Ropeti, E. 1995. Management Strategies for Inshore Fisheries in Tropical Pacific Islands. In *Workshop Proceedings on the Management of South Pacific Inshore Fisheries, Noumea, New Caledonia, 26 June–7 July 1995, volume II*. Noumea: FFA/SPC. p 510.

7 Sedimentation is to be understood as the deposition of eroded soil materials suspended in water bodies. Sedimentation takes place when water velocity falls below a point at which the suspended particles can be carried.

8 The concept of sustainability defined by the International Union for the Conservation of Nature (IUCN) in the World Conservation Strategy published in 1980 links the maintenance of ecological processes and life support systems to the sustainable utilization of resources and the maintenance of genetic diversity. International Union for Conservation of Nature. 1980. *World conservation strategy : living resource conservation for sustainable development* Switzerland: IUCN.

9 Farrier, D. 1993. Introduction to Basic Concepts of Environmental Law. In Boer, B.,ed. *Strengthening Environmental Legislation in the Pacific Region: Workshop Proceedings* Samoa: SPREP/UNEP, p 41.

10 For further discussion on this issue, see Hewison, G. 1997. Environmental Law Reform in Vanuatu: The Challenges Facing a Small Island Developing Country. *Asia Pacific Journal of Environmental Law* 2(1): 27–38.

11 A notable exception is found in Ginther, K. Denters, E. & de Waart, P. (eds.) 1995. *Sustainable Development and Good Governance*. Dortrecht: Martinus Nijhoff Publishers.

12 See Boer, B. 1993. *Strengthening Environment Management Capabilities in Pacific Island Developing Countries*. Samoa: SPREP. p 79–99.

13 It is not within the scope of this chapter to embark upon a detailed analysis of the failures of decentralisation policies in the South Pacific. Breifly the criticism here is that while in theory there are good grounds to keep decentralisation within the good governance

agenda, its practical implementation falls short because of the failure to consider the changing life style aspirations of local communities and to enhance their capacity to make the informed choices about possible development options. In other words, devolution of power remains within the context of a top-down approach, which forgets to equip local communities with the capacity to become self-reliant the beyond traditional activities of subsistence economy.

14 Gilpin provides the following definition for an EIA: "the critical appraisal of the likely effects of a policy, plan, program, project or activity on the environment. To assist the decision-making authority, assessments are carried out independently of the proponent, who may have prepared an environmental impact statement. The decision making authority may be a level of government (local, state) or a government agency. Assessments take account of any adverse environmental effects on the community; any environmental impact on the ecosystem of the locality; any long term or cumulative effects on the environment". See Gilpin, A. 2000. *Dictionary of Environmental Law.* London: Edward Elgar. p 96.

15 South Pacific Regional Environment Program. 1993. *A Guide to EIA in the South Pacific.* Samoa: SPREP.

16 In Samoa, about 80 percent of land is customary land. Samoa's *Constitution* formalised the existence of three categories of land: customary, freehold and public land (Article 101(1)). Article 101(2) of the Samoan *Constitution* provides that customary land is held in accordance with Samoan custom and usage and with the law relating to Samoan custom and usage. In the Solomon Islands, about 87 % of land is under customary ownership. In Fiji, 83 percent of land is classified as "native land" meaning that it is owned by indigenous Fijians.

17 Article 53 of the *Constitution* of Vanuatu provides that "parliament shall provide for the establishment of village or island courts with jurisdiction over customary matters and shall provide for the role of chiefs in such courts".

18 For further discussion on the role and effectiveness of Island Courts in Vanuatu, see Jowitt, A. 2000. Island Courts in Vanuatu. *School of Law Occasional Paper Series Volume 2.* Vanuatu: University of the South Pacific.

19 See Fa'asili & Mulipola, A. 1999. The Use of Village By-Laws in Marine Conservation and Fisheries Management. In *First Heads of Fisheries Meeting, Pacific Community, Noumea, New Caledonia, 9–13 August 1999* Noumea: SPC.

20 Fa'asili & Mulipola, A. 1999. Above, n 18.

21 see Hunt, C. 1997. Cooperative Approaches to Marine Resources Management in the South Pacific. In Larmour, P. ed. *The Governance of Common Property in the Pacific Region.* Canberra: Asia Pacific Press. p 145–164.

22 This means that such resources can only be harvested by members of the clan. See Amos, M. 1995. Combination of Fisheries Management Regulation, Traditionally Based Management and Wild stock Enhancement using Hatchery Reared *Trochus Juveniles* as Precautionary Management Principle for Trochus Niloticus Resources in Vanuatu. In *Workshop Proceedings on the Management of Pacific Inshore Fisheries, Noumea, New Caledonia, 26 June–7 July 1995, volume II.* Noumea: FFA/SPC. p 169–179.

13. LEGAL DEVELOPMENTS IN THE CONSERVATION AND MANAGEMENT OF HIGHLY MIGRATORY AND STRADDLING FISH STOCKS IN THE WESTERN AND CENTRAL PACIFIC OCEAN

By: Laurence Cordonnery

KEY TERMS AND PHRASES

Archipelagic waters

Under article 49 of the United Nations Convention on the Law of the Sea (UNCLOS), the sovereignty of an archipelagic state extends to the waters enclosed by the archipelagic baselines drawn in accordance with article 47 and described as archipelagic waters. Archipelagic baselines may be drawn by joining the outermost points of the outermost islands and drying reefs of the archipelago provided that within such baselines are included the main islands and an area in which the ratio of the area of water to the area of land including atolls is between 1 to 1 and 9 to 1.

Artisanal

This term refers to the scale and techniques of fishing operations in the context of subsistence economy as opposed to industrial fishing operations.

Biomass

The term biomass refers to the total mass of living organisms of one or more species per unit of space.

Straddling stocks

Highly migratory species that move across vast expanses of ocean space and that cross international maritime boundaries, straddling the exclusive economic zones (EEZs) of one or more states and the high seas.

PACIFIC TUNA STOCKS: ECONOMIC SECURITY AND SUSTAINABLE DEVELOPMENT OF PACIFIC ISLAND COUNTRIES

The Pacific Ocean represents 12% of the world's oceans, and, its importance for Pacific islanders is such that in many ways, "it is the sea that holds the key to the future of Pacific Islands peoples".[1]

The importance of marine resources to Pacific island countries (PICs) has been recognised in Chapter 17 (Programme G) of Agenda 21, the action plan for implementing sustainable development in the 21st century adopted as a soft law instrument[2] of the 1992 Rio United Nations Conference on Environment and Development (UNCED). Chapter 17 focuses upon the protection of the oceans and provides that:

> Small Island States are ecologically fragile and vulnerable. Their small size, limited resources, geographic dispersion and isolation from markets, places them at a disadvantage economically and prevent economies of scale. For island developing states ocean and coastal environment is of strategic importance and constitutes a valuable development resource.[3]

The Western and Central Pacific Ocean (WCPO) provides the habitat for the world's largest and most valuable tuna resources, contributing over 50% of the world 3.4 million tonne catch.[4] According to the 1988–1997 data compiled by the Secretariat of the Pacific Community, the Exclusive Economic Zones (EEZs) of PICs yield 78 % of the WCPO tuna catch[5] with a 1998 estimated value of US$ 1.3 billion.[6] Given the limited economic development options available to PICs, as outlined in the previous quote, the importance of tuna resources and their exploitation to the economic security and sustainable development of the South Pacific are considerable and cannot be overstated. Indeed, as Aqorau and Bergin note, "for many of the PICs, tuna is not just a resource; it is the only resource that sustains their economies".[7]

PICs have traditionally exploited tuna resources for local consumption. However, artisanal fisheries in comparison with industrial fishing activities undertaken by Distant Water Fishing Nations (DWFNs) represent less than 10 % of the total tuna catch. The negotiation of bilateral and multilateral access agreements with DWFNs has therefore been the main strategy used by PICs to obtain benefits from the foreign exploitation of tuna stocks present in their EEZs. The Forum Fisheries Agency (FFA) has been particularly instrumental in facilitating the negotiation of such agreements. Its mandate is to promote regional cooperation and co-ordination amongst PICs in management, conservation and development of legislation and fisheries policies in connection with the tuna resources of its member countries as further discussed in this chapter.

The sustainability of the Pacific tuna stocks, although not immediately threatened except for the most valuable bigeye tuna species (mostly exploited for the sashimi market), must be considered in the global context of the collapse of northern hemisphere world fisheries (such as the north Atlantic cod) and the relocating to southern oceans of intensive industrial fishing activities (south Atlantic, Indian and 'southern' oceans).

The current exploitation rates of the three main tuna species (skipjack, yellowfin, albacore) are considered low to moderate with stocks capable of supporting further increases in catch. In contrast, the status of the bigeye tuna stock is uncertain with increases in catches of juvenile fish raising concerns of over-fishing and declines in adult biomass.[8] Despite the relative abundance of the Pacific tuna stocks, the fact that tuna species are considered highly migratory as well as straddling stocks raises a number of issues for the management and conservation of the tuna fisheries. Indeed, the mobility of tunas across their oceanic habitat characterises these species as an international resource to be harvested both within EEZs and in the high seas. Given this, the sustainability of tuna resources can only be ensured if management and conservation measures adopted within the EEZs are compatible with measures implemented on the high seas where the freedom of fishing prevails, subject to conditions that will be discussed in the next section of this chapter. In other words, the reliability of tuna fishing as an option for sustainable development for PICs is dependent upon the establishment of a legal framework for managing the resource that needs to be devised in collaboration with DWFNs. This negotiation process was initiated in 1994 with a series of Multilateral High Level Conferences (MHLC) which culminated in the adoption of the Regional Convention on the Conservation and Management of Tuna in the WCPO in August 2000.

RATIONALE FOR COOPERATION IN TUNA FISHERIES MANAGEMENT AND THE LAW OF THE SEA

The Convention on the Conservation and Management of Tuna in the WCPO is a regional outcome of a regulatory process in international fisheries that was first initiated at the global level by the adoption of the United Nations Convention on the Law of the Sea (UNCLOS) in 1982. It was followed by the Agreement for the Implementation of the UNCLOS relating to the conservation and management of straddling fish stocks and highly migratory fish species (commonly known as the Implementing Agreement) in 1995.

The UNCLOS entered into force on 16th November 1994.[9] It is a framework convention, which establishes rules governing all uses of the oceans and their resources. It embodies in one instrument traditional rules for the uses of the oceans (freedom of the high seas) and at the same time introduces new legal concepts (coastal states' sovereignty over EEZs, sea-bed as common heritage of mankind) and addresses new concerns such as the sustainable use of marine resources.

The EEZ concept brings under national jurisdiction large tracts of ocean space that previously belonged to the regime of the high seas. A coastal state has sovereign rights to explore and exploit, conserve and manage the natural resources in the EEZ (article 56.1(a)). In the exercise of such rights, UNCLOS permits coastal states to undertake enforcement measures, including boarding, inspection, arrest and judicial proceedings (article 73.1). UNCLOS also imposes an obligation upon coastal states to "ensure through proper conservation and management measures that the maintenance of the living resources in the EEZ is not endangered by over-exploitation" (article 61.2). From this general obligation, two more specific obligations are derived. First, the coastal state is required to determine the total allowable catch (TAC) of the living resources in its EEZ, taking into account the best scientific evidence available. Secondly, the coastal state has the obligation to ensure an optimum utilisation of the living resources in the EEZ (article 62.1). If the coastal state cannot harvest the entire TAC, the coastal state is obliged to give access to the surplus to other states by agreement (article 62.2).

While the principle of sovereignty is useful to regulate an exclusive use of the 200 nautical miles zone seaward from the coastal state territorial sea baseline, it is of little relevance in regulating the exploitation of highly migratory fish species beyond the EEZ. This is because the principle of freedom of fishing in the high seas remains a central part of the "freedoms of the high seas" codified in Article 87 of UNCLOS.[10] This freedom of fishing is only subject to the duty for fishing states "to seek to agree" with coastal states upon the conservation of these stocks in the adjacent area to the coastal states' EEZs, in accordance with article 63.2 of UNCLOS. The limitation of the EEZ concept in managing highly migratory fish species is further demonstrated in article 64 of UNCLOS. This provides that coastal states and states whose nationals fish in the high seas shall cooperate to ensure conservation and promote the objective of optimum utilisation of such species within and beyond the exclusive economic zone. As pointed out by Hewison, the principle of freedom of fishing in the high seas was based on the assumption that the ocean's resources were inexhaustible.[11] This assumption has now been replaced by a realisation that conservation and allocation measures were required to prevent over-exploitation. In the South Pacific, the issue of driftnet fishing and the subsequent ban imposed by PICs on this particularly devastating fishing method for marine resources certainly triggered this awareness.[12]

Moreover, the new competence of coastal states to maintain or restore populations of harvested species at levels that can produce the maximum sustainable yield, as provided in article 61.3 of UNCLOS, puts limitations on the access of DWFNs to fisheries resources. Subsequently DWFNs had to adjust strategically and search for alternative fishing grounds, the tendency being for DWFNs to fish immediately outside the 200 NM zones. This strategy of margin fishing (or unregulated fishing) cannot be considered illegal yet it is damaging to the interests of coastal states. For stocks whose biomass occurring outside the EEZ is sufficiently large, unregulated fishing in the high seas can seriously deplete the stock and render ineffective management measures taken inside the EEZ. In the case of Pacific tuna stocks, depletion of the stocks due to unregulated high seas fishing is unlikely to occur given the spatial distribution of the catch with a high proportion taken in the EEZs and archipelagic waters of coastal states. However, the lack of enforcement capacity of PICs in the regulation of fishing within their large EEZs calls for an increased cooperation amongst PICs themselves as well as with DWFNs to make conservation and management measures applicable and effective.

While the principle of cooperation between coastal states and DWFNs was first laid down by UNCLOS, it has been further elaborated under the 1995 Implementing Agreement.[13] Indeed with the Implementing Agreement,[14] cooperation becomes a prerequisite to ensure the compatibility of the conservation and management measures for straddling and highly migratory fish stocks between areas under coastal states' jurisdiction (EEZs) and on the high seas (article 7.2). In other words, the Implementing Agreement acknowledges the necessity to consider highly migratory fish stocks as one biological unit over its entire range of distribution. This is clearly stated in Article 7.2 (d), which provides that:

> In determining compatible conservation and management measures, states shall take into account the biological unity and other biological characteristics of the stocks and the relationship between the distribution of the stocks, the fisheries and the geographical particularities of the region concerned, including the extent to which the stocks occur and are fished in areas under national jurisdiction.

One issue raised by the requirement to ensure the compatibility of conservation and management measures on the high seas and in the EEZs is the setting of the total allowable catch (TAC). The Implementing Agreement does not specify whether or not the TAC should be set jointly by coastal states and DWFNs. As discussed further below, the setting of the TAC for Pacific tuna stocks has similarly been a contentious issue during the MHLC negotiations.

Another limitation of the Implementing Agreement is in the lack of enforcement rights to enable coastal states to impose compliance by states fishing for straddling stocks in the area beyond and adjacent to their fisheries zone. Under the Implementing Agreement, enforcement remains the prerogative of the flag state,[15] as provided in article 19. Yet it is common knowledge that flag state enforcement has typically been characterised by its lack of effectiveness in international fisheries. Since enforcement of provisions is left to the state in which the vessel is registered (or whose flag it is entitled to fly), fishing operators tend to exert political pressures on flag state governments for them to be complacent when it comes to enforcement. In addition, most flag states do not have the technological ability to ensure that their nationals comply with international and foreign regulations of fishing activities often undertaken at a considerable distance.

The Implementing Agreement however provides the jurisdiction for port state enforcement. Under article 23 (2), a port state may inspect documents, fishing gear and catch on board. A port state may also adopt regulations to prohibit fishing vessels from landing catches or transshipping catches where it has been established that the catch has been taken in a manner that undermines the effectiveness of conservation and management measures on the high seas (article 23.3). Despite greater power granted to coastal states under these provisions, port state enforcement is only applicable to vessels fishing in the high seas that choose to use a coastal state port for landing catches. It is common knowledge that today industrial fishing fleets are capable of undertaking transshipment of catches at sea, an activity that can easily escape port state[16] and flag state control.

Perhaps the most proactive features of the Implementing Agreement in terms of enforcement are to be found in the provisions for international cooperation and regional agreements. Regarding international cooperation, states are to assist each other in the conduct of an investigation of an alleged violation of conservation and management measures and in the identification of vessels reported to have engaged in activities undermining the effectiveness of such measures (article 20.2 and 20.4). States are to establish arrangements to make available to prosecuting countries of any other state evidence relating to alleged violations of conservation and management measures (article 20.5). In addition, state members of a regional fisheries management organisation ought to take action to deter vessels that have violated conservation and management measures through recourse to regional proceedings established for that purpose (article 20.7). Finally, a flag state may authorise a coastal state to board and inspect a vessel on the high seas, providing there are reasonable grounds for believing that the vessel has been engaged in unauthorised fishing within an area under the jurisdiction of a coastal state (article 20.6).

Clearly the provisions of the Implementing Agreement regarding enforcement through regional cooperation provide some extended powers to coastal states, despite the fact that the exercise of such powers is dependent on the extent to which the flag state does or does not fulfill its enforcement obligations.

As discussed before, the central aim of the Implementing Agreement is to encourage international and, foremost, regional cooperation in the management of highly migratory fish species. In doing so, the Implementing Agreement primarily grants extended enforcement powers to coastal states that are parties to a regional arrangement or organisation for managing straddling and highly migratory fish species. This provides both an opportunity and an incentive for PICs to negotiate with DWFNs a regulatory regime for managing the Pacific tuna fishery. Indeed, such a strategy may be analysed as a logical outcome of the collaborative achievements of PICs themselves that were orchestrated by the FFA.

INTRA-REGIONAL COOPERATION BETWEEN PICS: THE ROLE AND ACHIEVEMENTS OF THE FFA IN RELATION TO THE PACIFIC TUNA FISHERIES

Since its establishment in 1979 under the Forum Fisheries Agency Convention,[17] the FFA has played a pivotal role in promoting intra-regional cooperation and coordination, particularly with respect to the harmonisation of fisheries management policies, surveillance and enforcement, and relations with DWFNs. Major outcomes in the work of FFA include the adoption of harmonised Minimum Terms and Conditions (MTCs) of access for foreign fishing vessels that impose a list of rules on all foreign fishing vessels, aimed at controlling the operations of such vessels in the EEZs of FFA member states.[18]

The MTCs were initially adopted in 1982 and revised in 1990 to strengthen the control of FFA member states over fishing operations by prohibiting transshipment at sea and requiring the maintenance and submission of catch logs on high seas fishing. In 1983, MTCs were complemented with a Regional Register used as a database and compliance mechanism holding details of all foreign fishing vessels operating in the region. The requirement of good standing being a prerequisite to obtain a licence to fish in the region, once the good standing status is withdrawn, the licencing bans remains with vessels even if sold or renamed.[19] The prospect of change in status of the vessel on the Register and subsequently having access denied to the entire region has been sufficient to make vessel operators comply with the fisheries laws of FFA member states. This also facilitates compliance with court orders or the settlement of negotiations regarding the payment of compensation for infringements.[20]

In 1995, the FFA launched a major initiative to implement a satellite-based vessel monitoring system (VMS) that will strengthen the effectiveness of existing monitoring and enforcement programmes such as military air and sea surveillance on fishing activities undertaken by New Zealand, Australia and France. The VMS will monitor the positions of fishing vessels using a global positioning system in near real time. Once implemented, the FFA VMS will require that any foreign fishing vessel wishing to apply for a licence (to fish in the waters of an FFA member country) be fitted with a VMS in addition to the licencing procedures normally required to become part of the Regional Register.

The FFA also provides assistance to members in drawing up bilateral and multilateral access agreements with DWFNs. Until recently, FFA member states have been leasing fishing rights to DWFNs through bilateral agreements. They are now interested in multilateral access agreements to promote more stability in fisheries relations. This trend was initiated in 1987 with the adoption of the Treaty on Fisheries Between the Governments of Certain Pacific Island States and the Government of the United States. This treaty has been considered as a major achievement since it put an end to the dispute between PICs and the United States over the jurisdiction of tuna. For the first time the USA recognised the right of coastal states over highly migratory species contained within their EEZ and also agreed to pay for the right to fish them (*via* fishing licences). The treaty gave access to 50 US vessels to be licenced and to fish in the EEZs of 16 FFA member countries. Access is subject to regulatory conditions. Vessels are only permitted to catch tuna using purse-seiners. They must comply with the good standing requirements of the Regional register, they cannot fish within closed areas (internal waters, territorial sea and archipelagic waters) and they must carry FFA observers on board.

Despite such impressive achievements, it is important to emphasise the limitations of the FFA in so far as conservation and management of tuna stocks is concerned. The limitations of the FFA stem from its lack of a decision-making role. The FFA's functions are administrative, facilitative and advisory. These functions prevent it from becoming a management agency. The need for an international management arrangement distinct from the FFA is even recognised in article III(2) of the Forum Fisheries Agency Convention which provides that:

> ...effective cooperation for the conservation and optimum utilisation of highly migratory species of the region will require the establishment of additional machinery to provide for co-operation between all coastal states in the region and all states involved in the harvesting of such resources.[21]

Indeed, one missing element if such a machinery was to be devised within the FFA would be the accession of DWFNs to the FFA Convention as a prerequisite to their participation. Although nothing in the Forum Fisheries Agency Convention prevents other states from acceding to it, one has to recall the initial controversy as to whether DWFNs could become members of FFA. The argument raised at that time was that the inclusion of DWFNs would dilute the agency's regional unity and weaken its bargaining position for asserting ownership of migratory tuna. That argument prevailed and the DWFNs were excluded from FFA membership. It was therefore necessary to envisage new avenues for cooperation beyond the FFA.

COOPERATION BETWEEN PICS AND DWFNS: THE MHLC NEGOTIATION PROCESS

In September 1996, South Pacific Forum leaders called the second Multilateral High Level Conference on the Conservation and Management of Highly Migratory Fish Stocks of the Central and Western Pacific (MHLC2), which was held in Majuro, Marshall Islands, during 10th–13th June 1997. The conference brought together member countries of the South Pacific Forum, other coastal states and territories, and those DWFNs with legitimate interest in the region's tuna fisheries, with a view to developing cooperative conservation and management measures consistent with international law.

The outcome of the conference resulted in the adoption of a Declaration of Principles (the 'Majuro Declaration') setting a framework on which future negotiations were to be based, with the aim to have them concluded by June 2000. From 1997 onwards, negotiations took place following the initial framework set by the Majuro Declaration which covered the following matters:

(a) species and stocks to be covered by the arrangement;

(b) geographical area to be covered;

(c) membership and participation by observers;

(d) mechanisms for decision-making and procedures for the settlement of disputes;

(e) mechanisms for the collection and exchange of fisheries data, scientific research and stock assessment;

(f) determination of conservation and management measures, including the application of the precautionary approach;

(g) relationship with other regional and global fisheries organisations and arrangements;

(h) procedures for monitoring, control, surveillance and enforcement; and

(i) financial and administrative arrangements.

States participating in the negotiation process included all 16 member states of the FFA,[22] the three French Pacific territories (New Caledonia, French Polynesia, Wallis and Futuna) and France, DWFNs (Canada, China, Japan, Korea, Taiwan, United States of America) and other coastal states in the region (Philippines and Indonesia). The United Kingdom did not attend despite being an eligible participant due to the presence of its one remaining territory in the region, Pitcairn Island.

From 30th August to 5th September 2000, a final round of negotiations was convened in Hawaii (MHLC 7) which resulted in the adoption of the Convention on the Conservation and Management of Tuna in the Central and Western Pacific Ocean. Despite every effort made by the Chairman, Ambassador Satya Nandan, to have the Convention adopted by consensus in accordance with the rules of procedure of the Implementing Agreement, the persistent opposition of a number of states to the final draft prevented this approach. The Convention was therefore adopted by a two third majority vote, with 19 states in favor, 2 states voting against (Japan and Korea) and 3 abstentions (China, France and Tonga).

The final negotiation process necessarily involved protracted debates on a number of outstanding issues, which included decision-making, the status of fishing entities and participation by territories. The absence of consensus on the above issues resulted in the abstention or rejection of the final text by the states listed above. These issues will now be analysed in the light of the objectives set in the Convention.

The main objective of the Convention is listed in article 2, which provides:

> the objective of this Convention is to ensure, through effective management, the long term conservation and sustainable use of highly migratory fish stocks in the western and central Pacific Ocean in accordance with the 1982 Convention and the Agreement.

Amongst the principles for conservation and management listed under article 5, it is provided that members of the Commission shall apply the precautionary approach in accordance with this Convention and all relevant internationally agreed standards and recommended practices and procedures.[23] The Convention is more than a framework agreement in that it provides for institutional arrangements to facilitate the implementation of the Convention provisions. A Commission is to be established with a secretariat and two committees dealing with compliance and scientific issues.[24] The Commission will be the decision-making body and will:

- determine the TAC in the Convention area and adopt such conservation and management measures as may be necessary to ensure the long-term sustainability of stocks (article 10.1(a));

- ensure that conservation and management measures on the high seas are compatible with areas under national jurisdiction (article 10.1(b));

- establish cooperative mechanisms for effective monitoring, control and surveillance and enforcement, including a vessel monitoring system (article 10.1(i));

- promote peaceful settlement of disputes (article 10.1(n));

- be responsible for compiling and disseminating statistical data while maintaining confidentiality (article 10.1(e)).

Further to article 10.1, paragraph 2 specifically lists the type of measures that the Commission may adopt in giving effect to article 10.1. These measures include: determining the quantity of any species or stocks which may be caught, the level of fishing effort, limitations of fishing capacity, including number of fishing vessels, types and sizes, areas and periods in which fishing may occur, the size of fish of any species that may be taken, the fishing gear which may be used.

DECISION-MAKING

At the outset, decision-making within the Commission has been identified as a delicate issue requiring adequate representation for all members as well as ensuring that decisions can be made in an efficient manner. Article 20 of the Convention provides that decision-making shall be by consensus as a general rule and refers to a three-fourths majority vote for decisions on questions of substance once efforts to reach a decision by consensus have been exhausted. In addition, mandatory consensus is required for all decisions pertaining to the rules of procedure for the conduct of the Commission and its subsidiary bodies' meetings (article 9.8), the budget of the Commission (article 18.1) and the allocation of the TAC (article 10.4). Given the scope of the decisions on conservation and management that may be taken by the Commission it is not surprising that some DWFNs, particularly Japan, felt threatened by the future power of the Commission and sought to obtain a decision-making process that would best secure their interests. This is illustrated by the Japanese proposal presented at the final round of negotiations which demanded the inclusion of an objection clause allowing for an objecting party to opt out of a decision. This proposal was supported by Korea but vigorously opposed by the Forum Fishery Committee (FFC) (which included all FFA member states) on the basis that a substantial compromise had already been reached during the previous session, which resulted in an increase of issues for which mandatory consensus was required, including budgetary arrangements and allocation of fishing opportunities. In addition, the FFC argued that most fora use a two-thirds majority rule for adopting substantive matters. Yet, in the case of substantive matters to be decided by the Commission the threshold had already been raised to a four-fifths majority in addition to decisions that are subject to consensus.

Not surprisingly, the FFC refused the Japanese proposal of inserting an objection clause in article 20 on decision-making on the grounds that it would make the regime ineffective in the light of previous international fisheries regimes. In addition, the FFC exerted some pressure to revert to a two-thirds majority vote as provided in the earlier drafts.

Yet, an ultimate compromise was made in order to secure the approval of Japan and Korea. A proposal was raised by the head of the American delegation for a voting system by chambers, which would be arithmetically detrimental to the FFC member states. The modified text proposed a three-fourths majority vote by chambers on questions of substance, instead of a four-fifths majority vote of members present and voting, as stipulated in the earlier draft convention adopted during MHLC 6. More specifically, the final text of the Convention identifies two chambers: one composed of FFA member states and the other chamber composed of non-members of the FFA.[25] Article 20.1 further states that "in no circumstances shall a proposal be defeated by two or fewer votes in either chamber".

Despite the inclusion of these provisions Japan and Korea voted against the adoption of the Convention. In addition, Tonga made a statement referring to the vote in chambers as the tyranny of the majority and the surrender of the negotiation on decision-making process, and decided to abstain from voting on the final text of the Convention.

STATUS OF CHINESE TAIPEI AS A FISHING ENTITY

Given the substantial fishing activities of Taiwan in the region[26], it is therefore imperative for the effectiveness of the regime to ensure her participation in and compliance with the decisions taken by the future Commission. This proved difficult to achieve because of the diplomatic position of China. In the MHLC jargon, Taiwan is referred to as Chinese Taipei as a result of the non-recognition by China of Taiwan. One has to note here that while five FFC member states (Palau, Solomon Islands, Tuvalu, Nauru and the Marshall Islands) have diplomatic ties with Chinese Taipei and supported its inclusion as a contracting party, other FFC member states support the 'one China policy'. At the outset, Chinese Taipei, which has participated as a full member in the MHLC process, sought to obtain contracting party status as a fishing entity. China has maintained throughout the negotiations that Chinese Taipei may only be allowed observer status, emphasising that the inter-governmental nature of the Convention amongst sovereign states ought to be preserved. During the FFC meetings of MHLC 7 a common position emerged that for Chinese Taipei's participation to be secured, the text of the Convention would have to be modified in order to clarify the rights, duties and obligations of fishing entities. Such accommodation of Taiwanese interests is reflected in Annex I of the final text of the Convention, which provides that after the entry into force of this Convention, any fishing entity may agree to be bound by the regime established by this Convention. In addition, paragraph two of Annex I stipulates that any such fishing entity shall participate in the work of the Commission, including decision-making. To avoid any further confusion, the text adds "[r]eferences thereto by the Commission or members of the Commission include, for the purposes of this Convention, such fishing entity as well as Contracting Parties".[27] Despite such clarifications aimed at ensuring the full participation of Taiwan in the decision-making process of the Commission, the Taiwanese delegation made a declaration noting its disappointment regarding the status granted to Taiwan in the final text. The declaration stated that had Taiwan such capacity it would vote against the adoption of the Convention if such a procedure were used. On the other hand, Taiwan declared, she would have to approve the Convention if adopted by consensus. China remained opposed to the participation of fishing entities in the decision making process and on that basis decided to abstain from voting.

Having analysed the position of the states that either abstained or voted against the Convention, one needs to examine their likely implications on the future of the regime. It may be useful at this point to quote article 8(4) of the Implementing Agreement, which sets the requirement of participation in regional arrangements as a prerequisite to having access to regional fisheries as follows:

> Only those States which are members of such organization or participants in such arrangement, or which agree to apply the conservation and management measures established by such organization or arrangement, shall have access to the fishery resources to which those measures apply.[28]

Despite the Implementing Agreement not having entered into force, this provision can be seen as a strong incentive for the future accession of the two DWFNs that voted against the Convention, Japan and Korea, as well as China. Incidentally, the option of demanding DWFNs' participation in the Convention as a prerequisite to access to the EEZs of coastal states was raised by the Papua New Guinea delegate during one of the MHLC 7 FFC meetings. This was, however, in order to encourage the FFC Chairman to table the text as it was then, and to refuse any further dilution of the decision-making process. Before this option can be applied though, it would certainly have to be weighed against the benefits of Japanese aid in Pacific Island countries and the strings attached to it.

POTENTIAL BENEFITS AND SHORTCOMINGS OF THE WCPO TUNA CONVENTION

Precautionary Approach to fisheries management

A major strength of the WCPO Tuna Convention rests in the application of a precautionary approach for the conservation and management of fish stocks as referred to in article 5(c) and detailed in article 6 of the Convention. This is in line with article 6 and Annex II of the Implementing Agreement, which sets a precedent by incorporating this approach in the management and conservation of straddling and highly migratory fish stocks. The precautionary approach illustrates a paradigm shift from the maximum sustainable yield (MSY) approach, previously used as a method for determining the potential reproductive productivity of a stock and setting a catch limit based on this determination. As Macdonald notes,[29] using MSY as a management tool led to many variables being ignored in allocation decisions, particularly biological variables such as minimum reproductive biomass, safe biological limits, optimum recruitment[30] levels and maximum statistical probability of ecological and economic collapse. The MSY approach led to the adoption of politically motivated catch quotas and in a vast number of species being overexploited.[31] Because of past failures of fisheries management to act in the face of scientific uncertainty in stock assessments, a new paradigm began to emerge relying upon a precautionary approach to fisheries management. In other words, caution is required when information is uncertain, unreliable or inadequate. This approach is reflected in article 6(2) of the Convention, which provides that "the absence of adequate scientific information shall not be used as a reason for postponing or failing to take conservation and management measures". When contrasting this approach with the previously prevailing attitude that fishing activities were left unregulated until there was an absolute proof of over-fishing, the paradigm shift is quite obvious. Yet it does not seem to be fully achieved since a strict interpretation of the precautionary principle would shift the burden of the proof to the proponent to prove that the proposed action (in this case fishing) does not degrade or have a negative impact on the resource. Macdonald[32] rightly argued that such a strict interpretation of the precautionary principle is not applicable to fisheries management, except in extreme cases as in the case of the high seas driftnet fishing ban imposed by the Convention for the Prohibition of Fishing with Long Driftnets in the South Pacific.[33] Instead, a more pragmatic interpretation has been applied in both the Implementing Agreement (article 6.3(b)) and the WCPO Tuna Convention (article 6.1(a), (b)) which require the setting of precautionary reference points to prevent over-fishing. The precautionary reference points are target levels of fishing effort designed to ensure that the abundance of fish stocks is maintained to a level above that which can produce the MSY. In setting precautionary reference points the resilience and reproductive capacity of stocks as well as major sources of uncertainty related to the knowledge of the stocks and the fisheries exploiting them are taken into account. In addition, article 6.3 of the Convention provides that:

> members of the Commission shall take measures to ensure that, when reference points are approached, they will not be exceeded. In the event they are exceeded, members of the Commission shall, without delay, take the action determined under paragraph 1(a) to restore the stocks.

Finally, the development of data collection and research programmes to assess the impact of fishing on non-target and associated (or dependent) species and the adoption of plans to protect habitats of special concern are other applications of the precautionary approach provided for in article 6.1(c) of the Convention.

If effectively implemented, the provisions listed above will certainly have major implications for fishing activities in the WCPO, which explains the concerns raised by Japan over the application of the precautionary approach and its attempts to delete paragraph 1 of article 6 from the text of the Convention.[34] However, the likelihood of implementation of the precautionary approach will depend on the decisions adopted by the Commission, subject to a vote by chambers where consensus fails. Furthermore, the Commission in adopting decisions will take into account the reports and any recommendations made by the Scientific Committee. The Scientific Committee in turn will review assessments and analyses prepared by scientific experts before making any recommendation to the Commission.[35]

This raises at least two questions. Will the Commission be capable of adopting conservation measures in the face of scientific uncertainty? Past experience in fisheries management has shown that lack of data and the consequent scientific uncertainty provide powerful arguments to reluctant states not to adopt proposed conservation measures. The example of the Commission for the Conservation of Antarctic Marine Living Resources, and the delay of eleven years after the Convention on the Conservation of Antarctic Marine Living Resources (CCAMLR) in adopting precautionary catch limits on krill, reveals the difficulty of implementing a precautionary approach to fisheries management.[36]

Secondly, will the members of the Commission provide accurate data concerning catch of target and non-target species and fishing effort in order to facilitate the work of the Scientific Committee? It is noteworthy that the Convention provides an incentive to that effect in article 10.3(e). This article lists the contributions of participants to conservation and management of the stocks, including the provision by them of accurate data and their contribution to the conduct of scientific research among the criteria to be taken into account by the Commission for the allocation of the TAC.[38]

The setting of the TAC

As demonstrated by Tony Lewis, the spatial distribution of the tuna catches shows a high proportion of the catch taken in the EEZs of coastal states. The legal implications of this are considerable in terms of ensuring the compatibility of the conservation measures throughout the range of stock, that is within EEZs and in the high seas.[39] This concern is addressed in article 8.3 of the Convention, which provides that coastal states should ensure that the measures applied to highly migratory fish stocks within areas under national jurisdiction do not undermine the effectiveness of measures adopted by the Commission in respect of the same stocks.

One issue raised by the requirement to ensure the compatibility of conservation and management measures on the high seas and in the EEZs is the setting of the TAC which has been a contentious issue during the MHLC negotiations. FFA member states maintained that the Commission should only be allowed to set fishing quotas for the high seas, leaving coastal states the sovereign right to set national quotas and determine the conditions of access to their EEZs. Yet, one difficulty in this argument is the fact that only a few PICs have actually set their own TAC within their EEZ, even if most are currently reviewing and amending their fisheries legislation and adopting national tuna management plans to address this issue. Fishing nations on the other hand argued that the Commission should allocate quotas throughout the region, both in zone and on the high seas, thus questioning the sovereign right of coastal states to set national fishing quotas. The Convention implicitly recognises the right of coastal states to set national quotas by reference to compliance with national laws as part of the terms and conditions for fishing prescribed in Annex III. However, it does not clearly spell out a precise formula to be used by the Commission for determining the TAC within the Convention area. Despite this, article 10.3 refers to criteria to be developed by the Commission for the setting of the TAC. Such criteria are to be developed mainly taking into account:

- the status of the stocks and the existing level of fishing effort in the fishery;
- the historic catch in an area;
- the needs of small island developing states whose economies are highly dependent on the exploitation of marine resources;
- the fishing interests and aspirations of coastal states in whose areas of national jurisdiction the stocks also occur.

In addition, any decisions relating to the allocation of the TAC are to be taken by consensus, as mentioned before. Past experience in fisheries regimes operating under consensus shows that the threat of veto by one or more fishing nations is likely to succeed in preventing the imposition of quotas. From a conservation perspective, the fact that the Commission will only be empowered to limit catch or effort in the area of application of the Convention in general also presents some difficulties given the somewhat unclear delimitation of the Convention area itself as discussed in the next section.

Area of application of the convention

In order to be effective, conservation and management measures ideally need to cover the full range of tuna stocks, that is an area covering the 50°N to 50°S and from the coasts of Asia to the longitude of 150°W. For the skipjack tuna, its main distribution is between 45 degrees of latitude north and 40 degrees latitude south, the stock being concentrated west of 150 degrees longitude west. The Convention area therefore covers most of the skipjack stock since the easternmost boundary of the Convention is at 130 degrees longitude west. Similarly, for the yellowfin tuna whose distribution is between 40 degrees latitude north and 40 degrees latitude south, with higher abundance in the western Pacific, most of the stock distribution is covered within the Convention area.

However, the main problem area for the skipjack and the yellowfin tuna is with respect to the western boundary. Twenty-three *per cent* of the total skipjack catches and 32% of yellowfin catches occur outside the Convention area, in the Philippines and Indonesia archipelagic waters. As pointed out by Hampton:

> Unless compatible management of these fisheries can be guaranteed, having such large portions of the total catch outside of the management regime has the potential to severely limit the effectiveness of management measures.[40]

A boundary problem also occurs for the bigeye since its distribution is continuous from the east coast of the Pacific ocean to the west coast, to capture the entire stock distribution ideally the Convention area would have to be extended to the coast of the Americas. The eastern boundary stops at 130 degrees longitude West and only 150 degrees longitude West at the latitude of Kiribati. Cooperation will therefore be required with the Inter-American Tropical Tuna Commission (IATTC) in the management of the bigeye stock, already considered endangered and the most valuable species. In addition, 16% of the total bigeye catch occurs to the west of the Convention area in the archipelagic waters of Philippines and Indonesia.[41] For the albacore, 10 to 20 % of the total north Pacific catch occurs east of the Convention area and cooperative management with the North American trawl fleet would be required.[42]

Despite attempts being made to set a northern boundary at 50 degrees north, this was rejected by some delegations and the final text of the Convention only defines the western and northern boundaries of the Convention area by reference to the migratory range of the stocks. Such open-ended boundaries raise concerns about possible enforcement of the measures adopted by the Commission in the future. In an attempt to address this issue, a proposition was made at MHLC 5 to establish sub-committees to deal with the both northern and western areas. This proposition was initially opposed by the FFC as it was felt it would weaken the decision-making power of the Commission and was only partly retained with the establishment of the Northern Committee. The Northern Committee is to be composed of member states situated in such area and those fishing in the area.[43] Its role is:

> ...to make recommendations on the implementation of conservation and management measures that may be adopted by the Commission for the area north of 20 degrees parallel north latitude and on the formulation of such measures in respect of stocks which occur mostly in this area.[44]

Concerns were raised during FFC meetings of MHLC 7 over recommendations that may be formulated by the Northern Committee in relation to stocks also occurring within the jurisdiction of FFA member states. According to Lewis,[45] the stocks concerned would represent 20% of skipjack, 14% of bigeye and 12% of yellowfin since these species occur throughout the range. The risk of establishing a Northern Committee mostly composed of fishing nations with potential to overturn the decisions made by the Commission was therefore identified. To a large extent, these concerns are set aside by the fact that the Northern Committee has no decision-making power but only acts as an advisory body to the Commission. Besides, recommendations formulated by the Committee must be adopted by consensus and the Commission is entitled to take decisions regarding stocks occurring north of 20 degrees latitude north in the absence of any recommendation formulated by the Committee. Yet, in case the Commission does not accept the recommendation of the Committee on any matter, it shall return the matter to the Committee for further consideration. The Convention does not explicitly state how such matters should be dealt with and article 11.7 simply provides that "the Committee shall reconsider the matter in the light of the views expressed by the Commission".

As illustrated above, the limitations in the boundaries of the Convention area show the need to develop cooperative and compatible management measures with the IATTC which are not secured at present. These geographical and biological limitations in the area of application of the Convention also reflect the unsuccessful attempt to fully cover the species range by bringing into the negotiations additional coastal states that may have different interests to those of PICs. This is so in the case of Indonesia and the Philippines who refused to have their archipelagic waters included within the Convention area despite their vote in favour of the adoption of the Convention. Reference to the particular status of Indonesia and the Philippines is made, albeit rather implicitly, in article 3.2 of the Convention, which provides that:

> nothing in this Convention shall constitute recognition of the claims or positions of any members of the Commission concerning the legal status and extent of waters and zones claimed by any such members.

Despite the fact that the Convention does not clearly spell out the non-applicability of conservation and management measures to the archipelagic waters, this has been clearly expressed by Indonesia in the following statement made at MHLC 6:

> We therefore like to interpret, as far as we are concerned, and in conformity with article 64 [of the Law of the Sea Convention] that the notion of 'throughout the range of stocks' cannot be interpreted to include these stocks within archipelagic waters.[46]

Another western boundary limitation to note concerns the exclusion of South-East Asia waters from the Convention area which are not part of the Pacific Ocean. There was a general agreement among MHLC participants that the benefits that may have been gained in terms of fisheries management and conservation did not outweigh the difficulties in bringing into the negotiation states claiming sovereignty in the South China Sea, an area currently subject to territorial disputes.[47]

Compliance and Enforcement

Compliance and enforcement mechanisms devised by the WCPO Tuna Convention range from the establishment of an observer programme, the requirement of VMS and the regulation of transshipment, to high seas boarding and inspections provisions. The establishment of a regional observer programme was initially opposed by some DWFNs, mainly Japan, Korea, China and Chinese Taipei because it was perceived as a challenge to flag state authority. Despite this, the idea of establishing an observer programme was retained although concessions were made for the Commission to develop further procedures and guidelines in order to ensure the confidentiality of the data collected by observers.[48] The role of observers is to collect catch and other scientific data and to monitor the implementation of the conservation and management measures adopted by the Commission. In other words, it is an important tool to facilitate compliance with the fisheries regime. However, no agreement was reached on the issue of funding for the observer programme, an issue that is left to the Commission to resolve.

The VMS is incorporated as one of the instruments for facilitating compliance through the requirement for fishing vessels operating on the high seas to use near real-time satellite position fixing transmitters. This requirement is listed in article 24.8 as part of the duties of flag states. The VMS will be operated by the Commission, under rules of procedures for protecting the confidentiality of information received. Compatibility between national and high seas VMS is ensured though cooperation between the members of the Commission. Each member of the Commission whose flagged fishing vessels operate in areas under the national jurisdiction of another member shall require those vessels to use near real-time satellite position fixing transmitters in accordance with the standards and procedures determined by the coastal state. Finally, any member of the Commission may request that waters under its national jurisdiction be included within the area covered by a VMS. Simultaneous and direct transmission of information on vessels' positions to the Commission and the flag state raised concerns during the negotiations from Japan and other fishing nations who maintained that that this would undermine flag state jurisdiction. Article 24.8 strikes a compromise by providing that the Commission should directly receive from the VMS, and simultaneously with the flag state where that state so requires.

The regulation of transshipment on the high seas (also referred to as transhipment at sea) is provided for under article 29 and article 4 of Annex III of the Convention. Prohibition of transshipment at sea is already part of the MTCs of fisheries access to EEZs set by FFA member states. Consequently the FFC's position was to support the prohibition of transshipment on the high seas so as to ensure accurate reporting of catch. However, that proposal was generally rejected, except for the transshipment at sea by purse-seiner vessels operating in the Convention area, which is prohibited under article 29.5. For other fishing activities, article 29.1 of the Convention does not impose a similar prohibition but only refers to members of the Convention which "shall encourage their fishing vessels, to the extent applicable, to conduct transhipment in port". Transshipment at sea is thus generally permitted (except for purse-seiners) provided it takes place in accordance with the terms and conditions set out in article 4 of Annex III of the Convention. Such terms and conditions create an obligation for the vessel operator to comply with any procedures established by the Commission to verify the quantity and species transshipped, hence allowing access and use of facilities and equipment necessary for any person authorised by the Commission to undertake such duties.[49]

Compliance and enforcement provisions are detailed in article 25 of the Convention, based on flag state responsibility to investigate any alleged violation by fishing vessels flying its flag of the Convention's provisions or conservation and management measures adopted by the Commission. Serious violations of the provisions of the Convention are defined in the Convention by reference to article 21.11(a) to (h) of the Implementing Agreement.[50] For fishing vessels on the high seas that have been engaged in unauthorised fishing within an area under the national jurisdiction of a member of the Commission, cooperation is required between the flag state and the member of the Commission concerned regarding boarding and inspection on the high seas. It will be one of the Commission's tasks to establish procedures for boarding and inspection of fishing vessels on the high seas in the Convention area within two years of the Convention coming into force. If after two years the Commission cannot agree on any procedures or alternative mechanism to boarding and inspection, the provisions of article 21 and 22 of the Implementing Agreement will be applied as if they were part of the Convention.

CONCLUSION

The analysis of overlapping legal, spatial and biological boundary issues shows the complexity of devising a legal regime for tuna in the WCPO that is both effective and accommodating to the interests of all parties. However, despite major concessions made to fishing states and entities in the decision-making process of the Commission, the latter has the potential to develop an effective conservation regime by applying a precautionary approach to fisheries management.

The fact that two DWFNs, Japan and Korea, voted against the adoption of the Convention should not be seen as a major obstacle to the future of the regime, given the legal basis existing for linking access to fisheries in the region to their participation in the regional fisheries' organisation that the Convention creates. In addition, had the Convention not been signed and negotiations reopened in a few years, it would have been extremely difficult for PICs to defend their long term interest in the sustainability of the fisheries given the increasing level of fishing activities that would have certainly taken place by then.

The coming into force of the Convention, upon ratification by three states north of the 20 degrees parallel North latitude and seven states South of that latitude, along with funding arrangements, will ultimately determine the political willingness of states participating in the MHLC process to make the new regime effective. Meanwhile, the interim regime established by way of a Preparatory Conference will be responsible for preparing practical and administrative arrangements for the future of the Commission[51] so that when the Convention comes into force, the Commission will be able to start its work.

ENDNOTES

1   South, G.R. 1993. Custodians of the Ocean in Wadell, E. Naidu, V. and Hau'ofa, E. (eds.) *A New Oceania: rediscovering our sea of islands*. Suva: University of the South Pacific, p 106.

2   In public international law, a soft law instrument is one that has no legally binding force. The Rio Declaration on Environment and Development and the Forest Principles are also soft law instruments adopted during the UNCED.

3   United Nations A/CONF.151/26. 1992. <u>Report of the United Nations Conference on Environment and Development: Chapter 17 Protection of the oceans, all kinds of seas, including enclosed and semi-enclosed seas, and coastal areas and their protection, rational use and development of their living resources</u>, para 17.130.

4   Lawson, T.A. (ed.) 1999. *Tuna fishery Yearbook 1998*. Noumea, New Caledonia: Oceanic Fisheries Programme, Secretariat of the Pacific Community.

5   Lewis, A.D. 1999 The Status of Pacific Tuna Stocks: The interaction of biological, boundary and legal issues in the conservation and management of highly migratory species. Paper presented at the *Pacem in Maribus XXVII* Conference, 7th–12th November 1999. University of the South Pacific, Suva, Fiji.

6   Van Santen, G. and Muller P. 2000. Working Apart or Together: The case for a Common Approach to Management of the Tuna Resources in Exclusive Economic Zones of Pacific Island Countries Pacific Islands. *Discussion Paper Series No. 10*. Washington: The World Bank.

7   Aqorau, T. and Bergin, A. 1998. The UN Fish Stocks Agreement – A New Era for International Cooperation to Conserve Tuna in the Central Western Pacific Ocean *Ocean Development and International Law* 29:21–42, p 36.

8   Lawson, T.A. (ed) 1999. Above, n 4 at p 5.

9   The Convention today has 132 parties. In the Pacific, the following countries are parties to UNCLOS: Cook Islands, Fiji Islands, Marshall Islands, FSM, Nauru, PNG, Samoa, Solomon Islands, Tonga, Tuvalu and Vanuatu.

10 The freedoms of the high seas defined in Article 87 of UNCLOS include: freedom of navigation; freedom of overflight; freedom to lay submarine cables and pipelines; freedom to construct artificial islands and other installations; freedom of fishing; and freedom of scientific research.

11 Hewison, G.J. 1999. Balancing the freedom of fishing and coastal state jurisdiction. In Hey, E. (ed.) *Developments in International Fisheries Law*. The Netherlands: Kluwer Law International. p 166.

12 About the issue of driftnet fishing see Hewison, G.J. 1993. High Seas Driftnet Fishing in the South Pacific and the Law of the Sea. *Georgetown International Environmental Law Review* Vol. 5: 313–374.

13 According to article 40, the Implementing Agreement shall enter into force 30 days after the date of deposit of the thirtieth instrument of ratification or accession. As at April 2001, there have been 28 ratifications.

14 Agreement for the Implementation of the Provisions of the United Nations Convention on the Law of the Sea of 10th December 1982 relating to the Conservation and Management of Straddling Fish Stocks and Highly Migratory Fish Stocks, opened for signature 4th December 1995. UN Doc. A/CONF. 164/33(1995), 34 I.L.M. 1542.

15 Under article 91.1 of UNCLOS, every state shall fix the conditions for the grant of its nationality to ships, for the registration of ships in its territory, and the right to fly its flag. Ships have the nationality of the state whose flag they are entitled to fly. There must be a genuine link between the state and the ship. Further, Article 94 details the duties of the flag state which shall effectively exercise its jurisdiction and control in administrative, technical and social matters over ships flying its flag.

16 Under article 23 of the Implementing Agreement, a port state may, *inter alia*, inspect documents, fishing gear and catch on board fishing vessels, when such vessels are voluntarily in its ports or at its offshore terminals. States may adopt regulations empowering the relevant national authorities to prohibit landings and transshipments where it has been established that the catch has been taken in a manner which undermines the effectiveness of subregional, regional or global conservation and management measures on the high seas.

17 South Pacific Forum Fisheries Agency Convention. In Campbell, B. and Lodge, M. (eds.) 1993. *Regional Compendium of Fisheries Legislation (Western Pacific Region)*. Rome: Food and Agriculture Organisation.

18 For example, requirements for vessel identification, catch and position reporting, catch and effort logsheets, transshipment and observers.

19 Withdrawal of good standing may be proposed by any FFA member state, based on alleged infringements. After the alleged infringement has been investigated and supportive evidence provided, the Director of FFA must notify the vessel operator of a withdrawal request. Approval for withdrawal of good standing requires a favourable response from at least 10 of the FFA member countries.

20 For example, in 1991, an unlicenced Taiwanese purse-seiner was photographed by an Australian surveillance plane inside Tuvalu's EEZ. The owners paid $AUS 75,000 to avoid the threat of blacklisting on the register.

21 Article III(2) of the South Pacific Forum Fisheries Agency Convention in Campbell, B. & Lodge, M. (eds.) 1993. Above, n 17.

22 Australia, Cook Islands, FSM, Fiji Islands, Kiribati, Marshall Islands, Nauru, New Zealand, Niue, Palau, PNG, Solomon Islands, Tonga, Tuvalu, Vanuatu.

23 Article 5(c).

24 See article 9 "Establishment of the Commission"; article 10 "Functions of the Commission"; article 11 "Subsidiary bodies of the Commission"; article 12 "Functions of the Scientific Committee"; article 14 "Functions of the Technical and Compliance Committee"; article 15 "the Secretariat".

25 Article 20.2.

26 The Taiwanese purse-seiner catch represented 167,037 metric tonnes (mt) in 1997 and 258,693 mt in 1998, having increased their catch by nearly 100,000 mt and making larger gains than Korea, Japan and the USA, the main DWFNs involved in the fishery.

27 Annex I (2), Final Text of the Convention on the Conservation and Management of Highly Migratory Fish Stocks in the Western and Central Pacific Ocean.

28 See above, n 14, article 8(4).

29 Macdonald, J. 1995. Appreciating the Precautionary Principle as an Ethical Evolution in Ocean Management. *Ocean Development and International Law* 26:255–286.

30 The term 'recruitment' refers to the addition to a population from all causes (reproduction, immigration, stocking) and more specifically in this context to numbers born.

31 For supportive evidence of the limitations of the MSY approach in fisheries management, see Macdonald, J. 1995. Above, n 29 at p.271; and Hewison, G.J. 1993. Above, n 11 at p 166.

32 Macdonald, J. 1995. Above, n 29 at p 263.

33 The Convention for the Prohibition of Fishing with Long Driftnets in the South Pacific, opened for signature 29th November 1989, 29 I.L.M. 1454 (entered into force 4th May 1990).

34 For example, Japan would no longer be able to argue that, in the absence of scientific data, no conservation and management measures can be adopted since this position would be in contradiction of article 6.1 of the Convention.

35 See article 12.2(b). This includes findings on the status of target and non-target or associated species, in accordance with article 12.2(e).

36 For a discussion on the effectiveness of the CCAMLR regime, see Cordonnery, L. 1998. Environmental Protection in Antarctica: drawing lessons from the CCAMLR model for the implementation of the Madrid Protocol. *Ocean Development and International Law* 29:125–146.

37 As provided in article 5(i) of the Convention.

38 Article 10.3(e).

39 Lewis, A.D. 1999. The Status of Pacific Tuna Stocks: The interaction of biological, boundary and legal issues in the conservation and management of highly migratory species. Paper presented at the XXVII *Pacem in Maribus* Conference, 7th–12th November 1999, University of the South Pacific, Suva, Fiji.

40 Hampton, J. 1999. Working Paper MHLC–2: The Convention Area. Paper presented at the *12th Meeting of the Standing Committee on Tuna and Billfish*, 16th–23rd June 1999, Papeete, Tahiti, Oceanic Fisheries Program: Secretariat of the Pacific Community, Noumea, New Caledonia.

41 Hampton, J. 1995. Above, n 40.

42 Hampton, J. 1995. Above, n 40.

43 That is: USA, Canada, Japan, Korea, Taiwan, China, in addition to New Zealand because of New Zealand flagged fishing vessels operating in the northern Pacific Ocean.

44 Article 11.7 of the Convention.

45 Lewis, T. personal communication 1st September, 2000.

46 Statement by the delegation of Indonesia. *Sixth Session of the MHLC*, 12th–19th April 2000, Honolulu, Hawaii, p 15.

47 See Valencia, M. 2000. Domestic Politics Fuels Northeast Asian Maritime Disputes. *Asia Pacific Issues: Analysis from the East-West Center* No.43, April 2000.

48 Article 28.7 (a, b).

49 That is: full access to the bridge, fish on board and areas which may be used to hold, process, weigh and store fish and full access to the vessel's records, including its log and documentation for the purpose of inspection and photocopying, as detailed in article 4.2 of Annex III of the Convention.

50 A serious violation under article 21.11 of the Implementing Agreement means either: "(a) fishing without a license, authorisation or permit issued by the flag state; (b) failing to maintain accurate record of catch and catch related data; (c) fishing in a closed area or during a closed season or after attainment of a quota established by a relevant regional organisation; (d) directed fishing for a stock subject to a moratorium; (e) using prohibited fishing gear; (f) falsifying or concealing the markings, identification or registration of a fishing vessel; (g) concealing, tampering or disposing of evidence relating to an investigation; (h) multiple violations which together constitute a serious disregard of conservation and management measures; or (i) such other violations as may be specified in procedures established by the relevant organisation".

51 Such as institutional arrangements for the establishment of the Commission, its rules of procedure, meetings, initial budget, location of the headquarters, *et cetera*.

Review questions

1. What is the relevance of traditional and customary practices for managing natural resources in the South Pacific region?

2. What are the advantages of establishing mandatory EIAs for development projects? What problems are associated with undertaking EIAs in the Pacific region?

3. What is the relationship between sustainable development and good governance? To what extent do co-management initiatives fall within the aims of decentralisation?

4. Explain the importance for sustainable fisheries management of ensuring that conservation and management measures applicable in the EEZs are compatible with those that apply on the high seas. Compare the relevant provisions of the Implementing Agreement and the Convention on the Conservation and Management of Highly Migratory Fish Stocks in the Western and Central Pacific Ocean. Focus on the criteria and factors to be taken into consideration in fulfilling this compatibility requirement.

Further readings

Boer, B. 1996. *Environmental Law in the South Pacific*. Gland, Switzerland and Cambridge, UK: SPREP/International Union for the Conservation of Nature.

Boer, B., Ramsay, R., Rothwell, D. 1998. *International Environmental Law in the Asia-Pacific*. London: Kluwer Law International.

Burt, B. and Clerk, C. eds. 1997. E*nvironment and Development in the Pacific Islands*. Canberra: University of Papua New Guinea/Australian National University.

Campbell, H.F. 2000. Managing tuna fisheries: a new strategy for the Western and Central Pacific Ocean. *Marine Policy* 24 159–163.

Crocombe, R. and Meleisa, M. 1994. *Land Issues in the Pacific*. Christchurch and Suva: Macmillan Brown Centre for Pacific Studies, University of Canterbury and Institute of Pacific Studies, University of the South Pacific.

Hey, E. 1999. *Developments in International Fisheries Law*. The Hague, London, Boston: Kluwer Law International.

Taconni, L., and Bennett, J. eds. 1997. *Protected Area Assessment and Establishment in Vanuatu: a Socioeconomic Approach*. Canberra: Australian Centre for International Agricultural Research.

SECTION 6
REBUILDING NATION STATES

14. BUILDING BRIDGES – LAW AND JUSTICE REFORM IN PAPUA NEW GUINEA
Sinclair Dinnen

15. CONSTITUTIONS AS LIMITS ON THE STATE IN MELANESIA: COMPARATIVE PERSPECTIVES ON CONSTITUTIONALISM, PARTICIPATION AND CIVIL SOCIETY
Anthony Regan

16. LEGAL PLURALISM AND THE PROBLEM OF IDENTITY
Robert Hughes

The final section of this book expands on some of the ideas introduced in Graham Hassall's chapter on the links between governance, legitimacy of the state and corruption. His argument is that a lack of consitutional legitimacy has created a situation in which the order embodied within the constitution is not respected. This disorder can be expressed in multiple ways or on multiple levels. Often countries will experience disorder on multiple levels at the same time, with, maybe, disorder on one level encouraging a lack of respect for order on other levels. To address this seemingly endemic problem of disorder it appears that we need to fundamentally reconceive our notions of the state and of the key institutions operating within it. The three chapters within this section examine different aspects of the problem of disorder in the Pacific.

This section begins with a chapter by Sinclair Dinnen that discusses the problem of lawlessnesss and crime in Papua New Guinea, which of all the Pacific island countries, probably has the longest history of problems of social order. Dinnen places this issue into the wider context of governance and legitimacy, pointing out that even if individual institutions are reformed the law and order problem will not be solved unless the underlying issues relating to governance and legitimacy that have arisen from the uneasy relationship between 'modern' conceptions of the state and indigenous cultures are addressed.

The next chapter, by Anthony Regan, examines constitutionalism and the actions of government in Melanesia. As well as comparing different Melanesian countries this chapter makes comparisons with consitutionalism in Africa, a region that is generally noted for its post colonial difficulties in the area of governance. The farily recent development of constitutionalism in western history is also noted. This comparative approach provides us with a perspective on why difficulties with constitutionalism in Melanesia exist that sites the region within a global context.

Finally the chapter by Professor Hughes offers us a somewhat radical position on the theory of the state. He argues that modern constitutionalism requires a unitary conception of the state and identity that is false. In order for modern states to gain legitimacy within this pluralistic environment, the state must be reconceptualised so as to allow for recognition of this plurality. Possibly this theoretical perspective offers us a way to approach the (re)building of Pacific island states in such a way that constitutional legitimacy, and thereby order, will be established.

14. BUILDING BRIDGES – LAW AND JUSTICE REFORM IN PAPUA NEW GUINEA

By: Sinclair Dinnen

KEY TERMS AND PHRASES

Governance

The manner in which power is exercised (in a country, community or any other organisation) for the management of social and economic resources.

Kiap

The Melanesian pidgin term used to describe patrol and district officers in colonial Papua and New Guinea.

Polity

According to the Oxford dictionary this is the term for a form or process of civil government, a condition of civil order. Here it is used to refer to a particular political order, whether of a village, tribe, island or nation.

INTRODUCTION

Problems of lawlessness loom large in current accounts of Papua New Guinea. Concerns about these problems have induced high levels of personal insecurity, as well as providing a major disincentive to foreign investment. While such problems cannot be resolved by law and justice solutions alone, the continuing deterioration of PNG's 'law and order'[1] situation raises questions about the adequacy of the formal regulatory system. Successive governments have been loud with 'tough' rhetoric, like many of their counterparts elsewhere. Practical responses have been essentially reactive and short term.[2] Australia, PNG's largest aid donor, has claimed to concentrate on institutional strengthening projects with individual law and justice agencies. While there have been achievements it is clear that improving the performance of law and justice processes is a complex and long term task and one that needs to be integrated with other areas of governance reform.

Building a more effective law and justice sector requires strategies that go beyond the strengthening of particular institutions. Given the operational interdependence of law and justice agencies, a broader sectoral focus is needed. In addition, while the state is the central player, there is a need to recognise the contributions of other stakeholders to the management of conflict and maintenance of peace at local levels. PNG's non-government sector, comprising 'traditional' structures of governance, community groups, churches, NGOs and the private sector, already plays a significant, if often unacknowledged, role. A sustainable law and justice framework needs to delineate responsibilities between different organisations and develop appropriate and mutually reinforcing linkages between government and non-government sectors.

This chapter examines the challenges facing PNG's law and justice sector and identifies key directions for reform. Section one describes the broader context of PNG's problems of order, including the acute fragility of the nation-state and the high levels of social and legal pluralism. Attention is drawn to the restorative character of many 'traditional' justice practices and the manner of their interactions with colonial institutions of social control. Section two examines the workings of the modern criminal justice system. Its shortcomings are attributed as much to a lack of legitimacy and strong social foundations as to its patent lack of institutional capacity. The final section looks at the recently endorsed National Law and Justice Policy and Plan of Action and the prospects for building a more socially attuned and effective law and justice system.

THE CONTEXT OF CHANGE

The broader context is one of rapid change induced by a combination of local and global forces that have left few individuals or communities untouched. PNG was granted independence in 1975 after a relatively short and uneven period of colonial administration. Over 800 languages are spoken among a population of just over five million people scattered across the eastern half of the island of New Guinea. The institutions and traditions of small, self-regulating societies have demonstrated remarkable resilience and adaptability in the face of colonial and post-colonial change. Twenty-seven years after independence, the primary allegiances and identities of most Papua New Guineans remain firmly implanted in local kin-based associations.

Building the institutional framework of modern statehood, including a uniform system of law and justice, commenced in earnest during an intensive period of institutional modernisation in the twenty years preceding Independence. As in other parts of Melanesia, the birth of the new 'nation' occurred in the absence of any shared sense of identity among its 'citizens'. Binding so many disparate communities into an effective political and ideological unit remains a formidable challenge.[3]

Despite the many gloomy forecasts, Papua New Guinea has stayed intact and retains an impressive record of uninterrupted democratic government. Serious challenges nevertheless remain, many of these stemming from the fragility of the post-colonial nation-state. The tragic and costly 12-year Bougainville war provides the most dramatic example. A weak national economy is hostage to the vagaries of regional and international markets. Levels of debt have risen as successive governments have been forced to seek loans from the multilateral development banks and bilateral donors. Economic mismanagement has contributed to growing popular discontent. Social indicators suggest a serious reversal of early advances, particularly in the areas of health and education. On a global scale, PNG's human development profile ranks in the lower one-third of all nations and is the lowest of all the Pacific island countries.[4] Government services are in a perilous state in many rural areas, where over 85% of the population live. Whilst the reformist government of Sir Mekere Morauta struggles to reverse this pattern of decline, political instability, corruption and lawlessness continue to pose a major threat.

CRIME AND LAWLESSNESS

The most visible manifestation of PNG's 'law and order' problems is the growth of so-called *raskol* crime in the main urban centres.[5] Serious outbreaks of inter-group conflict have also occurred in parts of the Highlands. The spread of lawlessness has tended to follow larger patterns of development. Hence the concentration of organised crime in the expanding urban centres, armed hold-ups along the arterial highways, and inter-group conflict in the vicinity of large-scale resource development projects. The incidence of corruption, fraud and 'white-collar' crime has also increased significantly in recent years.

Quantifying the extent of these problems is difficult given the paucity and partial coverage of available statistics. Criminal justice data is largely confined to the urban areas, where less than 15% of the total population live. They nevertheless suggest a marked growth in crime, with a 65% increase in the number of serious offences reported to the police over the last decade.[6] Port Moresby, the national capital, accounts for 40% of all reported serious crimes. Mount Hagen (Western Highlands) and Lae (Morobe) rank second and third respectively. With a conservatively estimated population of over 313,000,[7] Port Moresby has been described as one of the most dangerous cities in the world.[8] Between 1996 and 1998, the capital alone accounted for a recorded total of 232 murders; 3,361 robberies; 2,131 break and enters; 556 cases of causing grievous bodily harm; 816 serious sexual assaults; 585 drug offences; and 307 cases of illegal use of firearms.[9]

Media and anecdotal accounts draw attention to the violent and predatory activities of *raskol* gangs. Although they tend to be concentrated in urban centres, criminal gangs are found in many rural areas as well. Sexual assaults against women and girls appear to be widespread, and are by no means confined to gangs.[10] Gangs operate with relative impunity in the absence of effective deterrence from either the police or informal community controls. The typical probability of being arrested for crimes of larceny has been estimated recently at just over 3%.[11] Contrary to their depiction in popular stereotypes, gangs are often well integrated into their local communities. As well as ties of kinship and personal association, *raskols* engage in selective acts of redistribution, providing material and other benefits to their neighbours in, often, the poorest and most socially deprived urban communities.[12]

At a macro level, urban *raskolism* has developed in an environment where access to legitimate economic opportunities is severely restricted. A recent survey estimated that 18% of the Port Moresby population rely on crime as their principal source of income.[13] *Raskolism* has become, in effect, the largest occupational category in the informal urban economy. Rampant corruption among the political elite has also fuelled the rise of *raskolism*, providing a powerful rationalisation for street criminals.[14] Falling commodity prices, deteriorating government services and infrastructure have contributed to rural poverty and the spread of *raskolism* from urban centres to rural areas. These developments, in turn, have placed enormous pressure on an already weak criminal justice system.

As well as the devastating impact on individual victims, concerns about lawlessness have undermined commercial and investor confidence. They have become major constraints to the achievement of national and local development objectives. Employers in PNG recently ranked theft and crime, followed by corruption and then poor infrastructure, as the most significant obstacles to doing business.[15] A reinforcing downward spiral has developed whereby rising crime reduces legitimate economic activities which, in turn, leads to further crime and so on.

Many of the issues underlying PNG's current problems are shared with other developing and newly democratising countries. They include a potent cocktail of local and global factors contributing to uneven development and growing levels of division, exclusion and poverty. While domestic policymakers and international donors scramble for practical and timely solutions, it is clear that there are no quick fixes.

FORMAL AND INFORMAL JUSTICE SECTORS

The encounter between different traditions of justice brought about by colonialism in Melanesia, as elsewhere, generated many new tensions. It also gave rise to new synergies and the possibility for creative interaction between different regulatory traditions. Ideas and practices of law and justice relate to particular social and political orders. In western societies, the legal system provides the official framework for the regulation of relations between citizens, corporate entities and the state. In practice, many subordinate regulatory systems operate alongside, and interact with, this formal system.[16] The state is nevertheless central to understandings, structures and processes of law and justice in such a polity. In the case of crime, for example, it is the state that defines the categories of prohibited behaviour, prosecutes those who allegedly engage in them, and administers punishment to those who are found guilty.

In 'traditional' Melanesia, perceptions and practices of justice reflected the social and political organisation of small, essentially 'stateless', societies. Rather than being centralised in a single entity, authority was typically dispersed throughout the social body. 'Law' was an indivisible part of social and political life in these societies. Kinship and social relations were fundamental to the determination of an individual's rights and obligations in respect of others. There was no concept of 'crime' *per se*. Disputes were defined and resolved within an elaborate framework of kinship, status and relationships.[17] Notions of reciprocity and equivalence were also central to the redress of perceived wrongs, as they were to other social activities. Given that parties to a dispute were likely to continue to live in close proximity and interdependence, an important objective of dispute settlement was the restoration of relations between them. Compensation or the exchange of gifts was a common form of redress and was generally the result of protracted negotiation and mediation between the parties and their respective kin networks. Principles of restorative justice were thus central to the settlement of disputes between members of a recognised group or community. Where, on the other hand, there was no morally binding relationship between the parties, as with strangers or members of rival groups, retribution or 'payback' was a more likely response.

Interactions between western law and justice institutions and Melanesian processes of self-regulation provide insight into the challenges currently facing the formal legal system in PNG. They also reveal important areas of continuity in indigenous responses to conflict and wrongdoing and these, in turn, provide lessons for law and justice reform today. The formal system is largely a legacy of the period of institutional modernisation that preceded Independence. Throughout most of the colonial era there was in fact no discrete system of judicial administration applying to indigenous subjects. Instead, the policing, judicial and penal powers of government were part of an undifferentiated and decentralised system of 'native administration'. This system was personified in the Australian district officer — the *kiap* — who acted simultaneously as administrator, policeman, magistrate and gaoler at local levels. A special set of regulations (the Native Regulations), applying exclusively to Melanesians, was administered in separate courts presided over by the *kiaps*.

'Custom' was never officially accorded the status of law and no attempt was made to incorporate customary institutions into the formal government system. At the same time, 'traditional' structures were only interfered with when perceived as a threat to colonial authority or European prestige[18] and continued to shape the daily existence of most Melanesians. The evolutionary premise of the colonial 'civilising mission' was that the indigenous population would remain subject to their 'traditional' practices until such time as they had 'advanced' sufficiently to be fully integrated into the 'modern' legal system.[19] Integral to colonial thinking was the assumption that there was nothing in indigenous methods of governance that could provide the basis for a uniform system of justice. Linked to this was the belief that 'custom' would eventually die out under the impact of 'civilisation' or, in a later phase, 'modernisation'.

While some district officials argued for the recognition of indigenous regulatory processes,[20] opposition was expressed by the long serving Australian Minister for Territories, Paul Hasluck (1951–1963). Hasluck, the principal architect of modernisation, was intent on building a system of justice consistent with what he saw as the future political needs of the Territory.[21] This entailed the gradual replacement of the discriminatory system of 'native administration' by a modern system of centralised government, which, in turn, would provide the institutional foundations for eventual statehood.[22] While *kiap* justice was a pragmatic strategy for the gradual expansion and consolidation of administrative influence, it was not seen as an appropriate option for the long-term governance of the Territory. Establishing a centralised judicial system administering a uniform body of law was, in Hasluck's view, a necessary condition for the self-government that would one day follow. The adoption of an essentially Anglo-Australian model of law and justice was proposed in a review of the system of judicial administration commissioned by Hasluck, the so-called Derham Report of 1960.[23]

Ironically, while official thinking maintained that indigenous institutions were inadequate to the task, the colonial administration was dependent on them in practice for the maintenance of peace in most rural areas.[24] A high level of cooperation and interdependence developed between many *kiaps*, Melanesian policemen and 'traditional' leaders, including unofficial village 'magistrates', at local levels.[25] Had official thinking been more receptive it would certainly have been possible to develop a framework combining elements of both introduced and indigenous systems.

Such a possibility was out of the question, however, because it "was in fundamental conflict with the official political goals and therefore restricted to an underground existence."[26] The growing emphasis on nation-building that emerged during this period served simultaneously to draw attention away from the role of indigenous structures of governance, including mechanisms for dealing with conflict. The subordination of local institutions within the larger nation-building project has prevailed throughout the post-Independence period and conforms to a broader pattern of neglect evident in other Melanesian countries.[27]

For many observers, the decision to establish a modern centralised system contributed to the erosion of local social controls and the subsequent growth of PNG's 'law and order' problems.[28] While there have been many other factors at work, there is little doubt about the weakening of local regulatory systems. Related to this is the marked failure of the modern system to facilitate the mutually supportive interactions that developed in practice between *kiap* and indigenous ways of doing justice. While the Australian *kiap* may not always have been aware of the extent and character of these engagements, they were generally conducive to the maintenance of peace at local levels.

Contributing to the relative success of the *kiap* system in dealing with disputes was the large repertoire of agency functions and powers that these officials could draw upon.[29] These extended well beyond their official magisterial powers. The *kiap* also had considerable discretion in the exercise of his powers. He could, for example, link dispute resolution to the provision or withdrawal of various government services and facilities. He could persuade and reward, as well as punish. He could address remedies to either individuals or groups. *Kiap* justice accorded more closely with indigenous practices because it approached dispute resolution in a more holistic way than was possible under formal western juridical practice. In doing so, it produced outcomes that were generally acceptable in local terms. There are important continuities between *kiap* justice, particularly its holistic and problem solving approach, and many of the informal restorative justice practices that have emerged in Papua New Guinea since Independence.

Kiap justice's capacity to negotiate the seemingly unbridgeable space between the requirements of colonial order and indigenous perceptions of justice provides an illustration of what Sally Falk Moore has described as a "semi-autonomous social field":

> The semi-autonomous social field has rule-making capacities, and the means to induce or coerce compliance; but it is simultaneously set in a larger social matrix that can, and does, affect and invade it, sometimes at the invitation of persons inside it, sometimes at its own instance.[30]

In practice, if not necessarily by design, *kiap* justice allowed for a high degree of articulation between formal and informal fields of justice that was, in turn, an important contributor to the administration's much-lauded *Pax Australiana*.[31]

By contrast, the incremental processes of centralisation and specialisation that followed the endorsement of Derham's proposals served to close down or weaken many of the points of articulation between formal and informal systems that had contributed to peace. In the process, the differences between these regulatory systems became more apparent, as did the deficiencies of the formal system in the eyes of many local litigants. Thus the professional magistrate, who replaced the *kiap*, was constrained by all manner of substantive, evidential and procedural rules. Professional, as opposed to *kiap* justice, took much longer and entailed a cumbersome and formalistic process, all conducted in a foreign language. Professional officials, in the form of lawyers, magistrates, police officers and so on, now dominated proceedings, leaving little scope for meaningful participation by parties to the dispute and their wider support groups. Local litigants viewed this new system as exclusionary, confusing, and often profoundly unjust.[32] Speaking of the Western Highlands, Marilyn Strathern noted that:

The Kiap's handling of trouble cases in the past combined both a concern for public order and a capacity to deal with minor offences. In fact, these derived from different aspects of his roles (administrator and magistrate), but it meant that he "settled disputes" roughly along lines familiar to Hageners. The paradox is that although the modern official courts are ostensibly concerned with law and order, they fail in Hagener's eyes to take cognisance of matters directly related to both of these elements.[33]

Not surprisingly, dissatisfaction with the process and outcome of professional justice led to a return to older traditions of self-help in some areas. Many of these involved the use of violence as enhanced mobility created new opportunities for conflict. So-called tribal fighting — a practice which had been effectively suppressed under the *kiap* system — reemerged in parts of the Highlands in the early 1970s. The availability of modern firearms provided an additional lethal ingredient.

Twenty-seven years after Independence, minor disputes in rural areas are still dealt with largely by informal means as they have adapted to changing circumstances. The formal law and justice sector remains geographically, as well as socially, distant for many villagers. It also suffers from chronic under-resourcing that has seriously affected its operations. Informal means vary in different places but are likely to include a combination of methods: negotiation or mediation by kin, 'traditional' leaders or church officials; village moots; or the decisions of local *komitis*. Village Courts are also used widely and constitute the most important hybrid institution established in the post-independence period (see below). The effectiveness of informal processes is largely a consequence of the degree of social cohesion of rural communities. Social and economic change has had a seriously corrosive effect in many places. A common complaint relates to the lack of respect shown to village leaders and customary authority, particularly by youngsters exposed to the urban-oriented education system and the hedonistic values of global culture. Likewise, alcohol abuse has weakened social cohesion in both rural and urban communities, becoming a major cause of violence against women and children.[34]

The formal system proclaims a monopoly over the processing of the most serious incidents of conflict and dispute. Its record in this regard, however, leaves much to be desired. It has proved particularly ineffectual in dealing with the large inter-group conflicts that have broken out periodically in parts of the Highlands. There is evidence in some rural areas of an increasingly destructive entanglement between the social control processes of state and local kin-based associations. Rather than leading to a strengthening of overlapping social fields, as in the case of *kiap* justice, this process ultimately weakens both and generates further conflict. This is most evident in cases where officials endowed with state powers use these powers for essentially 'private' or other 'unofficial' ends. This would include, for example, the case of a police officer using a police raid to punish an adversary in a marital dispute,[35] or a Village Court magistrate responsible for maintaining peace and good order who is simultaneously a local fight leader.[36]

It is clear that many ordinary Papua New Guineans have little faith in either the efficiency or fairness of the formal justice system. There is a popular perception of a widening gap between 'law' and 'justice'. In addition to the brutality and violence of many police actions, there is a view that those with power and influence can manipulate the formal system to their own advantage.[37] In this respect, the deficiencies of the present system relate as much to lack of legitimacy as to lack of institutional capacity.

At the policy level, the incessant debate about 'law and order' in Papua New Guinea has focused on the issue of declining state capacity. Restoring law and order has been portrayed as a challenge primarily for the state. Practical proposals have thus concentrated on strengthening the formal sector. Continuing a long tradition of neglect, the role of informal institutions has been seen as peripheral at best.

Donor assistance to the law and justice agencies has reinforced the centrality of the state in this respect. Most assistance continues to be in the form of capacity building within state institutions. The outstanding challenge today is to develop appropriate strategies for enhancing the capacity of both the formal and informal sectors and linkages between them.

THE LAW AND JUSTICE AGENCIES

The Royal Papua New Guinea Constabulary

The Royal Papua New Guinea Constabulary faces enormous challenges. The scale of existing problems of order and PNG's demanding topography would stretch any modern police force. In some areas the police have been literally outgunned by groups armed with automatic weapons. Many of the factors contributing to lawlessness are issues of development that go well beyond the realm of law enforcement. Expectations of the police are often unrealistically high. Lasting improvement in the performance of the constabulary requires changes in the wider environment and the mobilisation of a range of other stakeholders. There is a pressing need to overcome popular distrust of the police and to develop more cooperative and productive linkages with community and non-government organisations.

At Independence, police coverage extended to only 10% of the total land area and 40% of the population.[38] Police resources are still concentrated in the towns and many rural areas are accessible only with considerable difficulty and expense. The size of the force has failed to match the demands of a growing population and escalating lawlessness. In 1975, when crime rates were relatively low, there were 4,100 police officers covering a national population of slightly more than 2 million people. At the end of 1998, with a total population of over 4.6 million and serious problems of order, there were still only 5,000 police officers, of which 20% were either reserves or auxiliary officers.[39] Singapore, with a similar population, has more than double the number of police operating on a small island with excellent transport and communication infrastructure.[40]

Lack of adequate government support has been a major constraint. The bulk of spending in the annual budget goes on salaries and wages, which, according to some accounts, consume 80% of the total police budget.[41] Funds for petrol, airfares, office equipment and other basic necessities are scarce and officers-in-charge are forced to seek external assistance, often from local business houses. The physical condition of many police stations and houses is appalling. Health authorities condemn police facilities regularly as unfit for human habitation. Barrack-type accommodation reinforces the separation between police and the surrounding community. While many dedicated officers struggle to maintain standards, poor working conditions have had a corrosive impact on morale and operational efficiency.

Disappointing performance in basic crime prevention, record keeping, investigation, and prosecution are, in part, a consequence of the shortage of experienced and specialist officers.[42] It also reflects the constabulary's colonial origins as an institution whose primary role was the extension of government control and only secondarily the control of crime. Lack of adequate on-the-job supervision has also contributed to ill discipline. Allegations of serious human rights abuses against individuals and groups are commonplace.[43]

An internal affairs division is responsible for managing public complaints against the police. In practice, less than 15% of complaints are resolved and lengthy procedural delays are usual.[44] Another disturbing trend in recent years has been the theft or disappearance of weapons from police armouries. Suspicions abound that unscrupulous officers have been selling or hiring weapons to criminal groups and those involved in inter-group conflicts.

Lack of capacity and poor community relations have contributed to the tendency to be confrontational in dealings with individual suspects and groups. The superficial 'strength' of reactive policing disguises the actual weakness of the institution. Reactive approaches have contributed to popular distrust and fear of the police. Police violence fuels criminal violence in a reinforcing spiral that becomes increasingly difficult to break.[45] Violent encounters with the police have become part of the process of induction into *raskolism*. While there are now serious efforts to develop community policing, the concept itself remains unclear in the eyes of most people, including many officers. The 1984 Clifford Report remarked that many police saw it as "the police being close enough to control the community — or at least to instruct it how to behave".[46] The same is true of many officers today, over sixteen years later, particularly in the Highlands. The dominance of this retributive approach in contemporary policing practice, with its continuous undermining of police/community relations, remains the most significant source of the constabulary's current weakness.

Correctional Services

The Correctional Service (CS) has been the most neglected of PNG's law and justice agencies. Low annual appropriations have been barely sufficient to cover wages and basic institutional costs. The condition of prison facilities and staff housing has deteriorated alarmingly over the years with predictable effects on the morale of staff and detainees.[47]

As a method of punishment, imprisonment elicits ambivalent views in the wider community, being seen as too harsh in some cases and too 'soft' in others.[48] This ambivalence also signifies differences in approaches to wrongdoing between formal and informal systems of justice. Removing offenders from society and locking them up in isolated institutions fails to deal with many of the issues that are central to informal dispute settlement processes. There is, for example, no role for the community or the parties most directly affected by the wrongdoing. Many Papua New Guineans view imprisonment as a form of punishment for and by the state, one that does little to 'resolve' the infraction or dispute in question. As such, it does not preclude the application of additional informal sanctions, such as compensation.

In practice, imprisonment has also served to reinforce, rather than reduce, criminal commitment and organisation. *Raskol* affiliations thrive in the major prisons.[49] As elsewhere, prisons provide a fertile environment for the building of criminal identity, the expansion of criminal networks and the transmission of new criminal skills. Just as policing is implicated in the generation of lawlessness, prisons have also contributed to the reproduction of criminality and violence in contemporary PNG.

Despite the 'correctional' tag, the primary role of prison is still viewed as being the provision of secure and punitive custody. Lack of resources, including trained personnel, has contributed to the neglect of rehabilitation programs. Activities that do take place — vocational training, spiritual counselling, and gardening — tend to be dependent on the voluntary participation of individuals and groups from the wider community. There are few follow-up activities or organised support programmes for released prisoners.

The CS operates as an integral component of the overall law and justice system. As the end-of-the-line agency,[50] many of the problems it faces are a consequence of inefficiencies in other parts of the system. Currently, over one-third of the prison population comprises remandees awaiting trial. Delays in court proceedings have added greatly to the pressures on the prison system, as well as contributing indirectly to prison breakouts. Overcrowded institutions experience difficulties in feeding and providing uniforms for the growing number of detainees. Many remandees would be more appropriately dealt with in separate remand centres or on bail in the community. Likewise, many minor offenders could be diverted from prison through the provision of adequately supervised community-based sentences or by decriminalising many minor summary offences, such as defaulting on debts and minor thefts.

The Law and the Courts

The development of a 'home-grown' legal system was an important theme in PNG's rhetoric of decolonisation. It was envisaged that 'custom' or customary law would play a major role in the post-colonial legal order. Indeed, the new *Constitution* explicitly adopted 'custom' as part of the underlying law that was to be developed when no existing law was applicable. The National Goals and Directive Principles in the preamble to the *Constitution* expressly called for "development to take place primarily through the use of Papua New Guinean forms of social and political organisation".[51] They also recognised the importance of community structures, calling for "traditional villages and communities to remain as viable units of Papua New Guinea society, and for active steps to be taken to improve their cultural, social, economic and ethical quality".[52] The constitutional scheme was thus receptive to the development of a more holistic and restorative approach to crime control and conflict resolution, including a greater degree of community participation.

Under the direction of Bernard Narokobi the Law Reform Commission was an early advocate of greater integration between western and Melanesian legal traditions. A 1977 report argued that the formal justice system should take greater account of the role of community mechanisms for dealing with conflict.[53] The same report called for wholesale law reform to narrow the perceived gap between the values governing indigenous communities and those embodied in the introduced criminal law.

Despite the idealism of the 1970s, there has been little practical progress towards fulfilling these aspirations. Few of the recommendations of the Law Reform Commission were implemented and, in recent years, the Commission has lacked adequate funds, effective leadership and political commitment. The slow pace of the development of the underlying law has been blamed on Parliament's failure to enact enabling legislation. This situation has been remedied recently with the enactment of the *Underlying Law Act* 2000.[54] Others have criticised the constitutional scheme, pointing to the non-justiciable character of the National Goals and Directive Principles, the wholesale adoption of pre-independence laws, and the subordinate role of the underlying law in the constitutional scheme.[55]

The superior courts — the supreme and national courts — are occasionally lauded as one of the success stories of the post-independence period. There are growing signs, however, that the generic problems affecting other state institutions are having an impact at even the highest judicial levels. An expanding caseload has placed great pressure on the court system and led to lengthy delays in proceedings. The present Chief Justice, Sir Arnold Amet, complained recently that "the judicial system is swamped" and recommended the development of alternative dispute resolution mechanisms.[56] Finding suitably qualified citizens to sit as judges has long been a problem and there is a growing reluctance to recruit overseas candidates. A recent survey by the Institute for National Affairs (INA) found great concern among business executives about the declining predictability of judicial decision-making.[57]

These difficulties have been even more marked for the magistrates and staff of the subordinate courts who process the bulk of formal court cases. There are currently 130 District Court[58] magistrates. This works out at only 1 magistrate per 36,5000 people and less than 1.5 per administrative district.[59] The deteriorating condition of court buildings and staff accommodation has also had an adverse impact in many areas.

The courts in the national judicial system have a range of non-custodial penalties available to them including, for example, probation, community work orders, and good behaviour bonds. A shortage of trained supervisory staff and other resources has inhibited their use in practice. The idea of probation was proposed initially after independence on the grounds that it was consistent with the spirit of the *Constitution* and older traditions of managing disputes in the community. The *Probation Act* was passed in 1979. The first operational probation service was established in 1981 by a local NGO, the Eastern Highlands Province Rehabilitation Committee. This initiative developed a strong community network and became the model for the development of a national service.[60]

Probation offices have now been established in every province, with the exception of Western Province.[61] While the use of probation is gradually increasing, lack of capacity remains a major constraint. In practice, there is often only one operational officer available in each province to carry out a large number of tasks.[62]

The weak capacity of the probation service has also had an impact on the workings of the *Criminal Law (Compensation) Act* of 1991. For many years the courts have taken account of any customary compensation paid by an offender to his/her victim as a mitigating factor when determining the appropriate judicial penalty.[63] The 1991 Act goes a step further and empowers the national and district courts to make compensation orders in addition to other penalties imposed for an offence.[64] In order to assist the courts to determine the appropriateness and amount of compensation, the Act requires the Chief Probation Officer to submit a means assessment report. The ability of the probation service to fulfil this requirement has been seriously affected by its resource problems.[65]

Arguably the most significant institutional innovation in the law and justice sector since independence has been the establishment of the village courts. The primary function of these courts is to "ensure peace and harmony", and endeavour to obtain "amicable settlement of disputes" and apply custom "as determined in accordance with the *Native Customs (Recognition) Act* of 1963".[66] Village courts are intended to provide an accessible forum for dealing with minor disputes and infractions and one that is responsive to the needs and expectations of local communities. They are presided over by village leaders appointed as village court magistrates after consultation with the people. While designed primarily for rural areas, these courts also operate in the urban centres. There are currently 1,082 village courts covering approximately 84% of the country.[67]

Responsibility for the payment of allowances to village court officials was transferred from the national government to provincial and local governments under the *Organic Law on Provincial and Local Level Government* 1995. Provincial and local level governments claim that when these functions were transferred, no actual funding was transferred with them. As a result, many village court officials have not been receiving their allowances. While some continue to work, others refuse to hear cases until they receive payment.[68]

District court magistrates are responsible for supervising the village courts but in practice rarely have the capacity to do so. It is not realistic to expect 130 district court magistrates to supervise the work of 1,082 village courts. At the same time, supervision is clearly required. There have been many instances of village courts exceeding their powers under the *Village Courts Act* by, for example, hearing cases that should be tried before the formal courts, or by unlawfully sentencing offenders to imprisonment.

Many early observers complained about the formalism creeping into village court procedures.[69] Illustrations included the construction of separate bush material courthouses and the holding of regular court sittings. Others, however, point to the successful synthesis between different traditions represented by these courts and their overall flexibility.[70] The formalism that worries some observers may be more a reflection of local expectations and the practice of 'forum shopping' than a deliberate attempt by village magistrates to slavishly imitate the formal courts. Many villagers simply expect these courts to be more formal than the informal local forums that they operate alongside.

A common criticism of the village courts, particularly in the Highlands, is that they reinforce the subordination of women and children.[71] There have been reports of women accused of adultery being imprisoned while their male partners go unpunished. Likewise, children have been locked up for minor offences. The problem here is that the courts have become too responsive to local power structures dominated by older men. In the process, they have compounded the grievances of the weakest groups in the community, notably women and children. The solution lies in a combination of better training that will discourage such inequitable outcomes and an effective system of supervision that will provide remedies to aggrieved parties. It is the weakness of the linkage between these courts and the formal system that is the source of many of their problems. Their strength lies in the provision of an accessible legal forum that is highly responsive to local expectations. Their location between the national court system and local dispute resolution mechanisms makes them an important point for creative interaction between formal and informal justice sectors. With appropriate support and supervision, these courts can provide 'semi-autonomous social fields' that are capable of integrating different regulatory regimes at local levels, like *kiap* justice in an earlier era.

DIRECTIONS FOR REFORM

There have been numerous reports and reviews about law and justice issues in PNG over the years. As mentioned previously, the practical response of governments has been the adoption of short-term measures aimed at suppressing lawlessness in particular areas. These have entailed a familiar repertoire of curfews, liquor bans, and special policing operations.

The well-known weakness of the PNG policy-making environment[72] has been accentuated by the sheer number of institutions and agencies comprising the law and justice sector. Separate departments and ministers exist for justice, the police and the correctional service. Each minister exercises a high degree of autonomy and no formal mechanism exists for ensuring coordination or even regular consultation between the various institutional components of the sector. In the absence of an overall sectoral vision and strategy, each agency has been able to develop their corporate plans and programmes independently of each other. Frequent changes in ministers, agency heads, and senior departmental officials have undermined further policy coherence in the sector.

The National Law and Justice Policy and Plan of Action 2000

Although policy instability continues to pose a major challenge, a window of opportunity presented itself with the election of the reformist Morauta government in 1999. The new government committed itself to an ambitious reform programme as part of its strategy to restore the integrity of state institutions and improve overall government sector performance. Establishing a secure and peaceful environment was recognised as a fundamental condition for the pursuit of other social and economic goals. A small working group of senior law and justice officials was tasked with preparing a draft national policy for the sector. Earlier proposals were reviewed, including the 1993 policy, and extensive consultations took place with a range of stakeholders. The Morauta cabinet endorsed the new policy and plan of action on 21st August 2000. The policy provides the vision statement for the sector as a whole, while the plan of action consists of a detailed set of proposals for achieving this vision.[73] These proposals are organised around three main pillars.

(a) Improving the Efficiency of the Deterrence System

The first pillar emphasises the need to improve the efficiency of the formal criminal justice system and is consistent with ongoing and proposed institutional capacity building activities. Australia has been funding development projects in the law and justice sector since the late 1980s. While initial assistance focused on the police, capacity building projects are now being provided to the Ombudsman Commission, the National Judicial Staff Service, the Legal Training Institute and the Attorney General's Department.

The new policy recognises that the state has a vital role to play in the maintenance of peace and good order and that its agencies must be appropriately equipped in terms of human and material resources. The strengthening measures proposed in the policy, however, are directed to the sector as a whole, rather than to individual agencies. These include strategies to revitalise the juvenile justice system and the Law Reform Commission, as well as the development of a national rehabilitation policy and multi-agency approaches to tackling corruption.

Increasing community participation in law and justice processes lies at the heart of the new policy and is seen as an integral part of institutional strengthening. Emphasis is placed on the building of mutually reinforcing linkages between state and non-state entities around activities aimed at preventing or resolving conflict in a variety of social and institutional contexts.

(b) Coordination

The second pillar relates to the critical issue of sectoral coordination. This is premised partly on the high level of inter dependence between criminal justice agencies in practice. Coordination between agencies is essential for ensuring that they operate effectively as an integrated system. As well as horizontal coordination, there is a need for vertical coordination between agencies and non-government actors operating at different social and geographical levels. *The Organic Law on Provincial and Local Level Government*, which is currently only partially implemented, mandates a major redistribution of functions and responsibilities from national to provincial, district and local level authorities. This larger exercise in decentralisation provides the broad framework for implementing the policy's vision of devolved law and justice and increased community participation.

At the national level, the policy recommends the establishment of a National Coordination Authority comprising the chief executives of the law and justice agencies, related government departments and co-opted members. This body will be responsible for the monitoring and review of sectoral policy, planning and budgeting, and the coordination of law and justice data and research. It will also provide oversight of sectoral training, liaison with other stakeholders at the national level, and cross-sectoral issues. Provincial level coordination will be based on the existing Provincial Peace and Good Order Committees. In addition to representatives from the law and justice agencies and provincial authorities, these committees will include a representative group of non-government stakeholders. Their functions will be broadly similar to those of the national authority. They will also serve as a conduit for the flow of information between national and local levels.

District level authorities are proposed to assist in the coordination of law and justice services in conjunction with local level governments. They will be involved in identifying and responding to local law and justice priorities, allocating resources, and the coordination of programs such as community policing, community based corrections and local preventive and restorative justice initiatives. At the time of writing, a number of 'community justice centre' pilot projects are being designed and these will be used to test and refine suitable local-level mechanisms. It is recognised that these mechanisms need to be sufficiently adaptable to accommodate different local circumstances.

(c) Prevention and Restorative Justice

The third pillar of the new policy relates to crime prevention and restorative justice. It seeks to strengthen the capacity of informal community based and other non-government structures to prevent and resolve conflict at local levels. 'Restorative justice' is the term used to describe the broad criminal justice reform movement that has emerged in many countries in recent years. It is often contrasted, somewhat simplistically, with retributive justice whose principal rationale is the deterrence of wrongdoing through punishment. While most modern criminal justice systems combine retributive and restorative principles in practice, it is their organisation around processes of identifying and punishing individual offenders that is used to distinguish them from restorative alternatives. Hence the traditional focus of the criminal process on apprehending suspects (the role of the police), ascertaining their responsibility under the law (the role of the courts) and, if found guilty, the administration of punishment (the role of the correctional service). There is usually little scope for the participation of either the immediate victim(s) of the wrongdoing or the wider community in this process.

By contrast, restorative justice provides a major role for the community and those who have been most directly affected by an offence or dispute. Ironically, the restorative justice movement in countries like Australia, New Zealand, Canada and the United States draws inspiration from the dispute resolution methods of indigenous, small-scale societies. An important objective of dispute resolution is seen as the restoration of balance and harmony in the community affected and, wherever possible, the healing of relationships damaged by wrongdoing or conflict. This involves allowing an offender to make amends for his/her infraction and, thereafter, to be reintegrated back into the community. Violence and other forms of wrongdoing are understood as doing damage to the fabric of a community and restorative practices are necessary to accomplish the necessary repairs. This is where law and justice activities have the potential for intersecting with other community building objectives. Empowering communities to manage conflict in this way can thus become an important force for community development.

Clearly not all conflicts or infractions are suitable for, or amenable to, restorative techniques. Retributive justice will always remain an option for dealing with the most dangerous and intractable offenders. In addition, where there are significant imbalances in power between particular groups, as in the case of women appearing before village courts, 'restoring' relations may simply serve to reinforce these underlying inequities. In such a case, a form of justice is needed that contributes actively to the transformation of the imbalances (e.g. 'transformative' justice). For the vast majority of minor offences and disputes, however, there remains enormous potential for developing restorative solutions that avoid the amplifying outcomes of retributive practice. Restorative justice in this broad sense is not a new idea in Papua New Guinea. As we have seen, practices like compensation, shaming and reconciliation have strong social foundations in Melanesian communities.

There are many examples of restorative justice institutions and practices in PNG today. Some of these operate independently of the state and are, in part, responses to the perceived failings or absence of state solutions. Others involve linkages or partnerships between state and non-state entities. As most of these practices are informal and occur in rural areas, they are often invisible to the planners and officials based in the central government offices in Port Moresby or in provincial headquarters. At the same time, they provide a rich reservoir of experience and innovation with much to offer the current reform process.

Mass surrenders and gang retreats are a fascinating illustration of an incipient restorative practice that has been developed in recent years.[74] In the case of the former, groups of self-professed criminals surrender themselves and their weapons at public ceremonies. Surrendering groups ask forgiveness for their criminal deeds and assistance for their rehabilitation strategies. Surrenders are often brokered by church groups or individual pastors. Brokers are instrumental in persuading the group to renounce crime and, in return, offer help in securing access to legitimate economic or educational opportunities. The violence involved in a life of crime is often given as a reason for surrendering. Where court proceedings eventuate, magistrates are likely to take the fact of surrender into account. Business houses and others in positions to help are often sympathetic to the plight of such 'reformed criminals'.

Gang retreats bring criminals together with state officials, business and political leaders. As in the case of surrenders, church representatives often broker retreats. Criminals engage in frank discussions with those in positions of authority and influence, outlining their grievances and identifying what is required to get them to abandon crime. Like the surrender, the outcome of a retreat can be a commitment to leave crime in return for access to legitimate opportunities. Unlike criminal justice practice, these informal institutions are potentially restorative with the capacity for breaking the reinforcing pattern of retributive violence between *raskols* and police. They also offer the prospect of sustainable solutions by linking exit from crime explicitly to employment, education, micro-credit and social development options.

In some areas voluntary associations have been formed to assist in the rehabilitation of ex-prisoners and ex-criminals. For example, in 1984 a group of former prisoners set up the Western Highlands Ex-Criminal Self Help Task Force. This group continues to operate today, producing a weekly programme on the local radio and engaging in a variety of spiritual, vocational and agricultural training programs for 'youth at risk' and released prisoners. The group also visits those in police custody and prison and provides informal representation for members of surrendering groups appearing in court.

Contrary to their depiction in current stereotypes as disorganised and lawless communities, many urban settlements have well-developed capacities for self-policing. John Ivoro, a leader in Port Moresby's Saraga settlement, documents the successful mediation of disputes by a local dispute settlement committee in a large multi-cultural urban community.[75] He also tells the story of a mutually beneficial partnership forged between the committee and a neighbouring private company. The company approached the committee over their concerns about thefts and break-ins at the company premises. After listening to community representatives, the company agreed to engage local youth in casual employment as security guards and provide sponsorship to church and sporting activities. As a result, criminal activities diminished and a relationship previously based on distrust and hostility was transformed.

Members of the Saraga dispute settlement committee received their mediation training from the Peace Foundation Melanesia, an NGO that has been helping local communities deal with conflict since the mid-1990s.[76] The Foundation offers training modules in people skills, conflict resolution, community development planning, training of trainers, and mediation and restorative justice. These modules have been developed with the full participation of villagers from many different parts of the country and are all linked to the general goal of building community cohesion and promoting community development. In practice, they work through existing community structures and local churches. The Peace Foundation has also worked with mining companies, the police, staff and detainees in prisons and university students. Training members of particular communities or institutions as trainers has given these initiatives a high degree of sustainability in practice.

While the Peace Foundation is probably the best-known NGO in this area, there are many others operating at local levels. East New Britain's *Sosel Eksen Komiti* is a good example. Initially established in 1986 as the Social Concern Committee of the East New Britain Provincial Assembly, they were incorporated as an NGO in 1991. Over the years, *Sosel Eksen* has built an extensive network of grassroots volunteers throughout rural East New Britain. Among its many programmes, it runs workshops and training courses directed at reducing drug and alcohol abuse, child abuse, and 'domestic' violence. There are approximately 120 trained extension volunteers living and working in villages throughout the province.

The peace process that has emerged out of the tragic conflict on Bougainville provides a rich source of restorative ideas and practices. While the conflict centred on the struggle between armed secessionists and the PNG security forces, it also served as a catalyst for many sub-conflicts between and within Bougainvillean communities. The collapse of state authority left the way open for the creation, and revival, of a host of local structures and processes of governance in different parts of the island. As such, it provides a unique opportunity for viewing the dynamics of order without state. The ongoing peace process has given rise to many innovative and culturally based strategies for reconciling the many different kinds of conflict provoked by the war. While subject to enormous variation, 'traditional' authority, in the form of chiefs, has played an important role in many areas:

> It reduced the tensions that were often the driving force in violent localised conflict, including that between BRA and Resistance Forces. In some cases the roles of chiefs in promoting peace went much further. Some exerted control over local BRA or Resistance Forces, limiting them to defensive roles. Some played major parts in initiating reconciliation between groups in conflict, a role now increasing as the peace process gathers momentum.[77]

Women's groups, churches and NGO's have been active in reconciliation and rehabilitation activities with individuals, families, ex-combatants, and villages. The role of women in the current peace process recalls the long history (and longer pre-history) of women as peace-makers in Melanesia.[78]

The Peace Foundation has also been involved in the Bougainville peace process, working with chiefs, women's groups and others in the area of mediation, conflict resolution and restorative justice.[79] John Tombot, a traditional chief and former village court magistrate in the Siwai district of southwest Bougainville, underwent training with the Foundation. Since 1997 he has been involved in over 300 mediations including many cases of homicide occurring during the conflict.[80] He tells how many local people in his area believed the imposition of fines by the formal courts was primarily an income generating activity for magistrates. When the war broke out, many magistrates were openly attacked and disputes that had been dealt with by the courts were resumed, often with violent consequences. According to Tombot, restorative practices that accord closely with 'traditional' methods are much more successful than formal adjudication in achieving sustainable resolutions.

In other parts of Papua New Guinea, the lack of tangible support from distant headquarters in Port Moresby has also served to stimulate local officials into developing creative solutions. In one large provincial prison, the commander and his senior officers have gone to great lengths to build supportive relations with the surrounding community. A local NGO has been providing training courses for prison staff and their families, as well as detainees. Selected inmates have helped build and repair local community schools and perform various public works. The prison has been contracted by a local company to provide detainees for sign writing on vehicles. A nearby agricultural research centre has been allowed to use prison land and detainee labour to grow hybrid guavas. From being a depressingly insular institution concerned solely with security, this prison has become a hive of activity. Regular interactions have diminished fears and insecurities among the local community about the proximity of a large prison. Likewise, the morale of detainees, prison staff and their families has risen dramatically.

These are a selection of some of the restorative initiatives occurring in different parts of PNG. Many other examples could be cited. These practices have been developed under very different local circumstances and involve a range of both state and non-state actors. The challenge now facing policy makers, law and justice practitioners and community and non-government sector leaders, is how to integrate these various practices within an overall regulatory system. It is the challenge of developing 'semi-autonomous social fields' that allows the existence of complimentary layers of social regulation under the rule of law. These levels inevitably draw on different traditions and experiences but should ultimately be directed at achieving the same overall objective — the promotion of peace and good order. The new national policy contains specific recommendations aimed at 'community-building'. These involve the identification of particular community needs and priorities and the provision of appropriate training and other support designed to increase local capacities for self-regulation. The policy also introduces the notion of 'partnerships for peace' whereby support will be targeted at preventative and restorative initiatives between state and non-state entities. Wherever practical, support will be directed at these partnerships thereby building the capacities of formal and informal sectors simultaneously and, in the process, nurturing a process of mutual learning.

CONCLUSIONS

It would be naïve to expect that law and justice reform alone could overcome PNG's problems of order. These problems are diverse and complex and need to be addressed in different ways. At the same time, fundamental reform is clearly needed. The formal justice system, particularly in its criminal justice role, has not only failed to stem lawlessness and conflict but has, in many ways, become a contributor to them.

At the heart of PNG's challenges of governance — including that of 'law and order' — lies the uneasy fit between the institutions and ideology of the modern 'nation-state' and the multiplicity of indigenous polities that constitute modern Papua New Guinea. The formal law and justice system is a relative newcomer and has been superimposed onto a patchwork of self-regulating local systems that have by no means 'disappeared' under the onslaught of modernity and externally induced change. On the contrary, the latter have been remarkably resilient and have engaged actively with institutions of more recent origin. Although many of these interactions are consistent with building a larger and sustainable social order, others are not.

While the role of the state internationally has undergone dramatic changes over the past two decades, its central role in national development is widely accepted. For many observers, PNG is a classic example of a 'weak state'.[81] This weakness is manifested in the difficulties it experiences in carrying out the most basic tasks of statehood, including the maintenance of public order, preserving political stability, providing basic services, and managing the national economy. Building the capacity of state institutions, including the law and justice agencies, is a necessary response to this weakness. Problems arise, however, when the state is treated in isolation from its social environment. Lack of state capacity is often viewed as a 'technical' problem to be remedied by strategic inputs targeted exclusively at state institutions. The question of a state's relations to its wider society and the extent to which these might themselves be a source of its limited capacity is rarely raised. The fragile legitimacy of the state in Papua New Guinea has all too often been ignored in the haste to build its institutional structures.

An implicit argument in this paper is that the weak performance of PNG's formal law and justice system, particularly its criminal justice system, is as much an outcome of its lack of legitimacy, as it is a consequence of shortage of resources, 'technical' or otherwise. There are growing levels of distrust and disaffection with the workings of the formal system. This can be seen in the turning away from state remedies, the revival of older ways of dealing with conflict, as well as in the creation of new ones. Restoring faith in the law and justice system requires that priority be given to improving relations with the wider society it exists to serve. Building trust and confidence in the principal agencies is an integral part of any sustainable institutional strengthening activities. Community participation in law and justice processes is a necessary part of building the social foundations whose absence is a significant contributor to the sector's current weakness.

While the weakness of the state is widely acknowledged, the weakness of PNG communities has received less attention. Building the conditions for sustainable peace and good order requires both a strong state and strong communities. Rapid social and economic change has taken its toll on even the most distant village. Combined with the deficiencies of formal processes, the erosion of community cohesion has meant a growing absence of effective conflict resolution capacities in many areas. Empowering communities to deal with local problems of order within an overall framework of national law is an important priority in the National Law and Justice Policy. As we have seen, there are already many community based organisations involved in conflict resolution and restorative justice initiatives in different parts of the country. Some of them already work with state officials and agencies, while others work with the private sector. Developing partnerships of this kind, as envisaged in the policy, is an important way of building the capacities of state and civil society simultaneously and in a mutually supportive way.

PNG's colonial and post-colonial history provides important lessons in the importance of developing law and justice strategies that can accommodate a degree of semi-autonomy at local levels within an overall national system of regulation. The relative success of *kiap* justice had less to do with the personal attributes of these agents of pacification, as with their ability to link the needs of colonial order with those of local power structures in a mutually reinforcing way. Their ability to approach disputes in a holistic manner allowed them to contribute to resolutions that were broadly acceptable and conducive to the maintenance of peace and good order. Local leaders were active participants in these processes, rather than merely passive bystanders.[82] *Kiap* justice was thus able to integrate the requirements of an encompassing 'administrative' order with those of particular 'local' orders in a way that the post-independence justice system has singularly failed to do.

There are strong echoes of this holistic approach to conflict resolution in many of the restorative justice initiatives that have developed informally in PNG in recent years, often in response to the failings of the formal system. While restorative justice approaches elsewhere have attracted criticism for individualising responsibility for conflict, the novelty of these responses in PNG has been their deliberate attempt to address underlying causes, including the structural conditions that contribute to crime (e.g. by providing pathways back to legitimate economic activities). An important source of the weakness of the formal system has been its failure to address the broader issues of social justice that are widely seen as contributing to crime and conflict. Indeed, many Papua New Guineans view the formal system as reinforcing these grievances by, for example, punishing the minor criminals while leaving alone those who engage in serious abuse of public office. The ability of restorative responses to engage directly with social justice issues provides an important way of building the legitimacy of the law and justice system. Contrary to a negative perception of law and justice as being solely about control and suppression, restorative justice also provides a way of integrating law and justice processes with more positive and productive development activities.

ENDNOTES

1 'Law and order' is the phrase that is used widely in PNG to refer to problems of criminal violence. Framed in this way, 'law and order' solutions generally entail emphasis on strengthening police capacity and punitive measures.

2 Examples include the imposition of curfews and the use of special policing operations.

3 This challenge is experienced, in varying degrees, in all the Melanesian countries, including Vanuatu and Solomon Islands.

4 GoPNG/UNDP. 1999. <u>Papua New Guinea Human Development Report 1998</u> Hong Kong: UN at p 76.

5 *Raskols* is the term popularly used to describe members of criminal gangs. See, further, Harris, B.M. 1988. The Rise of Rascalism: Action and Reaction in the Evolution of Rascal Gangs. *Discussion Paper 54.* Port Moresby: Institute of Applied Social and Economic Research; Goddard, M. 1992. Big-Man, Thief: the Social Organization of Gangs in Port Moresby. *Canberra Anthropology* 15(1): 20–34 and Dinnen, S. 2001. *Law and Order in a Weak State: Crime and Politics in Papua New Guinea.* Honolulu: University of Hawai'i Press.

6 World Bank. 1999. *Papua New Guinea – Improving Governance and Performance.* Washington DC: World Bank at p 108.

7 See above, n 4 at p 175.

8 Zvekic, U. and Alvazzi del Frate, A. 1995. *Criminal Victimization in the Developing World.* New York: United Nations Interregional Crime and Justice Research Institute.

9 Sikani, R. 1999. Criminal Threat in Papua New Guinea. In Boeha, B. (ed.) *Australia – Papua New Guinea: Crime and the Bilateral Relationship.* Port Moresby: National Research Institute at p 18.

10 Borrey, A. 2000. Sexual violence in perspective: the case of Papua New Guinea. In Dinnen, S. and Ley, A. (eds.) *Reflections on Violence in Melanesia.* Sydney: Hawkins Press and Asia Pacific Press.

11 Levantis, T. 1997. Urban employment in Papua New Guinea – it's criminal. *Pacific Economic Bulletin* 12(2): 73–84.

12 Dinnen, S. 2001. Above, n 5 at pp 76–77.

13 Dinnen, S. 2001. Above, n 5 at pp 76–77; Levantis, T. 1998. Tourism in Papua New Guinea. *Pacific Economic Bulletin* 13(1): 98–05.

14 Dinnen, S. 2001. Above, n 5 at p 1.

15 INA. 1999. *Factors Contributing to the Lack of Investment in Papua New Guinea: A Private Sector Survey.* Port Moresby: Institute for National Affairs at pp 14–15.

16 Moore, S. F. 1978. *Law as Process: An Anthropological Approach.* London: Routledge and Kegan Paul.

17 Epstein, A.L. 1974. Introduction. In Epstein, A.L. (ed.) *Contention and Dispute: aspects of law and social control in Melanesia.* Canberra: Australian National University Press at p 12.

18 The suppression of so-called tribal fighting is one example. The different ways in which sexual advances/assaults were dealt when a European (as opposed to an indigenous) woman was involved is another.

19 Sack, P. 1989. Law, Custom and Good Government: The Derham Report in its Historical Context. In Latufeku, S. (ed.) *Papua New Guinea: A Century of Colonial Impact 1884–1984.* Port Moresby: The National Research Institute and the University of Papua New Guinea at pp 381–2.

20 Fenbury, D.M. 1978. *Practice without Policy: Genesis of Local Government in Papua New Guinea.* Canberra: Australian National University.

21 Hasluck, P. 1976. *A Time for Building: Australian Administration in Papua New Guinea 1951–1963.* Melbourne: Melbourne University Press.

22 Dinnen, S. 2001. Above n 5 at p 25.

23 Derham, D. P. 1960. Report on the System for the Administration of Justice in the Territory of Papua and New Guinea, Canberra: Department of Territories.

24 Downs, I. 1980. *The Australian Trusteeship: Papua New Guinea 1945–75.* Canberra: Government Publishing Service at p 150; Gordon, R. J. 1983. The Decline of the Kiapdom and the Resurgence of 'Tribal Fighting'. *Oceania* 53: 205–223 at p 211.

25 Kituai, A. I. 1998. *My Gun, My Brother: The World of the Papua New Guinea Colonial Police, 1920–1960.* Honolulu: University of Hawai'i Press.

26 Sack, P. 1989. Above, n 19 at p 382.

27 Liloqula, R. and Pollard, A. 2000. Understanding Conflict in Solomon Islands: A Practical Means to Peacemaking. *State Society and Governance in Melanesia Project Discussion Paper 00/7* Canberra: Australian National University.

28 Gordon, R. J. and Meggitt, M. 1985. *Law and Order in the New Guinea Highlands.* Hanover, NH: University Press of New England.

29 Gordon, R.J. 1983. Above, n 24 at p 220.

30 Moore, S. F. 1973. Law and Social Change: the Semi-Autonomous Social Field as an Appropriate Subject of Study. *Law and Society Review* Summer 1973: 719–746 at p 720.

31 The establishment of peace, particularly among formerly belligerent groups in the New Guinea Highlands, was viewed as one of the most significant achievements of the Australian colonial administration.

32 Strathern, M. 1972. *Official and Unofficial Courts: Legal Assumptions and Expectations in a Highlands Community* Port Moresby: New Guinea Research Unit; Strathern, M. 1976. Crime and Corrections: The Place of Prisons in Papua New Guinea. *Melanesian Law Journal* 4(1): 67–93.

33 See above, n 32, Strathern, M. 1972 at p 143.

34 AusAID. 1997. *Papua New Guinea Law and Justice Baseline Survey of Community Initiatives.* Canberra: Australian Agency for International Development.

35 Standish, W. A. 1994. Papua New Guinea: The Search for Security in a Weak State. In Thompson, A. (ed.) *Papua New Guinea: Issues for Australian Security Planners.* Canberra: Australian Defence Studies Centre at p 72.

36 Reay, M. 1987. Laying Down the Law in Their Own Fashion. In Langness, L.L. and Hayes, T.E. (eds.) *Anthropology in the High Valleys.* Novato CA: Chandler & Sharp at p 74.

37 World Bank. 1999. Above, n 6 at p 110.

38 Dorney, S. 1990. *Papua New Guinea: People, Politics and History since 1975.* Sydney: Random House at p 296.

39 Dorney, S. 1990. Above, n 38 at p 110.

40 Curtin, T. 1999. Project appraisal and human capital theory. Public sector reform in Papua New Guinea (unpublished seminar paper) Australian National University, Canberra as cited in Levantis, T. 2000. Crime catastrophe – reviewing Papua New Guinea's most serious social and economic problem *Pacific Economic Bulletin* 15(2): 130–142 at pp 139–140.

41 Taku, P. 1990. Royal Papua New Guinea Constabulary: Personnel and Policies (unpublished paper dated 4th December, 1990).

42 See, for example, "Lawman laments cases" *Post-Courier* 12th December 2000.

43 Dinnen, S. 2001. Above, n 5.

44 World Bank. 1999. Above, n 6 at p 10.

45 Dinnen, S. 2000. Breaking the Cycle of Violence: Crime and State in Papua New Guinea. In C. Banks (ed.) *Developing Cultural Criminology: Theory and Practice in Papua New Guinea.* Institute of Criminology Monograph Series No. 13 Sydney: Institute of Criminology.

46 Clifford, W., Morauta, L. and Stuart, B. 1984. *Law and Order in Papua New Guinea* (The Clifford Report) Port Moresby: Institute of National Affairs and Institute of Applied Social and Economic Research at p 119.

47 For example, "Judge says prison 'unfit for humans'" *Post-Courier* 6th November, 2000.

48 Strathern, M. 1976. Above, n 32.

49 Dinnen, S. 2001. Above, n 5 at p 107.

50 That is, the agency that comes in at the end of the criminal justice process after the police and courts have performed their role.

51 *Constitution* (PNG), s 1(6).

52 *Constitution* (PNG), s 5(4).

53 Law Reform Commission of PNG. 1977. The Role of Customary Law in the Legal System Report No. 7 Port Moresby: LRC, p 63.

54 No. 13 of 2000, certified on 18th August, 2000.

55 Weisbrot, D. 1982. The Impact of the Papua New Guinea Constitution on the Recognition and Application of Customary Law. In P. Sack (ed.) *Pacific Constitutions.* Canberra: Law Department, Research School of Social Sciences, Australian National University.

56 *National* 31st October, 2000.

57 INA. 1999. Above, n 15 at p 14.

58 The District Courts process summary offences and certain indictable offences. Decisions of the District Court can be appealed to the National Court presided over by a single judge.

59 This information is contained in a letter from the Secretary of the Department of Provincial and Local Government Affairs, Leo Meninga, dated 26th October, 2000.

60 Giddings, A. 1986. Some Alternatives to States of Emergency. In L. Morauta (ed.) *Law and Order in a Changing Society* Political and Social Change Monograph 6. Canberra: Research School of Pacific and Asian Studies, Australian National University.

61   The Clifford Report. Above, n 46 at p 77.

62   These include advising courts on community sentences; supervising clients; preparing pre-sentence and pre-parole reports; training and supervising volunteers; attending to administrative matters and liaising with communities. See Pitts, M. 2000 *Informal Methods of Crime Control In Papua New Guinea*. Unpublished MA thesis University of Newcastle, at p 96.

63   Dinnen, S. 1988. Sentencing, Custom and the Rule of Law in Papua New Guinea. *Journal of Legal Pluralism and Unofficial Law* 27: 19–54.

64   See, also, Newton Cain, T. elsewhere in this volume.

65   Banks, C. 1998. Custom in the Courts: *Criminal Law (Compensation) Act* of Papua New Guinea. *British Journal of Criminology* 38(2): 299–316 at p 313.

66   *Village Court Act* 1973.

67   Department of Attorney General. 1999. <u>Brief to Minister for Justice, Hon. Kilroy K. Genia MP</u>. pp 93–94.

68   A local newspaper recently reported an attack on the Eastern Highlands provincial administration offices by Village Court officials angry about unpaid allowances, some of which had allegedly been outstanding for 5 years. See *National* 15th December, 2000.

69   Paliwala, A. 1982. Law and Order in the Village: Papua New Guinea's village courts. In Sumner, C. (ed.) *Crime, Justice and Underdevelopment*. London: Heinemann.

70   Goddard, M. 2000. Three urban village courts in Papua New Guinea. In S. Dinnen and A. Ley (eds.) *Reflections on Violence in Melanesia*. Sydney: Hawkins Press and Asia Pacific Press at p 243.

71   Garap, S. 2000. Struggles of women and girls – Simbu Province, Papua New Guinea. In Dinnen, S. and Ley, A. (eds.) *Reflections on Violence in Melanesia*. Sydney: Hawkins Press and Asia Pacific Press.

72   Regan, A.J. 1997. The Papua New Guinea policy-making environment as a window on the Sandline controversy. In Dinnen, S. May, R. and Regan, A. J. (eds.) *Challenging the State: the Sandline Affair in Papua New Guinea*. Canberra: Research School of Pacific and Asian Studies, Australian National University.

73   GoPNG. 1999. *The National Law and Justice Policy and Plan of Action – Toward Restorative Justice 2000–2005*. Waigani: Department of National Planning and Monitoring.

74   Dinnen, S. 1997. Restorative Justice in Papua New Guinea. *International Journal of the Sociology of Law* 25: 245–262; above, n 5 Dinnen, S. 2001.

75   Ivoro, J. 2000. Conflict Resolution in a Multi-Cultural Urban Settlement. Unpublished paper presented at the *Conflict Management and Restorative Justice in the Pacific conference* held at the University of the South Pacific, Port Vila, Vanuatu, June 2000.

76   Howley, P. 2001. Breaking Spears and Mending Hearts – Peace Foundation, Peace Makers, Custom Law and restorative Justice in Bougainville. Unpublished manuscript.

77   Regan, A.J. 2000. 'Traditional' leaders and conflict resolution in Bougainville: reforming the present by rewriting the past? In Dinnen, S. and Ley, A. (eds.) *Reflections on Violence in Melanesia*. Sydney: Hawkins Press and Asia Pacific Press at p 297.

78 Rumsey, A. 2000. Women as peacemakers – a case from the Nebilyer Valley, Western Highlands, Papua New Guinea. In Dinnen, S. and Ley, A. (eds.) *Reflections on Violence in Melanesia* Sydney: Hawkins Press and Asia Pacific Press.

79 Howley, P. 2001. Above, n 76.

80 Tombot, J. 2000. Restorative Justice Bougainville Style – A Marriage of Custom and Introduced Skills. Unpublished paper presented at the *Conflict Management and Restorative Justice in the Pacific conference* at the University of the South Pacific, Port Vila, Vanuatu, June 2000.

81 Migdal, J.S. 1988. *Strong Societies and Weak States: State-Society Relations and State Capabilities in the Third World*. Princeton NJ: Princeton University Press.

82 Kituai, A.I. 1998. Above, n 25.

15. CONSTITUTIONS AS LIMITS ON THE STATE IN MELANESIA: COMPARATIVE PERSPECTIVES ON CONSTITUTIONALISM, PARTICIPATION AND CIVIL SOCIETY*

By: Anthony J. Regan

KEY TERMS AND PHRASES

Authoritarian

A government system based on an established system of authority rather than on the express or implied consent of the governed. The term is also applied to situations where established power is regarded as having an absolute right to assert itself.

Bourgeois/bourgeoisie

A French word meaning 'town dwellers' and the upper class of such persons. As used by Karl Marx (see 'Marxist' below) it refers to the class of property owners who rose with and developed the capitalist system of production, taking power from the feudal aristocracy. (Also see 'middle class').

Clientilism

A term describing informal and unequal power relations based on exchange of benefits. It is found in many forms, including some small-scale traditional societies where a high status person uses his or her authority and resources to offer protection to others who in return provide support and services.

Dictatorial

Dictatorship is a form of government in which a single person, office, faction or party has complete political power. The term is often used in a less precise way to describe someone who has enormous political power or influence even though they are acting within the legal restrictions of a democracy.

Marxist

A Marxist is a person who adheres to any of the versions of social theory that derive from the works of Karl Marx (1818–83). The central part of his complex theories is the view that history must be explained in materialistic terms. Each person exists as a member of an economic class with all classes always in competition with others.

* I am grateful to Sinclair Dinnen, Yash Ghai, Peter Larmour, Ron May and Robert McCorquodale for their insightful comments on an early draft of this chapter.

INTRODUCTION

Human societies have to balance two apparently contradictory needs. While 'rulers' are needed to manage the society, at the same time there is a need to limit the tendency of those with power to abuse it. The potential for abuse is particularly acute in complex modern societies where coercive power is great. Hence the discussion of the control of rulers in the present day tends to be about limiting state action.

Constitutionalism — the acceptance by government of limits on its actions set by constitutional rules — was anticipated as an outcome of adoption of 'Western' style independence constitutions for most post-colonial states. In much of Asia and Africa, these hopes were not fulfilled, with most independence constitutions being short-lived and limits on the state increasingly being ignored by those in power. But following the 1989 fall of the Berlin Wall, expectations were raised that the efficacy of constitutions as restraints on the state might be bolstered by democratic change, and especially by popular participation in government associated with democratisation and by the development of civil society, and not just in Eastern Europe, but also in Africa and Asia.

In the post-colonial states of the Pacific constitution-makers embraced the need for limits on government. Popular participation in government was expected to assist acceptance of constitutional limits by governments. By contrast with Africa and Asia, hopes for independence constitutions in the Pacific initially seemed to be fulfilled. Adherence to constitutional provisions on succession of government in the immediate post-independence era was seen as evidence of support for constitutionalism.[1] But since at least the late 1980s, the position has become less clear, especially in the four turbulent states of Melanesia (Fiji Islands, Papua New Guinea, Solomon Islands and Vanuatu). Not only was the Fiji independence constitution overthrown in the first of two coups in 1987, but there has been a further coup in Fiji Islands (May 2000) and a coup in Solomon Islands (June 2000). More generally, as discussed elsewhere in this chapter, there seems to be growing evidence of reduced acceptance of constitutional limits on government, so that constitutionalism increasingly seems problematic in Melanesia. As with other parts of the post-colonial world, some see possibilities that civil society will assist in a resurgence of constitutionalism.

This chapter examines the record of and prospects for constitutionalism in Melanesia with particular reference to acceptance of limits on the state in the form of constitutional rules on succession of government, accountability and human rights. It also examines the possibility that popular participation and civil society might offer hopes of increased acceptance of limits on the state in Melanesia in the future. The chapter does not purport to examine the full range of factors relevant to understanding the persistence or otherwise of constitutionalism, factors which now include various forms of pressure from the international community, as for example, with the conditionalities in both bilateral and multilateral aid associated with governance-related goals.

CONSTITUTIONALISM, PARTICIPATION AND CIVIL SOCIETY

Constitutionalism

Constitutionalism is the imposition of effective limits on state action through the rule of law under constitutional government. It is "a constitutional system in which the powers of the government and the legislature are defined and limited by the constitution, which enjoys the status of fundamental law, and by which the courts are authorised to enforce these limitations".[2]

De Smith emphasised the distinction between the "formal sense" of constitutionalism — rules intended to limit government action — and its operation as a "living reality".[3] Constitutionalism really lives only when "these rules curb the arbitrariness of discretion and are in fact observed by the wielders of power, and to the extent that within the forbidden zones upon which authority may not trespass there is significant room for the enjoyment of individual liberty".[4]

Critics of post-colonial states often forget that constitutionalism became a 'living reality' in Europe comparatively recently, at the time of the bourgeois revolutions, when its 'constituent elements' of secularisation, nationalisation, separation and limitation of public powers developed.[5] Secularisation was part of efforts by national monarchies to escape papal authority. Nationalisation of public powers was sought by the bourgeoisie as it pursued mercantilism from the 16th to the 18th centuries. Capitalism's needs were served by constitutionalism, as the bourgeoisie sought limits on arbitrary or discretionary powers of either the monarchy or the centralised state in relation to property or contractual matters, general legal rules enforced by increasingly independent judges being well suited to such aims.[6] Hence constitutionalism did not emerge as part of a grand design, but rather as a slowly developing product of complex political and economic forces.

Constitutionalism is basically a description of a desirable outcome. The description alone does not help us understand how the outcome is achieved. The more important question for the purposes of this chapter is what is it that makes constitutionalism a 'living reality', especially in the post-colonial states of Melanesia, where the political and economic forces at work are very different from those of 16th to 18th century Europe?

Participation

Participation of the populace in political matters — through the ballot box, political parties, interest groups seeking to influence government, *et cetera*[7] — is almost universally accepted as essential to the accountability of government. Regular elections are seen to contribute to the legitimacy of constitutional government and to keeping it accountable (as policies of rulers subject to the real threat of replacement in elections need to exhibit some sensitivity to the needs of the society). Popular participation in sub-national governments — both directly and through elections — is said by many commentators on decentralisation and on autonomy arrangements to create centres of power able to check dictatorial tendencies of the central state and to make the local state responsive and accountable. Finally, popular participation in local level government is seen as vital to the strengthening of civil society, as discussed below.[8]

Popular participation was a goal of Melanesian constitution-makers, especially (but not only) Papua New Guinea's Constitutional Planning Committee (CPC), whose 1974 Final Report[9] provided the basis for much of Papua New Guinea's 1975 independence constitution. With a jaundiced view of the state based on experience of colonial rule, the CPC was concerned that constitutional law alone might not be a sufficient restraint on the state, and envisaged popular participation making the state more accountable. Its recommendations on constitutionally entrenched sub-national (provincial) government were intended to encourage political forces that could act as checks on authoritarian tendencies at the centre.[10]

Civil Society

Civil society in the 'developed' industrial states can be seen as the range of interests in society distinct from government, which in various ways combine and place limits on government. There is little consensus, however, about either exactly what the term 'civil society' means or how it acts to limit the state, even in relation to the industrialised democracies of Europe. An analysis by Woods[11] comparing civil society in Europe and Africa is helpful.

The concept springs from a differentiation between public and private interests that began to be made at the time of the emergence of the middle class two to three hundred years ago, and the idealisation of this separation as the monarchy and semi-feudal institutions were gradually restricted from treating the political and governmental arenas as private domains. As patrimonial rule[12] diminished, the notion developed that political authorities should be accountable to the public.[13] As to the manner in which civil society acts to limit state action, Woods emphasises the significance of the involvement of individuals in the public sphere through "articulated associational groups which could rely on an informed leadership to shape public opinion".[14] Civil society articulates "a set of norms which affect the way the state functions and how other groups will interact".[15] In other words, the contributions of groups and networks of private individuals to public debate helps shape values and standards of behaviour that become so widely accepted that they cannot be ignored, even by the state. So, for example, the higher degree of adherence to such things as democratic norms and limits on corruption in industrialised countries than in post colonial states is often explained in terms of a more 'developed' civil society.

Links are made between civil society and popular participation, it being claimed that civil society is strengthened by participation in local level government:

> Civil society provides an especially strong foundation for democracy when it generates opportunities for participation and influence at all levels of governance, not least the local level. For it is at the local level that the historically marginalized

are most likely to be able to affect public policy and to develop a sense of efficacy as well as actual political skills. The democratization of local government thus goes hand in hand with the development of civil society as an important condition for the deepening of democracy and the "transition from clientelism to citizenship" in Latin America, as well as elsewhere in the developing and post-communist worlds.[16]

Interest in civil society in the context of debate on limits on the post-colonial state originates with the role of popular protest in the fall of the Eastern European 'Marxist' regimes. This was widely seen as evidence of the emergence of a potentially powerful civil society, and the move to a free market economy in those states since 1989 as likely to strengthen civil society as an effective limit on the state. As discussed later in this chapter, many observers debate whether or not there is evidence for similar trends in Africa[17] and other areas of the post-colonial world, including Melanesia.

Perhaps the most striking instance of speculation about the potential for civil society to limit state action in Melanesia arose from events in Papua New Guinea in early 1997 in relation to the Sandline affair. In the wake of action by army elements to oust mercenaries engaged under a government contract with United Kingdom company Sandline International, popular unrest in the main cities, much of it led by the same army elements and also involving some non-governmental organisations (NGOs), led to the standing aside of Prime Minister Chan.[18]

Before considering whether the expectations of popular participation and civil society as limits on government in Melanesia are realistic, it is helpful first to discuss the effectiveness of more than 25 years of post-independence experience of constitutional limits on state action in Melanesia.

CONSTITUTIONAL LIMITS – SUCCESSION OF GOVERNMENT, ACCOUNTABILITY AND HUMAN RIGHTS

Among the central sets of rules in constitutions intended to set limits on state action are those on: succession of governments; accountability of politicians and public servants for use of state resources; and protection of human rights. One way to evaluate constitutionalism is by reference to the extent to which these rules have been effective restraints on the state.

The Rules in the Melanesian Constitutions

In relation to succession, three of the four Melanesian constitutions provide for variants of the Westminster system, with prime ministers taking office as a result of election by the legislature.[19] The exception is the 1997 Fiji Islands *Constitution*, where the situation is closer to the original Westminster system, with a (largely ceremonial) President appointing as Prime Minister a member of the lower house of the legislature who in the opinion of the President can form a government with the confidence of the legislature.[20] In general, prime ministers and governments can only be removed following a general election or through votes of no confidence[21] (again the President of Fiji Islands has limited discretionary powers in this area).

Concerning accountability, the four constitutions place unusual emphasis on the issue in that they:

- carefully codify variants of the principles of parliamentary control of the executive in various ways, including provision for collective responsibility of the political executive (often called the 'Cabinet'),[22] removal through votes of no confidence,[23] scrutiny of public finance,[24] and committee systems;[25]

- all provide for both ombudsman institutions and codes of conduct for leaders.[26]

- all provide for offices of the auditor general[27] and of the public prosecutor,[28] each independent from direction and control;

- all provide for independent judicial arms,[29] with extensive powers of judicial review and to interpret and apply the constitutions;[30]

- all provide for constitutional offices with roles concerning accountability of the main arms of government (especially of the executive) and that are independent from direction and control, the constitutions of Fiji Islands and Papua New Guinea containing especially elaborate arrangements in this regard.[31]

As for human rights, the four constitutions contain elaborate bills of rights that guarantee protection of the standard political rights[32] and enforcement in case of breach of rights.[33] In addition, the constitutions of Papua New Guinea and Fiji Islands are unusual in that they make provision directed to securing some aspects of economic, social and cultural rights, although those provisions are limited in extent in Fiji Islands and largely unenforceable in Papua New Guinea.[34]

Rules Versus 'Living Reality'

It is clear then, that de Smith's 'formal sense' of constitutionalism is well established in Melanesia. But what of the 'living reality'? Do rules limiting government action really curb the actions of the rulers? Are the zones of activity forbidden to those in power leaving increasing room for the exercise of liberty in Melanesian states?

The post-independence record of adherence to constitutional limits by the Melanesian states contrasts favourably with Ghai's 1993 assessment of the Third World generally. Not only did just a handful of post-colonial states retain their independence constitutions,[35] but in addition:

> Overwhelming evidence of the gross violations of law on the part of government officials; arbitrary and capricious exercises of power are frequent; there are many detentions without trial (and occasionally torture of detainees); massive direct or indirect censorship is obtained and it is difficult to exercise the right of association if the government does not like the officials or the purposes of the association; succession to office is seldom the result of elections; judiciaries are weak and some are compliant. One person or one party rule dominates the political system of most of these countries.[36]

A starting point for contrasting the situation in the Melanesian states is that all save Fiji Islands retain their independence constitutions. The picture with regard to democratic rule is also different, there being no instance of sustained one person or one party rule. Further, where coups have occurred (Fiji Islands in 1987 and 2000, and Solomon Islands in 2000) there have been popular pressures for restoration of constitutional rule and the holding of elections.

In relation to rules on succession of government, until the 1987 coups in Fiji Islands the record was remarkable compared to most other post-colonial states (and hence the early 1980s suggestion of new hope for constitutionalism on the basis of experience in the then ten post-colonial states of the Pacific).[37] Provisions for accountability generally operated reasonably well, especially in Papua New Guinea, where the Ombudsman Commission and the Leadership Code were generally regarded as having achieved much.[38] The position concerning human rights was well regarded in all states until the late 1980s.[39]

It would appear, however, that if there ever was a ready acceptance of constitutional limits in Melanesia it has been reducing since at least the late 1980s. The evidence includes the overthrow of the independence constitution in Fiji Islands in 1987, the attempted overthrow of the 1997 Fiji Islands *Constitution* in 2000, and the severe undermining of the Solomon Islands *Constitution* by and following the 2000 coup.[40] Each of these cases has involved attempts to take control of the state in large part related to ethnic conflict.

Rules on succession of government have been challenged in various ways, most notably in the Fiji Islands and Solomon Islands coups. In Papua New Guinea there has been: an inept coup attempt by the Police Commissioner in 1990; the attempted manipulation of constitutional provisions by the Prime Minister in 1993 in order to gain 18 months in office free from motions of no confidence;[41] the adjournment of Parliament for periods of seven to eight months in order to escape motions of no confidence (the Skate Government from December 1998 to July 1999 and the Morauta Government from November 2000 to July 2001); and the standing aside of the Prime Minister in April 1997 forced by urban unrest following the Sandline affair.[42] In Vanuatu in 1995 and in 2001 the constitutional rules on succession have been bent or ignored by members of Parliament until court decisions have resolved the problems.[43]

Even adherence to rules on succession of government prior to 1987 may not tell us much about the effectiveness of constitutional limits generally. Indeed, as discussed later, the more likely explanation is that managed competition for power within the constitutional framework suits the political and economic interests of the segments of the elite competing for political power.

Concerning the rules on accountability of government, their impact seems to be reducing as corruption in government and bureaucracy increases. The reports of the Vanuatu Ombudsman and the Papua New Guinea Ombudsman Commission and the decisions of leadership tribunals in Papua New Guinea dealing with prosecutions for misconduct in office by leaders provide powerful support for the proposition that state powers and resources are increasingly being used almost routinely for the personal enrichment of those with access to state power.[44] There seems little doubt that only a fraction of those involved in such activities are ever dealt with under the criminal law and the Leadership Codes. Those cases that do get dealt with suggest generalised patterns of abuse of office, from misappropriation of government funds to the soliciting of bribes and favours from interests seeking to extract natural resources wealth. There is increasing pressure on ombudsmen (for example, constant public criticism of the Papua New Guinea Ombudsman Commission suggesting it is too harsh in dealing with political leaders under the Papua New Guinea Leadership Code) and other accountability institutions, some of which have achieved little,[45] and a growing sense that the standards they seek to enforce are not consistent with those of a large proportion of public office-holders.

As for the record concerning human rights, there had been a generally poor human rights record in the colonial period in Melanesia, and much interest in changing this situation at the time of the de-colonising constitution-making exercises. For much of the post-independence period Melanesian countries have had a good record of respect for most civil and political rights. Since the late 1980s, however, there has been increasing evidence of a reduction in standards. The post-coup situation in Fiji Islands both in 1987 and 2000 has given rise to many abuses of rights.[46] In the Bougainville conflict in Papua New Guinea terrible abuses have occurred on all sides, including hundreds of extra-judicial killings, torture, rape and destruction of property.[47] The ethnic conflict occurring in Solomon Islands since late 1998 has resulted in appalling breaches of rights.

The situation in Papua New Guinea is of special concern, going well beyond the problems of the Bougainville conflict. A few examples drawn from a July 1995 report on Papua New Guinea by the United Nations Centre for Human Rights (UNCHR) illustrate the nature and scope of the problems. Police beatings and rapes of persons held in connection with investigation of criminal offences and their violent raids on villages in search of suspects, evidence and retribution were noted. Common violations of rights of prisoners by personnel of the Correctional Institutions Service included severe overcrowding, and routine rough treatment and confiscation of belongings.[48] The institutions that could have been expected to redress human rights abuses (the legal profession, the Public Solicitor, the Public Prosecutor, the Ombudsman Commission and the courts) had had a limited impact on human rights problems, not a single case relating to breaches of human rights arising from the Bougainville conflict having been conducted to completion.[49]

Additional, seldom highlighted but yet important facets of the human rights picture in the region were identified by the UNCHR report. First, it suggested that the severe law and order problems in Papua New Guinea involve violations of "the most fundamental rights of people — to life, to liberty and to security of the person".[50] Secondly, the right of citizens to equality was seen as "far from being a living reality, and there is no real evidence of, or apparent support for affirmative action", despite "severe and growing disparities among various social groups, and between various areas of the country". The "social, economic and political disadvantages" of women and the "widespread evidence of violence" against them suggested they suffered particular problems in this regard.[51] Thirdly, there was a "general failure to secure economic, social and cultural rights", suggesting "a failure of policies or of management or both".[52] Although they are intended to be to some degree enforceable through the National Goals and Directive Principles in the Preamble to the Papua New Guinea *Constitution*, there was little evidence of post-independence progress towards making those rights effective.[53]

While there is evidence of reducing acceptance of constitutional limits since the late 1980s, the record in Melanesia since then has been mixed. For example, even in the post-coup situations in Fiji Islands and Solomon Islands there have been serious attempts to restore constitutional rule. This is most notable in Fiji Islands, where court rulings early in 2001 on the continued applicability of the 1997 *Constitution* were accepted by the interim government installed after the coup of May 2000 in that instead of continuing to develop a new constitution, fresh elections were conducted under the 1997 *Constitution* as a result of the rulings.[54] Courts have resolved crises or conflicts on the succession rules in Papua New Guinea and Solomon Islands.[55] The fact that ombudsman institutions, public prosecutors and courts continue to take action in support of accountability offers hope to many concerned about the trends. Despite growing human rights problems, abuses by the state probably continue to be less serious and fewer in number than in many other post-colonial states, and are still capable of being dealt with under the law by independent courts, at least in Papua New Guinea, Vanuatu and Fiji Islands (although access problems remain severe).

For the purposes of this chapter, two major questions arise from this assessment of the record of constitutional limits in Melanesia. First, why has the record of constitutionalism in the Pacific apparently been relatively better than that of so many other post-colonial states, and especially, until recently, in relation to succession of government? Secondly, why has the effectiveness of restraints on state action apparently reduced since the late 1980s?

Insights into these questions may be gained by considering the factors that influence the roles of constitutions in both the industrialised 'democracies' and post-colonial states. In the space available, only a selective analysis is possible, highlighting just a few salient factors.

SOME FACTORS INFLUENCING EFFECTIVENESS OF CONSTITUTIONAL LIMITS

At the time of independence in most post-colonial states, there was a tendency to assume that the passing of constitutions on the model of those of the colonial powers would produce outcomes similar to those generally assumed to flow from the constitutions of the metropolitan powers.[56] In other words, it tends to be assumed that the 'living reality' of constitutionalism automatically flows from the formal rules set out in a constitution.

In fact, however, there is little consensus about what it is that makes the rule of law apparently a strong force in Western industrialised countries,[57] or what makes its effectiveness lesser in so many post-colonial countries. Most theories of both politics and law would now accept that the totality of the impacts of law in any society is likely to be a factor of the relationship between law and numerous forces at work in the society where it operates. The differing consequences of constitutions in post-colonial societies compared to the colonising countries suggest that there are distinct forces at work in the two sets of countries. Those that support the rule of law in the former colonisers may not be present, or may work differently, in post-colonial states. Similarly, the record of better adherence to constitutional norms in the Melanesian states than in many other post-colonial states suggests that again there are different forces at work in the two sets of states.

Ghai argues that it is the coinciding of economic and political power in the 'West' that makes the rule of law possible there. The constitution supports the forces that dominate in civil society, especially those with economic power. Because they can achieve their economic and other interests through a wide range of means, they do not have to rely openly on political or state power; the coercive power of the state seldom needs to be deployed on their behalf. Hence the outward forms of state neutrality and impartiality in accordance with constitutional and legal norms (for example, in the shape of an apparently neutral and impartial judicial system) can be preserved.[58]

By contrast, where economic and political power do not coincide in the same way as in the West, and especially in countries where the private sector is relatively 'undeveloped', as has been the situation in most former colonies both at and after independence, politicians have little independent economic base. They instead tend to use their access to the state to accumulate both wealth and the further power associated with it. Corruption flows from both personal interests of politicians and "the imperatives of political survival, since the primary basis of a politician's support is generally not the party or another political platform, but clientelism, sustained by regular favours to one's followers".[59] Popular control and accountability tend to be contrary to the fundamental interests of those in control of the state, and opposition can only be dealt with by coercion, the state tending to become authoritarian.

This analysis tells us much about the factors underlying the different roles of law in industrial and post-colonial states. It also provides us with insights into the reasons for the declining adherence to rules about accountability and human rights in Melanesia, suggesting that there are some important similarities between the forces at work in the Pacific and other post-colonial states. The analysis does not address, however, the reasons for the apparently better record of constitutionalism in Melanesia than, for example, in much of Africa. Comparing the operation of constitutions in Africa and Melanesia should provide some insights in this regard.

The State and the Constitution in Africa

Much of the vast literature on the state in Africa argues that while the state is immensely powerful compared to any other single force in society, it is also relatively weak. So although it dominates aspects of the economy and controls considerable coercive force, it has a limited impact on the lives of the majority who are rural dwellers. Such people organise their lives through rapidly adapting but nevertheless resilient pre-state social structures with considerable autonomy from the state.

On the other hand, among the few 'uniting' factors beyond clan and tribe in many African countries are major ethnic/regional and religious identities. Sections of the elite have tended to mobilise people around such identities in struggles for state power. They have exploited fears as to what will happen if 'representatives' of another group gain, or are not removed from, power. In the process, existing divisions have often been exacerbated and new ones created. There have been few pressures on the elite to stay within constitutional frameworks in their competition for state power. In deeply divided countries, there has been strong pressure for the section of the elite in control of the state to use any means at hand to retain power. Such measures have included seeking control of an expanding repressive apparatus of the state (intelligence services and security forces).

In the 1960s and 1970s such tendencies were often bolstered by state ideologies of development, which emphasised the need for stability. Super-power competition provided financial resources and legitimacy to weak regimes, and often contributed to development and increased capacity of repressive apparatus. Patronage and subsidies (for example, of urban food prices) were used to shore up support from client groups and to reduce the likelihood of potentially destabilising urban dissent.

Constitutions became little more than legitimating devices in many countries. They were ignored, overthrown or replaced where they were obstacles to the accumulation of power and wealth by those in control. Abuses of rights on an appalling scale occurred in the struggles for power between sections of the elite.

The State and the Constitution in Melanesia

There are parallels between the situations in Melanesia and Africa, especially concerning the prevalence of the weak state and strong localised society based on resilient pre-state social structures. In Melanesia, however, the state is perhaps even weaker than in Africa, due to factors such as the limited sustainable capacity developed during the colonial era, as well as others, discussed below, which inhibit co-ordination of both policy and agencies of the state.

Linguistic, cultural and ethnic groups in Melanesia tend to be both small and multiple. These factors help to explain the absence of attempts on behalf of any ethnic group to control the state in the post-independence period prior to the 1987 coups in Fiji Islands. Of course, the large Indo-Fijian population in Fiji Islands enabled observers to treat that situation as an exceptional case in the Pacific. However, the increasing complexity and intensity of divisions among indigenous Fijians, the ethnic element in the conflict in Bougainville since 1988,[60] and the development of significant ethnic conflict in Solomon Islands since 1998 all point to the potential for ethnic tensions to become central to struggles for control of the state in Melanesia in a manner similar to Africa.

It is the absence of significant ethnic divides in national politics anywhere other than Fiji Islands that is the basic explanation for the good record of Melanesia (before the Solomon Islands coup of June 2000) in relation to adherence to rules on succession of government. Where such divides do not exist there is room for political competition between a wide range of sections of the elite. None is either subject to strong pressure to take exclusive control of the state or capable of doing so if it wishes to. (They are all unable to capture control of the repressive apparatus by ethnic stacking of positions, as in Africa.) Without a cohesive force controlling the state, needing always to fend off or destabilise competing claims on power, the stakes of political competition are not nearly as high as in many cases in Africa.

In the absence of class and other interests which cut across the multiple and fractured clan interests, no political party or ideology promotes cohesive interests at the national level. The first-past-the-post electoral system also works against development of such interests. As a result, the state is controlled by ever-changing bands of sections of the elite. Unable to control the whole, each element of the band in government for the time being tends to attempt to extract what it can from whatever part of the state apparatus and resources it can get access to. The societies from which the politicians (and even senior) officials originate also tend to apply pressure to them to extract state resources on their behalf. In the process, the weakness of the state is reinforced, but a kind of equilibrium is maintained.

There is little capacity to develop a coherent policy or to integrate the operations of state agencies. Indeed, coherent policy or integrated operations could limit the ability to extract resources from the state. Accordingly each agency tends to operate with a great deal of independence. Prime ministers might like to assert control over all parts of the state apparatus but, having no means of enforcing discipline over their coalition partners, they have little capacity to control the state agencies under particular ministers.

As a result of such factors, all factions tend to accept the constitutional framework for managing political succession. More correctly, the constitution is accepted as the arena for management of elite competition. But acceptance of the arena does not reflect acceptance of all constitutional limits. As already discussed, there is evidence that the constitutional norms concerning accountability and human rights have limited acceptance. They tend to stand in the way of accumulation of wealth by those in power. Further, the limited cohesion and co-ordination of state agencies encourages, or at least puts few obstacles in the way of, breach of such norms.

Without co-ordination and constructive policy, the pressures of rapid social and economic change tend to produce crises that the state has little capacity to analyse or manage. Semi-autonomous state agencies have little capacity to analyse and deal with such crises, and their responses tend to be poorly judged, often exacerbating the original problems. Abuses of human rights tend to occur in such circumstances, not because the state desires them, but precisely because there is ineffective co-ordination and control of weak and under-resourced state agencies. The way in which the Bougainville conflict in Papua New Guinea escalated from late 1988 is the most obvious example of this pattern of response by the state. Poorly judged and undisciplined responses by police riot squads helped transform a localised landowner conflict to a province-wide rebellion. Harsh responses by the initially better disciplined Defence Force to Bougainville Revolutionary Army action added to the problem.[61]

It is also true, however, that the absence of pressure to take exclusive control on behalf of any ethnic or other interest means there is little focussed effort to use the coercive power of the state against particular opponents. Hence, human rights abuses by security forces have in most cases been less systematic and less severe than has often been the case in Africa. They are most often products of the random and uncoordinated actions by disjointed and poorly trained elements of the state apparatus, rather than of organised state action.

Consequently we can say that some constitutional limits are accepted by those in power whereas protection from the constitution is largely an irrelevance for the vast majority of the population — the rural dwellers and the urban poor.

This is not to say that constitutions have not played, and do not continue to play, a significant role in Melanesia generally. Independence mythology (the debate and stories about independence that have given special meaning and status to events of the time) combined with longevity have given them legitimacy and status that have enabled them to have a degree of autonomy and therefore to have some significant impacts.[62] Thus, for example, independent institutions created by constitutions with accountability functions benefit from the protection of the constitution (even if, in some cases, their positions have tended to be weakened as more elements of the elite find it in their interests to evade the restrictions of constitutional limits).

PARTICIPATION AND CIVIL SOCIETY: SUPPORT FOR CONSTITUTIONALISM?

In the light of the preceding analysis of factors which may help to determine the differing roles of law in various post-colonial societies, the extent to which support for the rule of law may be offered by popular participation and civil society can be examined more realistically.

Popular Participation

As already discussed, participation in government is widely regarded as contributing to constitutionalism. Its importance tends to be assumed in the industrialised 'democracies'. However, there is limited consensus on the factors which result in the rule of law being accepted in such countries. Further, there is little reason to believe that governmental arrangements for popular participation that might have particular results in such countries will necessarily have the same outcomes in post-colonial societies.

Debate in Africa from the early 1990s about the possible consequences of popular participation in government arises from moves away from the highly centralised one-party states that emerged in many countries in the 1960s. Popular participation even in the form of national elections either did not occur at all or was tightly controlled. There was almost no experience of elected sub-national government of any kind. The question is whether the experience of multi-party elections and political decentralisation helps to restrict executive action.

In fact what can only be described as tentative moves towards democratisation in Africa since the late 1980s were sparked not so much by popular pressures as by the impact of several closely related factors. These were the end of the Cold War, the general fiscal crisis facing most states and the ascendancy of a global economy. With the Cold War over, the global economy reduced the significance of national borders for the flow of capital. Grossly unfair patterns of world trade and poor domestic management contributed to the fiscal crisis of the state, itself exacerbated by cessation of the Cold War super-power competition that had subsidised authoritarian but otherwise poorly managed and unsustainable regimes. Forced to turn to international financial institutions, African governments had little choice but to meet the conditions attached to aid informed by a new orthodoxy about good governance and a reduced role for the state being pre-conditions for economic development. The possibilities for state patronage and subsidies reduced as the size of the public sector shrank rapidly. Loyalty of security force members was often undermined by lack of pay. Urban dissent emerged.

Governments no longer capable of crushing or buying off dissent called national constitutional conventions (or were forced to accept them), or amended constitutions or were overthrown. A few — such as Zaire and Kenya — initially resisted change, but at the cost of interminable chaos. The result was a wave of 'democratisation'. It is far from certain, however, that the long-term outcomes will include effective constitutional limits on those in power.

A survey of popular protest and political reform in African countries after the Berlin Wall fell found little evidence of emergence of effective forces "aggregated across the full breadth of civil society". Based in the urban bourgeoisie, protest sought to "protect corporate privilege", being "a conservative reaction against economic austerity. The opportunism of opposition political leaders, their patronage followings, and their links with current elites all suggest that a change of leadership would probably perpetuate a clientilistic pattern of 'politics as usual'".[63]

When the dust of popular protest had settled new elite groups had taken control under multi-party political systems introduced by constitutional amendment (as in Zambia, Malawi and Tanzania) or under new constitutions, as in several francophone countries (Senegal, Mali etc.). Astute managers of reform, such as President Moi of

Kenya, managed the transition. Exploiting differences in the opposition he was returned to power in the first — and flawed — multi-party election in almost 30 years and thereafter continued to rule in much the same dictatorial manner as before under the new and supposedly democratic system.

Concerning popular participation in government in Melanesia there is limited evidence that the operation of the parliamentary democracy at the national level counters the pressures towards abuse of rules on accountability and human rights, as discussed already. Regular national elections in Westminster system variants have produced national legislative and executive institutions that tend to be unaccountable to the electors. Contributing to the outcome have been the lack of effective political parties, the first-past-the-post electoral system, small traditional societies (clans and sub-clans), the continuing strength of clan loyalties and the lack of class and other interests which cut across them.[64] There was some evidence that the provincial government system operating in Papua New Guinea until 1995 did have an impact in terms of acting as a check on power at the centre.[65] However, the reforms of the system in 1995 provided for in amendments to the *Constitution* and the *Organic Law on Provincial and Local-level Governments* 1995 has given members of the national legislature control of provincial governments. There is little evidence of sub-national governments elsewhere in Melanesia being effective checks on the national government.[66]

Civil Society

In like manner to the debate on democratisation, the lack of clarity in debate on civil society in industrialised countries has not prevented many assuming that emergence in post-colonial countries of a 'developed' civil society on the model of the former countries will necessarily result in support for constitutional limits on the state. Yet the evidence for the emergence of such a civil society in post-colonial countries is far from clear, and the role of civil society in such countries remains problematic.

The evidence for civil society in Africa is supposedly seen in the largely urban-based social unrest that has contributed to the fall or destabilisation of some one-party regimes since the late 1980s. The dominant notion of civil society in this discourse has been described as:

> ...civic organisations of professionals, workers, women and others which not only lobby the State but also seek to humanise society. A particular species of them, the NGOs, have achieved prominence in recent years, seen as champions of rights and democracy, and giving voice to the underprivileged.[67]

This notion is in the tradition of civil society in the model of the industrialised 'democracies', of associations which shape public opinion and establish norms affecting the way the state operates. As discussed already, there are supposed to be links between civil society and popular participation, especially through sub-national government.[68]

Many observers (including foreign donors — both foreign governments and aid organisations) of post-colonial states in Africa and elsewhere tend to believe that encouragement of local level NGOs and local level governments will not only assist in controlling the executive, but may also contribute to maintaining and restoring basic order in developing states where economic and other pressures are tending to undermine "the basic structures of nation states".[69]

Key strands of thought about the evidence for the emergence of civil society in post-colonial states can be criticised. First, as to social unrest since the late 1980s, rather than evidence of civil society, it may be better understood as a conservative reaction to economic austerity.[70] Secondly as to the role of NGOs, there is a need for caution in assessing their potential role, "as they proliferate under encouragement of or incentives from foreign donors, operate increasingly as consulting firms, and lose touch with, or accountability to, in local constituencies".[71] Thirdly, as to the role of local government in strengthening civil society, there is little experience of long-term political decentralisation in Africa. Deconcentration of administrative capacity — 'administrative decentralisation' — rather than political decentralisation has been the pattern since the end of the colonial era. In the Pacific and elsewhere in post-colonial countries, the uneven experience of political decentralisation[72] suggests the need for care in making assumptions about sustainability and outcomes of political decentralisation.

Little is understood about the way in which civil society might develop to the point where it supports constitutionalism in a significant way in either Africa or the Pacific. If, as Woods argues, the principal indicator of a 'developed' civil society is the manner in which individuals and groups "articulate a set of norms which effect the way the state functions and how other groups will interact",[73] then civil society in Africa "is still threatened by the particularism of ethnicity and atomistic actions".[74] The "relatively unarticulated character of economic differentiation on the continent" is a significant factor, for while the economic base "does not determine whether a civil society exists... it does influence the rate and manner in which class interests will intersect with normative claims in the Western European tradition".[75] In other words, in the absence of the economic conditions of Europe, civil society will probably not limit state action in the same way it may do in Europe.

Even Woods' interesting analysis tends to assume that the goal for African civil society is something on the model of Western Europe. The views of Woods and commentators with similar analyses have been criticised by Kasfir. He points out that most notions of civil society in Africa are based too much on idealised Western experience, do not incorporate much of the rich web of political activity which goes on in Africa, and are unrealistic about the extent of the problems likely to be involved in developing civil society organisations to the point where they are powerful enough to act as limits on the state. In Kasfir's view, it is not possible to exclude ethnic or religious associations from civil society. Such associations, if strong and democratically based, could in fact weaken the state, undermining its ability to reconcile conflicting interests in society.[76]

If civil society is to become more important in Africa or the Pacific, factors such as ethnic divisions, the limited economic base, the limited linkages between traditional society and the modern economy[77] and the still relatively pervasive role of the state, will tend to shape distinctive African and Pacific island forms of civil society. These may also work in different ways and have quite distinct consequences from civil society in Western Europe.

In particular, civil society in Africa and the Pacific may not necessarily limit state power on the model of civil society in the 'developed' world. Experience in Asia should warn against what Ghai terms "over-romanticisation of civil society", for it is not only the state that abuses human rights:

> ...massive violations also take place in and through civil society, sometimes with the connivance of the state, and frequently reflecting feudalistic and patriarchal dimensions of culture. Social conflicts, particularly those stemming from ethnic or caste differences, have politicised and militarised civil society in many states.[78]

There is, of course, civil society in Melanesia. But with the exception of Fiji Islands, the vast majority of the population in Melanesia live in rural areas and in pre-state social structures with limited engagement with the modern state. As a result, there is little in society to make it meet the criteria of 'civil' society. Society has limited cohesion, little which aggregates multifarious local interests in a way that can influence the state. Even in the few large urban centres, there is limited aggregation of interests. There are media organisations, trade unions, NGOs and — especially — churches, all of which seek to influence the state, but each on their own has a limited impact, and their concerns seldom coincide. These characteristics of civil society help to explain the lack of fulfilment of the hopes of some Papua New Guinea observers that the March 1997 popular protests against the Chan Government's role in Sandline signalled the emergence of civil society as a powerful force in Melanesia.

The emergence of a 'developed' civil society in Melanesia may occur at the expense of traditional society, for it would be likely to involve development of such things as class and other interests which cut across clan loyalties. On the other hand, growing social pressures arising from overlapping factors such as economic change associated with globalisation, increasing social stratification, land shortages, law and order problems are resulting in increased popular dissatisfaction being expressed in government. The popular protests associated with Sandline provide an example from PNG. As dissatisfaction spreads more widely it will probably tend to be mobilised by populist leaders. Depending on the leadership, the basis might be laid for emergence of new political forces. In the process, aggregations of interests powerful enough to influence the state may occur. There are, however, many possible alternative futures. For example, the struggles for power and control of resources likely to be involved could contribute to emergence of new ethnic identities. As in Fiji Islands and Solomon Islands, these may be manipulated in the course of such struggles and ultimately contribute to undermining of constitutional rule as in both of those countries or at least undermine the ability of the state to reconcile conflicting interests in society.[79]

CONCLUSIONS

The constitutions of Melanesia are impressive examples of the 'formal sense' of constitutionalism. While the record of the 'living reality' of constitutionalism may be less remarkable, it nevertheless compares more than favourably with that of much of the rest of the post-colonial world. While there may be some evidence of commitment to constitutionalism in Melanesia in the immediate post-colonial era, the analysis in this chapter would suggest that such commitment was always limited. In particular, the apparent commitment to constitutional rules of succession suited the interests of sections of the elite. Moreover, such rules are readily jettisoned, particularly as significant ethnic conflict becomes a factor in national politics. The effectiveness of rules on accountability and human rights also appears to be waning.

Just as it was assumed at the time of de-colonisation — in the Pacific as much as in other parts of the world — that the rule of law would be a consequence of acceptance of 'Western' constitutional models, there is a similar tendency to assume the efficacy of the model of the 'West' in the debates about the ability of popular participation and civil society to support constitutionalism in post-colonial states. There is little evidence, however, to suggest that the popular participation provided for under the post-independence Melanesian constitutions has had a significant impact on constitutionalism there, and little evidence so far for significant impact in that regard from a Melanesian civil society.

It seems likely that the particular political and economic forces at work in Europe in the last few hundred years were critical to the emergence of constitutionalism. If civil society is in fact a major factor in maintaining constitutionalism in the West, it is important to remember that it was probably a product of much the same economic and political forces as contributed to constitutionalism. Those forces do not exist in Melanesia. In particular, there is no developed private sector. Nor is there the same set of nationalising pressures as existed in Europe, and which contributed to the notion of nationalisation of power (one of the "constituent elements" of constitutionalism identified by Ghai).[80] Rather, in Melanesia, small pre-state structures with their own norms are the primary sources of identity and the main centre of loyalties of most individuals, often undercutting national identity and support for the state.[81] With such different political and economic forces at work, it is most unlikely that either constitutionalism or civil society will develop in the same way in the Melanesian countries as they have in the West.

The reasonably positive record of acceptance of constitutional limits in Melanesia up until the late 1980s can be related to particular factors in the post-independence situations, and especially the limited competition for control of the state by large ethnic and other interests. On the other hand, the same factors have contributed to the longevity of independence constitutions, thereby increasing their legitimacy and autonomy. These qualities have probably been factors in the popular pressure for return to constitutional order in post-coup situations, especially in Fiji Islands. It is also, in part, a response to expressions of concern from the international community, something that is likely to become an increasingly important factor in support for constitutionalism in post-colonial states. All of these factors can be expected to continue to operate, although developments since the 1980s suggest that their impact will not necessarily be enough to change existing trends towards a weakening of constitutionalism.

This is not to say that constitutionalism is a dead issue in Melanesia. Nor should it be concluded that there is no role at all for increased participation in government or for civil society in enhancing constitutionalism. Rather, the point is that they — and indeed constitutions generally — can be expected to operate differently from their equivalents in the West. Despite the absence of the same conditions that contributed to the development of both civil society and constitutionalism in the West, people in Melanesia can nevertheless be expected to find their own paths to constitutionalism. After all, they, like people everywhere, have a deep interest in ensuring that there are limits on those with access to state power.

Finally, not only can it be expected that the paths to constitutionalism will take account of the particular situation of each Melanesian state, but the process could also be slow and gradual. If constitutionalism in Europe was a slowly developing product of complex political and economic forces, much the same will probably be true if it is to become more of a 'living reality' in the Melanesian states.

ENDNOTES

1 Fry, G. 1983. Succession of Government in the Post-colonial States of the South Pacific: New Support for Constitutionalism? *Politics* 18:48–60.

2 Ghai, Y.P. 1993. The Theory of the State in the Third World and the Problematics of Constitutionalism. In Greenberg, D. Katz, S.N. & Oliviero, M.B. (eds). *Constitutionalism and Democracy: Transitions in the Contemporary World*. New York: Oxford University Press, 186–96 at 188.

3 DeSmith, S.A. 1962. Constitutionalism in the Commonwealth Today. *Malaya Law Review* 4(2):205–20, at 205.

4 DeSmith, S.A. 1962. Above, n 3.

5 Ghai, Y.P. 1993. Above, n 2.

6 Ghai, Y.P. 1993. Above, n 2.

7 See, for example, Hague, R. Harrop, M. and Breslin, S. 1998. *Comparative Government and Politics: An Introduction Fourth Edition*. London: MacMillan, chs 5–10.

8 Diamond, L. 1994. Rethinking Civil Society: Towards Democratic Consolidation. *Journal of Democracy* 5(3):4–17. For an example of discussion of the connections between popular participation through decentralisation and the development of civil society in Africa (in this case, Uganda) in the 1990s see Regan, A.J. 1998. Decentralization Policy: Reshaping State and Society. In Hansen, H.B. and Twaddle, M. (eds.) *Developing Uganda*. Oxford: James Currey.

9 Constitutional Planning Committee. 1974. <u>Final Report of the Constitutional Planning Committee 1974: Part I.</u> Port Moresby: Papua New Guinea Government Printer.

10 See analysis of the CPC views in Ghai, Y.P. and Regan, A.J. 1992. *The Law, Politics and Administration of Decentralisation in Papua New Guinea*. Monograph 30. Port Moresby: Papua New Guinea Research Institute at p 11, and pp 49–53. For a discussion of decentralisation as an issue during constitution making in other Melanesian states, see Ghai, Y.P. 1988. Constitution Making and Decolonisation. In Y.P. Ghai (ed.) *Law, Politics and Government in the Pacific Island States*. Suva: Institute of Pacific Studies University of the South Pacific at pp 30–32.

11 Woods, D. 1992. Civil Society in Europe and Africa: Limiting State Power Through a Public Sphere. *African Studies Review* 35(2): 77–100. Criticisms of aspects of Woods' analysis by Nelson Kasfir are discussed later (Kasfir, N. 1998. Civil Society, the State and Democracy in Africa. *Commonwealth and Comparative Politics* 36(2).)

12 Personal and discretionary rule, as opposed to rule based on legal-rational norms that limit the ruler's powers.

13 Woods, D. 1992. Above, n 11 at pp 78–79.

14 Woods, D. 1992. Above, n 11 at p 84.

15 Woods, D. 1992. Above, n 11 at p 97.

16 See above, Diamond, L. 1994. At pp.8–9.

17 For a discussion of links between decentralisation policy and the development of civil society in Uganda, see Regan, A.J. 1998. Above, n 8.

18 For detailed discussion of the Sandline affair and its aftermath, see Dinnen, S., May, R.and Regan, A.J. (eds) 1997. *Challenging the State: The Sandline Affair in Papua New Guinea.* Canberra: Research School of Pacific and Asian Studies, The Australian National University; Dorney, S. 1998. *The Sandline Affair: Politics and Mercenaries and the Bougainville Crisis.* Sydney: ABC Books; Ivarature, H. 1998. The Sandline International Controversy in Papua New Guinea. In P. Larmour (ed.) *Governance and Reform in the South Pacific.* Canberra: The Australian National University, NCDS and SSGM; O'Callaghan, M.L. 1999. *Enemies Within: Papua New Guinea, Australia, and the Sandline Crisis: the Inside Story.* Sydney: Doubleday.

19 *Constitution of the Independent State of Papua New Guinea* s 142; *Constitution of Solomon Islands* s 33 and Sch 2; *Constitution of Vanuatu* art 39 and Sch 2.

20 *Constitution of the Republic of Fiji Islands* 1997 s 98.

21 *Constitution of the Republic of Fiji Islands* 1997 ss 107–9; *Constitution of the Independent State of Papua New Guinea* s 145; *Constitution of Solomon Islands* s 34; *Constitution of the Republic of Vanuatu* art 41 (hereafter *Fiji, Papua New Guinea, Solomon Islands,* and *Vanuatu*).

22 *Fiji* ss 98 and 107–9; *Papua New Guinea* s 141; *Solomon Islands* s 34; *Vanuatu* art 41.

23 See above, n 21.

24 *Fiji* ss 175–182; *Papua New Guinea* ss 209–216; *Solomon Islands* ss 100–109; *Vanuatu* art 23.

25 *Papua New Guinea* ss 118–123; *Vanuatu* art 21.

26 *Fiji* ss 156–165; *Papua New Guinea* ss 26–28 and 217–220; *Solomon Islands* ss 93–98; *Vanuatu* arts 59–66.

27 *Fiji* ss 166–8; *Papua New Guinea* ss 213–4; *Solomon Islands* s 108; *Vanuatu* art 23.

28 *Fiji* s 114; *Papua New Guinea* ss 176–7; *Solomon Islands* s 91; *Vanuatu* art 53.

29 *Fiji* ss 117–139; *Papua New Guinea* ss 168–183; *Solomon Islands* ss 77–88 ; *Vanuatu* arts 45–7.

30 *Fiji* ss 2, 120(4) & 128; *Papua New Guinea* ss 18–24; *Solomon Islands* s 83; *Vanuatu* art 51.

31 *Fiji* ss 169–173; *Papua New Guinea* ss 221–225. For a discussion of the Papua New Guinea provisions, see Regan, A.J. 2001 Protection of Independence of Constitutional Office-holders in Regan, A.J. Jessep, O. and Kwa, E. (eds) *Twenty Years of the Papua New Guinea Constitution.* Sydney: Law Book Co.

32 *Fiji* ss 21–38 & 40; *Papua New Guinea* ss 32–56; *Solomon Islands* ss 3–15; *Vanuatu* art 5.

33 *Fiji* ss 41–43; *Papua New Guinea* ss 57–8; *Solomon Islands* ss 17–18; *Vanuatu* art 6.

34 *Fiji* ss 39 & 44; *Papua New Guinea* s 25.

35 Ghai, Y.P. 1993. Above, n 2 at p 190.

36 Ghai, Y.P. 1993. Above, n 2 at p 187.

37 Fry, G. 1983. Above, n 1.

38 Canning D. 2001. The Ombudsman Commission; and Toop, G. 2001. The Leadership Code; both in Regan, A.J. Jessep, O. and Kwa, E. (eds). *Twenty Years of the Papua New Guinea Constitution* Law Book Co: Sydney.

39 In the case of Papua New Guinea, for example, compare the assessment for 1979 made by the United States Department of State for the US Congress (Department of State. 1980. Papua New Guinea. In *Country Reports on Human Rights Practices for 1979*, US Government Printing Office: Washington) with that for 1999 (website www://dosfan.lib.uic.edu:70/00ftp%3A...%20Pacific%3Apapua_New_Guinea_%2832k%29 accessed 24/11/2000).

40 For discussion of the coups of 2000 in Fiji Islands and Solomon Islands, see Fry, G. 2000. Political Legitimacy and the Post-colonial State in the Pacific: Reflections on Some Common Threads in the Fiji and Solomon Island Coups. *Pacifica Review* 12(3):295–304.

41 The manner in which the then Prime Minister sought to remain in office was the subject of strong criticism by the Supreme Court see the decision which overruled the vote of the Parliament which installed the Prime Minister for the eighteen month period. In *Haiveta v. Wingti and Ors (no.3)* [1994] PNGLR 197.

42 See above, n 18.

43 Ambrose, D. 1996. A Coup that Failed? Recent Political Events in Vanuatu. *State, Society and Governance in Melanesia Discussion Paper 96/3*. Canberra: The Australian National University; Bohane, B. 2001. New Vanuatu Government Hanging by a Thread. *Sydney Morning Herald*. 18th April 2001 p 8.

44 Crossland, K.J. 2000. The Ombudsman Role: Vanuatu's Experiment. *State, Society and Governance in Melanesia Discussion Paper 00/5*. Canberra: The Australian National University. See also Toop, G. 2001. Above, n 38. For discussion of aspects of corruption in the Pacific, see Larmour, P. 1997. Corruption and Governance in the South Pacific. *State, Society and Governance in Melanesia Discussion Paper 97/5*. Canberra: The Australian National University.

45 An assessment made for the Asian Development Bank of accountability in Solomon Islands summarised the record of the Solomon Islands Ombudsman and Leadership Code Commission as having tended "to act on behalf of public servants, and political leaders, rather than as a means of making them accountable to the public" Larmour, P. 2000. Issues and mechanisms of Accountability: Examples from Solomon Islands. *State, Society and Governance in Melanesia Discussion Paper 00/1*. Canberra: The Australian National University at p 13.

46 Information on specific human rights abuses related to the 2000 coup can be found on the Amnesty International website at http://web.amnesty.org/ai.nsf/countries/fiji (Accessed 27/11/01) and in the U.S. Department of State Human Rights Report 2000, http://www.humanrights-usa.net/reports/fiji.html (Accessed 27/1//01) Both sites also contain more general information on human rights abuses during the 1987 coups.

47 DeGedare, D. 2000. Human Rights Violations in Papua New Guinea and Bougainville, 1989–1997. In Rynkiewich, M.A. and Seib, R. (eds) Politics in Papua New Guinea: Continuities, Changes and Challenges Point No.24. Goroka: The Melanesian Institute.

48 UNCHR. 1995. <u>United Nations Centre for Human Rights Technical Cooperation Programme. Report of a Needs Assessment Mission to Papua New Guinea 28th May–6 June 1995</u> at pp 12–16.

49 UNCHR. 1995. Above, n 48 at pp 18–20.

50 UNCHR. 1995. Above, n 48 at p 14.

51 UNCHR. 1995. Above, n 48 at p 14.

52 UNCHR. 1995. Above, n 48 at p 14.

53 UNCHR. 1995. Above, n 48 at p 14.

54 See *Republic of Fiji v Prasad* (Court of Appeal of Fiji, Civil Appeal No. ABU0078/20005 1 March 2001) and *Prasad v Republic of Fiji* [2001] NZAR 21. These decisions are analysed in Williams, G. 2001. The Case that Stopped a Coup? The Rule of Law and Constitutionalism in Fiji. *Oxford University Commonwealth Law Journal* 73–93. The Journal of South Pacific Law Special Interest Section "Fiji Islands Crisis 2000–2001" contains various judgments and comments on this topic. http://www.vanuatu.usp.ac.fj/journal_splaw/Special_Interest/ Fiji_2000/Fiji_Main.html (Accessed 29/11/01)

55 In Papua New Guinea, see, for example, *Haiveta v Wingti* (No.1) [1994] PNGLR 160, and *Haiveta v Wingti* (No.3) [1994] PNGLR 197. In Solomon Islands, see, for example, *Ulufa'alu v Attorney-General and ors*, Unreported, High Court of Solomon Islands, HC-CC No.195 of 2000, Nov 2001.

56 This tendency continues. While working as a constitutional adviser to the Government of Uganda in the early 1990s, I listened to a succession of visiting experts extol the virtues of the United States Constitution. The clear implication was that a presidential executive, a short constitution, federal arrangements and so on would all produce results in Uganda similar to those the US Constitution was believed to have produced for the US.

57 The record of such countries is, of course, far from uniform. Not only have there been coups and extremely authoritarian governments in various European countries, continuing into the 1970s, but human rights abuses on the part of the state occur in all countries.

58 Ghai, Y.P. 1993. Above, n 2 at p 189. For a discussion of such issues in the Pacific context, see Ghai, Y.P. 2001. Establishing a Liberal Political Order Through a Constitution: The Papua New Guinea Experience. In Regan, A.J. Jessep, O. and Kwa, E. *Twenty Years of the Papua New Guinea Constitution*. Sydney: Law Book Co.

59 Ghai, Y.P. 2001. Above, n 58 at p 44.

60 See Ghai, Y.P. and Regan, A.J. 2000. Bougainville and the Dialectics of Ethnicity, Autonomy and Separation. In Ghai, Y.P. (ed.) *Autonomy and Ethnicity: Negotiating Competing Claims in Multi-ethnic States*. Cambridge: Cambridge University Press and the sources cited therein.

61 Regan, A.J. 1998. Current Developments in the Pacific: Causes and Course of the Bougainville Conflict. *The Journal of Pacific History* 33(3): 269–85.

62 In relation to the legitimacy of the Papua New Guinea *Constitution*, see Ghai, Y.P. 2001. Above, n 58.

63 Bratton, M. and van de Walle, N. 1992. Popular Protest and Political Reform in Africa. *Comparative Politics* 419–442 at p 440. See also Bratton, M. and van de Walle, N. 1997. *Democratic Experiments in Africa: Regime Transitions in Comparative Perspective*. Cambridge: Cambridge University Press.

64 For analysis of the issues in the Papua New Guinea context, see Ghai, Y.P. 2001. Above, n 58. and Regan, A.J. 1997. The Papua New Guinea Policy-making Environment as a Window on the Sandline Controversy. In Dinnen, S. May, R. and Regan, A.J. (eds.) *Challenging the State: The Sandline Affair in Papua New Guinea.* Canberra: Research School of Pacific and Asian Studies, The Australian National University.

65 Ghai, Y.P. and Regan, A.J. 1992. Above, n 10 at chapters 8 and 9.

66 Larmour, P. and Qalo, R. 1985. *Decentralisation in the South Pacific.* Suva: University of the South Pacific.

67 Ghai, Y.P. 1994. Human Rights and Governance: The Asia Debate. *The Australian Yearbook of International Law* 15:1–34 at p 32.

68 Diamond, L. 1994. Above, n 8 at pp 8–9.

69 See, for example, Kilby, P. 1994. Human Rights and Participatory Development: Stemming the rise of the "New Anarchy". *Development Bulletin* 32:20–22 at p 20.

70 Bratton, M. and van de Walle, N. 1992. Above, n 63.

71 Ghai, Y.P. 1994. Above, n 76 at p 32. In other words, they manifest at least the same degree of fragmentation and factionalism as the wider society in which they operate.

72 Rondinelli, D.A., Nellis, J.R. and Cheema, G.S. 1983. Decentralisation in Developing Countries: A Review of Recent Experience. *World Bank Staff Working Paper No. 581*: Washington; Larmour, P. and Qalo, R. 1985. Above, n 66; Ghai, Y.P. and Regan, A.J. 1992. Above, n 10; Regan, A.J. 1998. Above, n 8.

73 Woods, D. 1992. Above, n 11 at p 97.

74 Woods, D. 1992. Above, n 11 at p 97.

75 Woods, D. 1992. Above, n 11 at p 97.

76 Kasfir, N. 1998. Above, n 11 at pp 123–149.

77 Woods, D. 1992. Above, n 11.

78 Ghai, Y.P. 1994. Above, n 67 at p 22.

79 Kasfir, N. 1998. Above, n 11.

80 Ghai, Y.P. 1993. Above, n 2 at p 188.

81 For a personal account, in the Papua New Guinea context, of issues involved here, see Nonggorr, J. 2000. The Sandline Affair: a Papua New Guinean Perspective. In Boeha, B. and McFarlane, J. (eds.) *Australia and Papua New Guinea; Crime and the Bilateral Relationship.* Canberra: Australian Defence Studies Centre.

16. LEGAL PLURALISM AND THE PROBLEM OF IDENTITY

By: Professor Robert Hughes

KEY TERMS AND PHRASES

Pluralism – legal

The term covers various theories of law which hold that there can be many independent spheres of law, such as local or customary law, which do not require or depend upon the existence of a central state as the primary law making body in a society.

Pluralism – political

A body of theory which holds that the existence of groups and associations within society perform an essential function in any democratic society by mediating between the public arena of government and the individual citizen.

Monistic state

The idea, generally opposed by legal pluralists, that the state is the sole and final repository of legal and political authority within any society.

Orthodoxy

A body of theory, set of ideas or ideology which is either unchallenged and/or ordinarily accepted as an explanation for some phenomenon.

Formalism

In the legal context formalist theory conveys the idea that law consists essentially of abstract and general principles which are not dependent on any substantive principles such as those based on social norms and practices, customs and moral or ethical ideas including principles of justice.

Ontology

In philosophy, ontology is that area which concerns itself with questions of being; that is to say, with questions as to what things must assumed to exist and not exist. Most theories about social phenomena usually convey assumptions about what things the theorist takes to be the fundamental elements of society.

Legal Postulates

Basic propositions advanced by a particular theory of law.

INTRODUCTION

In this chapter I will take up one aspect of the legal pluralist challenge to conventional views of law and legal institutions. My concern is primarily with the challenge to the unified conception of the state which many legal pluralists hold is pivotal to the orthodox theory of legal systems. The orthodox position (i.e. positivist jurisprudence) holds that the existence of a unified central or monistic state is necessary for the existence of law in the sense that law is logically antecedent to the state. One of the central concepts or principles underlying this orthodox conception of a state is that of a unified identity. In this chapter I am suggesting that this concept is fundamentally misconceived for a variety of reasons. I will suggest an alternative understanding of identity and outline the consequences of adopting such an alternative in our understanding of the state.

The challenge of legal pluralism is made difficult to assess because of the absence of a coherent body of legal pluralist theory. So far as the state is concerned legal pluralism often appears as a critique of the state rather than as a theory pretending to offer any alternative view. Its business seems to be incomplete in some ways. There are also many versions of pluralism which lead in possibly different directions. The view I wish to put forward, nevertheless, is that legal pluralism's challenge is to be taken seriously and that we ought to attempt to accommodate it. I will argue that the monistic conception of the state is, regardless of its orthodoxy, a misconception. What the state presupposes is not some all-embracing unity as such. What it should be taken to presuppose is, rather, an identity; but an identity understood in a particular way that is consistent with the idea of the state as a substantive association rather than as an abstract or formal corporate institution. The South Pacific experience of 'small' states simply reinforces our need to recast our fundamental conceptions of the state in this way. In larger and more complex 'Western' societies we often lose sight of the fact that a state is basically composed of human individuals who are associated in various ways. The tendency has thus long been to conceive of the state in wholly abstract formal terms, such as appears in corporate theories of the state. In South Pacific states, given their size and the relative familiarity involved in social relations between their citizens, this abstract conception seems immediately inappropriate.

LEGAL PLURALISM – CLAIMS AND CHALLENGES

We should initially look at some of the claims of legal pluralism in more detail in order to set the context of the following discussion. What is legal pluralism? Hooker defined legal pluralism as that which "refers to the situation where two or more laws interact."[1] Griffiths defined it as the presence in a social field of more than one legal order.[2] For Chiba legal pluralism is that body of theory which recognises that the total context in which law operates within a legal system consists of a plurality of different culturally determined 'layers' of practice which might consist of official laws, unofficial laws and legal postulates. These cannot be wholly controlled by the central state nor unified under its authority. In fact, these layers continue to develop independently of the state and its institutions. However, these different systems of laws can and do interact with one another. This seems not to be a necessary interaction but a possible one only. The interaction is sometimes harmonious and sometimes not.[3]

Legal pluralism, in its advocacy of what is sometimes called the 'local law', 'customary law' or 'the people's law', presents us with conceptions of law. Law, so it is claimed, is a culturally relative concept and in many cultures there are customs, practices, conventions and quasi-legal rules which perform a function similar to those of law elsewhere. This can be so notwithstanding the absence within those environments of a state with a concomitant monopoly on power and law-making authority.[4]

Thus legal pluralism clearly challenges one of the precious themes of standard legal theory; namely, that there must be a state understood as a centralised legal institution.[5] This centralised institution is the modern unified nation state that has as its primary function that of law-making or legislating.[6] This rule- or law- making function is allegedly paramount and supercedes the authority of any other form of law, including judge made law. As this supreme legislative function is usually one of parliament there is parliamentary sovereignty. As parliament is a supposedly representative body comprised of members elected by the people the state, and hence law, might be thought to be democratic. From a legal pluralist perspective however, nation states are increasingly challenged by the existence of cultural and social diversity which they find within themselves.[7] The orthodox theoretical articulation of the nature of a state in fact implies that there is a large gap between the state, as such, and culture. This gap is especially evident in so far as this understanding of the state cannot theoretically accommodate multicultural and multi-religious content.

According to legal pluralists, one consequence of this sovereignty principle is that it devalues custom, tradition and culture. It both elevates itself at the expense of culture and values and eschews any serious attempt to understand law or legal institutions in light of these 'non-rational' and contingent historical principles.[8] Custom, on the centralist view, is perceived as that which is typical of societies that are relatively undeveloped or under-developed. Custom based societies are those that have insufficiently progressed towards modernity. Thus the orthodoxy of state-centralism is revealed as substantially biased in favour of modern constitutional principles, which are in turn supported by a range of assumptions about modern culture as opposed to traditional or 'primitive' culture and custom.[9]

There are other associated orthodoxies occasionally challenged by legal pluralists, expressly or impliedly. One of them concerns the central importance of law itself. For example, it is sometimes contended by pluralists that it is only in European culture that the primary principle of social and political order is taken to be law in the sense of apparently value-neutral, rationally justifiable and publicly created rules or principles. Other cultures might have 'law', or something like the Western sense of it but it is not all that important either in the production of social order or in conflict resolution.[10] In another way, legal pluralism has presented an alternative theoretical perspective to challenge the legal positivist conception of the relationship between law and culture and law and society Whilst positivism eschews any meaningful or logical relationship between them, legal pluralists purport to establish quite the reverse.

Different concepts of legal pluralism

'Classical' and 'new' legal pluralism

Legal pluralism developed distinctly as a "law from the outside" perspective[11] mainly through legal sociologists and anthropologists who were studying traditional or stateless societies. They were often confronted with what appeared to be quasi-legal rules, practices and orders that seemed to warrant some consideration as law within these societies.[12] These so called 'classical legal pluralism' proponents asked us to suspend belief in our Eurocentric concepts of law and to entertain the claim that, in some cultures, custom, or at least some part of it, could be regarded as law. One theme, perhaps, was that we should restrain our Western philosophical tendency to universalise our own concepts — legal and otherwise — and accept some form of cultural relativism.

The focus of this classical legal pluralism was on the relationship between introduced legal systems and custom.[13] These different spheres aligned, and perhaps still do align, themselves readily with the politics of modernisation and development on the one hand, and the defence of traditional society and culture on the other. Sometimes the respective poles indicate alignments on issues of colonising values versus those of self-determination. Yet, ironically, the distinction, largely unacknowledged in classical legal positivism itself, between introduced and customary law was largely the creation of colonisers themselves, and custom mostly assumed the characteristic of reinvention tainted by the intervening colonial experience. The institutions raised to defend custom and tradition were often those created by the colonial government to achieve nothing more than administrative convenience.[14] The body of custom itself was affected by its interaction with colonial law, such that it could not be taken as a pre-existing body of customs or practices.

The body of Pacific jurisprudence that is concerned with the relationship between introduced and customary law largely fits within the tradition of classical legal positivism. We can also see the opposing tensions of modernisation and tradition within politics in the Pacific. The ironic nature of the custom/introduced law dichotomy is, perhaps, not as thoroughly examined, particularly as it weakens the foundations of the policies of tradition as compared to modernsation.

Some legal pluralists have since turned their attention to European legal systems, arguing that even those systems are pluralistic in important respects. Whilst legal pluralism was once an approach that was distinctively focused on questions as to the operation of law in post-colonial societies that is no longer the case. The theoretical approach has inspired some renewed thinking about the nature of legal systems in Western countries such as those of Europe and the United States. Writers such as Merry and Van den Bergh have seen pluralistic patterns operating in various industrialised societies.[15] This is sometimes called 'new legal pluralism.' Turned back on itself legal pluralism has seemed a suitable platform from which to investigate the plurality that consists in various non-state forms of social order existing within the larger and enveloping unity of the state. It has purported to reveal a plurality of legal orders which operate within late capitalist societies. Merry sees the new legal pluralism as having shifted from the classical problematic which was with the mutual relationship and interaction between separate spheres of order such as introduced/official law and custom or non-official law. It has become concerned with the relationship between the official legal system and "other forms of ordering that connect with but are in some ways separate and dependent on it".[16] It is concerned with a complex network of relationships which exist within and between overlapping groups and subordinate orders which also interact within the same overarching structure. Thus "this perspective sees plural forms of ordering as participating in the same social field."[17]

The new legal pluralism seeks to direct us away from the frequently assumed theoretical dualities of state and society, law and non-law, official and unofficial law, public and private towards more multifaceted terrain. One of the questions it compels us to ask is whether there can be a pluralistic logic applied to conceptions of European law and state which would displace that conventional logic which demands a mere unity both of the sovereign state and of the legal system.[18] But the consequence of new legal pluralism, ironic in some ways, is to eliminate some of the fundamental differences in cross-cultural perception. If all societies have pluralistic structures have we not, *via* the all-embracing techniques of social science, produced a new universal or modernist understanding of society and state?

Legal pluralism, political pluralism and political theory

In exaining different concepts of legal pluralism it should be noted that it cannot be viewed, historically at least, to be a product of what is known as political pluralism, which developed particularly in the United States and is characterised by minority and interest group politics. Political pluralism is a theory which promoted the role of such groups as a vital one in a democratic society. This is particularly because these groups or associations provided, firstly, an opportunity for some degree of participation by citizens in larger social purposes and, secondly, because they perform a mediating function between the public and private spheres in society. Legal pluralism, it is sometimes said, has had, and needs little or no input from, this particular movement. Baxsi, for example, suggested:

> I believe that although liberal doctrine and dogma of interest group pluralism has run aground, there is no need to import this crisis into the domain of legal pluralism. While thinking on legal pluralism has been influenced here and there by liberal doctrine, literature on legal pluralism has, by and large, arisen from the sociology of law (including legal anthropologists) and comparative lawyers. No leading liberal theorist has bothered much about legal pluralism let alone with the relative autonomy of law in an analysis of the state... Legal pluralism does make

certain assumptions about the nature of the state and civil society, but these assumptions are rarely tied to a specific version of interest group pluralism.[19]

However I think it is also a fallacy to assume that legal pluralism can or need pretend to be anything other than a form of political theory. Discourse and argument as to the nature and role of the state has long been taken as characteristic of political theory. Legal pluralist argument, whatever use it might have had for comparative law, seems fundamentally to challenge our thinking about the state, if also its relationship to law, so is a branch of political theory.[20]

Juridical and social science and strong and weak versions of legal pluralism

Aligned to the classical and the new versions of legal pluralism, as mentioned above, there is the juridical version and the social science version. The juridical version is that which is concerned, as Griffiths suggested, with the drawing of links between parallel systems in the context of the overall system. Law and the state provide a kind of coordinating role in respect of diverse sub-systems of law. The social science version is more concerned with revealing the content of the complex web of relationships which exist between orders whilst admitting that there might be some more general linkage between them, for example, in terms of law.

Along the same lines there is sometimes said to be a weak version and a strong version of legal pluralism. Weak legal pluralism would hold that there can be 'parallel systems' of law; primarily state law and non-state law, introduced law and customary law. It endorses the recognition of alternative systems within a state, although they are systems which are not dependent on the state as such for their authority. The strong version, on the other hand, would hold that even the distinction between law and non-law postulated by state centralism itself is, in fact, socially constituted or constructed. Clearly the category of the social assumes a primary force here, which indicates also the sociological bias in the analysis. It insists on a 'mutually constitutive' nature of law and society.[21] Such a view usually places considerable emphasis on the plurality or diversity of distinct legal orders existing independently of the state. The disunity of the 'system' in general leads readily to the conclusion that law can and does exist without the need for a state at all. Hence, so it is claimed, the state cannot achieve the basic unifying function which orthodox theories attribute to it.

Legal pluralism and polycentricity

It is usual to differentiate legal pluralism from legal polycentricity, although the basis for the differentiation is often confused. Legal pluralism describes and accepts multiple legal orders within some more general community or association and proceeds to consider the ways in which these might intersect. At the national level, this community is obviously a state, but in some cases this is extended to the international or global context or community as well. Polycentricity focuses rather on the law itself. It seeks to indicate that law manifests something other than the unity and coherence which it is often assumed to have. Rather than achieving stability through this alleged unifying function law can be shown to contain an inherent elements of inconsistency, disunity and, therefore, instability. Others in this vein refer, more specifically, to the factor of fragmentation and to the lack of any cohesive moral foundation for law.[22] If legal pluralism is a view of the legal order from without then polycentricity is a view from within, which seems to suggest that perhaps it is law or the legal *Weltanschauung* (world view) which accounts for the plurality of the world.[23] Yet the two are sometimes difficult to disentangle.

Legal Pluralism – Comprehensive Theory or Marginal Critique?

There are now several different dimensions or contexts of legal pluralist argument along with a shift in the focus of attention. There is that which is dualistic and has largely focused on the coexistence of local decentralised systems of law and central state based law within a given system. But there is also that which shifts attention to another context, which is the global and seemingly stateless context. This is what Chiba has termed "legal pluralism in triple structure".[24] This structure assumes the dualistic structure of operation of legal pluralism but extends beyond it. In this context Teubner, for example, argues:

> Global law can only be adequately explained by a theory of legal pluralism which has recently successfully turned from the law of colonial societies to the laws of diverse ethnic, cultural and religious communities in modern nation-states. It needs to make another turn — from groups to discourses. It should focus its attention on a new body of law that emerges from various globalization processes to multiple sectors of civil society independently of the laws of nation states.[25]

It could be thought that legal pluralism is not in any particular need of any theoretical perspective to do its work. Perhaps many legal pluralists merely accept that different peoples have different senses of law, setting out from there to understand what that sense of law is. This lack of theoretical perspective is a possible deficiency of legal pluralism as acknowledged, for example, by Griffiths. There is a lack of clear definition of just what pluralism entails and in particular what it propounds as an alternative to the legal centrism that it sets out to correct.[26] But perhaps this is not a problem. Bergh suggests instead some kind of Hegelean solution to the lack of a single theoretical perspective. The legal pluralist position would thus be seen not as one of adopting a pluralistic logic of categories of laws which would potentially and, perhaps inevitably, lead to conflict. Pluralism is rather to be seen as a process that develops in and over time.[27] It is not a static situation or set of interrelated categories but a complex pattern of interaction taking place constantly.[28]

In summary, legal pluralism claims to reveal the operation of a number of legal orders within a society. Those legal orders are administered in several sets of institutions.[29] This implies a system of complex interactions within a legal system, the notion of a 'system' here being taken in a rather loose or open sense. Sometimes the parts of the system interact closely with one another and sometimes they do not. As one writer puts it "law in modern society is plural rather than monolithic,… it is private as well as public in character and… the national (public, official) legal system is often a secondary rather than a focus of regulation."[30] In principle, such a conception of a legal system has a ring of familiarity to it to most who have engaged in the practice of law. From such a perspective, the idea that there is any coherent unifying principle operating in the legal system would be the product of idle fancy. At times there appear connections between areas of law but there are also substantial gaps between areas of law and between law and practice. At times, usually during periods of judicial radicalism, the courts appear to assume a reductionist stance proposing that there are deep connections between principles in tort, contract and equity, for example. But it has generally defied jurisprudence to show that there is uniformity (rather than equivalence) across the different sub-domains of a legal system. From the practical standpoint the legal system would be better conceived in terms of diverse practices which sometimes overlap and interact and sometimes they do not. Discrete groups or sub-groups do operate even within all legal systems. Sometimes they stand in direct connection the state, and sometimes independent of it. The division between groups and also between state law and local law cannot be cast in rigid terms or as harsh conceptual divisions.[31] It is the complicated interaction of the legal system as such which renders the term 'pluralism' appropriate.

Despite this, within so-called Western societies, legal pluralism has not developed much beyond a marginal critique. The recognition of plurality of legal orders as an empirical phenomenon can perhaps be dismissed as an unfortunate complexity — another case of facts not being allowed to get in the way of a good theory. Legal pluralism runs foul of the dominant view that different legal systems cannot co-exist within the structure of a sovereign state without challenging the continuing authority and legitimacy of the state. Moreover, from an international perspective, legal pluralism might seem to erode the claimed need for absolute independence of a nation state by weakening the inner unitary core of the state. The claim to a plurality of legal orders, in other words, appears contrary to the idea that the law should derive its authority ultimately from a single source.[32] Furthermore, in the originally fertile ground of legal pluralist research, the so-called traditional societies themselves, there seems a strengthening of state centralism as new governing elites seek out rapid development, international financing, structural reform and rapid assimilation to the liberal capitalist model of the state. All of this seems to imply a strengthening of legal positivism within these societies,[33] although not without resistance form other sectors within the society.[34] Thus the actual tendency of many such societies, especially after independence, has been towards a positivist rather than a legal pluralist paradigm.

Legal positivism and the Pacific

In the Pacific context positivism is that which reinforces the supremacy of introduced law and systems of government that are part of the colonial heritage. They are no longer colonial societies but they are not traditional either. Colonialism has left behind legal/political systems in which elements of custom and modernity are intermingled in an ambivalent and uncertain relationship with a central state system. Nowhere is custom exactly pre-colonial custom and, as is common in 'new' states post-independence, traditions need to be invented and reinvented to forge some kind of community out of the colonial residue. Legal pluralists have not been able to agree themselves on the future of this relationship between introduced law and custom. Some in fact have argued that custom will inevitably be eliminated by introduced law.[35] The co-existence of these two produces in these societies a thorough-going systemic confusion of authority. Legal pluralism plays to some extent, and perhaps originally, on connections between custom or tradition and self-determination or independence.[36] Thus the tension between custom and the introduced legal system is represented as that between independence and some form of lingering cultural imperialism.

Inevitably, however, there is ambivalence in the Pacific region about playing this song of independence to the end. On the international political scene it is still important for the small Pacific countries to engage in the statehood game so as to maintain recognition as states. This has strategic significance not only in terms of internationally sourced funding for aid and development. It also impacts directly on the content and structure of internal politics. Introduced government systems or central state structures lend themselves to a certain sort of politics. They provide a playing field suited to certain sorts of players — particularly educated and non-traditional elites — who play according to a different set of rules. Those who are empowered in this way are those who frequently preach the gospel of custom and tradition whilst in practice ignoring it. Thus it becomes less likely that the introduced legal system will be subjected to modification or change or that the tension between custom and the introduced legal system will be resolved. One thing that the Pacific countries do make obvious — perhaps as a result of their size — is the fact that pluralism within these states has a certain explanatory power. They are small societies but they are highly complex and diverse in their composition. Thus the so-called official view of traditional jurisprudence that has tended to apprehend political societies or states in terms of their apprehended unity and uniformity seems remarkably deficient in this environment.

THE TRADITIONAL CONCEPT OF THE STATE

We have seen that legal pluralism rejects the concept of a monolithic state. This can be contrasted with the traditional jurisprudential view of the modern state, which sets out to justify the idea of the modern state which, in turn, finds as its key principle, historically and theoretically, the principle of sovereignty.[37] In modernist terms sovereignty embodies certain key ideas, not the least of which is its essential unity or indivisibility. It must do, so the argument goes, because now sovereignty has the sense of absolute and final political and legal authority.

This concept of the modern state is based on the works of those such as Hobbes, Locke and Rousseau. It is a formal or imaginative conception which makes certain assumptions about the necessary uniformity of human nature as a defining condition of membership or citizenship. This is only possible if we treat a state as a formal association, and define the individuals who comprise it in terms that are themselves essentially formal.

The essential unity of the sovereign state is clearly enough expressed, for example, in Hobbes' corporate view of civil or political association; a theory which clearly involves borrowings from Cicero and the later medieval jurists.[38] Faced with the fact of impenetrable human diversity, the answer of theorists such as Hobbes was to appeal to artifice rather than nature, and more particularly to personation theory provided by the classical jurists.

The natural unity of humanity was a thesis of Platonically inspired natural law theory. It was rejected by Hobbes on the basis variously of its absurd, unscientific and irrational metaphysical doctrines.[39] To Hobbes, the many can become one if they are united in an artificial sovereign *persona* which is the product of their own covenant and to which they assign power over themselves. As an artificial person the sovereign body is a kind of Hobbesean individual writ large, its mortal imperfections perfected in the abstract in light of reason and imagination. It has a kind of completeness of power which is also the final and ultimate source of all political legitimacy. Unity is possible for such a being because it is both separate from and above the diversity of natural (or 'private') human existence in the so-called State of Nature. The primary function of this 'thing' is, moreover, to legislate.[40]

Modern constitutionalism

The fundamentals of Hobbes' political theory provide the platform for modern constitutionalism. In his book *Strange Multiplicities*[41] James Tully draws out what he takes to be the seven conventions of modern constitutionalist doctrine. This doctrine, he claims, constitutes an orthodoxy which is adhered to in varying ways by contemporary liberals, nationalists and communitarians. Each of these three groups in fact have slightly different but consistent enough versions of popular sovereignty. It is these seven features which together enabled adherents of modern constitutional theory to suppress arguments based on ancient constitutionalist principles including tradition and custom. They continue to exclude the voice of diverse minority interests and intercultural groups from constitutionalist argument. But further they supported the claim that the principles thus developed are of universal validity, thus diverting attention away from intercultural as well as regional diversity on the global scale. These seven conventions are as follows[42]:

1. There is adherence to the basic notion of sovereignty as a modern principle of statehood.

2. The modern constitution is defined in contrast to ancient or historically earlier constitutional types which are sometimes treated as 'earlier' and as belonging in a lower phase of historical development. It also sets up a distinction between that which is distinctly European, and that which is not. Ancient constitutions are also most often treated as implying irregularity or disorder. The traditional and the customary become something pre-modern but more significantly also primitive, underdeveloped, incompletely formed. Hence there is what Tully calls an imperial element in the argument.

3. There is a contrast between the modern constitution with its features of unity, uniformity and order, and the ancient constitution(s) which has features of disunity, differentiation, plurality, multiplicity, disorder.

4. There is the recognition of custom within a general theory of progress. It appears as a lower phase of historical development and, more especially as something which is overtaken or rendered irrelevant by progress.

5. Modern constitutionalism becomes identified with respect to a particular set of European political principles as essential features of what was sometimes called a 'republican constitution'. This includes the likes of rule of law, separation of powers, representative government, equal citizenship with fundamental rights and a distinctive public realm.

6. The sixth convention is one that he takes to have come especially to the fore since the French and American revolutions. This is that:

   > a constitutional state possesses an individual identity as a 'nation', an imaginary community to which all nationals belong and in which they enjoy equal dignity as citizens. Although the nation is interpreted differently in each society... it engenders a sense of belonging and allegiance by means of the nation's individual name, national historical narrative and public symbols. By naming the constitutional association and giving it a historical narrative, the nation and its citizens, who take on its name when they become members, possess a corporate identity or personality. From Pufendorf onward, this corporate identity of nation and nationals in a state is seen as necessary to the unity of a modern constitutional association.[43]

7. The final convention is that which aligns or assimilates modern constitutions and democracy. As he puts it, "the modern constitution comes into being at some founding moment — and stands behind and provides the rules — for democratic politics."[44] The modern constitution appears as a precondition rather than a part of democratic politics. It lays the ground and prescribes the domain of debate on democratic politics at the same time excluding the classical dimensions of democratic debate.

Tully acknowledges in fact that legal pluralists are those who have challenged this uniformity supposed to exist in modern states conceived under the dominant rhetoric of modern constitutionalism. It is the rhetoric of modern constitutionalism that devalues alternative conceptions of a state based on principles which acknowledge and respect diversity just as the principles of modernity purport rationally to exclude the likes of custom, traditional and the diversity which this entails both internally and globally. It is modernity and the logic of both universalism and uniformity that drives this rhetoric, which purports in a wider global context to devalue and debase cultural and social diversity.

Modern consitutionalism and the state in the Pacific

We can see the impact of the need for unity in the concept of the modern state in independence movements in the Pacific. This concept shaped the political imagination and the resultant form of the emerging nations. For example, in Vanuatu the politics of nationalism were expressed in 1971 by the newly formed New Hebrides National Party. One of its first public statements began:

> Our aims in forming a National Party are to preserve the New Hebridean people; their culture and their ways of life are in danger of large scale settlement by Europeans.[45]

Nationhood was seen as being the end goal of decolonisation, with the national purpose being to protect and project the national cultural past of the New Hebridean people. The cultural underpinnings of nationhood, with its ideological insistence upon cultural homogeneity, inevitably affected the political imagination. Despite the fact that the group of islands that now make up Vanuatu did not form a single entity until they were defined as the New Hebrides by colonisers, a single New Hebridean people[46] and New Hebridean culture became the justification for the creation of Vanuatu.[47]

Also if we look at the current constitutions of the Pacific states themselves we will see the familiar proclamations of the unity, common destiny, common citizenship and heritage of the people; in all an assumed identity of the people under the adopted constitutional frameworks. They are complete with conventional proclamations of the rule of law, the common possession of fundamental rights and freedoms and equality of all before the law. Almost without exception these documents are masterpieces of liberal design reinforcing the various tenets of modern constitutionalism as Tully has described it. The central legal authority of the state is clearly established. The role of custom is recognised but generally, with the possible exception of Vanuatu in relation to land ownership, is subordinated to the central authority of the state.[48]

Yet the assumed identity constructed or at least assumed by these constitutions has been shown by recent events to be an unstable one. The relationship between modern constitutional theory and actual practice in the Pacific is tenuous. The civil war in Solomon Islands from 2000 onwards, and the events following the attempted coup in Fiji Islands in May 2000 have, for one thing, shown that assumptions about the underlying unity of a people at the national level are frequently misplaced. The forces of fragmentation and internal division were, if anything, shown to be much potent than any reading of the the constitutions themselves would have suggested.

THE PROBLEM OF IDENTITY

It is the sixth convention in Tully's analysis above which is of interest. He talks of a convention within the doctrine modern constitutionalism which is that of identity or at least a particular sense of it. The notion of identity that Tully is referring to here is what he calls corporate identity, but it might equally be called formal, nominalistic, artificial or abstract identity. It is a product largely of elevation of the writings of

Hobbes, Locke and Hume on identity into something of an orthodoxy amongst liberal philosophers.[49] This is a notion of identity as a simple unity in the sense I have already mentioned.

Tully seeks to solve the problem of a unitary concept of identity by developing a notion of identity using the theoretical perspectives of Wittgenstein, post-modernism, post-structuralism, interculturalism and feminism. He purports to reconstruct the idea of identity such that it is a product of, and contains difference. That is to say, it is a sense of identity that does not involve self-reflexive or essentialist notions of identity. Such a concept of identity allows for a state which can acccomodate intercultural ideas, ideas of cultural diversity and so on. I do not disagree with that conclusion but I think there are other ways of proceeding. The major points I wish to make are as follows:

First, modernist authors from Hobbes and Locke onwards have simply misrepresented the concept of identity as if it were, and could only logically be, a principle implying simple numerical unity. These writers were, for their own political ends, keen to reject the metaphysics of both Neoplatonism, Catholicism and natural law along with the challenges to secular political authority which these seemed to entailed. Thus they rejected, or at least redefined, what was one of the key defining principles of it; namely, the principle of identity taken in a properly collectivist sense.[50]

Second, this misconception of identity renders any conception of an association or a collectivity, human or otherwise, not so much impossible, but highly abstract. It is a creation of the philosophical imagination or of grand artifice because it is only in the imagination or in abstract thought that a corporate identity achieving such a unity could be conjured up out of the diversity of practical existence. Treated in this way identity could only be employed in our understanding of a state as if those which it unites are treated as fundamentally the same in some respect or other. To Hobbes, and perhaps correctly, this would be impossible with respect to natural individuals. But these individuals also assume a certain conformity if we attribute to each individual by virtue of the covenant a formal *persona* as citizens which appropriately affects their membership but also their subjection of the artificial corporate *persona*. But the corporate unity is, as I have indicated, a reflection of the simple atomic or numerical unity of the individual. It does not carry with it the multiplicity of the 'state of nature'. Nor does it carry any taint of the multiplicity of individual membership. It transcends even that because it is an essential unity. Thus as we say in modern corporate theory, according to the separate identity doctrine: it has an identity (i.e. a juristic status) distinct from its individual members or any aggregation of them.

Thirdly, there is another way of understanding identity that is not exclusive of diversity or difference at all. Such an employment of the concept is quite legitimate from an historical point of view as also from a logical point of view. It is that sense of identity which I suggest is more appropriate to our understanding of a state.

Concepts of Identity

I have elsewhere explored the relationship between identity and politics and implicitly, perhaps, the relationship between identity and the state.[51] There are many who would think that the connection between identity and political discourse is a recent one. It is common enough now to talk of 'identity politics' as a certain sort of political debate occurring particularly in the U.S.A. in the 1960s and 1970s as, for example, a politics of gay identity, race identity, ethnic identity and so on.

It is apparent that this recent theme of 'identity politics' has itself come to an end. One of the reasons for that is that the concept of identity that it employed is that of a simple or numerical unity or oneness. Given this, the suggestion appeared to be that identities such as racial, feminine or ethnic could be reduced to some seamless or pure conceptual base. This search for a numerical, finally specific, essentialist notion of identity was inevitably a failure, because it was found that within such identity categories there were considerable and significant differences to be accounted for. Thus it is an odd story. That which was alleged in itself to capture a definitive essence of something and thereby differentiate itself from the rest, merely collapsed. What it sought was impossible either to achieve or to sustain because an identity concept such as this, being one that admits no difference, diversity or change, is an impoverished one.[52]

But the connection between identity and politics is much longer and the potential for this concept far more considerable than these undertakings might indicate. Are there richer alternatives to the concept of identity? Here, maybe, we can look to Hegel. Identity has a seemingly peculiar and difficult sense in Hegel's conception of the dialectic. The dialectical method is integral to Hegel's understanding of philosophy, or the so-called philosophy of the 'Absolute Idea'. Thus it is integral also to Hegel's philosophy of the state as expressed in the *Philosophy of Right*.[53] The dialectic is a process or movement from unity to diversity to a higher phase of unity. All might be change in some sense but it is an orderly, logical process of change. Thus it is more appropriately a sense of development. It is that higher phase, which is a unity of the diversity which can gone before it,[54] which is specifically called "identity" by Hegel.

Many have set out to ridicule Hegel's concept of identity as if concepts such as unity-in-diversity, unity-in-difference or sameness-through-change entail a basic contradiction in terms. Identity, Hegel's critics hold, means a numerical unity (hence exactly the same, oneness). Thus it can hardly be something found in, or compatible with, difference. But this is clearly not what Hegel was arguing at all, as far as I can tell. He was arguing that identity, at its simplest, is that process whereby thought moves from a point of unity to a point of differentiation from that unity, and thence to a higher, fuller unity. Identity is precisely the outcome of this process and necessarily implicit in all of the stages of this process. As a process it incorporates the moments of unity and difference. Furthermore, these critics simply fail to understand that the tradition of understanding that Hegel was drawing on here is a tradition in which identity is _not_ understood as a principle of simple unity, individuation or oneness. It is a tradition which builds on Aristotle and Neoplatonism (Christian and otherwise, classical and medieval) as much as Leibniz, Fichte, Kant and Schelling.

True, it is a tradition which can be understood in terms of its tendency towards unitary metaphysics. But another fruitful way of looking at it is that it is a tradition which attempts to balance or mediate the two sides of unity and diversity; sameness and difference.

Two Senses of Identity?

If we take an overview, we can say that there have been two differences of meaning assigned to the concept of identity. There is one which derives from Hobbes and Locke which treat identity as importing a type of simply mathematical idea unity i.e. oneness. There is the other, older, philosophical tradition in which identity is treated as that sense of unity that persists amidst difference. It is a unity-in-diversity in the sense in which we might speak of any form of human association as a form of unity-in-diversity, a unity of different individuals.

IDENTITY AND THE STATE

If we are to take identity in this alternative sense and apply it to the understanding of states where does it lead us? Taking identity as a unity-in-diversity means that we can, in some more reasonable way, retain the sense that the state is an association of individual human beings. In the case of small states such as those of the Pacific this original sense of a state as a 'polis' might be more obvious than in larger 'developed' countries where formalism and abstraction have reached special heights, possibly as a reaction to complexity. But formalism is neither an inevitability nor a necessity. Our rethinking of identity in relation to states will lead us towards a possible resolution of the real problem posed by legal pluralism. This is not that of recognition of plurality in the face of the omnipresent unity of the state. It is that of finding some degree of balance between plurality and unity. The problems in Fiji Islands and Solomon Islands adverted to above are, I think, indicative of the need to address these issues, rather than seeking solutions within the framework of existing constitutional structures.

Let me sketch out some ways in which a balance between plurality and unity might be achieved. I will have to consider first the notion of association and, second, what identity in this revised sense might bring to it. Third, I will consider the idea of culture which I think is tied up with identity issues. Finally I will comment on the role of law within a state thus reconsidered.

All associations are primarily unities of diverse things or, to be more specific, unities, combinations, collectivities (however we prefer to put it) of diverse human individuals. The very idea of individuality implies, as I have said, an extreme of diversity and multiplicity. Individuals are allegedly unique and this clearly implies diversity. Hence where I am asserting that identity can be attributed to a state, and that it is a far more basic or workable way of conceiving of a state, I am suggesting that it properly captures the sense of the state as an association — a unity of diverse things. I am also asserting that this diversity is such that it might consist of individuals certainly, but also sub-associations of individuals in a wide and perhaps indeterminate array or relationships. In other words, we might prefer to think of states as associations of associations and of individuals, given the manifold ways in which human beings conduct themselves.

However that might be, we are still engaged here at a level of formal abstraction. An association is a unity-in-diversity which traditionally lawyers have been prepared to conceive of themselves, making clear distinctions between incorporated bodies and other forms of association. These associations are identities which are not distinct from the aggregates which compose them. But implied in this notion of unity-in-diversity is also the fact that what we are talking about is a systematisation of human conduct and experience[55] which, in some sense, brings together form and content. We need to consider how this might be so. The way forward here is in terms of the fact that identity is a relational principle. It asserts a relationship between (different) things.

Once this is understood we can proceed to the second point. This is that identity does not merely assert an association. It asserts association in some respect or other. Thus it asserts association by virtue of something that is held in common — some characteristic of sameness that is held by those who are associated. This is how unity is achieved and how the identity as a relational concept is to be grasped as identity with respect to a particular something or other. This is basic to the sense of identity I am seeking to articulate. In common parlance the identity of something is answerable by reference to the acknowledgement that it is something of a certain sort or type which it shares with other things. This is in large part why idealist philosophers constantly refer to identity as asserting a qualitative, rather than a numerical, unity. Identity is identity in respect of some common or shared characteristic or feature.

One can perhaps assume that things can be associated by chance or associated simply by being somewhere — a chance conjunction. One can also assume that there can be simple associations as a matter of principle. But on closer analysis even these things tend to be associated by virtue of some common or shared characteristic such as being in the same place, or being together at the same time or being human. Associations of human beings are meaningful, though not always purposeful, associations. They persist perhaps because they are attributed meaning by those who are associated even if the original circumstance of the association might have been one of chance or choice.

Third, it is this characteristic of being associated in a certain respect that brings out a connection between culture and identity. Culture consists of shared ideas or beliefs which are, in other words, held in common. Commonness is closely related to community. Culture is a community of ideas, beliefs and so on. These go to establish the content of identity. Whilst there is some conjecture about the possibility of natural identities in political associations I think that it is much more sensible to admit that all political identities are composed by human thought out of historical practices. Whether they actually represent human practices is quite another question. But what sort of identity is this? The content of such identity is cultural constructs which are created, challenged, adjusted and recreated. The whole idea of attempting to build political associations as if they were logical extensions of families and other allegedly natural forms of association is one which is dead and buried if indeed it ever were viable. Liberal theory has had its moment in putting this idea to rest.

The sense of identity here does not transcend culture because identity in the sense in which I am employing it has the characteristic of immanence. Immanence implies being contained within and confined by some more general context. Thus we can say that this cultural identity is indeed a diverse unity. Identity is embedded in culture. The form is determined within and by the content. It is identity which changes with the culture itself. It has the feature of relative continuity. It is persistent but it is not permanent. In the first place we must acknowledge the fact that identities vary considerably from one place and from one association to another. The variance is cultural. Additionally ideas both persist and are transmissible over time regardless of the comings and going of the generations or those who from time to time comprise the substance of an association.

It is primarily ideational culture understood as a community of shared ideas, beliefs and opinions that both provides and preserves the identity of the state.[56] It is culture that transcends the individual experience of those who are the variety of associations within a state and indeed constitutive of the state itself, without destroying or denying them. We can say here that identity manifests a certain sameness but not sameness in any rigid or static sense. And it is certainly not sameness *per se* whatever that might be. Without a sustainable identity in that sense, the structure of a state and the prospects of its continuance are poor. Without any such identity the putative state and its institutions lack legitimacy.

It appears to me that cultural identity must exist to some reasonable degree before one can even begin to acknowledge the constitutional viability of a country. Without that underlying system or pattern of commonness or community then unity in any sense is impossible. Individual, ethnic and other forms of diversity are basic within the overarching identity of a state and play a vital role in the construction of the sustaining cultural identity. But at some point or other they could, if unrestrained, cause it to fragment.

How are we to treat law in such a scenario? Law is a set or a system of relatively abstract system of ideas. It is, I think, merely a subdivision or an aspect of a culture. This fact accompanied with the role of language in law lends itself directly to analysis in terms of culture. As a system of ideas law is very 'loosely' systematised. Its unity as a system is weak. This is because it the product of a history of abstractions from practice without any unifying or guiding logic and without clearly established axioms or assumptions from which to generate rules or formulae. Law is not like a logical system because it is affected by practice. It can never be the whole of culture even though in some respects it often pretends to function as if the abstractions it contains are somehow were representative or symbolic of the culture which surrounds and contains it. Legal culture captures the mutual and sometimes confused relationship according to which law is affected by and in turn affects culture. It is because of this mutuality in fact that law very often has influenced concepts of personal identity.

Law, in other words, is a component of culture, which in terms of relative priority must precede, not flow from, the existence of the state. This seems clear enough as an historical fact. Even legislation which is the product of a state occupies a place as part of culture and has no meaning or force apart from it. In certain cultures, such as modern Western cultures, law assumes a position of pre-eminence. It need not occupy such pre-eminence in all cultures, and indeed it does not as I have noted above.

Tully acknowledges in fact that legal pluralists are those who have challenged this uniformity supposed to exist in modern states conceived under the dominant rhetoric of modern constitutionalism. It is the rhetoric of modern constitutionalism that devalues alternative conceptions of a state based on principles which acknowledge and respect diversity just as the principles of modernity purport rationally to exclude the likes of custom, tradition and the diversity which this entails both internally and globally. It is modernity and the logic of both universalism and uniformity that drives this rhetoric, which purports in a wider global context to devalue and debase cultural and social diversity.

Furthermore in the Pacific context, it is obvious that the modern constitutional structures which they have adopted assume that law and centralised legal structures can somehow settle the question of identity in some satisfactory way. This, it seems to me, is a dangerous fallacy. It is a question which assumes that more fundamental cultural issues of identity, especially those at the national level, have been settled when in fact they have not. Pacific constitutions, as they presently stand, clearly assume that they have been. However, there is often mere fragmentation and high levels of diversity. The theoretical assumptions are clearly at odds with the reality. Moerover, the expectation that centrally imposed law, in terms of an homogenous central set of legal principles, can formally resolve such issues of identity, especially in societies where there remain deep divisions, and there is little pre-disposition towards law as a means of social ordering, is clearly a pipe dream.

CONCLUSION

The identity problem is, I think, a crucial one for small South Pacific countries. The orthodox conception of identity to which Tully referred is clearly a colonial legacy. Modern constitutionalism is clearly a major aspect of that legacy; a subsisting residue which has survived independence. It is part and parcel of the attempt to conceive of a state in abstract institutional terms and to position law as a central agency within this perspective. Theoretically it makes a range of assumptions as to uniformity under a coherent body of law, which are clearly at odds with the social and cultural reality of these countries.

The position I have attempted to argue is that the concept of identity which is employed within modern constitutionalism is one which ought to be rethought. In fact it needs to be rethought and reworked in order that these relatively new post-independence countries within the Pacific region can begin seriously to set about a task of nation building which incorporates and makes sense of their unique and diverse cultural traditions. Modern constitutional doctrine and the identity principle which goes with it serves, and has served, to exclude cultural diversity. It is only when we understand the identity principle as one of incorporating and preserving diversity, rather than excluding it, that the proper social and cultural dimensions of these constitutional systems can be preserved. The way to do that is, I believe, to understand identity as a contingent principle in the sense in which collective identities emerge as the products of history, rather than as the posulates of abstract philosophical reason. This is essentially what a principle of identity as a 'unity-in-diversity' must be taken to imply. Only understood in this way can it capture the historical reality of newly emergent states.

Does that mean that law therefore plays no place in such a scheme of things? I think not. It is fallacy to suggest that law or a legal system necessarily either requires or could achieve the kind of uniformity which many writers seem to assume. Law, surely, is only very loosely a coherent and/or unified system. It is what Stone referred to once as a "complex unity" or a unity which is "multi-fashioned".[57] It is itself in basic ways a product and sometimes a reflection of historical practices which have preserved within it vital elements of diversity and differentiation, if also at times tension and inconsistency. Thus the identity which law might provide within a state ought to be understood in just this way.

ENDNOTES

1   Hooker M.B. 1975. *Legal Pluralism: An Introduction to Colonial and Neo-Colonial Laws.* Oxford: Clarendon Press at p 6.

2   Griffiths, J. 1986. What is Legal Pluralism? *Journal of Legal Pluralism and Unofficial Law* 1: 1–56 at p 1. See also Pospisil, L. 1971. *Anthropology of Law: A Comparative Theory.* New York: Harper and Row. p 1; Van den Bergh, G.C.J.J. 1992. Legal Pluralism in Roman Law. In Verga, C. ed, *Comparative Legal Cultures.* New York: New York University Press. pp 338–50, p. 451; Galanter, M. 1981. Justice in Many Rooms: Courts, Private Ordering, and Indigenous Law. *Journal of Legal Pluralism and Unofficial Law* 19: 1–25 at p 1.

3   Chiba, M. (ed.) 1986. *Asian Indigenous Law: An Interaction with Received Law.* London and New York: KPI. p 1, 2.

4   See, for example, Llewellyn, K.N. and Hoebel, E.A. 1983. *The Cheyenne Way: Conflict and Case Law in Primitive Peoples.* Norman: University of Oklahoma Press. 212ff; and Fitzpatrick, P. 1980. *Law and State in Papua New Guinea.* London: Academic Press. p 100 and 117. Thus legal pluralism rejected the claims made by orthodox legal theorists, as well as by some sociologists or anthropologists in this regard, such as Hobhouse, Pound, Radcliffe-Brown. Hobhouse wrote that "such societies, of course have their customs, which are doubtless felt as binding my their members, but if we mean by law a body of rules enforced by an authority independent of personal ties of kinship and friendship, such an institution is not compatible with their social arrangement." Hobhouse, L.T. 1910. *Morals in Evolution.* London: Oxford University Press. p 73.

5   Whilst some legal pluralist views might tend to the form of anarchy there does not seem to be a general denial of some role for the state.

6   Not all sovereignty theorists — Austin for example — would agree on this. Austin thought that it was the obedience to a singular individual or body and absence of legal limitation was more important to the concept of sovereignty. Indeed he suggested that the legislative and the executive functions were so confused that one could not really hold out the legislative as that which gave sovereignty or independence to a state. See Rumble, W.E. (ed.) 1995. *Austin: The Province of Jurisprudence Determined.* Cambridge: Cambridge University Press. p 188, 197.

7   Tie, W. 1999. *Legal Pluralism: Toward a Multicultural Conception of Law.* Brookfield: Ashgate Publishing Co. at p 177–178. The "diversification of socio-cultural identity within nation-statehood" poses a growing problem for established legal orders which could ultimately bring about "the demise of that whole politico-legal system (and the onset of civil war, for example)."

8   Non-rational, that is, in the post-Enlightenment sense of rationality.

9   See, for example, Austin, above n 6, who refers to natural, "primitive", "domestic" or "savage" societies employing customary law which lacks the "habit of obedience to one and the same superior". Hence they have no law which is enforced by legal and political sanctions. Hence they have no law at all. Rumble, W.E. (ed) 1995. Above, n 6, at p 178. See similarly, Robson, W.A. 1935. *Civilisation and the Growth of Law.* New York: McMillan. p 7

10 See Surya Prakash Sinha. 1995. Legal Polycentricity. In Petersen H and Zahle H. (eds.) *Legal Polycentricity: Consequences of Pluralism in Law.* Aldershot: Dartmouth. 31ff.

11 This is a perspective of law as viewed by non-lawyers.

12 To mention but a few: Griffiths, J. 1986. What Is Legal Pluralism? *Journal of Legal Pluralism* 1: 1–56; Bohannen, P. Differing Realms of Law. 67 *American Anthropologist* 65; Pospisil, L. 1958. Kapauku Papuans and Their Law. *Yale University Publications in Anthopology* 54, 248; Nader, L. 1965. The Anthropological Study of Law. 67 *American Anthropologist* 3.

13 See Merry, S.E. 1988. Legal Pluralism. *Law and Society* XXII (5): 869–896 at p. 869. Merry contends that the focus originally was on the role which this dichotomy played in colonised and therefore also post-colonial societies. See also McLennan, G. 1995. *Pluralism*. Buckingham: Open University Press. Chapter 1.

14 That seems clearly to have been the case with respect to both the Great Council of Chiefs and the Native Lands Trust Board in Fiji, for example.

15 Merry, S.E. 1988. Above, n 13, at p.872; Van den Bergh, G.C.J.J. 1992. Above, n 2, at p 451.

16 Merry, S.E. 1988. Above, n 13, at p 872.

17 Merry, S.E. 1988. Above, n 13, at p 872.

18 And, indeed, the unity of the legal system under the ultimate authority of the state.

19 Baxsi, U. 1986. Discipline, Repression and Legal Pluralism. In Sack, P. and Minschin, E. *Legal Pluralism: Proceedings of the Canberra Workshop*, Canberra: Australian National University, p 51.

20 Thus it would meet one of Rohe's criteria for the meaning of politics. It involves discourse about states. It is therefore clear that we can speak of a politics of legal pluralism. See Rohe, K. 1994. *Politik: Begriffe und Wirklichkeiten*. Stuttgart: Verlag W. Kohlhammer. p 11, 12.

21 See, for example, Griffiths, A.O. 1997. *In the Shadow of Marriage: Gender and Justice in an African Community*. Chicago: University of Chicago Press. p. 35 and 133. Griffiths argues that this contention need not lead to the conclusion that law permeates the whole social fabric because the distinction between law and non law is socially constituted. (At p 213.)

22 De Lange, R. 1995. Divergence, Fragmentation and Pluralism. In Petersen, H. and Zahle, H. 1995. Above, n 10 at p 105.

23 Hirvonen, A. (ed.) 1988. *Polycentricity: The Multiple Scenes of Law*. London: Pluto Press. p 1, 2.

24 Chiba, M. 1995. Legal Pluralism in Mind: A Non-Western View. In Petersen, H. and Zahle, H. 1995. Above, n 10 at p 74.

25 Teubner, G. 1997. 'Global Bukowina': Legal Pluralism in World Society. In Teubner G. (ed.) *Global Law Without A State*. Dartmouth: Aldershot. p 4.

26 Griffiths, J. 1986. Above, n 2 at p 1, 2.

27 Process is also the position adopted by Tie in his attempt to show that legal pluralism can accommodate multicultural ideas.

28 Bergh, G.C.J.J. 1992. Above, n 2, at p 451–454

29 Griffiths, J. 1986. Above, n 2, at p 5.

30 Galanter, M. 1981. Above, n 2, at p 20. Similar points are made by Merry, S.E. 1988. Above n 13; and Pospisil, L. 1971. Above, n 2.

31 Griffiths, J. 1986. Above, n 2, at p 17–18.

32 Of course, it should be noted that this has hardly prevented such states from pushing the idea of legal pluralist systems in their former colonies.

33 See Sack, P. and Alick, J. 1992. (eds.) *Law and Anthropology*. Dartmouth: Aldershot. p xviii.

34 See Merry, S.E. 1988. Above, n 13, at p 872; Okotho-Ogendo, H.W.O. 1979. The Imposition of Property Law in Kenya. In Berman, S.S. and Harrell-Bond, B.E. (eds.) *The Imposition of Law*. New York: Academic Press. p 147–166; Skalnik, P. 1987. On the Inequality of the Concept of the 'Traditional State'. *Journal of Legal Pluralism and Unofficial Law* 26: 301–321; Geertz, C. 1983. *Local Knowledge: Further Essays on Interpretative Anthropology*. New York: Basic Books. p 228.

35 See Diamond, S. 1973. The Rule of Law versus the Order of Custom. In Black D. and Mileski M. (eds.) *The Social Organisation of Law*, New York: Academic Press, pp 318–344, at p 332. The various views here are discussed in Merry, S.E. 1988. Above, n 13, p 874ff.

36 Although in some respects arguments in this regard are troublesome. The concept of introduced law as simply *loa blong weit man* is not, given a long period of independence and self determination of many states, quite an accurate description of the situation. Some law might still be introduced law in the strict sense and constitutions might have been modelled on the European model but the characterisation simply as introduced law begs a number of questions.

37 Perhaps there is no need to say that jurisprudence has since moved on from there but this is only a partial truth.

38 We tend to refer to Hobbes as the founder of peculiarly modern ideas in political theory. Perhaps this is an overstatement of his own claims to genius and originality for he draws considerably on a long tradition of thought. That is certainly the case in respect both of his attention to secularism and his use of corporatist principles. The argument on these points is contained in Hughes, R.A. 1995. *Identity, Law and Politics*. Armidale: UNE Press. Chapter 4.

39 The immediate enemy appeared to be the Cambridge Neoplatonists whose abstruse scholastic doctrines appeared capable of justifying rule by divine right. It is significant that their response to Hobbes was to term his theories 'democritic' a play on Hobbes portrayal of the (human) universe in the State of Nature as behaving much in the fashion of Democritus' dissociated atoms. Hughes, R.A. 1995. Above, n 38, at chapter 4.

40 This reflects Hobbes' distaste for Coke's primacy of judicial reason.

41 Tully, J. 1995. *Strange Multiplicities: Constitutionalism in an Age of Diversity*. Oxford: Oxford University Press.

42 Tully, J. 1995. Above, n 41, at p 63ff.

43 Tully, J. 1995. Above, n 41 at p 68 Rousseau's conception of the general will appears as a slight variation on Hobbes' notion of personation. About the social contract, he said, "(at) once in place of the individual personality of each contracting party, this act of association creates a corporate and collective body, composed of as many members as the assembly creates voters, and receiving from this act its unity, its common identity, its life, and its will." Rousseau, J.J. 1975. *The Social Contract and Discourses*. London: Dent p 175.

44 Tully, J. 1995. Above, n 41, at p 69.

45 Van Trease, H. (ed) 1995. *Melanesian Politics: Stael Blong Vanautu*. New Zealand: Macmillan Brown Centre for Pacific Studies, University of Canterbury at p 21

46 The "New Hebridean people" were constructed as singular because of common descent/shared ethnicity.

47 Jowitt, A. 1999. Reconstructing Custom: The Politics of Homophobia in Vanuatu. Unpublished conference paper. *2nd ISSACS Conference*, Manchester, July 1999.

48 See, for example, the application of laws provisions in the *Constitution* of Solomon Islands, section 75 and Schedule 3 which assign customary law to such a subordinate position. See also the decision in *To'ofilu v Oimae* Unreported, High Court of Solomon Islands, Civil Appeal Case No. 5 of 1996 19th June, 1997.

49 Locke seems to have been the first to employ identity as a concept in relation to a person. It was more usually applied with respect to collective entities some of which were exceedingly general, such as the human species. This redeployment converts it from a universal concept into something particularistic.

50 Hughes, R.A. 1995. Above, n 38. Chapter 4 deals with the political context of the rejection of classical and religious metaphysics in the philosophy of Hobbes, Locke and Hume and the relevance of identity in this context.

51 Hughes, R.A. 1995. Above n 38.

52 See Danielsen D. and Engle K. 1995. *After Identity*. New York: Routledge, p xiv. This of course hardly prevents the search for new identity concepts or the search for new identities as such.

53 On Hegel's use of identity see Hughes, R. A. 1995. Above, n 38, chapter 5.

54 The dialectical process in Hegel's *Philosophy of Right* begins specifically with the greatest degree of diversity in human affairs, the individual.

55 All systems are in some basic sense unities in, or of, diversity.

56 Some might prefer the term 'ideology' but culture is more acceptable because ideology has a negative sense in some areas of political theory where the understanding of ideology is itself ideological.

57 Stone, J. 1964. *Legal System and Legal Reasoning*. London: Stevens and Sons. p 21 and 25 respectively. Such a state of complexity has led Stamford to suggest that the term legal system was itself highly misleading and misrepresentative. In fact he suggests, law is better imagined as "a vast web of relations (or perhaps a multi-dimensional maze)" Stamford, C. 1989. Oxford: Basil Blackwell. p 223.

Review questions

1. Identify and discuss restorative justice practices in different parts of the Pacific islands. To what extent do you think that such approaches can be used to reconstitute or stabilise states that are experiencing coups, civil wars or other major social unrest?

2. Are the institutions of the modern state and 'Western' constitutions appropriate or sustainable in the Melanesian states?

3. What are the most important factors and forces at work in your own country which influence the extent to which constitutional limits on the state are accepted by those in power?

4. Consider the extent to which Pacific constitutions assume, or perhaps impose, some underlying principle of identity. Do the assumptions made by the constitutions in this regard, if any, reflect the actual conditions of the society in question?

5. Identity is a principle which seeks to balance out the interests of unity and diversity in a society. Both elements are necessary in any society and neither can be ignored. To what extent does or could law contribute to a solution to this balancing problem?

Further readings

Dinnen, S. 2001. *Law and Order in a Weak State: Crime and Politics in Papua New Guinea* Honolulu: University of Hawaii Press.

McLennan, G. 1995. *Pluralism*. Buckingham: Open University Press.

Moore, S.F. 1978. *Law as Process: An Anthropological Approach* London, Henley and Boston: Routledge and Kegan Paul.

Petersen, H. and Zahle, H. (eds.) 1995. *Legal Polycentricity: Consequences of Pluralism in Law*. Aldershot: Dartmouth.

Sack, P. and Minschin, E. 1986. *Legal Pluralism: Proceedings of the Canberra Workshop*. Canberra: Australian National University.

Tully, J. 1995. *Strange Multiplicities: Constitutionalism in an Age of Diversity*. Oxford: Oxford University Press.

Weisbrot, D., Paliwala, A. and Sawyer, A. (eds.) 1982. *Law and Social Change in Papua New Guinea* Sydney: Butterworths.

INDEX

INDEX

www.ingramcontent.com/pod-product-compliance
Lightning Source LLC
Chambersburg PA
CBHW061239270326

41926CB00053B/4667